AUTHORITY AND LEGITIMACY OF ENVIRONMENTAL POST-TREATY RULES

In the international law of the 21st century, more and more regulation comes in the form of post-treaty rules. Developed in environmental law, this trend increasingly spreads to areas ranging from tobacco regulation to arms trade. This book offers the first systematic examination of these decisions, resolutions and recommendations adopted by treaty bodies, to assess their effectiveness. The study shows that the authority of such rules is in question as, in practice, treaty parties retain almost complete discretion when it comes to their implementation. This conclusion gives rise to two key questions. To what extent does this ambiguous authority affect adherence to procedural principles like legal certainty, non-arbitrariness and the duty to state reasons? And can the legitimacy of the process and content of post-treaty rules fill the gaps in their authority? In assessing these questions, the study shines a light on this crucial but neglected area in international law scholarship and forms a starting point for improvements and reform.

Authority and Legitimacy of Environmental Post-Treaty Rules

Tim Staal

•HART•
OXFORD • LONDON • NEW YORK • NEW DELHI • SYDNEY

HART PUBLISHING

Bloomsbury Publishing Plc

Kemp House, Chawley Park, Cumnor Hill, Oxford, OX2 9PH, UK

HART PUBLISHING, the Hart/Stag logo, BLOOMSBURY and the Diana logo are trademarks of Bloomsbury Publishing Plc

First published in Great Britain 2019

A catalogue record for this book is available from the British Library.

Library of Congress Cataloging-in-Publication data

Names: Staal, Tim, author.

Title: Authority and legitimacy of environmental post-treaty rules / Tim Staal.

Description: Oxford, UK ; Chicago, Illinois : Hart Publishing, 2019. | Based on author's thesis (Doctoral – Universiteit van Amsterdam). | Includes bibliographical references and index.

Identifiers: LCCN 2018057411 (print) | LCCN 2018058981 (ebook) | ISBN 9781509925575 (EPub) | ISBN 9781509925568 (hardback)

Subjects: LCSH: Environmental law, International—Interpretation and construction. | Treaties. | International and municipal law. | Delegated legislation. | BISAC: LAW / Environmental. | LAW / International.

Classification: LCC K3585 (ebook) | LCC K3585 .S73 2019 (print) | DDC 344.04/6—dc23

LC record available at https://lccn.loc.gov/2018057411

ISBN: HB: 978-1-50992-556-8
ePDF: 978-1-50992-558-2
ePub: 978-1-50992-557-5

Typeset by Compuscript Ltd, Shannon

To Joni, Halina, Eleni, Jonas, Iason, Amélie, Fenne, Simon, Jayda, Jasper and Nicanor Máximo, the generation for whom this book hopes to make a small difference

PREFACE AND ACKNOWLEDGEMENTS

In the late summer of 2010, I returned to the Universiteit van Amsterdam fresh out of a post-Masters in International and European law at the Vrije Universiteit Brussels. International and European Environmental Law professors Harri Kalimo and Sebastian Oberthür had infected me with their enthusiasm for research. I was ready to become a legal scientist.

A number of people helped me to find my bearings. Jean d'Aspremont and Christiane Ahlborn, two courteous scholars with an incredible amount of knowledge of international law and international legal theory. My colleague and friend Leon Castellanos-Jankiewic, who coached me through the materials of his entire International Law-making class at the Geneva Graduate Institute. I never met a more gracious and generous gentleman.

But my thesis did not just concern basic international law. I needed to read up on international environmental law, international relations and political science, legal philosophy, international organisations, the law of treaties and Global Administrative Law. I needed to get a grasp on the vast worlds of international environmental regimes as well, each with their own vocabularies, political dynamics and historical oddities, generating dozens of post-treaty rules and decisions every few years, filling handbooks of up to a thousand pages each. At the end of my first year the PhD Dean had just one remark on my research plan: 'I couldn't locate your research question, could you e-mail it to me?'

That this book lies before you despite my own stubbornness and penchant for fatalist thoughts is due to a great many people.

André Nollkaemper, my promotor, whose thoughtfulness and effective commentaries are unequalled. Ingo Venzke, my daily supervisor and co-promotor, who helped me tremendously in achieving conceptual 'parsimony'. I would like to warmly thank the members of the reading committee, Peter Sand, Ellen Hey, Jonathan Verschuuren, René Lefeber, Jean d'Aspremont and Kiki Brölmann, for taking part in my defence, and for taking the time to read my long manuscript.

Thanks should also go to the members of the Amsterdam Law Faculty's Architecture Group through the years, for hiring me and teaching me what it is to be an academic: Marija Bartl, Deirdre Curtin, Christina Eckes, Martijn Hesselink, Machiko Kanetake, Chantal Mak, Joana Mendes, Yannick Radi, Eljalil Tauschinsky and Maria Weimer – and the wonderful Angela Moisl, always ready to stand up for my interests.

And to my fellow PhDs at the faculty, with whom I spent many lunches: Sara, Willemijn, Nik, Maarten, Chris, Josse, Eljalil, Enrico, Sanne, Nienke, Isabelle, Kathelijne, Evelien, Vincent, Emma, Krit, Berenice, Erik, Nwamaka, Or, Geranne, Michelle, Louwrens, Cedric and many others in the department and the faculty. To Anne, my longest-lasting office-mate, who became a friend and *confidant*. Thanks to Willem, Mayra, Betty, Eric and Martine, the beating hearts of our department. To René Smits.

Thanks to the Amsterdams Universiteitsfonds, particularly the Julia Henriëtte Jaarsma-Adolfs Fonds, for enabling the last sprint to the finish.

To Heko, Stephan, Kiki, Anne, Isabelle, Natasa, Rosanne, Maarten, Antoinette, Louwrens, Olivier, Annemarie and Kirsten for the many Monday teacher meetings. I never thought I would discuss the *Interhandel* case for half an hour and enjoy it so much. To Yvonne Donders for granting me these teaching opportunities and supporting my scholarship from the AUF.

To my colleagues at platform for investigative journalism *Investico*: Femke Awater, Pamela Kalkman, Emy Koopman and Karlijn Kuijpers. You gave me the energy to finish the project on a high note. Marcel Metze and Thomas Muntz, thanks for the outlandish idea of specifically asking for lawyers in your ad.

For commenting on my work, in addition to my supervisors, many thanks to Anne van Mulligen, Leon Castellanos-Jankiewicz, Joop Ramondt, Pieter-Jan Kuijper, Isabelle Feichtner, Matthias Goldman, Dana Burghardt, Armin von Bogdandy, Kiki Brölmann, and René Lefeber, as well as the attendants and participants of my ACIL Luncheon Meeting on the *Whaling Case*, the Max Planck Institute's IPA 3+ Workshop on *International Public Authority*, the Architecture Symposium on *Postnational Rulemaking between Authority and Autonomy*, the PhD Training School on *The vices and virtues of international constitutionalism* at the EUI, and my 'Doctoral Presentation' at the Graduate Institute in Geneva. Thanks to Peter Sand and Daniel Bodansky for taking the time to discuss my work with me on their visits to Amsterdam.

To Menno Endt for spending far too much time on designing a – to my mind – stunning cover for this book, and to Miluska Kooij for painstakingly editing the text.

To my family: Heleen, Onk, Paul, Noam, Daniël, Evelien, Frank, Yoram, Joop, Jolijt, Camiel and Lyn. My deceased Opa, whose demands and judgments looked over my shoulders as an inspiration and a *nemesis* at once. 6 minus out of 10, he would have concluded, only half joking. Why write 400 pages? He only needed 86.

David, Thelma, Sander, Gijs, Daniël, thank you for being such loyal and good friends. Kobus, Matthijs, Tycho and Felix, thank you for many Weihenstephaner-fired conversations about life, science and politics, and your deep belief in me.

Merlijn, apart from being funny, persevering, smart, sweet, professional, thank you for your patience, your encouragements, your presentation trainings, and, last but not least, your belief in me and love for me. They were major forces behind this dissertation. Joni, you don't realise it yet but your arrival marked a turning point for this book, and in my life.

In preparing this title for publication, the assistance of Nuria de Jong was of tremendous help. Thanks also to Sinead Moloney, Savannah Rado, Sasha Jawed, and the other friendly and supportive people at Hart Publishing.

TABLE OF CONTENTS

Preface and Acknowledgements ... vii
List of Abbreviations ... xvii
Table of Cases ... xxi
Table of Treaties ... xxvii

Introduction ... 1
A. Shipments of Mahogany ... 1
B. Environmental Post-Treaty Rules ... 3
C. The Argument in a Nutshell ... 6
D. Defining Authority ... 8
E. Fundamental Conflicts within the PTR Practice ... 10
F. Research Context and Broader Relevance ... 11
G. Methodological Considerations ... 15
H. Selection of Examples ... 16
1. Regimes ... 16
2. PTRs ... 18
3. Domestic Court Cases ... 19

PART I
ENVIRONMENTAL POST-TREATY RULES
AND THEIR AUTHORITY

1. Environmental Post-Treaty Rules: Concept and Context ... 23
A. Multilateral Environmental Agreements ... 24
1. Multilateral Environmental Agreements and International Environmental Regimes ... 24
2. Three MEA Techniques for Developing IEL ... 25
a. The Convention-Annex Technique ... 25
b. The Framework-Protocol Technique ... 27
c. The Montreal Protocol 'Adjustment' Technique ... 28
B. Plenary Treaty Meetings ... 30
C. Rule Making by Plenary Treaty Meetings ... 36
1. Explicit Enabling Clauses ... 36
2. Open-Ended Clauses (Implicit Enabling Clauses) ... 37

D. The Concept of Post-Treaty Rules 39
  1. A Common Concept and Standard Instruments 39
  2. Post-Treaty Instruments 40
  3. Post-Treaty Decisions and Post-Treaty Rules 44
  4. External and Internal Post-Treaty Rules 45
E. The Normative Relationship between MEAs and Environmental Post-Treaty Rules 46
  1. 'Clarification'? 46
  2. 'Implementation'? 47
  3. Regulatory Acts: Interpretation, Supplementation or Modification 48
  4. Substantive Limits to Modifying PTRs 52

2. The Compartmentalised Authority of Environmental Post-Treaty Rules 56
A. Investigating Authority: Three Normative Orders 56
  1. Defining Internal Normative Orders 57
  2. Relevance of the Three Orders for International Environmental Law 61
  3. Observing the Authority of PTRs in the Three Orders 64
B. Eternal Interpretation: The Ramsar Convention and CITES 67
  1. The Ramsar Convention: *Identification Criteria* and *Designating Conditions* for 'Wetlands of International Importance' 68
    a. Resolutions on the Identification and Designation of Wetlands of International Importance 71
    b. The 'Identification Criteria' and 'Designation Requirements' in the Internal Order of the Ramsar Regime 73
    c. The *Designation Conditions* before the Australian Federal Courts: A Designated Wetland? 78
  2. CITES: *The 'Primarily Commercial Purposes' Resolution* and the *Reason to Believe Paragraph* 80
    a. Resolutions on the Import and Export of Protected Species 82
    b. The 'Primarily Commercial Purposes' Resolution 85
    c. The *Reason to Believe Paragraph* 88
C. Closing the Gap: The Montreal and Kyoto Protocols 95
  1. The Montreal Protocol: *Critical Use Exemptions for Methyl Bromide* 95
    a. Resolutions Concerning Methyl Bromide 97
    b. Authority of the *Criteria* and the *Exemption Decisions* in the Montreal Normative Order 98
    c. The *Exemption Decisions* in United States Courts: The Natural Resources Defense Council's Challenge to US Methyl Bromide Policy 100

2. The Kyoto Protocol: *The Land Use and Forestry Decisions* (*LULUCF*) and *Accounting Modalities* 103
a. Resolutions Concerning Forestry and Accounting 105
b. Authority of the *LULUCF* and *Accounting Modalities* in the Kyoto Normative Order 109
c. Authority of Kyoto COP/MOP Decisions in the EU and the Netherlands 110
D. Conclusion 111

PART II
THE SOURCES OF THE AUTHORITY OF ENVIRONMENTAL POST-TREATY RULES

3. The Silence of the Enabling Clauses: Delegated Authority and the Doctrine of Sources 119
A. PTRs as International Delegated Acts 119
B. PTRs' Delegated Authority According to the Sources of International Law 122
1. Treaties or Treaty Amendments? 122
2. (Binding) Decisions of International Organisations? 124
3. Customary Law or Soft Law? 124
C. PTRs' Delegated Authority in the Internal Normative Orders of MEAs 125
1. Correspondence between Delegation and Delegated Act? 126
2. Is Compliance with PTRs Obligatory? 129
D. National Legal Orders 133
1. Transposition of and 'References' to MEAs and PTRs 134
2. Particular Issues Concerning Monist States: Validity and Direct Applicability 136
E. Conclusion 138

4. 'Taking into Account': Interpretive Authority and Wording 140
A. PTRs as Interpretive Agreements in the International Legal Order 142
1. PTRs as 'Subsequent Agreements' 142
a. 'Agreement' 144
b. 'Between the Parties' 144
c. 'Regarding the Interpretation of the Treaty or the Application of its Provisions' 149
2. The Riddle of 'Taking into Account' 153
B. PTRs as Interpretive Agreements in National Courts 159

C. The Effect of Wording on PTRs' Interpretive Authority 164
1. Mandatory Quality and Specificity 165
2. Variations in Mandatory Quality and Specificity 168
a. The Ramsar Convention 169
b. CITES 171
c. Kyoto Protocol 173
d. Montreal Protocol 176
e. Comparative Observations 177
3. Significance of Wording as a Source of the Authority of PTRs 178
D. Conclusion 182

5. Invisible Authority: Social Legitimacy and Social Pressures 184
A. Social Legitimacy and Authority 184
B. Social Legitimacy and Social Pressures in the Three Normative Orders 188
1. Internal Normative Orders 188
a. Social Legitimacy 190
b. Social Pressures 194
2. International Legal Order 195
a. Stance of Governments in International Dispute Settlement 196
b. The ICJ's Justifications for Applying PTRs 197
3. National Legal Orders 201
a. Stance of Governments in Domestic Legal Orders 201
b. Domestic Courts' Justifications for Applying PTRs 202
C. Conclusion 207

PART III
CRITICAL PERSPECTIVES ON THE AUTHORITY OF ENVIRONMENTAL POST-TREATY RULES

6. Vulnerable Authority: Discretion in Domestic Implementation and Violation of Procedural Principles 211
A. Is Authority Based on Social Legitimacy Different? 211
B. Wide Governmental Discretion 213
1. The Commodification of International Rules 213
2. Governmental Discretion in Domestic Legal Orders 216
C. Infringement of Fundamental Procedural Principles 221
1. The Principle of Promulgation 223
2. The Duty to State the Law and to State Reasons 224
3. The Principle of Legal Certainty 225
D. Conclusion 226

7. Challenges to the Normative Legitimacy of Environmental Post-Treaty Rules 227
A. Input Legitimacy 230
1. The Insufficiency of State Consent to the Underlying Treaty....232
2. The Reality of Consensual Decision Making....233
a. Adopting PTRs by Consensus....233
b. What is Consensual Decision Making and How Should its Legitimacy be Assessed?....236
c. Input Legitimacy of Kyoto Protocol COP/MOP Decisions....242
d. Consensus and Global Interests....245
3. Courts' Misunderstanding of the Consensual Process....246
4. Executive Branch Dominance....249
B. Output Legitimacy....252
1. Analysing Effectiveness *Ex Ante*....253
2. PTRs as Complements....257
3. PTRs as Antagonists....258
4. National Courts and the Effectiveness of PTRs....263
5. The Consensual Process and Output Legitimacy....264
C. Conclusion....266

Conclusion....269

Bibliography....276
Index....289

LIST OF ABBREVIATIONS

AATA	Administrative Appeals Tribunal of Australia
ABRvS	Afdeling Bestuursrechtspraak Raad van State (Judicial Department of the Council of State, the Netherlands)
APHIS	Animal and Plant Health Inspection Service (United States)
ATT	Arms Trade Treaty
CBD	Convention on Biological Diversity
CCE	Commissioners of Customs and Excise (United Kingdom)
CDM	Clean Development Mechanism
CDM EB	CDM Executive Body
CFI	Court of First Instance of the European Union
CFR	Code of Federal Regulations
CITES	Convention on International Trade in Endangered Species
CMP	COP/MOP
COP	Conference of the Parties
COP/MOP	Conference of the Parties meeting as the parties to the (Kyoto/Cartagena) Protocol
CUP	Cambridge University Press
DC Cir.	District of Columbia Circuit Court (United States)
DDC	District Court for the District of Columbia (United States)
EB	Enforcement Branch (of the Kyoto Protocol Compliance Committee)
EC	European Community
ECJ	European Court of Justice
EIA	Environmental Impact Assessment
EPA	Environmental Protection Agency (United States)

EPBC	Environment Protection and Biodiversity Conservation Act 1999 (Australia)
ERT	Expert Review Team (under the Kyoto Protocol)
EU	European Union
EWCA	Court of Appeal of England and Wales (United Kingdom)
FAO	Food and Agricultural Organization
FCA	Federal Court of Australia
FCFCA	Full Court of the Federal Court of Australia
FWS	Fish and Wildlife Service (United States)
GTAN	Spanish Acronym of 'High-Level Technical Group'
HUP	Harvard University Press
IBAMA	Brazilian Institute of the Environment and Renewable Natural Resources (Instituto Brasileiro do Meio Ambiente e dos Recursos Naturais Renováveis)
ICJ	International Court of Justice
ICRW	International Convention on the Regulation of Whaling
IEL	International Environmental Law
ILC	International Law Commission
IMF	International Monetary Fund
INSC	Supreme Court of India
IO	International Organisation
IPCC	Intergovernmental Panel on Climate Change
IUCN	International Union for Conservation of Nature
IWC	International Whaling Commission
LJ	Lord Justice (United Kingdom)
LJN	Landelijk Jurisprudentie Nummer (register of Dutch court cases)
MEA	Multilateral Environmental Agreement
MOP	Meeting of the Parties (to the Montreal Protocol)
NGO	Non-Governmental Organisation
NRDC	Natural Resources Defense Council

OEWG	Open-Ended Working Group (under the Montreal Protocol)
OJ	Official Journal of the European Union
OUP	Oxford University Press
PTD	Post-Treaty Decision
PTI	Post-Treaty Instrument
PTR	Post-Treaty Rule
Res Conf	Resolution of the Conference of the Parties (to CITES)
RIS	Ramsar Information Sheet
SBSTA	Subsidiary Body for Scientific and Technological Assistance (under the UNFCCC and the Kyoto Protocol)
TEAP	Technology and Economic Assessment Panel (Montreal Protocol)
UN	United Nations
UNCLOS	United Nations Convention on the Law of the Sea
UNEP	United Nations Environmental Programme
UNFCCC	United Nations Framework Convention on Climate Change
USC	United States Code
VCLT	Vienna Convention on the Law of Treaties
WHO	World Health Organization
World Bank	IBRD, International Bank for Reconstruction and Development
WTO	World Trade Organization

TABLE OF CASES

Permanent Court of International Justice

Jurisdiction of the Courts of Danzig (Advisory Opinion) PCIJ Rep Series B No 15, 3 March 1928 137

International Court of Justice

Reparation for Injuries Suffered in the Service of the United Nations (Advisory Opinion) [1949] ICJ Rep 174 .... 31, 189
Voting Procedure on Questions relating to Reports and Petitions concerning the Territory of South West Africa (Dissenting Opinion of Judge Lauterpacht) [1955] ICJ Rep 90 154
Certain Expenses of the United Nations (Article 17, paragraph 2, of the Charter) (Advisory Opinion) [1962] ICJ Rep 151 145
Legal Consequences for States of the Continued Presence of South Africa in Namibia (South West Africa) notwithstanding Security Council Resolution 276 (1970) (Advisory Opinion) [1971] ICJ Rep 16 .... 55, 165
Interpretation of the Agreement of 25 March 1951 between the WHO and Egypt (Advisory Opinion) [1980] ICJ Rep 73 154
Legal Consequences of the Construction of a Wall in the Occupied Palestinian Territory (Advisory Opinion) [2004] ICJ Rep 136 145
Pulp Mills on the River Uruguay (Memorial of Argentina) [2007] ICJ Rep 1 197
Pulp Mills on the River Uruguay (Counter-Memorial of Uruguay) [2007] ICJ Rep 1 197
Dispute Regarding Navigational and Related Rights (Costa Rica v Nicaragua) (Separate Opinion of Judge Skotnikov) [2009] ICJ Rep 283 157
Dispute Regarding Navigational and Related Rights (Costa Rica v Nicaragua) (Declaration of Judge *ad hoc* Guillaume) [2009] ICJ Rep 290 157
Whaling in the Antarctic (Australia v Japan: New Zealand intervening) (Memorial of Australia) [2011] ICJ Rep 1 .... 59, 124, 196
Whaling in the Antarctic (Australia v Japan: New Zealand intervening) (Counter-Memorial of Japan) [2012] ICJ Rep 1 .... 124, 196–97
Whaling in the Antarctic (Australia v Japan: New Zealand intervening) (Dissenting Opinion of Judge Bennouna) [2014] ICJ Rep 341 155

Whaling in the Antarctic (Australia v Japan: New Zealand intervening) (Separate Opinion of Judge Cançado Trindade) [2014] ICJ Rep 348 200
Whaling in the Antarctic (Australia v Japan: New Zealand intervening) (Dissenting Opinion of Judge Yusuf) [2014] ICJ Rep 383............155
Whaling in the Antarctic (Australia v Japan: New Zealand intervening) (Dissenting Opinion of Judge Greenwood) [2014] ICJ Rep 405 ....152, 156, 263
Whaling in the Antarctic (Australia v Japan: New Zealand intervening) (Dissenting Opinion of Judge Xue) [2014] ICJ Rep 420............155
Whaling in the Antarctic (Australia v Japan: New Zealand intervening) (Separate Opinion of Judge Sebutinde) [2014] ICJ Rep 431 155
Whaling in the Antarctic (Australia v Japan: New Zealand intervening) (Separate Opinion of Judge *ad hoc* Charlesworth) [2014] ICJ Rep 453 ....156, 198

Court of Justice of the European Union/European Court of Justice

Case C-9/70 *Franz Grad v Finanzamt Traunstein*, Judgment of the Court of 6 October 1970............110
Joined Cases C-21/72 to 24/72 *International Fruit Co v Produktschap voor Groenten en Fruit (No 3)*, Judgment of the Court of 12 December 1972.......137
Case C-182/89 *Commission v France (Bolivian Wildcats)*, Opinion of Advocate-General Mischo of 18 October 1990, Judgment of the Court of 29 November 1990 201
Case C-149/96 *Portugal v Council*, Judgment of the Court of 23 November 1999............164
Case C-154/02 *Criminal proceedings against Jan Nilsson*, Judgment of the Court of 23 October 2003 163
Case C-80/06 *Carp Snc di L. Moleri e V. Corsi v Ecorad Srl.*, Judgment of the Court of 7 June 2007............110
Joined Cases C-120/06 P and C-121/06 P *Fabbrica italiana accumulatori motocarri Montecchio SpA (FIAMM) and Fedon v Council and Others*, Judgment of the Court of 9 September 2008............137
Case C-308/06 *Intertanko and Others*, Judgment of the Court of 3 June 2008 ....137, 164

General Court of the European Union/Court of First Instance of the European Union

Case T-216/05 *Mebrom NV v Commission*, Judgment of the Court of 22 May 2007............135

Domestic courts

[NB. For the domestic court decisions, a citation style is chosen that guarantees a certain homogeneity, while safeguarding essential information to find the decisions in their respective national databases.]

Australia

Federal Court of Australia

Minister for the Environment and Heritage v Greentree (No 2) [2004] FCA 741, 11 June 2004 .... 79–80, 160, 167, 180, 218, 223
Greentree v Minister for the Environment and Heritage [2005] FCAFC 128 (Full Court), 13 July 2005 .... 79–80, 160, 218
Spencer v Commonwealth of Australia [2008] FCA 1256, 26 August 2008 .... 113, 163

Administrative Appeals Tribunal of Australia

And Jombi and Minister for the Environment and Heritage [2004] AATA 1380, 20 December 2004 163
The International Fund for Animal Welfare (Australia) Pty Ltd and Ors and Minister for Environment and Heritage and Ors [2005] AATA 1210, 7 December 2005 .... 87, 180

India

Supreme Court of India

Indian Handicrafts Emporium & Ors v Union of India & Ors [2003] INSC 419, 27 August 2003

The Netherlands

Crown Court/Council of State

Spoedwet wegverbreding A2, LJN: BM1321 (ABRvS [Judicial Department of the Council of State]), 15 September 2004

Lac/Sorobon (Bestuurscollege van het Eilandgebied Bonaire tegen de Gouverneur van de Nederlandse Antillen), Staatsblad 347, Kroonberoep Raad van State van het Koninkrijk der Nederlanden, 11 September 2007. [See also (2008) 35 *Milieu en Recht* 28 (with Annotation by JM Verschuuren).] 201

Rechtbanken (lower courts)

X. tegen de Staat (Import Kaviaar), LJN: AX8598 (Rb. Haarlem), 11 May 2006........135
Stichting The Black Fish c.s. tegen de staatssecretaris van Economische zaken, Landbouw en Innovatie (Orka), LJN: BU5150 (Rb. Amsterdam), Voorlopige Voorziening [provisional order], 21 November 2011........182, 202
Face the Future BV v De Staat der Nederlanden, LJN: BX1737 (Rb. 's Gravenhage), 6 June 2012........111–12, 114, 138, 180, 218

United Kingdom

Court of Appeal

R (on the application of Greenpeace Ltd) v Secretary of State for the Environment, Food and Rural Affairs, EWCA Civ 1036 (Civil Division), 25 July 2002........1, 90–91, 163, 204

High Court

Deutsche Bank AG v Total Global Steel Ltd, EWHC 1201 (Commercial Court), 11 May 2012........113, 135

United States

United States Supreme Court

Foster v Neilson 27 U.S. (2 Pet.) 253 (1829), 314
Zicherman v Korean Air Lines Co., 516 U.S. 217, 116 S.Ct. 629 (1996), 16 January 1996........93, 161, 225
Medellin v Texas, 552 U.S. 491, 128 S.Ct. 1346 (2008), 24 March 2008........220

United States Courts of Appeal

F.R.C. Intern, Inc. v U.S., 278 F.3d 641, (C.A.6 Ohio), 30 January 2002........203, 206, 217–18
Castlewood Products Llc v A Norton, 365 F.3d 1076 (DC Cir), 30 April 2004........1, 91, 93–94, 202–03, 217, 223, 264, 274

Natural Resources Defense Council v Environmental Protection Agency (Judgment after rehearing), 464 F.3d 1 (DC Cir), 29 August 2006 ... 37, 51, 67, 100–02, 112, 114–15, 134, 136–37, 150, 161, 201, 205–06, 218, 220, 225, 248–49, 271

United States District Courts

Cayman Turtle Farm, Ltd v Andrus, 478 F. Supp. 125 (D.D.C.), 29 May 1979 ... 160, 217
FRC Int'l, Inc. v United States, 82 American Federal Tax Report 2d 98-7074 (N.D. Ohio), 29 October 1998 ... 204
Castlewood Products v Norton, 264 F.Supp.2d 9 (D.D.C.), 16 April 2003 ... 1, 91, 93, 111, 114, 161, 202–03, 217, 225, 274
Born Free USA v Norton, 278 F.Supp.2d 5 (D.D.C.), 8 August 2003 ... 87–88, 111–12, 160, 180, 182–83, 202–03, 217
U.S. v 1866.75 Board Feet and 11 Doors and Casings, More or Less, of Dipteryx Panamensis Imported from Nicaragua, 587 F.Supp.2d 740 (E.D.Va.), 24 November 2008 ... 136
Conservation Force v Salazar, 677 F.Supp.2d 1203 (N.D.Cal.), 30 December 2009 ... 204–05, 217
Franks v Salazar, 751 F. Supp.2d 62 (D.D.C.), 5 November 2010
Franks v Salazar, 816 F.Supp.2d 49 (D.D.C.), October 6, 2011 ... 206, 217
U.S. v One Etched Ivory Tusk of African Elephant (Loxodonta Africana), 871 F.Supp.2d 128 (E.D.N.Y.), 17 May 2012 ... 112, 220

TABLE OF TREATIES

Charter of the United Nations (adopted 26 June 1945, entered into force 24 October 1945) (UN Charter) 124, 145–46, 154, 230

International Convention for the Regulation of Whaling (adopted 2 December 1946, entered into force 10 November 1948) 161 UNTS 72 (ICRW) 17–18, 53–54, 59, 62, 86, 146–49, 153, 155–56, 196, 198, 200

Convention on International Trade in Endangered Species of Wild Fauna and Flora (adopted 3 March 1973, entered into force 1 July 1975) 993 UNTS 243 (CITES) 2–5, 12, 16–18, 25–26, 30, 33, 38–39, 44–46, 48, 51–52, 56, 59, 61–63, 65, 67–95, 112–14, 121, 124, 126–28, 130–31, 134–36, 160–63, 166, 168–69, 171–73, 178–83, 189–90, 193–94, 201, 203–05, 217–19, 223–26, 234–35, 245–46, 250, 254–60, 264, 268, 270–72, 274–75

Convention on Wetlands of International Importance especially as Waterfowl Habitat (adopted 2 February 1971, entered into force 21 December 1975) 996 UNTS 245 (Ramsar Convention) 4–5, 12, 16–17, 26, 30, 38, 50, 52, 54, 60, 62–63, 65, 67, 69–93, 95, 111, 113, 126–28, 131, 134, 137, 169–71, 181, 201, 203, 205, 233–34, 250, 256, 259–64, 272

Vienna Convention on the Law of Treaties (adopted 23 May 1969, entered into force 27 January 1980) 1155 UNTS 331 (VCLT) 6, 34, 38–39, 41–42, 52, 59, 62, 79, 86, 102, 114, 142–46, 149–53, 156–58, 160–61, 164, 198, 204, 247

Vienna Convention for the Protection of the Ozone Layer (adopted 22 March 1985, entered into force 22 September 1988) 1513 UNTS 293 .... 28, 96

Montreal Protocol on Substances that Deplete the Ozone Layer (adopted 16 September 1987, entered into force 1 January 1989) 1522 UNTS 3 (Montreal Protocol) 4–5, 11–12, 15–17, 24, 28–30, 34, 37–38, 44–45, 47–48, 51–52, 60–61, 63, 65, 67, 95–101, 106, 111–13, 121, 123–24, 127–29, 132, 134–36, 146, 150, 166, 168, 176–77, 189, 194, 206, 214–15, 226, 233–35, 238, 248, 251, 255–56, 259, 272

Convention on the Control of Transboundary Movements of Hazardous Wastes and their Disposal (adopted 22 March 1989, entered into force 5 May 1992) 1673 UNTS 57 (Basel Convention) 53
Convention on Biological Diversity (adopted 5 June 1992, entered into force 29 December 1993) 1760 UNTS 79 (CBD)..........................26, 28, 233–34, 250, 265
United Nations Framework Convention on Climate Change (adopted 9 May 1992, entered into force 21 March 1994) 1771 UNTS 107 (UNFCCC).......................4, 15–16, 26–28, 39, 53, 58–59, 103, 107, 110, 132, 135, 175, 192, 194, 223–24, 229, 233–34, 237, 241–44, 250, 265–67, 273
United Nations Convention to Combat Desertification in those Countries Experiencing Serious Drought and/or Desertification, Particularly in Africa (adopted 14 October 1994, entered into force 26 December 1996) 1954 UNTS 3 (UNCCD)..28
Convention on Access to Information, Public Participation in Decision-Making and Access to Justice in Environmental Matters (adopted 25 June 1998, entered into force 30 October 2001) 2161 UNTS 447 (Aarhus Convention)...222, 224, 272
Cartagena Protocol on Biosafety to the Convention on Biological Diversity (adopted 29 January 2000, entered into force 11 September 2003) 2226 UNTS 208 (Cartagena Protocol) 16, 37, 42, 127–28, 214, 233–34, 250, 266
Kyoto Protocol to the United Nations Framework Convention on Climate Change (adopted 11 December 1997, entered into force 16 February 2005) 2303 UNTS 162 (Kyoto Protocol)......... 4, 12, 14–18, 27–28, 30, 36–43, 45, 47, 52–53, 58–59, 62–63, 65, 67, 95–114, 123, 127–29, 134–35, 138, 143, 149–50, 157, 168–69, 173–76, 189, 192, 195, 212, 223–24, 229, 233–34, 236, 242–44, 250–51, 254–55, 259–61, 266–67
Framework Convention on Tobacco Control (adopted 21 May 2003, entered into force 27 February 2005) 2302 UNTS 166 (FCTC) 13–14, 44, 158, 270
Arms Trade Treaty (adopted 2 April 2013, entered into force 24 December 2014) (not yet reported)................................. 13, 44, 237–39, 242
Paris Agreement (adopted 12 December 2015, entered into force 4 November 2016)..4, 14, 41, 103, 229

Introduction

A. Shipments of Mahogany

In the early months of 2002, several shipments of Brazilian bigleaf mahogany began to arrive at United States ports. Between February and July 2002, the US Animal and Plant Health Inspection Service (APHIS), alerted by the Brazilian Institute of Environmental and Renewable Resources (IBAMA), intercepted 16 shipments of mahogany timber and veneer, and placed the shipments in quarantined storage. APHIS' sister agency, the Fish and Wildlife Service (FWS), suspected that the wood might have been harvested after the effective date of a moratorium on the logging of bigleaf mahogany in Brazil recently imposed by its government. On 23 July 2002, several trading corporations brought an action before the US District Court for the District of Columbia to compel delivery of their shipments. The central question before the Court was whether the APHIS and FWS were *allowed* to put a hold on these shipments. The traders lost in first instance, appealed, and lost again. Yes, the federal agencies were allowed to do so.[1]

At around the same time, on 27 December 2001 to be exact, a cargo of at least 584 cubic feet[2] (about 117 wheelbarrows) of Brazilian bigleaf mahogany was shipped to the United Kingdom. Her Majesty's Commissioners of Customs and Excise (the Commissioners), which, like its US counterparts, had been expressly informed by IBAMA of the serious suspicions that the hardwood was illegally obtained, chose to sit still. The shipment was awaiting a seemingly hassle-free customs clearance at Birkenhead docks when Greenpeace UK sought to prohibit it by bringing a case before the Queen's Bench Division. It centred on the question of whether the Commissioners were *required* to put a hold on these shipments. Greenpeace lost in first instance, appealed, and lost again. No, the Commissioners were not required to do so.[3]

[1] *Castlewood Products v Norton*, 264 F.Supp.2d 9 (D.D.C.), 16 April 2003; *Castlewood Products Llc v A Norton*, 365 F.3d 1076 (DC Cir), 30 April 2004.

[2] *R (on the application of Greenpeace Ltd) v Secretary of State for the Environment, Food and Rural Affairs*, EWCA Civ 1036 (England and Wales Court of Appeal, Civil Division), 25 July 2002. Greenpeace UK mentioned the number of 811 cubic feet.

[3] *R (on the application of Greenpeace Ltd) v Secretary of State for the Environment, Food and Rural Affairs*, EWCA Civ 1036 (England and Wales Court of Appeal, Civil Division), 25 July 2002.

At the time, bigleaf mahogany was listed in 'Appendix III' of the Convention on International Trade in Endangered Species (CITES).[4] According to the Convention, import of 'specimens' (one or more trees) of this species required the prior presentation of a certificate of origin[5] and an export permit. Such an export permit, in turn, was to be granted only when the so-called 'Management Authority' of the *state of export* (in this case IBAMA) was 'satisfied that the specimen was not obtained in contravention of [its] laws'.[6] In other words, evidence had to be presented that the tree was legally taken *according to IBAMA*.

Recent changes in Brazilian policy with regard to mahogany had led to a complicated legal situation. In October 2001, alerted by reports of massive illegal logging, IBAMA suspended all transportation and processing of, and domestic and international trade in mahogany for an indefinite period. By this time, however, a large amount of mahogany had already been harvested, awaiting export. Was this stock covered by the ban? IBAMA issued a second decree, suspending all authorisations to export already cut-down mahogany that was not yet 'in the course of certification or in conclusive phase of certification'.[7] A number of timber companies, including the owners of what later became the earlier-mentioned US and UK shipments, petitioned a Brazilian court to require IBAMA to issue export permits anyway. This court concluded that the prohibitions 'flagrantly contravened' the trading companies' constitutional right to carry on economic activity and issued preliminary injunctions that IBAMA must grant export permits. IBAMA now had no choice but to do so. Yet, it informed its foreign counterparts in the US and the UK that its granting of the export permits did not reflect its independent judgment that the mahogany had been obtained lawfully:[8]

> We hereby confirm the authenticity of the CITES [permits] issued to [SEMASA], in respect of which the Security Stamps are BR9130404 AND BR913175.
>
> Despite the fact that the export of mahogany (Swielenia macrophylla) is prohibited, the CITES [export permits, TS] in question were authorised by a decision of the courts in favour of the company.[9]

Considering this background and their exchanges with IBAMA, the 'Management Authorities' of the importing states – the FWS and APHIS in the US, and Her Majesty's Commissioners in the UK – had every reason to doubt that IBAMA had been 'satisfied' that the mahogany was not obtained in contravention of Brazilian law when the shipments began to arrive. However, the question remained whether it was up to them to take action. According to the text of Article V CITES, it was

[4] At the 12th meeting of the CITES Conference of the Parties, in Santiago, Chile, bigleaf mahogany was upgraded to Appendix II, making it subject to stricter exporting and importing conditions.

[5] The certificate is of no concern in the present cases.

[6] Art III.2(b) Convention on International Trade in Endangered Species of Wild Fauna and Flora (adopted 3 March 1973, entered into force 1 July 1975) 993 UNTS 243 (CITES).

[7] IBAMA, *Decree IN 22*. See *Greenpeace*, para 10.

[8] *Greenpeace*, paras 8-10.

[9] E-mail of IBAMA of 28 January 2002. Cited in *Greenpeace*, para 11.

not: the Management Authorities of the importing states just check that there is a valid export permit; it is up to the Management Authority of the *exporting state* to 'satisfy' itself that it only issues a permit for specimens not obtained in contravention of its laws. That is not surprising: ordinarily it would be quite an inroad into state sovereignty to question the lawfulness of a foreign governmental agency's decision to issue a permit. Of course, the particularity of the present situation was that IBAMA had openly stated that it had issued the permits against its own assessment of illegality.

The Conference of the Parties to CITES (CITES COP), the Convention's plenary meeting that consists of representatives of all the treaty parties, had for some time expressed its awareness of the possibility that export permits – usually issued by developing countries with less than bullet-proof legal systems – were issued without such 'satisfaction' of legal acquisition. Since its Tenth meeting in 1997,[10] the CITES COP had adopted a series of resolutions on *Permits and Certificates* containing the *recommendation* that 'Parties not authorise the import of any specimen if they have reason to believe that it was not legally acquired in the country of origin'.[11] In other words, the CITES COP recommends that Management Authorities in the country of import add another condition in addition to the conditions for granting an import permit laid down in the Convention. A condition, moreover, for which the text of the *Convention* places sole responsibility with the Management Authority of the country of *export*.

If ever there was a situation in which importing Management Authorities had 'reason to believe' that specimens were *not* legally acquired in the country of origin, it was this mahogany situation. The relevance of the *Reason to Believe Paragraph* in these CITES resolutions was beyond dispute, and the legal questions before the courts in both countries were nearly identical. These cases are therefore an illustrative test for a question that has long puzzled international (environmental) legal scholars, international relations scholars, courts, and NGOs: what authority do such resolutions, and other comparable instruments adopted as follow-up to environmental treaties, hold over states, governmental agencies and affected individuals and businesses? In the mahogany cases, the answer to this question meant the difference between the effectiveness and ineffectiveness of Brazilian rainforest protection policy.

B. Environmental Post-Treaty Rules

Resolutions, recommendations, guidelines, modalities, decisions, criteria and many differently named non-legally binding instruments are being widely used

[10] CITES COP Res Conf 10.2, *Permits and Certificates*, para II(h).

[11] Similar formulations are found in other CITES COP Resolutions: CITES COP Res Conf 11.3, *Compliance and Enforcement*, para (e); CITES COP Res Conf 12.3, *Permits and Certificates*, para II(j).

in international environmental governance, often assembled under the uninformative rubric of 'environmental soft law'. There are independently negotiated instruments such as the 10-yearly Stockholm, Rio, and Johannesburg Declarations. The United Nations Environmental Programme (UNEP) produces numerous guidelines. There are countless private and public-private initiatives, such as the Forest Stewardship Criteria.

Yet, by far the largest volume of legally non-binding instruments in international environmental governance is produced by plenary treaty meetings (like the CITES COP), through consensual decision-making processes, on the basis of enabling clauses in Multilateral Environmental Agreements (MEAs). This study labels such instruments *environmental post-treaty instruments*. The Montreal Protocol Meeting of the Parties alone has adopted some 720 decisions, guidelines and criteria in the less than 30 years of its existence.[12] The UN Framework Convention on Climate Change (UNFCCC) COP, in its own capacity and when serving as Meeting of the Parties to the Kyoto Protocol (Kyoto COP/MOP), has produced 585 decisions and counting.[13] The regularly updated *Guide to CITES* is a handbook of almost 1,000 pages explaining how all its resolutions, recommendations, guidelines, criteria and decisions work together.[14] The Ramsar Convention COP has produced 325 resolutions and recommendations between 1980 and 2015.[15] And these examples are just four of the dozens of similar Conferences and Meetings of the Parties with voluminous output.

This study takes the mass of environmental post-treaty instruments apart, and focuses on instruments with a rule-making character (*post-treaty rules*), such as the CITES *Permits and Certificates* Resolution, as opposed to post-treaty *decisions* which specifically address a *single* actor, species, wetland, substance or situation – such as the specific decision to list bigleaf mahogany in CITES Appendix III.

It is fair to say that after a Multilateral Environmental Agreement enters into force, the development of the agreement's obligations depends for a very large part on these post-treaty rules. Formal treaty amendments on substantive issues have become rare. Post-treaty rules were the instruments used to turn the Kyoto Protocol from a possible success into a certain failure,[16] and will be a decisive factor in the effectiveness of the Paris Agreement.[17] Post-treaty rules are also the instruments used to determine whether the species that most need protection will end up on CITES' lists of protected species, including economically important

[12] The number on 10 August 2016.

[13] That was the number on 10 August 2016.

[14] Willem Wijnstekers, *The Evolution of CITES* (9th edn, International Council for Game and Wildlife Conservation 2011).

[15] See: www.ramsar.org/search?f[0]=type%3Adocument&f[1]=field_document_type%3A530&search_api_views_fulltext, accessed 26 August 2018.

[16] See further, ch 2, section C.2; ch 7, section A.2.

[17] Paris Agreement (adopted 12 December 2015, entered into force 4 November 2016).

commodities such as tuna and timber species like mahogany; to determine for how long developed and developing states will continue to receive exemptions to emit highly ozone-depleting substances into the atmosphere, enabling them to grow agricultural products, despite their official phase-out under the Montreal Protocol; and to determine the extent to which unique and valuable wetland ecosystems may be 'sustainably' used after having been placed on the Ramsar Convention's List of Wetlands of International Importance.

Regardless of post-treaty rules' centrality in international environmental governance, international lawyers tend to be very vague about the authority – legal or otherwise – of post-treaty decisions. One of the most consulted handbooks on international environmental law does not venture further than a hesitant conclusion that they are '*intended* in *many* cases to have *some* normative significance'.[18] Such standard works also tend to make little differentiation between post-treaty rules and other forms of (environmental) soft law.[19] The matter is often not further addressed than statements such as 'they have *assisted* in establishing the CITES legal regime' (emphasis added).[20]

As with much of global governance, such an enormous body of instruments with uncertain legal authority, opaque to all but the most well-versed insiders, presents a huge challenge to international environmental lawyers and observers of global governance trying to make sense of it. Satisfaction with the indeterminate statements above will not do, for this body of rules and decisions raises many pressing questions. To what extent does it change the legal obligations of the treaty parties? Has it become an – equally authoritative – functional equivalent of the underlying treaties?[21] Which parts of it affect the rights and obligations of individuals and businesses and what legal recourse do they have when this is the case?[22] In which direction is this mass of instruments developing international environmental law – towards more or less environmental protection?[23] Is it meaningless but harmless, or far-reaching and serving parochial interests? How does the process of adopting such instruments affect power configurations between states and within the nation state alike?

[18] Patricia Birnie, Alan Boyle and Patricia Redgwell, *International Law and the Environment* (3rd edn, OUP 2009), 34.

[19] See, eg, Michael Bowman, Peter Davies and Catherine Redgwell, *Lyster's International Wildlife Law* 2nd edn (CUP, 2010), 36 ('[Soft law] is the term applied to the mass of recommendations, declarations and related measures addressed to states which, while lacking mandatory force, are nevertheless intended to influence their conduct'.).

[20] ibid, 488.

[21] Matthias Goldmann, 'We Need to Cut Off the Head of the King: Past, Present, and Future Approaches to International Soft Law' (2012) 25 *Leiden Journal of International Law* 335.

[22] Armin Von Bogdandy, Philipp Dann and Matthias Goldmann, 'Developing the Publicness of Public International Law: Towards a Legal Framework for Global Governance Activities' in Armin Von Bogdandy et al (eds), *The Exercise of Public Authority by International Institutions, Advancing International Institutional Law* (Springer, 2010), 3.

[23] Gregory C Shaffer and Mark A Pollack, 'Hard vs. Soft Law: Alternatives, Complements, and Antagonists in International Governance' (2010) 94 *Minnesota Law Review* 706.

C. The Argument in a Nutshell

After further conceptualising and contextualising the phenomenon of environmental post-treaty rules (chapter one), this book takes up the three most pressing of these questions. First, what is the authority of environmental post-treaty rules in treaty bodies, in the international legal order, and in domestic legal orders? Second, what are the sources of this authority, what is it based on? Third, is the authority of environmental post-treaty rules, and are the sources on which it rests, justified?

The answer to the first question, in short, is that environmental post-treaty rules have weaker authority the further they stray from the treaty regimes in which they originate (chapter two). Despite the differences between PTRs in terms of authority, the most obvious commonality noted is how the authority of one single PTR varies greatly along its journey through the practices of the 'environmental regime' (clear/high),[24] and the international legal order and the national legal orders (ambiguous/low). This phenomenon of a single PTR possessing different degrees of authority in different normative orders, without that PTR's authority in one normative order noticeably affecting its authority in another normative order, is labelled *compartmentalised authority*.

The second question has a more complex answer. Because PTRs are adopted on the basis of an act of delegation in the underlying environmental treaty, the source of the authority of PTRs is first sought in that link (chapter three). Does the way in which that delegation is shaped qualify PTRs as sources of international law, primarily treaty amendments or binding decisions of international organisations? Do environmental treaties contain hints that could explain why the authority of PTRs is higher inside the environmental regimes than outside of it? By and large concluding that this is not so, chapter four continues the search into the terrain of *interpretive authority*. It finds that PTRs do qualify as 'subsequent agreements' in accordance with the Vienna Convention on the Law of Treaties. Still interpretation as source of the authority of PTRs ultimately also reaches a dead end, because Article 31 of the VCLT does not specify the *degree* of authority that 'subsequent agreements' possess compared to other means of interpretation. The wording of PTRs – mandatory versus hortatory, precise versus vague, etc – in some cases makes the difference in trumping the balance in favour of PTRs over other means of interpretation. Yet practice shows many cases in which PTRs phrased as recommendations nonetheless achieved high authority, or PTRs with mandatory wording were set aside as mere political commitments.

Rather than these 'traditional' sources of the authority of international rules, the authority of PTRs is foremost determined by their social legitimacy

[24] In Stephen Krasner's work, international regimes are defined as 'principles, norms, rules, and decision-making procedures around which actor expectations converge in a given issue-area.' Stephen D Krasner, 'Structural Causes and Regime Consequences: Regimes as Intervening Variables' in Stephen D Krasner (ed), *International regimes* (Cornell University Press, 1983), 1.

(chapter five). That sounds vague, but is simply an amplified version of what happens to sustain the authority of any kind of norm, including norms that, different from PTRs, are legally binding. Social legitimacy is what participants in normative processes believe to constitute legitimate authority. What is defining for the case of PTRs is that their authority is based on *social legitimacy* directly, not on the legal status of a norm signalling social legitimacy. Without social legitimacy, a treaty would still be binding, because international law *as a whole* enjoys social legitimacy among states, whether in the environmental regimes, the international legal order or even in the domestic legal orders. Without social legitimacy, a PTR's authority is close to zero.

The third and final question shifts from a descriptive, analytical perspective to a normative, evaluative perspective and is divided into two sub-questions concerning the vulnerability of authority resting on legitimacy beliefs (*implementation* and *procedural rights*), and legitimacy deficits (*democratic legitimacy* and *effectiveness*).

First, is it a problem for the effective implementation of international environmental law that the authority of PTRs rests on social legitimacy to such an extreme extent? Chapter six argues that it is. Norms whose authority rests on the legitimacy beliefs of the direct participants are neither prohibited from being applied, nor obligated to be applied. Extensive research into domestic case law finds that potential obligations based on PTRs are easily avoided by states at the level where PTRs are ultimately to be implemented: the domestic legal orders. This makes it almost impossible for citizens and NGOs to nudge governments into implementing these all-important detailed rules. At the same time, no domestic court stops its government from acting on the basis of PTRs. Fundamental procedural rights of affected persons – such as legality, the duty to state reasons and legal certainty – are also violated due to this arbitrariness.

Second, should we – those of us not directly participating in the normative process of adopting and applying PTRs – agree with the legitimacy beliefs of the participants? Here the answer is not an easy yes or no and must be given on a case-by-case basis (chapter seven). This book provides critical perspectives to assess instances of PTR adoption on their legitimacy, and the content of particular PTRs on their effectiveness. Some PTRs are adopted through inclusive consensual processes; with others there is only consensus on paper. Some PTRs harden the obligations of the parties, others weaken them or are used to safeguard economic interests.

This book starts with a conceptualisation and description of practice (the *existence* of authority, Part I), to continue with a legal and theoretical analysis into what could support and explain the authority found (the *sources* of authority, Part II), to end with critical perspectives on the authority found (*critical evaluation* of authority, Part III). Clearly establishing that PTRs are widely and deeply important to the practice of international environmental governance and how, is its primary goal, because that is what creates the urgency of analysing the sources of their authority. The findings relating to the first two questions should then organically trigger the questions into the desirability of the system for developing environmental treaty norms currently in place.

D. Defining Authority

As already mentioned, international (environmental) legal scholars have long had trouble making legal sense of PTRs. On second thoughts, that is not at all surprising. In adopting PTRs, the parties to international environmental treaties have emphatically not chosen for any particular legal form. By opting out of the legal form, it becomes difficult, perhaps impossible, to fit PTRs neatly into legal doctrine and sources. Doctrinal legal analysis thus has to be supplemented with a broader perspective in order to get a grip on the exact normative importance of PTRs and the explanatory factors for that importance: authority and its sources. The choice for authority as an umbrella concept, with *legal* authority being one type of authority, is in other words a response to changes in the development of international norms that traditional legal conceptualisations have been less and less able to reflect and process. Moreover, authority allows for an empirical, practice-oriented approach to the study of global governance norms, yet without *equating* law with practice by equating compliance with obligation. Ultimately, the goal of authority studies into global governance is to bring back some link between authoritative instruments and the requirements of international law.

This book has, however, few theoretical ambitions of its own. For its central concept of 'authority' it relies on previous definitional work by others. The degree to which a PTR has authority is:

> The degree to which it is a reference point in the development of (environmental treaty) norms that is difficult to escape for legal subjects and law-appliers, affecting their freedom.

This definition builds on, and is a specification of, the definitions developed by various collaborators on the International Public Authority project (IPA).[25] The definition can be broken down into three elements.

(1) *'The degree to which it is a reference point'*: Claims to authority of instrument of global governance are rarely absolute, and often compete for authority with

[25] This definition borrows heavily from the definitions provided in Von Bogdandy, Dann and Goldmann, 'Developing the Publicness'; Armin von Bogdandy and Ingo Venzke, 'In Whose Name? An Investigation of International Courts' Public Authority and Its Democratic Justification' (2012) 23 *European Journal of International Law* 7; and Ingo Venzke, 'Between Power and Persuasion: On International Institutions' Authority in Making Law' (2013) 4 *Transnational Legal Theory* 354. The most recent contribution to this work in progress is Armin Von Bogdandy, Matthias Goldmann and Ingo Venzke, 'From Public International to International Public Law: Translating World Public Opinion into International Public Authority' (2016) *Max Planck Institute for Comparative Public Law & International Law (MPIL) Research Paper* No 2016-02.

other instruments. The authority of a PTR is therefore better understood as the degree[26] to which it makes it difficult for legal subjects and law-appliers to escape that PTR. A further significant point is that authority in this definition merely concerns the capacity of a PTR being difficult to escape as reference point; this capacity is not *per se* justified. That is the difference between authority and legitimate authority.[27]

(2) *'[I]n the development of (environmental treaty) norms'*: A distinction must be made between the authority of actors and institutions on the one hand, and the authority of their actions and output on the other hand. They are two different bearers, or objects, of authority. In the context of PTRs, the plenary treaty meetings (the COPs, COP/MOPs and MOPs) adopting a PTR may or may not have 'the authority' (i.e. competence) to do so. In the same vein, compliance bodies and courts may or may not have 'the authority' (competence or jurisdiction) to control compliance of states with international environmental law. The object of authority central to this study, however, is the instrument through which the plenary meetings exercise their authority: the post-treaty rule. An advantage of the above definition is precisely its acknowledgement that a norm's authority is not identical to the authority of the actor that issued it. The fact that an actor possesses authority to adopt a certain instrument is only one of multiple factors determining a norm's eventual authority.

(3) *'that is difficult to escape for legal subjects and law-appliers, affecting their freedom'*: The definition is sympathetic to Krisch's definition of authority as 'the ability to induce deference',[28] but takes issue with the latter's failure to account for situations in which deference is not *actually* induced in practice. Incorporating actual deference into the authority concept risks blurring the distinction between authority and compliance. In the context of PTRs, 'compliance with a PTR' would mean for a treaty party to act in accordance with what that PTR prescribes.[29] It is important to clarify that the study of *compliance* remains outside the scope of this study. The focus of authority research is not directly on the actual compliance that may result from an exercise of authority, or whether a state actually changes its policies, but in the degree to which PTRs are *difficult to escape* as reference points in the development of environmental treaty norms. It only concerns this *capacity* to constrain: a PTR's expected impact rather than its actual impact. In accordance with Von Bogdandy, Goldmann and Venzke, to state that this capacity exists does

[26] For the position that authority is a matter of degree, see also Daniel Bodansky, 'The Concept of Legitimacy in International Law' in Rüdiger Wolfrum and Volker Röben (eds), *Legitimacy in International Law* (Springer, 2010), 309, 312; Nico Krisch, 'The Structure of Postnational Authority' (2015), at http://papers.ssrn.com/sol3/papers.cfm?abstract_id=2564579, 11.

[27] See further ch 7.

[28] Krisch, 'The Structure of Postnational Authority', 10.

[29] For a straightforward definition, see Daniel Bodansky, *The Art and Craft of International Environmental Law* (Harvard University Press, 2010), 253 ('whether outcomes conform to what a legal rule requires').

not require that the norms in question are 'backed by coercive mechanisms'. It is sufficient that they condition legal subjects and law appliers in their actions or legal situation, thus affecting their freedom.[30]

E. Fundamental Conflicts within the PTR Practice

Two fundamental conflicts resonate throughout the different steps in the analysis of the authority of PTRs. The first conflict results from the flexibility of the process of adopting PTRs compared to the process of amending a treaty: flexibility creates opportunity for progressive and retrogressive development alike. The second conflict results from the increased certainty of the content of environmental treaty obligations for which PTRs can be used, but which is mirrored by the decreased certainty of formal legal status (compared to the more certain legal status but less certain content of treaties).

The flexibility of PTRs is at once their strength and their weakness. Instruments like PTRs are necessary for the development of international law, especially international environmental law (IEL). Owing to the much less time-consuming and burdensome process of their adoption and their immediate 'entry into force', they create opportunities to prevent environmental treaties from becoming obsolete. Without PTRs, IEL would miss the detailed rules and the adaptation to changing scientific, political and environmental circumstances that are necessary to make it effective and keep it effective. They present an escape from the lowest common denominator nature that has come to characterise global treaty making for the last few decades, and from the deadlock of time-consuming treaty amendments that get stuck in the morass of failed ratifications. On closer examination, however, many PTRs are far from realising this promise of making IEL effective. If rules can be adapted more easily, more often, and through less formal processes, the process can also be (mis)used for creating exceptions and less burdensome obligations. PTRs can serve a wide range of non-environmental (economic) objectives, as much as the more environmentally effective solutions that they should ideally provide. With flexibility comes not only room for constant improvement, but also vulnerability to changing state preferences, and a constant situation of renegotiation. There is little protection against state parties forgetting how important it is to protect them from themselves.[31]

[30] Von Bogdandy and Venzke, 'In Whose Name?' (2012) 23 *European Journal of International Law* 7, 18.

[31] Compare debates about the European Convention and Court of Human Rights, or the Refugee Convention. Those who care about human rights or the plight of refugees are thankful every day that there are determinate rules in these treaties that can weather times in which there are many states that would grasp every opportunity they could to soften them.

PTRs are adopted in an ambiguous form.[32] It is their defining feature. What they gain in certainty of content, they lose in certainty of form. While the main problem with environmental *treaty* obligations is that they often fail to require specific and measurable action from the parties, the one thing they do not lack is the formal status of international law. Often, the nearly 200 parties to MEAs cannot reach sufficient political agreement to accept meaningful obligations in treaty form. With PTRs, it is the other way around. Most of the time phrased in relatively specific language, and for some types of PTRs in mandatory language, they lack the formal status of international law. In short, while MEAs lack the content to constitute meaningful obligations, PTRs lack the form to be legal obligations at all. And because the legal link between treaty and PTR is ambiguous, PTRs end up existing in a 'legal purgatory'.[33]

This study acknowledges both the opportunities and pitfalls inherent to the PTR practice. It does not lose sight of the opportunities of a well-functioning PTR practice for the development of international environmental law, while simultaneously monitoring its vulnerabilities due to the aforementioned conflicts. An important objective of this study is to contribute to a PTR practice and an international environmental law that respect important procedural principles, do not negatively affect power configurations, and maintain the centrality of its environmental rather than economic objectives.[34] In other words, to show the consequences of the conflicts in the PTR practice so that they may be ameliorated.

F. Research Context and Broader Relevance

Several studies of environmental post-treaty rules from over the last two decades form the foundations on which this study is built. This previous research already remarks on the curious difference between the seemingly 'internal bindingness' of PTRs within regime bodies, compared to their more limited effect outside of the regime.[35] Others insightfully examined the reasons for high levels of compliance

[32] Malgosia Fitzmaurice, 'Compliance with Multilateral Environmental Agreements' (2007) 20 *Hague Yearbook of International Law* 19, 23 ('what we are here considering is the situation in which the COP or MOP is charged with making decisions which purport to modify or extend the obligations of the parties, but where the treaty provisions so charging them do not either set out a clear procedure for their adoption, and/or do not specify their legal nature (whether parties [are] to be legally bound by them)'.).

[33] Bodansky, '*Art and Craft*', 99.

[34] 'Many scholars in or influencing critical geography have noted how economic concerns often supersede environmental concerns – even in international agreements with environmental clauses'. Brian J Gareau, 'Dangerous Holes in Global Environmental Governance: The Roles of Neoliberal Discourse, Science, and California Agriculture in the Montreal Protocol' (2008) 40 *Antipode* 102, 107.

[35] Geir Ulfstein, 'Reweaving the Fabric of International Law? Patterns of Consent in Environmental Framework Agreements, Comment by Geir Ulfstein' in Rüdiger Wolfrum and Volker Röben (eds), *Developments of International Law in Treaty Making* (Springer, 2005), 145.

with PTRs in the operation of international environmental regimes,[36] and argued that this could not but be based on social pressures replacing the pressure of legal obligation.[37] There are increasing suggestions among international environmental lawyers that lawyers could reach a better grasp of the 'level of obligation' of all kinds of instruments of international environmental governance by looking at the formulation of their content in terms of specificity and mandatory quality.[38] And the normative legitimacy of 'ongoing systems of governance,' such as the process of PTR adoptions, has also long been pointed out as one of the greatest challenges in international environmental law.[39] Last but not least, there have been earlier critical voices, showing that CITES COP resolutions, for instance, were regularly used for 'well-meaning peer-interpretation' – i.e. interpretations favourable to certain states' interests – rather than more demanding obligations.[40]

This study builds on these findings, but places them within a more systematic framework of authority and legitimacy. It compares multiple examples from different regimes, and at the same time follows a small number of illustrative PTRs much more closely: the context in which they originated, the circumstances of their adoption, their operation within the regime and their fate in international and domestic dispute settlement procedures. Assisted by the work of scholars specialised in the Ramsar Convention, CITES, the Kyoto Protocol and the Montreal Protocol, sketching the background of particular PTRs makes their role in normative development more tangible. By zooming in particularly on four different MEAs and their regimes, it is possible to simultaneously highlight differences between PTRs from, for instance, the Ramsar Convention and the Kyoto Protocol, and, even more importantly, similarities in how the compartmentalised authority of PTRs functions. Of course, the upside of comparing PTRs from four different regimes is mirrored to some extent by the downside of not being able to engage fully with any one of them. This disadvantage is mitigated by the fact that some shorter regime-specific studies have already been done.[41] It is the ambitious

[36] Thomas Gehring, 'Treaty-Making and Treaty-Evolution' in Daniel Bodansky, Jutta Brunnée and Ellen Hey (eds), *The Oxford Handbook of International Environmental Law* (OUP, 2007), 467.

[37] Jutta Brunnée, 'COPing with Consent: Law-Making Under Multilateral Environmental Agreements' (2002) 15 *Leiden Journal of International Law* 1.

[38] Annecoos Wiersema, 'The New International Law-Makers? Conferences of the Parties to Multilateral Environmental Agreements' (2009) 31 *Michigan Journal of International Law* 231.

[39] Daniel Bodansky, 'The Legitimacy of International Governance: A Coming Challenge for International Environmental Law?' (1999) 93 *American Journal of International Law* 596, 604.

[40] Peter H Sand, 'Institution-Building Compliance with International Environmental Law: Perspectives' (1996) 56 *Zeitschrift fur auslandisches offentliches Recht und Volkerrecht (ZaoRV)* 774.

[41] Christopher Joyner, 'Recommended Measures under the Antarctic Treaty: Hardening Compliance With Soft International Law' (1998) 19 *Michigan Journal of International Law* 401; Peter H S and, 'Whither CITES? The Evolution of a Treaty Regime in the Borderland of Trade and Environment' (1997) 8 *European Journal of International Law* 29; Christine Fuchs, 'Convention on International Trade in Endangered Species of Wild Fauna and Flora (CITES) – Conservation Efforts Undermine The Legality Principle' (2008) 31 *German Law Journal* 1565; Petra Lea Láncos, 'Flexibility and Legitimacy – The Emissions Trading System under the Kyoto Protocol' (2008) 9 *German Law Journal* 1625; René Lefeber, 'Creative Legal Engineering' (2000) 13 *Leiden Journal of International Law* 1.

common ground where new insights are to be gained. Therefore, the move toward the common concept of 'post-treaty rules' is suggested, enabling an overarching framework of analysis.

Having become such a widely used instrument, post-treaty rules are no longer a newly 'discovered' phenomenon. This study goes beyond the descriptive approach of most of the early scholarship on PTRs and takes a more evaluative and critical approach. Its emphasis is as much on treaty parties' exercise of international authority as on their avoidance of creating more of it than they like; as much on their achievements in strengthening environmental obligations as in softening them. As with the emergence of many new or relatively new forms of global governance, there is a growing realisation that their authority over states, societies and individuals should not be underestimated.[42] But the development of international public authority should not be exaggerated either. Post-treaty rules' authority *and* their lack thereof raise different but equally significant questions.[43]

While this is first and foremost a study of *environmental* post-treaty rules, in a time of stagnating multilateralism in a world of 200 states,[44] it is to be expected that new global treaties will increasingly reflect an inability to agree on detailed obligations. But states have become wary of creating formal international organisations with autonomously exercised powers, preferring less formalised settings in which states collectively maintain control over the process of negotiating and re-negotiating rules. Further rule-making efforts in plenary treaty meetings are therefore likely to spread to other areas of international law, as they have already done to some degree. Examples are the *Arms Trade Treaty*, a recently negotiated treaty full of openly phrased provisions on account of political disagreement.[45] Its success will come to depend on interpretations adopted by the parties.[46] The parties to the *Framework Convention on Tobacco Control* have already produced

[42] On closer inspection it turned out that the authority of some of these new instruments far exceeds previous expectations, such as the Forest Stewardship Criteria, various ISO Standards, and Basel Banking Supervision. See, respectively, Errol Meidinger, 'The Administrative Law of Global Private-Public Regulation: The Case of Forestry' (2006) 17 *European Journal of International Law* 47, 52–53; Jennifer Clapp, 'The Privatization of Global Environmental Governance: ISO 14000 and the Developing World' (1998) 4 *Global Governance* 295; Michael S Barr and Geoffrey P Miller, 'Global Administrative Law: The View from Basel' (2006) 17 *European Journal of International Law* 15, 17.

[43] In more detail Tim Staal, 'Exercising or Evading International Public Authority? The Many Faces of Environmental Post-Treaty Rules' (2016) 7 *Goettingen Journal of International Law* 303.

[44] Nico Krisch, 'The Decay of Consent: International Law in an Age of Global Public Goods' (2014) 108 *American Journal of International Law* 1.

[45] After the adoption of the Arms Trade Treaty's text, 98 of the negotiating states delivered a joint statement acknowledging that the final text 'does not fully meet everyone's expectations'. 'However, the Treaty enables us to make it stronger, and through its implementation, to adapt it to future developments. We look forward to working with all future State Parties to make it so. This is just the beginning. The hard work starts now'. *Adoption of the Arms Trade Treaty – Joint statement: A Joint Political Declaration delivered by Mexico*, New York, 2 April 2013.

[46] Ray Acheson, 'Starting Somewhere: The Arms Trade Treaty, Human Rights and Gender Based Violence' (2013) 22 *Human Rights Defender* 17.

a number of post-treaty rules and decisions.[47] Similar phenomena can be observed with regard to existing treaties such as the GATT, where the treaty amendment process has ground to a halt, to be replaced by executive committee level guidelines and decisions, in addition to the role of adjudication.[48] The move away from formal institutions and instruments – happening not just in private networks but also in state-centred rule-making – challenges governments, international lawyers, international and national courts to grapple with the question if and how to incorporate post-treaty rules into existing legal systems, such as the sources of international law, the law of treaties and the law of international organisations. This study aims to be a contribution to these broader challenges as well.

Within the field of international environmental law, a very important role for PTRs can be expected in the ongoing negotiations under the Paris Agreement on climate change. Just like the Kyoto Protocol, the Paris Agreement's success or failure will in part rely on the adoption of extensive sets of rules on topics such as accounting of emissions, adapted versions of flexibility mechanisms such as the Clean Development Mechanism, and on the clear and transparent provision of information, which is the single mechanism for compliance with the Agreement.[49] In fact, the Paris Decision,[50] which was adopted simultaneously with the Agreement, already raises many of the same questions regarding its authority. Even the very first action that parties to the Paris Agreement are bound to take, the communication of Nationally Determined Contributions, is to take place in accordance with relevant decisions of the Conference of the Parties.[51]

Although it is some 40 years since the first environmental PTRs were adopted, their volume is still expanding, both within international environmental law and in other areas of international law and EU law. With treaties on most important issues in existence, and moving further and further away from their date of adoption, while formal amendments become more and more challenging, we can expect PTRs to become the key to the way in which many of these treaties develop. It is adamant that international lawyers, scholars and practitioners as well as new generations of international law students get to terms with this development.

[47] Sam Foster Halabi, 'The World Health Organization's Framework Convention on Tobacco Control: An Analysis of Guidelines Adopted by the Conference of the Parties' (2010) 39 *Georgia Journal of International and Comparative Law* 121.

[48] Andrew Lang and Joanne Scott, 'The Hidden World of WTO Governance' (2009) 20 *European Journal of International Law* 575.

[49] Preamble and Art 6 of the *Paris Agreement* (2015).

[50] UNFCCC COP Decision 1/CP.21 *Adoption of the Paris Agreement* (2015).

[51] Preamble and Art 4 of the *Paris Agreement* (2015).

G. Methodological Considerations

While this is a legal study at heart, in many ways it feeds off other disciplines. It draws insights from such areas of international law as the law of treaties, the law of international organisations, the study of global governance, international authority and global administrative law, as well as numerous sub-fields of international environmental law (climate change, wildlife law). It also incorporates insights from international relations, such as the study of international regimes and the effectiveness of international (environmental) law. It uses illustrative examples from many different environmental regimes, without being a full-fledged comparative study. This multi-disciplinary approach is aimed at overcoming the hurdle that states operate outside the reach of one particular discipline. The treaty parties neither adopt PTRs in any specified legal form, nor specifically opt for a non-binding form. International and national courts rely on legitimacy considerations in addition to legal considerations in deciding whether or not to apply PTRs. Not to accommodate the research approach to such non-legal aspects of the research object would make little sense for a study setting out to understand the significance of PTRs for international environmental governance. If the PTR practice were a thick forest, this study simply uses different types of *machetes* and *parangs* to cut paths through it.

Despite the comparative aspects of this study, it is not a fully fledged comparative study. It is as much interested in commonalities between the PTR practices that have developed under various MEAs as in their differences. Establishing whether treaty parties do things differently under the Montreal Protocol than under the Kyoto Protocol is not a primary aim. The move toward the common concept of 'post-treaty instruments' (and post-treaty rules) and their analysis through a common framework is in part precisely a counter-move to the fragmentation of international environmental governance into so many treaty regimes.[52] The authority of the hundreds of PTRs might become more streamlined and predictable, if such a common concept is accepted.

The focus on commonalities does not mean that the study has lost sight of the significant differences between MEAs, and between the regimes that have formed around them. First, the nature of the different environmental issues brings its own political dynamic to the decision-making process. In the Montreal Protocol, the extent of political agreement on the reduction of the use of ozone-depleting substances was and is much greater than on the reduction of greenhouse gas emissions in the UNFCCC.[53] Second, the four MEAs from which most of the

[52] Frank Biermann et al, 'The Fragmentation of Global Governance Architectures: A Framework for Analysis' (2009) 9 *Global Environmental Politics* 14.

[53] Scott Barrett, *Why Cooperate? Incentives to Supply Global Public Goods* (OUP, 2007); Daniel Bodansky, 'What's in a Concept? Global Public Goods, International Law, and Legitimacy' (2012) 23 *European Journal of International Law* 651.

examples are drawn originated in very different periods, have a different architecture and diverge in terms of the powers that states have delegated to the plenary treaty meetings and their subsidiary bodies. For instance, the Ramsar Convention leaves its treaty parties much more room for sovereign decision making on 'wetlands' than CITES does for endangered species. These caveats do not, however, prevent an effective analysis of the commonalities, it is suggested, as long as the differences are also duly noted.

H. Selection of Examples

1. Regimes

Most of the supporting or illustrative examples throughout this book come from four environmental regimes: the Convention on Wetlands of International Importance especially as Waterfowl Habitat 1971 (Ramsar Convention); the Convention on International Trade in Endangered Species 1973 (CITES); Montreal Protocol on Substances that Deplete the Ozone Layer 1987 (Montreal Protocol); and the Kyoto Protocol to the United Nations Framework Convention on Climate Change 1998 (Kyoto Protocol).

The main criterion in the selection of these regimes, and the particular PTRs selected from these regimes to focus on, was that they had to be helpful in answering the research questions of the thesis. They have not been picked randomly, representatively or according to any other official method for case study selection. To be helpful in answering the research questions, a regime had to have produced a considerable *volume and scope* of PTR practice, including on important substantive issues. Because the research question is interested in PTRs in general, the examples had to be *diverse* in terms of types of regimes and types of PTRs predominantly used in those regimes. To be reasonably comparable, the sample had to consist of *global* MEAs (alternatively, the choice could have been for MEAs from a single region). Finally, the existence of insightful *compliance cases, and international and domestic court cases* involving PTRs from a regime was important.

In cases where other regimes provided more useful examples for the purposes of addressing a particular sub-question, however, exceptionally it was preferred to use those examples rather than keeping strictly to this selection of four.

The Ramsar COP, the CITES COP, the Montreal MOP and the Kyoto COP/MOP all produced a *large volume and scope* of PTRs relating to the core substantive issues in their underlying MEAs.[54] In terms of volume of post-treaty *instruments*, the Montreal Protocol MOP, for instance, produced more than 720 post-treaty

[54] The Cartagena Protocol on Biosafety to the Convention on Biological Diversity (adopted 29 January 2000, entered into force 11 September 2003) 2226 UNTS 208 (Cartagena Protocol), for instance, contains only two explicit enabling clauses on important substantive issues.

instruments up to and including its 22nd meeting, the Ramsar Convention COP 324 recommendations and resolutions, the CITES COP had 90 resolutions and 198 decisions in force, and the Kyoto COP/MOP 160 decisions. The majority of these examples are specific decisions, however, not post-treaty *rules*. On the ozone-depleting substance methyl bromide alone – a recurring example in this study – seven Montreal MOP decisions containing rules[55] and 14 decisions applying those rules have been adopted so far. Of the 90 CITES COP resolutions, 30 are of a rule-making character.

Equally important, the *types of PTRs* that are prominent in each of the regimes *diverge* sufficiently that the range of different kinds of PTRs is covered – in terms of how they are worded, being based on an explicit mandate in the MEA (explicit enabling clauses), or rather on open-ended language in the MEA (implicit enabling clauses). For a more detailed typology, see chapter one. The Kyoto Protocol contains the greatest number of explicit enabling clauses to adopt PTRs for an unprecedented range of substantive issues, such as the extent to which sinks, like planting new forests, can be used for achieving reductions in greenhouse gas emissions. The majority of its PTRs tend to be phrased in mandatory language. The Ramsar Convention and CITES stand out because they have the longest running PTR practices, and because most of their PTRs are based on 'implicit enabling clauses': indeterminate treaty provisions leaving space for more specific rules, fine tuning open-ended treaty concepts such as 'threatened with extinction' or 'wise use'. The majority of their PTRs tend to be phrased as recommendations. The Montreal Protocol MOP, by contrast, has produced some of the most firmly worded PTRs, based on both explicit and implicit enabling clauses.

This diversity does not mean that the four regimes are fully representative of all environmental regimes and all the PTRs they have produced. Evidently, there are other environmental regimes with – in some aspects – unique PTR practices, such as those that have emerged around the International Convention on the Regulation of Whaling (ICRW), the Antarctic Treaty, and the Long-Range Transboundary Air Pollution (LRTAP) Convention. But those were excluded because a further criterion was the *global representativeness of the treaty parties* to an MEA. The Kyoto Protocol (197 parties and one observer state) and the Montreal Protocol (197 parties) have (near) universal membership, and with 169 and 183 parties respectively, the Ramsar Convention and CITES also have a widespread membership that is still growing.[56]

A final important selection criterion was the *existence of non-compliance cases, international court cases and domestic court cases* involving PTRs from these regimes. The Montreal Protocol and the Kyoto Protocol have active and powerful compliance systems, including compliance control with post-treaty rules.

[55] Montreal MOP Decisions VIII/16; IX/7; XIII/11; XV/54; Ex.I/4; XVI/3; XVI/6.

[56] Last checked on 26 August 2018.

For CITES, several bodies (the COP, the Standing Committee and the Secretariat) together check compliance with PTRs on issues such as adoption of national legislation that penalises trade in endangered species and controls the functioning of national Management Authorities. In the Ramsar regime, compliance control is notably weaker. At the level of international courts, the most relevant cases for the PTR practice concern the ICRW (*Whaling in the Antarctic*) and the bilateral 1975 Statute of the River Uruguay between Uruguay and Argentina (*Pulp Mills on the River Uruguay*). Therefore, these examples from outside the four selected regimes were unavoidable. In particular the Ramsar, CITES and Montreal PTRs are regularly subject to domestic court decisions.

2. PTRs

Considering that the Montreal MOP alone has produced more than 720 decisions so far, where to start the selection of particular PTRs to use as examples? To start with, most of those 720 are not post-treaty *rules*, but other kinds of post-treaty *instruments* (PTIs), such as *specific decisions* related to individual treaty parties, to yearly quota for a certain substance or species, to single incidents, single wetlands or single species. Often, such specific decisions are closer to rule *application* than rule *making* (which is not to say that these instances of application cannot affect the future interpretation of the PTRs so applied). Of the 21 Montreal MOP decisions relating to the ozone-depleting substance methyl bromide, seven consist – partly or completely – of general rules. The other 14 apply these rules on a yearly basis to set specific amounts of methyl bromide exempted for so-called 'critical use'. Thus, only those first seven are post-treaty *rules*, while the latter 14 are post-treaty *decisions*. Applying this same distinction to the total body of CITES resolutions and Recommendations, around 30 CITES resolutions setting general rules[57] are currently operative, most of which have been adjusted or replaced several times.

The next step in the selection process was to focus on PTRs addressing substantive rather than procedural issues. By means of example, for the Kyoto Protocol, the COP/MOP Decisions on *Land Use, Land Use Change and Forestry* (LULUCF) were selected over the COP/MOP Decisions on *Procedures and mechanisms relating to compliance*. This criterion has only limited usefulness because many PTRs contain substantive as well as procedural aspects, and because procedural and substantive issues are often hard to separate. For example, CITES Resolution 12.3, which played such a central role in the mahogany cases, contains the provision that 'Parties not authorise the import of any specimen if they have reason to

[57] An exact number would require very precise criteria on what are 'specific decisions' and on what are 'general rules'. For this calculation, rules for specific species or groups of species, such as sharks or elephants, were left out.

believe that it was not legally acquired in the country of origin' (*Reason to Believe Paragraph*). Resolution 12.3 is called *Permits and Certificates* and mostly addresses the procedure of how to issue and treat such documents. However, the particular recommendation to look beyond the formal permit in case of doubt about the lawful acquisition of a specimen is thoroughly substantive in nature.

The final, detailed selection was based on how well a PTR could contribute to addressing the central questions of one or more chapters, in accordance with the study's multi-disciplinary approach. In chapter one, the examples were selected for their divergent treaty bases, explicit enabling clauses versus implicit enabling clauses, and whether they had been the subject of debates over procedural or substantive validity. In chapter two, the criterion was to find PTRs whose authority could be shown in as many stages as possible in a PTR's existence. In examining the degree of legal obligation of PTRs (chapters three and four), the leading criterion was to look for PTRs that were considered in reaching a decision in compliance cases, international court cases and domestic court cases. In chapter four, one selection criterion was to show the widest array of PTRs on the scale of mandatory quality and precision, another one was to portray PTRs with wording representative for most PTRs from the regime they were taken from. In chapters five and six, all examples came from compliance cases providing insight into the role of social legitimacy for authority, and court cases providing insight into the role of legitimacy considerations in decisions to apply PTRs. In chapter seven, finally, the guiding principle was to look for PTRs that were exemplary for weaknesses or strengths in the normative legitimacy of the PTR practice, such as PTRs adopted through less inclusive decision-making processes, or PTRs softening the obligations of some or all of the parties.

3. Domestic Court Cases

The selection of domestic court cases did not involve much selection, considering the limited number of domestic court cases concerning PTRs available in national case databases that were available in English or Dutch. The claim to a 'representative sample' of domestic court cases is for that reason much stronger than the selected regimes and post-treaty rules, at least for the domestic jurisdictions that were included in the search. However, a quick note is needed to explain the minimal requirements for a case to be considered a case 'concerning PTRs'.

In order to be selected for study, cases at least had to *mention* one or more PTRs in their section on the legal sources relevant for deciding the case, with which judgments in most legal traditions open, *and* at least once in the judgment's analysis of the case. In order to actually be actually used for analysis or even as examples in the thesis, the judgments in the case at least had to (briefly) treat the PTR(s) in question: it had to at least *refer* to them in reaching judgment, or explain *why* it did or did not consider them relevant in reaching judgment. The search along these lines yielded a 'long list' of 27 cases. Of this list, 22 were considered to add to the depth or breadth of the analysis, some only to stipulate or corroborate minor points, some more extensively. The cases are from the Netherlands, the United Kingdom, the United States, India, Australia, the European Union and the Benelux Union.

That there are so few cases explicitly involving PTRs is in itself noteworthy. One explanation is that some PTRs are inserted into national law, directly or through (dynamic) references. The possibility exists that there are cases in which such transposed PTRs were involved, without mention of the name of the MEA in which they originated. Another explanation is that claimants and defendants may often not be aware of the existence of PTRs that could support their argument. Government agencies may prefer not to act solely on the basis of a non-legally binding document or may not know about them either. Finally, claimants may be aware of them, but not dispute the legality of government action on their basis, so that fewer cases end up in court.

PART I

Environmental Post-Treaty Rules and Their Authority

1

Environmental Post-Treaty Rules: Concept and Context

The aim of this chapter is to present and define the central concept of Environmental Post-Treaty Rules, and place these 'PTRs' into the context of the Multilateral Environmental Agreements (MEAs) on which they are based, and the Plenary Treaty Meetings (COPs, COP/MOPs and MOPs) in which they are adopted. In doing so, insights from international law, regime theory and delegation theory are used. This chapter does not yet reach any conclusions as regards the authority of PTRs, but together with the following chapter, lays the groundwork for doing so.

A short history of the techniques that states parties use for developing Multilateral Environmental Agreements – Amendments, Annexes, Protocols and Adjustments – shows that these techniques have limited use for the continuous development of treaty rules. Amendments are time-consuming and politically unattainable; annexes are suitable for listing species, substances or states subject to certain rules, but not so much for setting the rules. Protocols are generally more detailed than framework conventions but are subject to the same inflexible amendment procedures, and 'adjustments' are only possible under conditions of strong political agreement. In addition to these techniques, environmental treaty parties have increasingly turned to adopting COP, COP/MOP and MOP decisions in large quantities, using 'plenary meetings' of a diplomatic nature and 'enabling clauses' in the MEA.

Although the term 'Post-Treaty Rule' is not an official name for any of those decisions, the relevance of a common concept is to be able to place them within a common framework for analysis, as well as to connect them to a broader movement advocating similar legal conditions for instruments with similar effects on addressees.[1] This study defines PTRs as *general rules, adopted by consensus in plenary treaty meetings and their subsidiaries, usually on the basis of an enabling clause in an underlying treaty, which does not specify their legal status.* External PTRs directly address the conduct of the treaty parties, or their domestic regulation of the conduct of others. Internal PTRs address the functioning and operation

[1] Matthias Goldmann, 'Inside Relative Normativity: From Sources to Standard Instruments for the Exercise of International Public Authority' in Armin Von Bogdandy et al (ed), *The Exercise of Public Authority by International Institutions* (Springer, 2010), 661 (suggesting a move towards 'standard instruments' with similar effects on addressees, that should meet similar legal conditions).

of the plenary treaty meeting, its subsidiary bodies, and even parties in their capacity as participants in these meetings and bodies.

Finally, this chapter examines the nature of the normative relationship between MEAs and PTRs and discusses the latter's substantive limits. PTRs do not 'clarify' or 'implement' MEAs; they are regulative in nature, whether they are interpretive, gap-filling or modifying.

A. Multilateral Environmental Agreements

1. Multilateral Environmental Agreements and International Environmental Regimes

International law and political science use different concepts for talking about international environmental treaty systems. International lawyers speak of Multilateral Environmental Agreements (MEAs): treaties with multiple parties and a primarily environmental subject matter.[2] They also speak of other phenomena related to the MEAs, but primarily in terms of their legal relevance: are COPs, COP/MOPs and MOPs international organisations or not? Are they subject to the law of international organisations or the law of treaties? Are the decisions they adopt legally binding? What is the difference between responsibility, breach of treaty and non-compliance?[3]

Political scientists and international relations scholars speak of international environmental regimes,[4] a much broader concept. The political scientist Krasner was the first to define regimes as 'principles, norms, rules, and decision-making procedures around which *actor expectations* converge in a given issue-area' (emphasis added).[5] International environmental regimes comprise not just the MEA or MEAs (treaties, protocols, and annexes), but also the Conferences of the Parties established through the MEA, its subsidiary bodies, and any decisions they produce, regardless of their legal status. It is not that international lawyers disregard these additional phenomena, but, as lawyers, they tend to discuss them more separately and view each of them from the perspective of their legal importance.

[2] Robin R Churchill and Geir Ulfstein, 'Autonomous Institutional Arrangements in Multilateral Environmental Agreements: A Little-Noticed Phenomenon in International Law' (2000) 94 *American Journal of International Law* 623, 623–25.

[3] Martti Koskenniemi, 'Breach of Treaty or Non-Compliance? Reflections on the Enforcement of the Montreal Protocol' (1992) 3 *Yearbook of International Environmental Law* 123.

[4] Thomas Gehring, 'International Environmental Regimes: Dynamic Sectoral Legal Regimes' (1990) 1 *Yearbook of International Environmental Law* 35; Helmut Breitmeier and others, 'The International Regimes Database as a Tool for the Study of International Cooperation Acknowledgments' (1996), *International Institute for Applied Systems Analysis Working Paper* 1996/160.

[5] Stephen D Krasner, 'Structural Causes and Regime Consequences: Regimes as Intervening Variables' (2009) 36 *International Organization* 185, 185.

The regime approach is interested in a different perspective: the perspective of the regime participants and their expectations. For them, the MEA is not necessarily more relevant for the regime than other exercises of authority the regime produces; it is the expectations that the regime participants have of them that matter most.[6]

Both approaches have strengths and weaknesses. The strengths of the regime approach are the recognition of the importance of instruments that lack a clear legal status, and a willingness to look at what influences 'actor expectations'. The weakness lies in muddled boundaries because all sorts of utterances may have relevance, but no hierarchies are established. The weakness of the legal approach is that it tries to fit everything into existing legal categories, at the risk of disregarding actual obligations of the parties, and with no avenue for critique. However, the emphasis on seeking new categories and legal certainty is a strength.

A combination of these approaches is most suitable for this study. It would be a mistake to stop the investigation where the legal approach cannot presently fit parts of environmental regimes into existing legal categories, even if actor expectations make evident that those parts contain some of the main obligations from their viewpoint. The legal approach must learn from the regime approach. In chapter two, the two approaches are combined by introducing the concept of the 'internal normative order', defined as *a semi-closed order in which rules may have a different degree of authority than they possess according to international law*. In this internal normative order, instruments gain authority based on 'actor expectations'.

2. Three MEA Techniques for Developing IEL

Multilateral Environmental Agreements have formed the basis for further development of international environmental law by introducing three techniques or approaches: the Convention-Annex technique, the Framework-Protocol technique, and the 'adjustment' technique. All have played an important part in the development of IEL, and still do so today, but the promise that each carried at the time of their introduction has not been realised.

a. The Convention-Annex Technique

The predecessors of most nature conservation treaties currently in force are widely thought to have been unsuccessful due to rigidness and lack of institutions for implementation. The design of one of the earliest modern environmental treaties, the Convention on International Trade in Endangered Species (CITES),[7] was clearly informed by the fate of its predecessors. As Sand relates, the 1933 London

[6] Thomas Gehring, 'Treaty-Making and Treaty-Evolution' in Daniel Bodansky, Jutta Brunnée and Ellen Hey (eds), *The Oxford Handbook of International Environmental Law* (OUP, 2007), 467, 492–95.

[7] Convention on International Trade in Endangered Species of Wild Fauna and Flora (adopted 3 March 1973, entered into force 1 July 1975) 993 UNTS 243 (CITES).

Convention Relative to the Preservation of Fauna and Flora in their Natural State, for instance, 'failed to provide for decision-making institutions and secretariat services. Consequently, proposals for implementation and adjustment formulated during two follow-up meetings … were unsuccessful'.[8] Others describe older environmental treaties as 'sleeping treaties'.[9]

The cure to this problem was thought to be what could be described as the 'convention-annex' approach, a 'split between the general obligations in the main body of a treaty and more specific rules set forth in an allegedly technical annex',[10] with the latter frequently being subjected to a simplified amendment procedure.[11] The novelty of these annexes lay in reversing the burden of participation.[12] Rather than 'opting in', i.e. to give express consent, parties unwilling to be bound had to expressly opt out within a rather short time frame, sometimes under significant political pressure not to do so. Should they refrain from actively opting out, they were presumed to have tacitly consented, and accordingly would be bound by the amendment. For instance, when a new species was added to Appendix I or II of CITES – CITES annexes are titled 'Appendix' – the contracting parties would be bound by the amended annex unless they expressly opted out.

Annexes tend to contain the species, substances or areas of land falling within a convention's remit, and sometimes procedural issues. They are rarely used for laying down or changing the *rules* to which those species, substances or areas of land are subject. For example, the Ramsar Convention's main Annex (called 'the List') contains all listed wetlands, but no rules that apply to those wetlands or criteria for their listing. Likewise, CITES' Appendices I, II and III contain all listed species, but not the rules that apply to trade in those species or criteria for listing those species in the first place. Appendix IV of CITES contains a model permit to be issued by national authorities, but this model permit is based on rules developed through CITES COP resolutions.[13] Although on its own, the use of the 'Annex' element of the 'convention-annex' type of environmental treaty lies in expediting the process of adding new species, substances, or habitats, for it to be truly effective it needs to be coupled with expedited systems for *rule making and rule developing*.

Later MEAs, such as the UNFCCC and the CBD, even if not characterised as 'convention-annex' MEAs, still used annexes for distinguishing between categories of states to which different rules apply, to list substances, or to list targets. The UNFCCC distinguishes between Annex I and Annex II parties (industrial and

[8] Peter H Sand, 'Whither CITES? The Evolution of a Treaty Regime in the Borderland of Trade and Environment' (1997) 8 *European Journal of International Law* 29, 32.

[9] Michael Bowman, Peter Davies and Catherine Redgwell, *Lyster's International Wildlife Law* 2nd edn (CUP, 2010), 261.

[10] Geir Ulfstein, 'Reweaving the Fabric of International Law? Patterns of Consent in Environmental Framework Agreements, Comment by Geir Ulfstein' in Rüdiger Wolfrum and Volker Röben (eds), *Developments of International Law in Treaty Making* (Springer, 2005), 145, 147.

[11] eg Art XV.3 CITES, which allows Parties to make a reservation with respect to Appendix amendments within 90 days after the meeting in which the amendment was adopted.

[12] Ulfstein, 'Reweaving', 147.

[13] See CITES Res. Conf. 12.3 Rev. CoP15, *Permits and certificates*.

developing countries). Kyoto Protocol Annex A and B respectively list substances to which that Protocol applies, and reduction commitments for the Annex I parties. In that sense, all MEAs use the convention-annex technique to some extent.

b. The Framework-Protocol Technique

The more eye-catching characteristic of the other main type of MEA – the Framework-Protocol technique – is the evasive nature of the substantive obligations in the initial framework convention, presented as a tactic to lure as many states as possible into the process: the 'transformational design strategy'.[14] According to Sand, the idea of a 'framework convention' (supplemented by optional 'protocols') first emerged in 1974.[15] There is widespread agreement on its four main characteristics:[16] (1) It establishes a structure for further cooperation; (2) it outlines some competences that these structures can exercise, and some procedure rules; (3) it sets an agenda for *possible* future action, including the adoption of protocols; (4) it establishes main principles and 'obligations', carefully crafted not to require any particular course of action.

The absence of meaningful obligations is the hallmark of the framework-protocol technique. They are policy objectives, statements of aims to reach more specific obligations at a future moment somewhere within the broad outlines of the initial policy formulation. This can be illustrated by the example of the UNFCCC.[17] In the words of Brunnée and Toope, 'the UNFCCC does not impose ambitious substantive commitments on parties. Rather, it contains principles and objectives to guide global climate policy, facilitates gathering and exchange of scientific information, and establishes institutions and processes for further treaty development, including through the adoption of protocols'.[18]

The main idea behind this approach was that as many states as possible become party to the framework convention. The idea can be traced directly to the constructivist beliefs that became influential in the period of the negotiations of

[14] George W Downs, Kyle W Danish and Peter N Barsoom, 'The Transformational Model of International Regime Design: Triumph of Hope or Experience?' (2000) 38 *Columbia Journal of Transnational Law* 465, 488–93.

[15] Peter H Sand, 'The Evolution of International Environmental Law' in Daniel Bodansky, Jutta Brunnée and Ellen Hey (eds), *The Oxford Handbook of International Environmental Law* (OUP, 2007) 29, 36.

[16] Gehring, 'Treaty-Making and Treaty-Evolution', 478–79 ('merely establish the institutional machinery of the treaty system and some auxiliary obligations'); Daniel Bodansky, 'The United Nations Framework Convention on Climate Change: A Commentary' (1993) 1 *Yale Journal of International Law* 451, 493 ('a largely procedural convention, establishing a basis for future action'); W Lang, 'International Environmental Cooperation' in Sjostedt, G and Uno, S (eds), *International Environmental Negotiations: Process, Issues and Contexts* (The Swedish Institute of International Affairs 1993), 1919 ('a framework convention sets the tone, establishes certain principles and even enunciates certain commitments … As a rule, it does not contain specific obligations … nor does it contain detailed prescriptions of certain activities').

[17] United Nations Framework Convention on Climate Change (adopted 9 May 1992, entered into force 21 March 1994) 1771 UNTS 107 (UNFCCC).

[18] Jutta Brunnée and Stephen J Toope, *Legitimacy and Legality in International Law* (CUP, 2010), 131.

the great framework conventions: the Vienna Convention on the Ozone Layer,[19] the UNFCCC, the Convention on Biological Diversity (CBD),[20] and the UN Convention Combating Desertification (UNCCD).[21] According to constructivist international relations scholars and international lawyers, ongoing processes of social practice and interaction have more influence over international cooperation than realists would have us believe. They maintain that, in particular, interaction between states on a set of shared, albeit rudimentary, understandings can slowly bring their self-identification and interests closer to each other, and enable a deeper level of shared understandings in the future.[22] This is not the place to extensively discuss the merits of this theory, although the record shows that the framework protocol approach at the very least has not been more successful than other approaches.[23]

If protocols can be agreed upon, a big if as the meagre harvest of Protocols under the UNFCCC and CBD testifies,[24] they do as a rule set forth much more specific prescriptions than framework agreements. But even protocols often leave the thorniest issues, issues that make the difference between failure and success, to be solved at a later time. Until the Paris Accord, the primary example was the Kyoto Protocol, which left open important questions about many central issues – accounting of greenhouse gases, flexibility mechanisms such as emissions trading, and caps on those mechanisms[25] – the solution to which could mean the success or failure of the protocol. In the end, they signalled its failure.

c. *The Montreal Protocol 'Adjustment' Technique*

Only one MEA, the Montreal Protocol,[26] allows for – what some went as far as to call – real 'international legislation', defined as majority rule with binding outcomes,

[19] Vienna Convention for the Protection of the Ozone Layer (adopted 22 March 1985, entered into force 22 September 1988) 1513 UNTS 293.

[20] Convention on Biological Diversity (adopted 5 June 1992, entered into force 29 December 1993) 1760 UNTS 79 (CBD).

[21] United Nations Convention to Combat Desertification in those Countries Experiencing Serious Drought and/or Desertification, Particularly in Africa (adopted 14 October 1994, entered into force 26 December 1996) 1954 UNTS 3 (UNCCD).

[22] Jutta Brunnée and Stephen Toope, 'International Law and Constructivism: Elements of an Interactional Theory of International Law" (2000) 39 *Columbia Journal of Transnational Law* 19.

[23] Downs, Danish and Barsoom, 'The Transformational Model'.

[24] The UNFCCC produced only a single protocol in more than 20 years, the Kyoto Protocol, before the arrival of the Paris Accord, which due to its lack of obligations misses many characteristics of a protocol. The Convention on Biological Diversity produced two protocols, but only on narrow issues such as 'biosafety' (trade in GMOs) and 'access to benefit-sharing', and one 'supplementary protocol', on 'liability and redress' relating to biosafety (GMOs).

[25] See Arts 3, 4, 6, 7, 12 and 17 Kyoto Protocol to the United Nations Framework Convention on Climate Change (adopted 11 December 1997, entered into force 16 February 2005) 2303 UNTS 162 (Kyoto Protocol).

[26] Montreal Protocol on Substances that Deplete the Ozone Layer (adopted 16 September 1987, entered into force 1 January 1989) 1522 UNTS 3 (Montreal Protocol).

in a move that at the time seemed of historic importance to commentators.[27] The Montreal Protocol allows the adoption of 'adjustments' to the parties' obligations by two thirds of the treaty parties (from developed and developing countries), by which, according to the protocol text, all become bound, without the possibility to opt out:

> Article 2.9. Montreal Protocol (Control Measures)
>
> ...
>
> (c) In taking such decisions, the Parties shall make every effort to reach agreement by consensus. If all efforts at consensus have been exhausted, and no agreement reached, such decisions shall, as a last resort, be adopted *by a two-thirds majority vote* of the Parties present and voting representing a majority of the Parties operating under Paragraph 1 of Article 5 present and voting and a majority of the Parties not so operating present and voting;
>
> (d) The decisions, which shall be *binding on all Parties*, shall forthwith be communicated to the Parties by the Depositary. Unless otherwise provided in the decisions, they shall *enter into force* on the expiry of six months from the date of the circulation of the communication by the Depositary.[28]

This possibility of majority vote was never used. In practice, the decisions to accelerate the ban on the various ozone-depleting substances were always taken by consensus. Through adjustment decisions, the parties have in fact accelerated reductions in production and consumption of the controlled substances many times over the years.[29] New adjustments continue to be adopted from time to time.

This construction, which was understandably welcomed as the start of a new era for international (environmental) law making for some time,[30] was never repeated in other MEAs after the Montreal Protocol. Looking back, it is to be regarded as the product of rather unique circumstances:[31] a broad coalition of industrial states (the US above all) and developing states that were promised temporary advantages, in combination with an issue relatively limited in scope compared to topics like biodiversity and climate change, and available alternatives for the dangerous substances.[32]

With more disagreement looming, in the Montreal Protocol itself, as well as in other (older and newer) MEAs, states turned to other, less revolutionary instruments for developing environmental rules. They sought an instrument more

[27] Julia Sommer, 'Environmental Law-Making by International Organisations' (1996) 56 *Zeitschrift für ausländisches öffentliches Recht und Volkerrecht (ZaöRV)* 628, 634.

[28] Art 2.9 Montreal Protocol.

[29] London Adjustments (MOP II, 1990); Copenhagen Adjustments (MOP IV, 1992); Vienna Adjustments (MOP VII, 1995); Montreal Adjustments (MOP IX, 1997); Beijing Adjustments (MOP XI, 1999); Montreal Adjustments (MOP XIX, 2007).

[30] Patrick Szell, 'Decision Making under Multilateral Environmental Agreements' (1996) 26 *Environmental Policy and Law* 210; Volker Röben, 'Institutional Developments under Modern International Environmental Law' (2000) 4 *Max Plank Yearbook of United Nations Law* 436, 372–73.

[31] Churchill and Ulfstein, 'Autonomous Institutional Arrangements', 640–41.

[32] Scott Barrett, *Why Cooperate? Incentives to Supply Global Public Goods* (OUP, 2007), ch 3.

diplomatic in nature than majority rule and definitely not with an autonomous international organisation either. International organisations had become far too unpredictable, with their almost boundless implied powers and threatening developing country majorities. Instead, dominant states turned to plenary treaty meetings, already for the CITES and the Ramsar Convention, and after that for the Montreal and Kyoto Protocols and many others too. In these meetings, diplomacy ruled, states made the rules, changed the rules, and determined who complied and who did not,[33] and the word 'binding' was banished to keep everyone on board.

B. Plenary Treaty Meetings

COPs, COP/MOPs and MOPs, the Conferences of the Parties and Meetings of the Parties that most modern MEAs establish, go back to the 1971 Ramsar Convention. Conferences and Meetings of the Parties are, as objectively formulated as possible, *meetings of representatives of all the treaty parties* that convene at regular intervals determined by the treaty. These intervals range from one to three years, depending on the MEA. The meetings can also decide to hold extraordinary meetings, which has happened from time to time for most of the studied MEAs. Apart from the treaty parties, observers from international organisations and non-governmental organisations may attend the meetings under certain conditions.

These institutions generally have the following competences according to the MEA:[34]

1) To discuss, review and consider information, implementation, progress, effectiveness;
2) To request information from parties, secretariat and international organizations;
3) To make recommendations, resolutions, decisions, guidelines, rules, modalities or principles on particular subjects;
4) Where appropriate, make recommendations 'to promote the functioning,' to 'improve the effectiveness,' 'for the achievement of the purposes,' or 'on any matters necessary for the implementation' of the MEA;
5) Consider and adopt amendments of Annexes (possibly subject to opt-in/opt-out procedures), or negotiate and adopt new Annexes and Protocols (subject to ratification);
6) Adopt rules of procedure and financial rules, and adopt the budget;
7) Review requests for technical assistance;
8) Seek cooperation with international organizations and NGOs.

[33] Jan Klabbers, 'Compliance Procedures' in Daniel Bodansky, Jutta Brunnée and Ellen Hey (eds), *The Oxford Handbook of International Environmental Law* (OUP, 2007) 995, 996, 998.

[34] The listed competences are taken from Art 6 Convention on Wetlands of International Importance especially as Waterfowl Habitat (adopted 2 February 1971, entered into force 21 December 1975) 996 UNTS 245 (Ramsar Convention), Art XI CITES, Art 13 Kyoto Protocol and Art 11 Montreal Protocol.

The competences under points 3) and 4) are obviously most relevant for this study, being part of the legal basis for adopting post-treaty rules. But before delving deeper into these competences, first, it is important to understand the nature of these Conferences and Meetings of the Parties, because that has a direct bearing on the applicable law and the authority of Post-Treaty Rules.

The international lawyers Churchill and Ulfstein put the topic of MEAs and their plenary meetings from a legal perspective on the agenda in the early 2000s. Their argument was that COPs, COP/MOPs and MOPs are *autonomous bodies or institutions*, and therefore parts of the law of international organisations should apply to them and their output, in addition to the law of treaties.[35] Close examination of the nature of COPs, COP/MOPs and MOPs should, it is argued, lead to a very different conclusion: they possess very little autonomy. It is important to elaborate upon that for two reasons. First, because, as Ulfstein and Churchill pointed out already, the extent of autonomy of treaty bodies from their composite elements – the states parties – determines in part whether treaty law or the law of international organisations applies to their decisions. Second, and it is suggested more important, the nature of treaty bodies, particularly their degree of autonomy from states, is central to how we should conceptualise their decisions. Because autonomy is the central issue in both questions, they can be answered simultaneously.

Although the full set of conditions for international organisationhood is broader, debate generally centres on two of them: 1) does the entity in question have one or more organs with a 'will of their own?';[36] and 2) does the entity possess international legal personality?[37] Traditionally these questions tend to be answered by looking at a combination of the intentions of the founders of the entity in question ('will theory'), and how the entity operates in practice ('objective theory').[38]

The common tests for the identification of international organisations through their possession of legal personality do not make much sense when applied to treaty bodies.[39] To begin with, the MEA provisions establishing COPs, COP/MOPs or MOPs do not expressly embody them with legal personality. Although that has no longer been a formal requirement since the *Reparations* case at the latest, in more recent times, it is quite unusual for states not to explicitly stipulate that a new IO has legal personality, if that is what they intend. From a more objective perspective, in terms of the *Reparation for Injuries* case,[40] a treaty meeting would have international legal personality if *it* is 'intended to exercise and enjoy, and is in

[35] Churchill and Ulfstein, 'Autonomous Institutional Arrangements', 623, 658–59.

[36] Jan Klabbers, *An Introduction to International Institutional Law* 2nd edn (CUP 2009), 11–12; Henry G Schermers and Niels M Blokker, *International Institutional Law* 3rd rev edn (1995), 36.

[37] *Reparation for Injuries Suffered in the Service of the United Nations* (Advisory Opinion) [1949] ICJ Rep 174.

[38] Klabbers, *An Introduction to International Institutional Law* 47–49.

[39] Daniel Bodansky, 'Is There an International Environmental Constitution?' (2009) 16 *Indiana Journal of Global Legal Studies* 565, 577 ('It is also unclear whether international environmental agreements even establish international organizations with an independent legal personality.').

[40] *Reparation for Injuries*, p 179.

fact exercising and enjoying, functions and rights which can only be explained on the basis of the possession of a large measure of international personality and the capacity to operate upon an international plane'.[41] The problem is neither the lack of functions and powers, nor whether these are exercised in practice. The problem is the nature of the Conferences and Meetings. What is the *entity* that exercises the functions listed above?

Trying to answer the question of legal personality thus inevitably leads back to the question of autonomy: do the Conferences and Meetings of the Parties constitute 'organs with a will of their own'? In Schermers and Blokker's classic definition, international organisations are 'forms of cooperation founded on an international agreement *creating at least one organ with a will of its own*, established under international law'.[42] While the first and last parts of this phrase are fulfilled for these institutions, that somewhat mystical element in the definition[43] poses serious problems for the organisationhood of the Conferences and Meetings. As Klabbers puts the question, the crucial point would be whether we are dealing with an 'organ which has a will distinct from the will of its member states' or that 'the collectivity merely express … the aggregate opinion of its members?'[44] Is a COP separable from a gathering of the treaty parties to an extent sufficient to maintain that the *conference* is exercising certain functions rather than that it is the *parties* (together or some of them) exercising those functions? Klabbers says: 'Otherwise, it becomes indistinguishable from other forms of co-operation'.[45]

The question should be answered by combining the *intentions* of the parties and the operation of the Conferences and Meetings in *practice*. To begin with intentions, there is no indication that states wanted to create international organisations.[46] The treaty parties evidently intended to create institutions that are barely autonomous from the collective will of the treaty parties.[47] The language used in MEAs clearly shows the 'objectified intention' of the treaty parties not to create an international organisation. COPs, COP/MOPs and MOPs have no 'member states' and have no conditions and procedures for membership. States that are party to an MEA continue to be called treaty parties. Erroneous are also the expressions '(environmental) treaty *bodies*' and 'institutions' uttered by many international lawyers. For instance, Werksman asserts that 'MEAs

[41] ibid.

[42] Schermers and Blokker, '*International Institutional Law*', 23. See also Chittharanjan F Amerasinghe, *Principles of the Institutional Law of International Organizations* 2nd edn (CUP, 2005), 9.

[43] Catherine Bröllmann, 'A Flat Earth? International Organizations in the System of International Law' (2001) 70 *Nordic Journal of International Law* 319, 321.

[44] Klabbers, '*Introduction to International Institutional Law*', 11.

[45] Klabbers, '*Introduction to International Institutional Law*', 11.

[46] Geir Ulfstein, 'Treaty Bodies and Regimes' in Duncan B Hollis (ed), *The Oxford Guide to Treaties* (2012) 428–29.

[47] Ulfstein recently nuanced the degree of 'autonomy' he awards environmental plenary bodies with. See Ulfstein, 'Treaty Bodies and Regimes', 428–29. ('[I]t may be asked whether the tenets of international institutional law as developed for IOs apply wholesale (or even partly) to treaty bodies. After all, if the parties have carefully determined not to establish an IO, why should the law of IOs … apply?').

establish independent intergovernmental bodies'.[48] These are not terms that the treaty parties have used to name these forums: the texts of MEAs speak of 'Conference' or 'Meeting'. The term 'conference' is traditionally used in international law for *diplomatic* conferences, where new treaties are negotiated.[49]

If states are negotiating a new treaty and consider creating institutions to further develop it, COPs, COP/MOPs and MOPs are amongst the *least* autonomous options they can choose. In fact, the concept of the COP was, to an important extent, a consequence of the unwillingness of states to concede powers to an international organisation in environmental matters.[50] Powerful states wanted to retain control over these forums.[51] There are no international civil servants appointed to represent their state for a number of years, such as in the IMF or World Bank for example. At least, not at the level of the Conferences and Meetings; in the subsidiary bodies, appointments for several years are more common. There is no Secretary-General with a leading role such as in the FAO, or an Executive Board such as in the IMF. The Secretariats of some regimes play an active role in performing some tasks,[52] such as the role of the CITES and Ramsar Secretariats in the listing of species and wetlands,[53] but they are not prominent in the rule-making process. COPs and similar bodies simply consist of, and act through, the representatives of the parties.

If one looks to infer intentions from the kinds of competences of the plenary meetings, it is further remarkable that those competences are almost identical to those states, in their capacity as treaty parties, would have had if no such thing as a COP or MOP had been established, apart from setting financial and procedural rules.[54] This is particularly so for the substantive rule-making competences at the core of this study. States parties to any treaty possess the power to issue 'authentic

[48] Jacob Werksman, 'The Conference of the Parties to Environmental Treaties', in *Greening International Institutions* (1996) 55, 55.

[49] Two famous ones are the Vienna Conference on the Law of Treaties, and the United Nations Conferences on the Law of the Sea.

[50] If there is one international environmental organisation with a separate will from its members, it is the United Nations Environmental Programme (UNEP). UNEP clearly possesses autonomous competences, but these are more of a coordinating character, and do not include the power to adopt binding decisions under multilateral treaties. UNGA Resolution 2997, Art I.2 (competences of the UNEP Governing Council).

[51] Bodansky, 'Is There an International Environmental Constitution?', 577 (stating of MEAs that they 'do not typically create systems of governance with significant independence from states. Multilateral environmental agreements addressing climate change, ozone depletion, hazardous chemicals, or endangered species are still very much state-driven'.).

[52] Frank Biermann and Bernd Siebenhüner, *Managers of Global Change: The Influence of International Environmental Bureaucracies* (MIT Press 2011).

[53] Bernd Siebenhüner, 'The Biodiversity Secretariat: Lean Shark in Troubled Water' in Frank Biermann and Bernd Siebenhüner (eds), *Managers of Global Change: the Influence of International Environmental Bureaucracies* (2009) 265.

[54] Jutta Brunnée, 'Reweaving the Fabric of International Law? Patterns of Consent in Environmental Framework Agreements' in Rüdiger Wolfrum and Volker Röben (eds), *Developments of International Law in Treaty Making* (Springer, 2005) 101, 107 ('But one might also say that a COP is nothing more than the forum in which lawmaking by states takes place').

interpretations' of that treaty, whether they establish a COP or MOP, or not. The law of treaties, both customary as in Article 31.3(a) VCLT, recognises that such authentic interpretations are relevant to the interpretation of the treaty. The same is the case for clauses in the treaty that explicitly enable rule making on a certain issue, which could have simply assigned rule-making competences to 'the Parties' instead of the 'Conference of the Parties'.

Apart from the intentions behind their establishment, COPs, COP/MOPs and MOPs also hardly function autonomously in practice, which in accordance with the objective theory of legal personality may be even more important. The Rules of Procedure of a number of MEAs suggest otherwise on paper, by allowing for (qualified) majority voting if consensus fails. In practice, however, COPs and MOPs almost always decide by consensus or acclaim,[55] the same decision-making mode as is common nowadays for diplomatic conferences, at least since the negotiation of the UN Convention on the Law of the Seas in the 1980s.[56] The chairmen of the plenaries also act just like chairmen of diplomatic conferences, assembling negotiating texts, actively seeking and declaring consensus. Just like the chairpersons of diplomatic conferences, they are not appointed for longer periods. For instance, in accordance with the Montreal Protocol Rules of Procedure, each new meeting of the plenary elects its own 'President' and 'Vice-Presidents'.[57] As Birnie, Boyle and Redgwell conclude, 'the regulatory body, whether a meeting of the parties or a commission, is in substance no more than a diplomatic conference … [T]hese institutions are in no sense independent of their member states'.[58]

Considering the evidence, the applicability of the law of international organisations to COPs, COP/MOPs and MOPs, and to Post-Treaty Rules, should be considered very limited. This leaves the law of treaties as the predominantly applicable law.[59] Support in practice for this position can be found in the International Court of Justice's judgment *Whaling in the Antarctic*. The Court treats resolutions adopted by the International Whaling Commission as subsequent agreements or practice in the interpretation of the International Convention on the Regulation of Whaling, not as decisions of an international organisation.[60] The Court only contingently refers to a 'duty to co-operate with the International Whaling Committee and the Scientific Committee' on the part of Japan, which suggests a

[55] See ch 7, section A.2.

[56] Karl Zemanek, 'Majority Rule and Consensus Technique in Law-Making Diplomacy' in Ronald St J MacDonald and Douglas M Johnston (eds), *The Structure and Process of International Law* (Martinus Nijhoff Publishers, 1986), 858, 865.

[57] Art 21.1, *Rules of Procedure* of meetings of the Conference of the Parties to the Vienna Convention and Meetings of the Parties to the Montreal Protocol.

[58] Patricia Birnie, Alan Boyle and Patricia Redgwell, *International Law and the Environment* 3rd edn (OUP, 2009), 87.

[59] Art 5 of the Vienna Convention on the Law of Treaties (adopted 23 May 1969, entered into force 27 January 1980) 1155 UNTS 331 (VCLT) states that '[t]he present Convention applies to any treaty which is the constituent instrument of an international organization and to any treaty adopted within an international organization without prejudice to any relevant rules of the organization'.

[60] *Whaling in the Antarctic (Australia v Japan: New Zealand intervening)* (Judgment) [2014] ICJ Rep 226, para 83.

duty towards these organs as such, rather than a duty to comply with particular treaty obligations.[61]

The common term used for the COPs, COP/MOPs and MOPs should also reflect their diplomatic character. The term 'body' would still suggest something permanent, something that exists even when its members are not present. Conferences and Meetings are not permanent at all, meeting once every year, two years or even three years. To speak simply of '*plenary meetings*' or '*plenary treaty meetings*' is therefore more appropriate.[62]

This is not to say that there are *no* differences between the dynamics of decision making in a COP and a diplomatic conference. However, these changes are not in the nature of more autonomy for the institution. For instance, an important change resulting from establishing a plenary treaty body is that the parties have a number of procedural obligations[63] to meet at regular intervals and discuss the issues on the agenda. If one follows the transformationalist logic that repetitive meetings increase the chances of shared understandings, the decision-making process can be regarded as taking a deterministic turn away from autonomy. Then again, it may also simply entail that the parties must come and meet. As Pan puts it, 'they save time by eliminating the need to set up negotiation procedures, but do not eliminate the political problem of needing to build consensus.'[64]

As French suggests, in international environmental law the question of autonomy should perhaps focus on the '*non-involvement*' or '*de-involvement*' of states in certain international activities, rather than on a shift of power towards an international entity.[65] To the extent that states have exercised their autonomy by giving up a part of their autonomous decision-making powers, to whom have they given it up?

For instance, particularly the weaker treaty parties, which can concern more than 100 states for the larger MEAs, may give up quite some autonomy because of the consensual decision-making model. The consensual model disables the withholding of state consent as a way out for *individual* states. (States may of course informally become part of groups that do have considerable power to avert consensus, in which case they give up autonomy to that group.) But these states

[61] ibid.

[62] See also A/CN.4/660, *Second report on subsequent agreements and subsequent practice in relation to treaty interpretation, of the Special Rapporteur, Mr Georg Nolte* (65th session of the ILC (2014)) pp 36–48, 37, referring to Conferences of States Parties as 'a meeting of States parties pursuant to a treaty'.

[63] Werksman, 'The Conference of the Parties', 57 ('states' parties become members of the COP, and entitled and subject to its unique procedural rights and obligations').

[64] Eric J Pan, 'Authoritative Interpretation of Agreements: Developing More Responsive International Administrative Regimes' (1997) 38 *Harvard International Law Journal* 503, 527.

[65] Duncan French, 'Finding Autonomy in International Environmental Law and Governance' (2009) 21 *Journal of Environmental Law* 255, 265 ('From this perspective, autonomy has a dual purpose, both focusing upon how far, and to what extent, States are "not" involved in international activity, be that at the policy-making, law-creation or law-compliance level and, equally important, how far, and to what extent, non-State actors, such as international organisations, non-governmental organisations (NGOs) and others (most notably, in the environmental field, epistemic groupings of scientific/technical experts) "are involved" in such international activity.').

do not give up autonomy to a separate international entity. Rather, they become outvoiced by economically or politically stronger parties, or gain it by being part of winning majority coalitions or using convincing arguments that end up representing the consensus position.[66] This is a *horizontal* battle between states with shared and opposing interests, rather than a *vertical* competition between states and an international organisation.[67] Churchill and Ulfstein's position is that plenary treaty meetings are 'autonomous institutional arrangements',[68] 'freestanding and distinct … from the states parties'[69] – i.e. not international organisations in name, but in essence the same is unjustified.

C. Rule Making by Plenary Treaty Meetings

Considering that the plenary treaty meetings are barely autonomous from the treaty parties, the question arises where these meetings derive the competence to adopt rules and decisions. In short, they derive from a combination of competences explicitly provided by the treaty and competences that treaty parties possess according to customary treaty law. MEAs contain two different types of clause that delegate authority to adopt PTRs of a regulatory character: enabling clauses and open-ended clauses (or implicit enabling clauses). Malgosia Fitzmaurice has aptly suggested the term 'enabling clauses'[70] for MEA provisions 'which give a specific mandate to [COPs, COP/MOPs and MOPs] to elaborate in more detail rules in particular areas without providing for specific amendment procedures'.[71] Building on Fitzmaurice's concept, a further distinction can be made between *explicit* and *implicit* enabling clauses.

1. Explicit Enabling Clauses

Explicit enabling clauses are (parts of) treaty provisions that specifically assign the task *to adopt decisions or general rules on an expressly specified issue or topic* to the

[66] See, eg, in relation to the Marrakesh Accords LULUCF negotiations under the Kyoto Protocol, Ian Fry, 'Twists and Turns in the Jungle: Exploring the Evolution of Land Use, Land-Use Change and Forestry Decisions within the Kyoto Protocol' (2002) 11 *RECIEL* 159, 159 (arguing that a number of 'less dissatisfied' parties used their 'considerable leverage to hold out until the final moment and wait for the others to crumble').

[67] French, 'Finding Autonomy in International Environmental Law and Governance', 266.

[68] Churchill and Ulfstein, 'Autonomous Institutional Arrangements'.

[69] ibid, 623.

[70] Fitzmaurice's use of the term 'enabling clause' should not be confused with the 'Enabling Clause' in WTO law (Decision of 28 November 1979, officially called the 'Decision on Differential and More Favourable Treatment, Reciprocity and Fuller Participation of Developing Countries').

[71] Malgosia Fitzmaurice, 'Treaties' in Rüdiger Wolfrum et al (ed), *Max Planck Encyclopedia of Public International Law* (Max Planck Institute/OUP 2010), para 53. For more elaborate discussion, see Malgosia Fitzmaurice, 'Compliance with Multilateral Environmental Agreements' (2007) 20 *Hague Yearbook of International Law* 19, 21–22.

COP, COP/MOP or MOP. They are found most abundantly in the Kyoto Protocol, Montreal Protocol and the Cartagena Protocol on Biosafety. As an example of such a clause, Article 18.2(a) of the Cartagena Protocol on documentation accompanying shipments of LMOs intended for direct use as food, feed, or for processing, states that '[t]he Conference of the Parties serving as the meeting of the Parties to this Protocol shall take a decision on the detailed requirements for this purpose, including specification of their identity and any unique identification, no later than two years after the date of entry into force of this Protocol'. Another example is Article 2H.5 of the Montreal Protocol, which states that, starting in 2005, the consumption and production of methyl bromide will be down to zero, 'save to the extent that the Parties decide to permit the level or production or consumption that is necessary to satisfy uses agreed by them to be critical uses'. An example from the Kyoto Protocol is Article 17 on emissions trading, which states that '[t]he Conference of the Parties shall define the relevant principles, modalities, rules and guidelines, in particular for verification, reporting and accountability for emissions trading'.

Although these clauses are rather specific as to the topic of the delegated rule-making activity, it is clear from these examples that they do not necessarily provide much direction on the content of the prospective PTRs.[72] Enabling clauses involve a great deal of discretion in terms of the future content of the rules to be adopted.[73] They usually result from the impossibility of reaching agreement at the time of negotiating the treaty text. Such clauses are explicit recognitions of the inability to agree on an issue that the prospective parties do appear to agree needs to be settled before the treaty can be implemented effectively.

2. Open-Ended Clauses (Implicit Enabling Clauses)

Implicit enabling clauses are MEA provisions containing open-ended terms lending themselves to extensive further interpretations and rule making by the treaty parties.[74] This category is more expansive and harder to delineate, because any MEA provisions with the slightest undefined term in it can be turned into an implicit enabling clause by using it that way. Examples are most abundantly found

[72] *cf* the analysis in *Natural Resources Defense Council v Environmental Protection Agency (Judgment after rehearing)*, 464 F3d 1 (DC Cir), 29 August 2006, p 14 ('The [Montreal] Protocol is silent on any specific conditions accompanying the critical-use exemption.').

[73] Darren G Hawkins et al, *Delegation and Agency in International Organizations* (CUP, 2006), 8 ('Discretion entails a grant of authority that specifies the principal's goals but not the specific actions the agent must take to accomplish those objectives.').

[74] *cf* Ingo Venzke, 'Between Power and Persuasion: On International Institutions' Authority in Making Law' (2013) 14 *Transnational Legal Theory* 354, 360 ('[D]elegation may well be implicit, for instance when state representatives conclude an agreement with rather generic language and grant international institutions … the competence to interpret the agreement, knowing that this will develop the vague terms and thus shape the content of their commitments.').

in CITES and the Ramsar Convention, which contain many undefined terms and phrases, but open-ended provisions in the Protocols have also commonly been approached as such by the parties.

Consider this short impression of the multitude of open-ended terms in MEAs: Article II CITES ('threatened with extinction'), Articles III CITES ('primarily commercial purposes'), Article 3 Ramsar Convention ('conservation', 'wise use' and 'ecological character') and Article 17 Kyoto Protocol (emissions trading shall be 'supplemental'). Even though these provisions do not expressly assign the COP the task of adopting more detailed rules, they certainly leave open room for it. What is more, without further interpretation, their international and national implementation would be inconceivable. Parties would constantly disagree over the meaning of the provisions, and it would be impossible for compliance bodies to find a party in non-compliance.

But are the plenary meetings allowed to turn open-ended treaty provisions into implicit enabling clauses and start adopting interpretations? Insofar as it concerns interpretations of a purely recommendatory character, each MEA provides the COP, COP/MOP or MOP with the general competence to improve the effectiveness or otherwise achieve the purposes of the treaty through recommendations. All MEAs since the Ramsar Convention contain a general Article on the competences of the COP, COP/MOP or MOP. These general provisions all contain a rule-making clause, assigning the plenary meeting the task of effectively implementing the MEA, including the competence to adopt recommendations, undertake action, or exercise additional functions to that end. These clauses could be called Residual Competences Clauses.[75] For instance, Article 13.4(j) of the Kyoto Protocol authorises the COP/MOP to '[e]xercise such other functions as may be required for the implementation of this Protocol'; and Article 11.4(j) of the Montreal Protocol authorises the MOP to 'consider and undertake any additional action that may be required for the achievement of the purposes of this Protocol'. The comparable provisions in the Ramsar Convention and CITES are slightly different: Article 6.2(f) of the Ramsar Convention states that its COP 'shall be competent to adopt other recommendations, or resolutions, to promote the functioning of this Convention'; and Article XI.3(e) CITES states that the parties 'may where appropriate, make recommendations for improving the effectiveness of the present Convention'.

The power of the treaty parties to adopt rules interpreting open-ended treaty terms is not, however, solely based on the powers of the treaty meetings according to the MEA. In their capacity of 'masters of the treaty', the treaty parties can collectively decide to adopt 'authentic interpretations'.[76] An 'authentic

[75] Churchill and Ulfstein, 'Autonomous Institutional Agreements', 639 (stating that it should be considered to be a 'residual competence').

[76] See, eg, Ulf Linderfalk, *On the Interpretation of Treaties: The Modern International Law as Expressed in the 1969 Vienna Convention on the Law of Treaties* (Springer, 2007), 192; Pan, 'Authoritative Interpretation of Agreements'.

interpretation' is an agreement between the parties to a treaty which requires no formal amendment, because it does not contradict the treaty.[77] That treaty parties possess that power is further recognised and confirmed in Article 31.3(a) VCLT, which includes among the means of treaty interpretation 'any subsequent agreement between the parties regarding the interpretation of the treaty or the application of its provisions'. Through the content of each PTR and the context in which it is adopted, the treaty parties must make clear whether a particular PTR is a recommended interpretation in the sense of the Residual Competences Clause, or an 'authentic interpretation'.[78]

A final reason as to why there can be little doubt about plenary treaty bodies' power to adopt PTRs based on open-ended treaty provisions, is simply that it occurs commonly in practice, unchallenged by treaty parties. In the long history of CITES adopting interpretations of open-ended treaty terms, Sand noted not one such challenge.[79] It is a well-accepted notion in international law that acquiescence can legalise a practice that may formerly not have existed. The power to adopt interpretations and rules is itself a 'subsequent' practice, constituting the practice of adopting PTRs coupled with the absence of objections, which together denote the 'agreement' of the parties.[80]

D. The Concept of Post-Treaty Rules

1. A Common Concept and Standard Instruments

So far, the literature on environmental regimes has not produced a single term for all the instruments adopted by COPs, COP/MOPs and MOPs, let alone further classification. What is usually done is to take the name of the particular body and the name of the instrument and put that together: 'COP decision', 'COP recommendation', 'decision of the COP/MOP', 'decision 16/CMP.1', 'COP guidelines', etc. Obviously, when discussing separate instruments or regimes, these are the most accurate denominations. Decisions, guidelines, and so on of subsidiary bodies – such as the SBSTA and SBI under the UNFCCC and the Kyoto Protocol, the Animals and Plants Committees under CITES, and so forth – are typically addressed as 'a decision of the Plants Committee', 'an SBI decision', 'guidance issued by the Executive Body of the CDM', etc. In other words, the official denominations used are followed.

[77] Linderfalk, *On the Interpretation of Treaties*, 192.

[78] As part of the discussion of the sources of authority of PTRs, this matter is discussed in ch 4.

[79] Peter H Sand, 'Institution-Building Compliance with International Environmental Law: Perspectives' (1996) 56 *Zeitschrift für ausländisches öffentliches Recht und Volkerrecht (ZaöRV)* 774, 779.

[80] International Law Commission, *Draft Articles on the Law of Treaties with Commentaries* (1966) II *Yearbook of the International Law Commission*, 221–22.

However, there are some common characteristics of all these instruments that justify the use of a common denominator, a common concept, for discussing characteristics and concerns at that common level. There are also differences that justify breaking down that common concept into further sub-categories. For that purpose, no particular official denomination would be appropriate, because many different official denominations are being used for instruments that in practice have the same characteristics, whereas the same official denominations are sometimes used for instruments that are widely different. It is therefore suggested that a common concept be introduced which, on a general level, covers the entire array of decisions taken by all the bodies established by, or on the basis of, a regime's constitutive treaty, and subsequently should be divided into relevant sub-categories.

What could the development of such a new common concept deliver? In the context of the burgeoning volumes of global governance in many different forms, Goldmann suggests, it is time to start making a move towards the creation of new categories of international law making: 'standard instruments'.[81] As he proposes to define it, '[a] standard instrument is a combination of a rule of identification for authoritative instruments of a specific type and a specific legal regime that is applicable to all instruments coming under the rule of identification'.[82] After completion of the categories, the same legal and normative conditions can be set for each category. This section takes the first step of arriving at a single rule of identification for the category of 'Post-Treaty Instruments' as a common concept for all COP, COP/MOP and MOP decisions.

2. Post-Treaty Instruments

The common characteristics of COP, COP/MOP and MOP decisions justify their shared analysis with the help of a single concept, and to choose the term 'Post-Treaty Instrument' for that concept. Post-Treaty Instruments are defined as: *instruments adopted by consensus or large majority in plenary treaty meetings and their subsidiaries*[83] *on the basis of an explicit or implicit enabling clause in an underlying treaty.*

These instruments have in common that they serve as a follow-up to formal international agreements (treaties or protocols), and are based on explicit or implicit enabling clauses in these agreements; that they are adopted in plenary treaty meetings or their subsidiaries by consensus or – on extraordinary occasions,

[81] Goldmann, 'Inside Relative Normativity'.

[82] ibid, 679.

[83] Because the plenary treaty bodies adopt the PTIs and PTRs that usually have the most profound effect on the obligations, little attention will be paid to PTIs and PTRs adopted by subsidiary bodies. However, in some regimes, notably the Kyoto Protocol climate change regime, the guidance provided by such subsidiary bodies can be crucial for the obligations of the treaty parties: for example, the Executive Body of the Clean Development Mechanism has a considerable impact on the conditions that proposed CDM projects must fulfil.

if consensus fails – by large or super majorities among all treaty parties; and that they are neither expressly binding[84] nor expressly non-binding in international law.[85]

There are a number of reasons (partly overlapping with these characteristics) to choose the term 'Post-Treaty Instrument' as the common concept for these instruments: their adoption after the adoption of the treaty, their close connection to the treaty in terms of substance and applicable law, the continuation between treaty and post-treaty methods of adoption, and recognition for the equivalent regulatory importance of these instruments and the underlying treaty.

First, the concept of 'post-treaty instrument' captures that, time-wise, these instruments are adopted in the post-treaty phase. COPs, COP/MOPs and MOPs can only take rule-making decisions that find some basis in 'their' treaty. They will only start doing so after the adoption of the treaty text, and with the notable exception of the first batch of COP/MOP decisions under the Kyoto Protocol and the Paris Decision that was adopted in connection to the Paris Agreement, only after the MEA or protocol enters into force.

Second, these instruments are intimately connected to the underlying treaty on which they are based in terms of substance.[86] As Wiersema writes, they are 'inextricably bound up with the underlying treaty obligations of the parties'.[87] To begin with, COP, COP/MOP and MOP decisions almost always concern a subject matter that is also addressed in the treaty. They are either changing the meaning of the treaty provision upon which they are based (implicit clause) or adding detailed rules as enabled by the treaty (explicit clause). As Wiersema suggests, '[t]he significance of the COP activity for the parties' obligations derives from the way in which that activity is connected to the treaty and how it consequently affects that treaty's terms'.[88]

This intimate connection between treaty and post-treaty instrument also exists in terms of the applicable legal framework. The most convincing explanation of the degree of legal obligation of COP, COP/MOP and MOP decisions in international law – as explained more extensively in chapter four – is that they are 'subsequent agreements' in accordance with Article 31.3(a) VCLT, and as such must be taken into account in the interpretation of the treaty. This legal conceptualisation of the decisions and rules of plenary treaty bodies should be reflected in their conceptualisation in general. The concept of 'post-treaty instrument' aims to do exactly that.

Why not simply opt for the term 'subsequent agreement'? First, the term subsequent agreement is tied specifically to the importance of an instrument as a means

[84] An annex is part of a treaty, and as such possesses the international legal status of treaty law. A protocol is a treaty in itself. Both fall outside the concept of post-treaty instrument.

[85] In the words of Bodansky, they represent 'a kind of legal purgatory'. Daniel Bodansky, *The Art and Craft of International Environmental Law* (Harvard University Press, 2010), 99.

[86] Wiersema, 'The New International Law-Makers', 248.

[87] *cf* ibid, 248.

[88] Annecoos Wiersema, 'The New International Law-Makers? Conferences of the Parties to Multilateral Environmental Agreements' (2009) 31 *Michigan Journal of International Law* 231, 248.

of interpretation in accordance with Article 31 Vienna Convention on the Law of Treaties. Second, it is a concept specific to the international legal order that neither necessarily has relevance in the internal normative orders which have formed around the treaty bodies (see chapter two, Section A), nor in the national legal orders, although the latter generally have developed similar concepts. In other words, post-treaty instruments have broader importance than as 'subsequent agreements' alone.

Third, the political nature of the process of negotiation and adoption of the text of the instrument is really a continuation of the process of treaty adoption. These instruments are negotiated and adopted by the parties by consensus, exactly how treaties are negotiated. Adopting a post-treaty instrument is the result of a political negotiation, not a technical implementing decision.[89] In the literature on the development of particular environmental treaty regimes, there is indeed widespread agreement that the main reason why the adoption of the precise regulatory material is postponed to a post-treaty stage is the lack of (political) agreement, and the need for more prolonged processes to achieve common ground for more precise rules.[90]

Fourth, using the term 'treaty' in the concept aims to connote the importance of this set of instruments for the treaty regimes of which they are part. It is not exaggeration to put post-treaty instruments on a par with the underlying treaty in terms of regulatory relevance.[91] They have become 'functionally equivalent': it is mostly a political outcome which regulatory aspect is discussed at which level of governance.[92] While 'decision', 'recommendation', 'guideline' or 'treaty body instrument' convey a sense of subordination to the treaty, the concept of 'post-treaty instrument' aims to convey this equal regulatory significance.

For the many issues for which PTIs are adopted, they set out much more than the treaty how the regime's bodies are supposed to operate, and what the obligations are with which the parties are expected to comply. The Kyoto Protocol, for instance, introduces flexibility mechanisms such as emissions trading, joint implementation, and the clean development mechanism,[93] thereby

[89] Martti Koskenniemi, 'The Mystery of Legal Obligation' (2011) 3 *International Theory* 319, 325.

[90] René Lefeber, 'Creative Legal Engineering' (2000) 13 *Leiden Journal of International Law* 1, 1 (pointing to political disagreement as the reason for the insertion of the enabling clause in Art 7(4) Cartagena Protocol); Gehring, 'Treaty-Making and Treaty-Evolution', 480 ('to postpone the settlement of pending conflicts').

[91] Nico Krisch, 'The Structure of Postnational Authority' (2015), at http://papers.ssrn.com/sol3/papers.cfm?abstract_id=2564579, 2 (noting this for many non-traditional forms of global governance generally); Matthias Goldmann, 'We Need to Cut Off the Head of the King: Past, Present, and Future Approaches to International Soft Law' (2012) 25 *Leiden Journal of International Law* 335, 336–37 (speaks of the 'functional equivalence' of much soft law compared to the sources of international law).

[92] Gehring, 'Treaty-Making and Treaty-Evolution', 481 ('Hence, the two levels of law-making become – to some degree – functional equivalents – that is, actors can increasingly choose the level at which they will deal with a given problem.').

[93] Arts 6, 12 and 17 Kyoto Protocol.

excluding other possible strategies such as requiring exclusively domestic action. Yet, it defines neither these mechanisms or their terms of operation, nor the crucial accounting modalities for calculating the utilisation of these mechanisms. When it comes to the question what parties can or cannot do to achieve compliance, the Kyoto Protocol articles provide very little information. The exact proportion with which emissions trading had to be 'supplemental to domestic action'[94] (left for determination by PTIs) has at least as much impact on what behaviour constitutes compliance as the possibility of emissions trading itself (introduced by the MEAs). For instance, had the flexibility mechanisms been limited to a small percentage of total reductions, the real modification of consumption patterns required within developed countries would have been much more radical. In the opposite scenario, without any PTIs, many more interpretations of the Kyoto Protocol's Articles 6, 12 and 17 would be acceptable, while that interpretive space has shrunk considerably on account of the PTIs' existence.[95]

An alternative option would be to conceptualise COP, COP/MOP and MOP decisions as (closely related to) decisions of international organisations. This would, however, contradict the above analysis of the non-autonomous nature of the plenary treaty meetings. A second reason not to equate rules and decisions of plenary treaty meetings with decisions of international organisations is that the nature of the former differs from most of the output of international organisations.[96] Overlooking the range of decisions of international organisations, on the one hand there are unequivocally binding decisions of international organisations, such as UN Security Council decisions, and on the other hand unequivocally non-binding decisions of international organisations, such as UN General Assembly resolutions. By contrast to UNSC resolutions, nothing in MEAs or protocols suggests that PTIs are legally *binding*. Yet, by contrast to UNGA resolutions and other clearly non-binding instruments emanating from international organisations, nothing in the language of underlying MEA or protocol provisions suggests that PTIs are *non-binding* either. The matter of bindingness is instead left entirely unmentioned. At the same time, the language used in PTIs can be much more mandatory than the language of most non-binding decisions of international organisations.

In conclusion, the term 'post-treaty instruments' (PTIs) best captures the phenomenon of COP, COP/MOP and MOP decisions considering the lack of autonomy of treaty bodies, the singular characteristics of their decisions which have effects and functions unlike the decisions of IOs, the chronological,

[94] Art 17 Kyoto Protocol.

[95] Compare Sand, 'Institution-Building Compliance', 780 ('considering that even "clarifications" of previously indeterminate treaty terms effectively reduce the range of interpretative options that were available to the Parties prior to the clarification').

[96] *cf* Wiersema, 'The New International Law-Makers', 251, 253–55.

substantive and legal connection to the underlying treaty, the highly political, treaty-negotiation-like decision-making process, and, finally, the regulatory importance at least on a par with treaties.

Post-treaty instruments are not exclusive to Multilateral Environmental Agreements. For instance, the parties to the *Framework Convention on Tobacco Control* have also regularly adopted post-treaty rules to interpret, supplement or modify the Convention.[97] The *Arms Trade Treaty* 'Conference of States Parties' (CSP) may 'adopt recommendations regarding the implementation and operation of this Treaty',[98] and has taken steps towards the adoption of a first wave of post-treaty instruments during its first CSP.[99]

3. Post-Treaty Decisions and Post-Treaty Rules

With a common concept for all COP, COP/MOP and MOP decisions in place, it can be broken down further into sub-categories for meaningful analysis. The first major distinction among PTIs is between rules (general) and decisions (addressing specific cases). Applied to Post-Treaty Instruments, this distinction produces the sub-categories of Post-Treaty Rules and Post-Treaty Decisions.

Post-Treaty Decisions (PTDs) are PTIs addressing specific cases or individual states. Examples include: instruments concerning a particular area of land, such as a decision to place particular wetlands on the Ramsar List of Wetlands of International Importance, or under the special scrutiny of the Montreux List; instruments that suspend all trade in CITES-listed species with a particular CITES treaty party for a certain period of time; instruments introducing an exceptional situation for a particular population of a certain species under CITES; instruments setting particular production or consumption limits of ozone-depleting substances for individual treaty parties under the Montreal Protocol; findings of (non-)compliance with regard to specific states by compliance bodies.

Post-Treaty Rules (PTRs) are PTIs that set general rules. The category of Post-Treaty Rules is the object of research of this study. A rough distinction between two kinds of PTRs can be made, respectively external and internal PTRs. Both can be based on implicit as well as explicit enabling clauses.

[97] Art 7 of the Framework Convention on Tobacco Control (adopted 21 May 2003, entered into force 27 February 2005) 2302 UNTS 166 (FCTC) confers on the COP the power to issue guidelines relating to non-price measures for reducing tobacco consumption contained in Arts 8–13 FCTC. The FCTC COP has extensively used these powers. Examples include guidelines adopted on the basis of Art 5.3 (Protection of tobacco control policies from commercial and other vested interests of the tobacco industry); Art 8 (Protection from exposure to tobacco smoke); Art 11 (Packaging and labelling of tobacco products); and Art 13 (Tobacco advertising, promotion and sponsorship). Afterwards, guidelines have also been adopted at the fourth COP for Arts 9 and 10 (Regulation and Disclosure); Art 12 (Public Education); and Art 14 (Cessation).

[98] Art 17 Arms Trade Treaty (adopted 2 April 2013, entered into force 24 December 2014) (not yet reported).

[99] Arms Trade Treaty CSP, First Conference of States Parties, Cancun, 24–27 August 2015.

4. External and Internal Post-Treaty Rules

External PTRs are general rules directly addressing the treaty parties, their obligations and conduct, or their domestic regulation of conduct of others.[100] For instance, the Ramsar COP's *General guidance for interpreting 'urgent national interests' under Article 2.5 of the Convention and considering compensation under Article 4.2* contains guidance on how to interpret the right of treaty parties to delete or restrict the boundaries of an already listed wetland on their territory, because of 'its urgent national interests', under Article 2.5 of the Convention. This deletion or restriction of the boundaries of a listed wetland is a right of each party, and is not a function of the Ramsar COP or its subsidiaries. Another example is the *Definitions, modalities, rules and guidelines relating to land use, land-use change and forestry activities (LULUCF)*,[101] which the Kyoto COP/MOP adopted on the basis of Articles 3.3 and 3.4 of the Kyoto Protocol. This PTR sets out general criteria in which forestry-related activities are relevant for meeting the emission reduction targets set through the Kyoto Protocol.

Internal PTRs are general rules addressing the functioning and operation of the plenary treaty meeting, its subsidiary bodies and even the parties, in their capacity as participants in these meetings and bodies.[102] The primary example of internal PTRs are the CITES COP *Criteria for amendment of Appendices I and II*,[103] the 'Listing Criteria' for short. The Listing Criteria are not addressing the environmental conduct of the parties in allowing trade in endangered species to and from their territory, but at the operation of the CITES COP, the CITES Secretariat and the treaty parties when they consider adding or removing species to or from the Appendices. Another example of an internal PTR is the Montreal Protocol MOP decision on *Critical-use exemptions for methyl bromide*.[104] This PTR contains a set of criteria addressing the Montreal MOP's yearly decision on the acceptable levels of production and consumption of methyl bromide by treaty parties that have indicated their need for methyl bromide despite its being phased out.

The distinction between internal and external PTRs is directly relevant for the analysis of their authority. For internal PTRs, aimed at governing activities within the regime, only their authority within the regime matters. For external PTRs addressing the environmental conduct of the treaty parties on their own territory or against the territory of other states, or their regulation of environmental

[100] Wiersema, 'The New International Law-Makers', 237–40. In Wiersema's version, external PTRs can be further divided into rules 'defining treaty terms that inform the external, substantive obligations of the parties' and rules making 'direct changes to the parties' external obligations'.

[101] Kyoto COP/MOP Decisions 13/CMP.1 and 2/CMP.7.

[102] *Internal PTRs* resemble the category of standard instruments that Goldmann calls 'internal operational rules', and are not unlike what Wiersema calls 'the internal operation of the treaty'. Goldmann, 'Inside Relative Normativity', 697–99; Wiersema, 'The New International Law-Makers', 241–45.

[103] CITES COP Res. Conf. 9.24 (Rev. 16), *Criteria for amendment of Appendices I and II.*

[104] Montreal MOP Decision IX/6, *Critical-use exemptions for methyl bromide.*

conduct by private actors, it is not enough to possess authority within the regime. Their degree of authority in the international and national legal orders is crucial for the outcomes of inter-state dispute settlement procedures and domestic court procedures.

E. The Normative Relationship between MEAs and Environmental Post-Treaty Rules

This final section discusses the nature of the normative relationship between MEAs and PTRs. As such, this section creates further sub-categories of PTRs useful to their authority analysis. Commentators of international environmental regimes tend to be unduly vague about the nature of the relationship between MEAs and PTRs. Some describe the function of PTRs in terms of 'clarification', 'concretisation' or 'implementation' of the underlying MEA. In other words, they see PTRs as acts of discovery of what is already prescribed by the MEA. Others recognise, rightly it is submitted, that PTRs go beyond clarification or implementation of pre-existing obligations, and accept that many PTRs expand and specify the obligations of the parties, and add new or even contradictory obligations.

1. 'Clarification'?

A first type of account of PTRs defends the position that COP, COP/MOP and MOP decisions are 'concretisations', 'elaborations' or 'clarifications'. This characterisation can be found for PTRs based on implicit enabling clauses in particular. Friedrich submits that 'if nonbinding instruments contain precise norms, they can deliver much needed *concretisations* of those terms and provisions in treaties that due to reluctance of states to agree on binding norms often remain vague and imprecise' (emphasis added).[105] Bothe speaks of 'a clarification process',[106] and Sommer of acts '*elaborating* a description of [an MEA's] content' (emphasis added).[107] The term 'clarification' supposes that PTRs merely explain a rule already prescribed by the treaty. 'Concretisation' supposes that only a single concretisation is possible. 'Elaborating' suggests there is something to build on.

For the majority of PTRs, this depiction is not correct. PTRs do not derive pre-existing meaning from MEA provisions. For instance, Article II.1 CITES

[105] Jürgen Friedrich, *International Environmental 'soft Law': The Functions and Limits of Nonbinding Instruments in International Environmental Governance and Law* (Springer, 2013), 171, 215–16.

[106] Michael Bothe, 'The United Nations Framework Convention on Climate Change – an Unprecedented Multilevel Regulatory Challenge' (2003) 63 *Zeitschrift für ausländisches öffentliches Recht und Volkerrecht* 239, 246.

[107] Sommer, 'Environmental Law-Making', 635.

states that species 'threatened with extinction' will be listed in appendices, and will receive special protection. This provision hardly provides a clue as to *which species* will actually be listed, or *which criteria* will be used for the listing decisions. Under what conditions is a species sufficiently threatened to be listed? What if it is threatened in one geographic area, but not in another? What if it is not threatened by *international* trade *per se*, but only by habitat change? How much information about the threat is needed? Many compositions of the list are possible, as well as many different sets of listing criteria, which would all be 'legally right'.[108]

Likewise, requiring that emissions trading is 'supplemental' to domestic emissions reduction activities, as Article 17 Kyoto Protocol states, is a far cry from determining how to balance the two. The discretion that such treaty provisions leave to future rule-making through post-treaty rules is great. Some explicit enabling clauses recognise this: Article 2H, paragraph 5 of the Montreal Protocol, allows the Montreal MOP to permit critical uses of methyl bromide as far as 'necessary to satisfy uses *agreed by them to be critical uses*' (emphasis added).[109] Insofar as scholars use the *term* interpretation, but define it as clarification,[110] this amounts to the same error of viewing interpretation as an act of discovery. As Venzke puts it, 'interpretation contributes to creating what it finds'.[111] It could not be otherwise, because the parties are not clairvoyant.

2. 'Implementation'?

A second often-encountered characterisation of COP, COP/MOP and MOP decisions is that they are 'implementing decisions'. For example, according to Werksman, '[t]here can be said to be two stages in the life of an MEA …: The first stage is the process of treaty-making, the negotiation and adoption of the text of an international agreement. The second stage is the more open-ended process of *implementing* the agreement's provisions'.[112] Of a number of post-treaty rules, Sommer likewise says that 'acts of this type may not be real law-making as they do not create general norms but rather *implement* norms through elaborating a description of their content',[113] and she describes plenary treaty meetings as

[108] Federick Schauer, *Thinking Like a Lawyer: A New Introduction to Legal Reasoning* (Harvard University Press, 2009), 190–91. Most implicit enabling clauses are very close to what in the literature are often called 'standards'. Standards, according to Schauer, are defined by the attribute that they allow for numerous decisions taken under their banner that are 'equally *legally* right'. They 'will let stand a multiplicity of quite different decisions'.

[109] Article 2H, paragraph 5 Montreal Protocol.

[110] For instance, Irina Buga, *The Modification of Treaties by Subsequent Practice: The Implications of Practice Going Beyond the Limits of Treaty Interpretation* (Dissertation, 2015), 151 ('where subsequent practice is used to clarify the treaty terms, it is to be characterized as an interpretation').

[111] Ingo Venzke, *How Interpretation Makes International Law: On Semantic Change and Normative Twists* (OUP, 2012), 239.

[112] Werksman, 'The Conference of the Parties', 56.

[113] Sommer, 'Environmental Law-Making', 635.

'organisations established under environmental conventions for the *implementation* of the substantive treaty provisions'.[114]

The term 'implementation' is bound to create confusion about the character of the activity that is described by it.[115] It is typically used to downplay the regulatory relevance of the activity described. A common characteristic of all implementation is that it is only possible where there exists a pre-existing act with a clear meaning, congruent with which outcomes can be brought about.[116] Implementation is about giving practical effect to, or to ensure the actual fulfilment of, some beforehand agreed upon outcome.[117] Therefore, only rules that define the required behaviour or outcome in a reasonably transparent and specific manner are amenable to direct implementation, without the need to adopt a more specifically formulated general rule first. For enabling clauses in MEAs and protocols, be it because of their overt indeterminacy or explicit call for more specific rules, such agreed standards of behaviour or outcome simply do not exist, so that their implementation by way of PTRs is impossible.

In fact, PTRs are the necessary step to make implementation *possible*, turning treaty provisions into specific rules. For instance, it is arguable that the listing or delisting of species shifted closer to a form of international implementation with the adoption of the CITES listing criteria.[118] Likewise, the setting of criteria for critical uses, and the critical uses determined on the basis of those criteria, of methyl bromide under the Montreal Protocol (international implementation), could henceforth be nationally implemented, subject to international compliance review.

In the PTR context, use of the term implementation should be limited to two phenomena. First, one may speak of the *national implementation* of international environmental law, including of environmental PTRs. Second, implementation might be used to describe the *application to particular cases* of existing regulative rules at the international level, such as the listing of a species based on the CITES listing criteria.

3. Regulatory Acts: Interpretation, Supplementation or Modification

PTRs are *regulatory* acts. For the many issues on which PTRs are adopted, *they* – not the underlying MEA – contain the detailed rules on how the plenary meetings

[114] ibid, 631. See also Churchill and Ulfstein, 'Autonomous Institutional Arrangements', 639 (stating that 'COPs may be authorized to adopt measures that relate to the implementation of the parties' substantive obligations').

[115] Jan-Erik Lane, 'The Concept of Implementation' (1983) 86 *Statsvetenskaplig tidskrift* 17, 17.

[116] ibid, 17.

[117] ibid, 18.

[118] *cf* Thomas Gehring and Eva Ruffing, 'When Arguments Prevail Over Power: The CITES Procedure for the Listing of Endangered Species' (2008) 8 *Global Environmental Politics* 123.

should operate, and how the parties should comply with their obligations. The states meeting in the plenary treaty meetings are not carrying out previously 'agreed-upon programs and projects';[119] they are defining what those 'programs and projects' really are. The relationship between MEAs and PTRs is thus comparable to the relationship between legislation and administrative rules at the domestic level. The MEA is the 'legislation' without which parties would not be in a position to take the further steps of adopting PTRs. But the PTRs do not implement existing rules, they interpret, supplement and modify.

The term 'regulatory' still has quite a broad meaning. Doctrinal debates between legal scholars on the nature of the relationship between treaties and instruments adopted by the treaty parties at a later stage are helpful in further specifying the relationship between MEAs and PTRs, between 1) *interpretation*, 2) *supplementation or gap-filling*, and 3) *modification*. PTRs based on implicit enabling clauses generally relate to the treaty in an interpretative or modifying manner. PTRs based on explicit enabling clauses generally relate to the treaty in a supplementing, or gap-filling, fashion.

There are three important reasons for breaking down the PTR concept not just between external and internal PTRs, but also between interpretive, supplementing and modifying PTRs. First, a PTR that qualifies as modification may face a problem of legality, since treaty law ordinarily prescribes a formal amendment for modifying a treaty. This is dealt with in the next section. Second, there is debate on whether interpretive and supplemental PTRs carry the same degree of legal obligation according to the law of treaties, to be addressed in chapter four. This section merely reports the different characterisations of the *relationship* between MEA and PTR. Third, it has been suggested that the authority of PTRs based on explicit enabling clauses is likely to be higher than PTRs based on implicit enabling clauses.

PTRs *based on implicit enabling clauses* – on open-ended terms in the underlying treaty – can normally be characterised as '*interpretive*' PTRs, and on rare occasions as '*modifying*' PTRs. As noted above, the interpretation of open-ended treaty terms by the treaty parties is based on their power to adopt 'authentic interpretations'. The main characteristic of an 'authentic interpretation' is that it is 'based on the communicative assumption that the treaty and the agreement do not logically contradict one another'.[120] This definition captures the essential difference between interpretation and modification, and thus between interpretive and modifying PTRs. An interpretive PTR needs to be *reconcilable* with the underlying treaty. A general rule or set of general rules adopted in the plenary treaty that *contradicts* the underlying treaty is a modifying PTR.

[119] The definition of policy implementation that Bradley and Kelley provide in their treatise on international delegation. Bradley and Kelley, *The Concept of Delegation*, 17.

[120] Linderfalk, '*On the Interpretation of Treaties*', 192. See also Pan, 'Authoritative Interpretation of Agreements', 509 ('authoritative interpretation does not change the constitutive agreement'); Julian Arato, 'Subsequent Practice and Evolutive Interpretation: Techniques of Treaty Interpretation over Time and Their Diverse Consequences' (2010) 9 *The Law & Practice of International Courts and Tribunals* 443, 462.

The distinction between interpretation and modification is, however, a difficult one. Whether a treaty and a PTR are reconcilable is in itself a question of interpretation of the terms of the treaty. There is no clear dividing line.[121] However, this does not mean that the conceptual divide as such makes no sense. It only means that there is a fine line, a grey zone[122] of PTRs for which an argument can be made either way.[123]

Some PTRs approach the dividing line between interpretation and modification, or even clearly cross over toward modification. An important example is the resolutions of the Ramsar COP, which have conflated the terms 'wise use' and 'conservation' in Article 3.1 of the Ramsar Convention. Article 3.1 states that the Contracting Parties shall 'promote the *conservation* of the wetlands included in the List, and as far as possible the *wise use* of wetlands in their territory'. Although these terms are not further defined in the Convention itself, Article 3.1 makes it quite clear that the terms, at least, connote different standards of protection,[124] with conservation being the more hands-off approach of the two. However, in the practice under the Convention, the parties have adopted countless resolutions referring to the 'wise use' of *listed sites*, conflating the two standards. According to Ramsar COP Resolution VII.11, for instance, the listing of a wetland is 'an appropriate first step along a conservation and sustainable use pathway, the endpoint of which is achieving the long-term wise (sustainable) use of the site'.[125] This is a clear contradiction of the terms of the convention, so that with some measure of confidence these can be categorised as modifying rather than interpretive PTRs. Yet, even for this apparently obvious example of modification, looking at the text of the treaty alone, doubts could arise on the basis of the text of 4(1) Ramsar Convention, which requires the treaty parties to 'promote the *conservation* of wetlands and waterfowl by establishing nature reserves on wetlands, *whether they are included in the List or not*' (emphasis added).[126]

For the great majority of PTRs, however, it is quite clear that they do not contradict the open-ended terms in the implicit enabling clause on which they are based, and that they constitute interpretations. The reason is obvious: as discussed in

[121] Wolfram Karl, *Vertrag Und Spätere Praxis Im Völkerrecht. Zum Einfluß Der Praxis Auf Inhalt Und Bestand Völkerrechtlicher Verträge* (Springer, 1983), 3 ('So wird es ein besonderes Anliegen dieser Arbeit sein zu zeigen, daß zwischen der Vertragsänderung und der Vertragsauslegung kein allgemeingültiger Trennungsstrich gezogen werden').

[122] Buga, *The Modification of Treaties by Subsequent Practice*, 156.

[123] International Law Commission, *Draft Articles on the Law of Treaties with Commentaries* (1966) II *Yearbook of the International Law Commission*, p 236, para 1: 'Although the line may sometimes be blurred between interpretation and amendment of a treaty through subsequent practice, legally the processes are distinct'.

[124] Alexandre S Timoshenko, 'Protection of Wetlands in International Law', *Legal Aspects of the Conservation of Wetlands* (IUCN 1991) 69.

[125] Ramsar COP Resolution VII.11, *Strategic Framework and Guidelines for the Future Development of the List of Wetlands of International Importance.*

[126] *cf* Bowman, Davies and Redgwell, *Lyster's International Wildlife Law*, 414.

Section C.2 of this chapter, a great many provisions in MEAs contain open-ended terms, phrases and obligations which allow for a very wide range of interpretations, without contradicting what the treaty prescribes. For instance, there are many different possible sets of criteria that could be agreed upon to determine whether a species is 'threatened with extinction' in the sense of Article II.1 CITES. Such a set of criteria can have a tremendous impact on which species are, and are not, thereafter listed in the Appendices of protected species. But, unless that set of criteria would allow for the listing of species that are very clearly not threatened with extinction, it would not contradict the Convention, and thus be an interpretive rather than a modifying PTR.

PTRs *based on explicit enabling clauses* – on an explicit assignment to the plenary treaty meeting – are best characterised as *supplementing* or *gap-filling* in their relation to the treaty.[127] PTRs based on explicit enabling clauses do not interpret treaty terms or phrases by specifying them, but instead adopt rules that fill a gap explicitly left open in the treaty. Just like interpretive PTRs – and unlike modification – supplementing PTRs do not contradict the terms of the treaty.[128] As the US Court of Appeals in *NRDC v EPA* dryly noted on the Montreal Protocol PTRs called the *Critical-use Exemptions*, which are based on an explicit enabling clause in the Protocol, '[l]ike any interpretive tool, however, the "decisions" are useful only to the extent they shed light on ambiguous terms in the Protocol. But the details of the critical-use exemption are not ambiguous. They are non-existent. The "decisions" do not interpret treaty language. They fill in treaty gaps.'[129] Article 2H.5 of the Montreal Protocol enabled the Montreal MOP to adopt a PTR on possible exemptions for so-called critical uses of the ozone-depleting substance methyl bromide. The treaty explicitly states that it did *not* already constitute an agreement which uses of methyl bromide amount to 'critical uses'.[130] The Court of Appeals stated: 'Article 2H(5) thus constitutes an "agreement to agree". In the Protocol, the parties agree to reach an agreement concerning the types of uses for which new production and consumption will be permitted, and the amounts that will be permitted'.

[127] Some international lawyers argue that supplementation is a type of modification. See Buga, *The Modification of Treaties by Subsequent Practice*, 119 ('The term 'modification' is taken here to refer to both altering treaty provisions, and supplementing them with an important 'novel' element or direction.').

[128] Buga argues against this position: ibid, 120 (submitting that 'the elaboration or supplementation of a rule by subsequent practice constitutes modification if it adds a new "dimension" to the rule being elaborated or to the treaty's object and purpose(s), rather than merely a concretization or clarification of the text'). However, this position overlooks that 1) PTRs are not clarifications, if such a thing as clarification without interpretation even exists; and 2) interpretations also add a new 'dimension' to the term being interpreted, so that classifying supplementation as modification would also collapse the difference between *interpretation* and modification.

[129] *NRDC v EPA*, p 15.

[130] Art 2H.5 Montreal Protocol, last sentence: 'This paragraph will apply save to the extent that the Parties decide to permit the level of production or consumption that is necessary to satisfy *uses agreed by them to be critical uses*' (emphasis added).

Gap-filling PTRs do not necessarily have less or more far-reaching consequences for the rules applying to the treaty parties than modifications or interpretations. But MEAs making much use of explicit enabling clauses, such as the Kyoto Protocol, and to a lesser extent the Montreal Protocol, leave open so many gaps that PTRs can completely transform the rules that apply to the treaty parties, without contradicting the protocol text in the slightest.

4. Substantive Limits to Modifying PTRs

This final section discusses the substantive limits that PTRs may not exceed in accordance with the respective MEAs and their rules of procedure. It explores boundaries for the legal authority of PTRs that go beyond the limit of an explicit enabling clause, or that contradict the terms of the treaty outright, and as such set out to modify it, risk invalidity in accordance with the law of treaties.[131] Even if PTRs would not be legally binding, the issue of substantive validity retains relevance, since an invalid PTR should also be prevented from gaining authority as a means of interpretation.[132]

The main argument against the validity of modifications, other than by formal amendment, is that most treaties contain a provision prescribing formal procedures for amending the treaty.[133] All MEAs have a provision in place setting out a formal procedure for amendment of the MEA.[134] In order for an amendment to enter into force, these provisions require large majorities of two thirds to three quarters of the parties to submit instruments of ratification. Amendments only enter into force for parties that have ratified them. These procedures are not followed in the adoption of PTRs. PTRs are adopted by consensus of the plenary treaty meeting, and become operative immediately, unless the PTR states otherwise.

Further support for this argument is found in the fate that met the once proposed Draft Article 38 VCLT at the Vienna Conference on the Law of Treaties. The envisaged Article, titled 'Modification of treaties by subsequent practice', provided that '[a] treaty may be modified by subsequent practice in the application of the treaty establishing the agreement of the parties to modify its provisions'.[135] It did not survive the substantial opposition from state representatives, exactly because they argued that modification should be reserved to formal

[131] Because plenary treaty meetings are not international organisations, the concept of *ultra vires* decisions developed in the law of international organisations is less suitable to the case of PTRs.

[132] See ch 4, section A.1.

[133] *cf* Venzke, *How Interpretation Makes International Law*, 236.

[134] Art 11.4(h) Montreal Protocol; Art 20 Kyoto Protocol; Art 10bis Ramsar Convention; Art 17 CITES.

[135] International Law Commission, *Draft Articles on the Law of Treaties with Commentaries* (1966) II *Yearbook of the International Law Commission*, 236.

amendment procedures.[136] This would lead to the conclusion that PTRs 'can develop a treaty in a way that stops short of modifications that require formal amendment'.[137]

Indeed, parties to various MEAs have charged a handful of PTRs with being invalid on account of bypassing the formal amendment procedure in the past decades, raising protests in the COP, COP/MOP or MOP.[138] Handl examined a number of PTRs that clearly contradicted treaty language, or were not based on any treaty provision, and the reactions they incited. In almost all these cases, protests erupted, and the targeted PTRs were withdrawn or re-adopted as a formal amendment.[139]

One interesting example is the decision taken by the parties at the second meeting of the COP of the Basel Convention on the Transboundary Movement of Hazardous Wastes and Their Disposal.[140] Decision II/12 introduced a ban on exports of hazardous wastes from OECD to non-OECD countries, a 'major revision of the original understanding'.[141] On this occasion, the Conference of the Parties ignored the obvious meaning of a number of Convention articles, which 'approaches regulation of international trade in waste through information and consent rather than through prohibitions and bans'.[142] Therefore, a number of treaty parties argued that the decision should have been subjected to a formal amendment, and this eventually happened.[143] Another well-known example that Handl discusses is the controversy about the decisions under the International Convention for the Regulation of Whaling (ICRW) to impose a moratorium on

[136] Wolfram Karl, *Vertrag Und Spätere Praxis Im Völkerrecht. Zum Einfluß Der Praxis Auf Inhalt Und Bestand Völkerrechtlicher Verträge* (1983), 291–94.

[137] Venzke, '*How Interpretation Makes International Law*', 238. As Jutta Brunnée states in the context of the Kyoto Protocol, 'the rules, guidelines or procedures that are to flesh out the Protocol must be compatible with the terms of both the Protocol and the UNFCCC'. See Jutta Brunnée, 'COPing with Consent: Law Making Under Multilateral Environmental Agreements' (2002) 15 *Leiden Journal of International Law* 1, 42.

[138] That there are so few of such incidents is not surprising in light of the many open-ended terms in MEAs, where widely differing interpretations are possible without contradicting the terms of the treaty.

[139] Günther Handl, 'International "Lawmaking" by Conferences of the Parties and Other Politically Mandated Bodies' in Rüdiger Wolfrum and Volker Röben (eds), *Developments of International Law in Treaty Making* (Springer 2005), 130–31. A number of his examples are, however, not of a general rule-setting character, but rather the establishing of a subsidiary body or a change of the procedural rules.

[140] UN Doc UNEP/IG.80/3, 22 March 1989.

[141] As Handl submits, '[a]lthough the Convention itself – in its preamble as well as in Art 15, para 7 – envisages the possibility of a partial or complete ban of transboundary movements of hazardous wastes, the COP's decision to ban such movements as essentially between North and South, constitutes a very major revision of the original understanding among the parties to the Convention'. Handl, 'International 'Lawmaking' by Conferences of the Parties', 131, fn 20 and accompanying text.

[142] Wiersema, 'The New International Law-Makers', 239. *cf* Werksman, 'The Conference of the Parties', 55, 63–64.

[143] Convention on the Control of Transboundary Movements of Hazardous Wastes and their Disposal (adopted 22 March 1989, entered into force 5 May 1992) 1673 UNTS 57 (Basel Convention) COP Decision III/1, 28 November 1995.

commercial whaling and to establish the Southern Ocean Sanctuary.[144] Treaty parties with whaling industries argued that these conservation measures disregarded Article V.2 of the ICRW, which requires that such measures 'be based on scientific findings'. The whaling nations also asserted that the moratorium and sanctuary decisions were incompatible with the ICRW's objectives and purposes in a broader sense: conservation not for conservation's sake, but for the maintenance of sustainable whaling stock.

As Handl concludes on the basis of the available evidence, instances of clear contradiction are rare and, when they have taken place, almost always have led to a situation where the COP, COP/MOP or MOP 'backtracked and sought to defuse the controversies by resorting to the formal law-making/amendment procedures'.[145]

The validity of PTRs becomes more complicated in the absence of protests from the treaty parties, or where PTRs fall within a grey zone between interpretation and modification. Contrary to the examples discussed by Handl, the examples of PTRs contradicting the Ramsar Convention relating to the 'conservation' and 'wise use' of wetlands, mentioned earlier, were never publicly contested by one or more treaty parties. Various theories about why such situations arise are possible. The treaty parties may have considered the PTRs in question to relate not in a modifying but in an interpretive manner to the treaty, because – as noted previously regarding interpretation and modification, 'it is next to impossible to distinguish one from the other, or at least to formulate such a distinction in general terms'.[146] Other parties may have doubted the validity of these PTRs, but decided to remain silent for various reasons, such as their support for the content of the modification or their political estimation of the slim chances of successful protest.

If a PTR constitutes a modification of the treaty, and thus formally violates the treaty by not following the prescribed amendment procedure, could silence on the part of the treaty parties constitute a particular form of acquiescence? Acquiescence means the silence or failure to protest by a state against an encroachment on its rights, in a situation *where active objection of that state is required*.[147] In some areas of international law, notably in territorial and boundary disputes, it is well accepted that acquiescence can even modify rights and obligations.[148] In the context of the adoption of PTRs, if a treaty party has not objected against the formation of consensus in the plenary treaty meeting, does that negate its right to protest at a later stage? Is the active objection of the treaty parties required to prevent the validity of a treaty modification? Strong doubts remain whether acquiescing parties merely lose their right to protest, or go as far as validating the modification. In the 1971 Namibia Opinion, the International Court of

[144] Handl, 'International "Lawmaking" by Conferences of the Parties', 133–34.
[145] ibid, 136.
[146] Venzke, '*How Interpretation Makes International Law*', 238.
[147] Sérgio N Marques Antunes, 'Acquiescence', *MPEPIL* (2015).
[148] ibid.

Justice practically supported the latter position. The Court stated that, by having 'consistently and uniformly interpreted the practice of voluntary abstention by a permanent member as not constituting a bar to the adoption of resolutions', this procedure had been 'generally accepted by Members of the United Nations and evidences a general practice of that Organization'.[149] This passage does not go so far as concluding that the Charter had been successfully modified, but that is the outcome in practice. In any case, without a right to protest, the validity of that modification is unlikely to be challenged anymore.

[149] *Legal Consequences for States of the Continued Presence of South Africa in Namibia (South West Africa) notwithstanding Security Council Resolution 276 (1970)* (Advisory Opinion) [1971] ICJ Rep 16.

2

The Compartmentalised Authority of Environmental Post-Treaty Rules

Environmental Post-Treaty Rules have very different degrees of authority in different normative orders. In short, their authority is very compartmentalised. That conclusion arises from an in-depth analysis of the authority of a number of PTRs from the four regimes selected for this study. In the internal normative orders that have developed in the international environmental regimes, there is no difference between the authority of PTRs and their underlying MEA at all. In the international and national legal orders, however, PTRs have a much lower degree of authority than MEAs. Particularly in the domestic legal orders, states can easily escape PTRs as reference points in the interpretation of the underlying MEA.

This chapter follows the existence of PTRs from the Ramsar, CITES, Kyoto and Montreal treaty meetings. Starting with a short discussion of the particular set-up of each regime, the reasons for the adoption of the PTRs in question, the circumstances of their adoption and their content, it continues with their authority in the internal order of the treaty bodies, in the international legal order and in national legal orders.

The closing observations bring the case studies together: the differences between the case studies; between the levels of authority of PTRs from the four regimes; between the authority of internal and external PTRs; between interpretive and supplemental PTRs; and – last but not least – between the three normative orders. But before embarking on this in-depth investigation of the authority of PTRs, it should be explained why and how this investigation must distinguish three partly separated normative orders.

A. Investigating Authority: Three Normative Orders

It is impossible to speak of *the* authority of PTRs. As Benedict Kingsbury suggests, in global governance, 'there is no single legal system … with [a single] rule of recognition'.[1] For international environmental law alone, a multitude of relevant

[1] Benedict Kingsbury, 'The Concept of 'Law' in Global Administrative Law' (2009) 20 *European Journal of International Law* 23, 29.

normative orders with their own rules of recognition exists: the internal orders of the various international environmental regimes, the international legal order, and all the different domestic legal orders. These orders are not completely closed off from each other, but they are sufficiently separate that a single PTR may have different authority in each of them, and that it makes sense to speak of separate normative orders.

All three orders have their own relevance for the effectiveness and implementation of international environmental law. But the internal orders are especially relevant to internal PTRs, that is PTRS aimed at the conduct of treaty parties acting within the meetings and subsidiary bodies of the treaty regime. The national legal orders, and to a lesser extent the international legal orders, are especially relevant to external PTRs, those PTRs aimed at the environmental conduct and policies of individual states. This plurality of normative orders is not a new phenomenon. As long as there has been a separation between the international and domestic legal orders, an instrument with international legal status does not always have domestic legal status even in monist states. This depends on a constitutional decision of the domestic political institutions.

1. Defining Internal Normative Orders

It is suggested that international environmental regimes – the 'principles, norms, rules, and decision-making procedures around which actor expectations converge in a given issue-area'[2] – constitute an 'internal normative order'.[3] Two questions arise with regard to the use of the term 'normative orders'. First, do international environmental regimes really constitute sufficiently separate normative spheres to speak of a separate 'order'? And second, why speak of normative orders, not of legal orders?

Do international environmental regimes constitute sufficiently separate spheres so as to speak of a separate 'normative order' at all? What separates them from the international legal order? To start with, complete separation of a normative order from other normative orders is not required to qualify as one. International organisations are widely accepted to establish their own internal normative orders, even legal order, regardless of being far from fully separated from the international legal order.[4] There is a longstanding and open-ended debate on the extent to which general international law or the respective constitutive treaties determine the legal situation of international organisations.[5]

[2] Stephen D Krasner, 'Structural Causes and Regime Consequences: Regimes as Intervening Variables' in Stephen D Krasner (ed), *International regimes* (Cornell University Press, 1983), 1, 185.

[3] This position should not be confused with the assertion in ch 1 that the plenary treaty meetings are not autonomous from their treaty parties.

[4] Christiane Ahlborn, 'The Rules of International Organizations and the Law of International Responsibility' (2011) 8 *International Organizations Law Review* 397, 417.

[5] Jean d'Aspremont, 'The Law of International Organizations and the Art of Reconciliation: From Dichotomies to Dialectics' (2014) 11 *International Organizations Law Review* 428 (distinguishing a

As Kingsbury and Casini suggest, the central requirement for a normative order is that a 'rule of recognition' has developed, along the lines of Hart's understanding of that concept, which is – at least to some extent – specific to a regime.[6] This rule of recognition is 'special' insofar as it does not (fully) overlap with the rules of recognition of other normative orders. As Kingsbury writes, '[t]here may well exist, however, different rules of recognition within different social-institutional-sectoral groupings in specific practice areas of global administrative law'.[7] This Hartian term denotes simply that:

> As to relatively technical areas of very specific IO practice, *the set of authoritative sources and their application* in doubtful cases may be determined by the recognition practice of the key actors in the specific community of expertise on the subject matter and normative regime involved. Thus there is a rule of recognition in Hart's sense, but for these purposes it is not a general rule of recognition covering the whole of international law, but a rule of recognition among a narrower set of specialized actors (emphasis added).[8]

As the case studies below testify, such a special 'rule of recognition' certainly exists for the internal normative orders of the treaty bodies. They show that the relevant norms, the norms that possess authority, can differ strongly between the internal normative order, the international legal order, and the national legal orders. Post-treaty rules have much more authority in the internal normative order of the treaty bodies than in the international and national legal orders.

One very strong example of the existence of a separate internal normative order can be found in a decision from the Kyoto Protocol Compliance Committee, Enforcement Branch, concerning the question of whether Croatia could achieve compliance with the Kyoto Protocol because it had acted in accordance with a PTR adopted by the *UNFCCC* COP. It concerns a Final Decision of the Enforcement Branch,[9] in which it stated that Croatia was barred from relying on a PTR from the *UNFCCC* COP in arguing that it was in compliance with Kyoto Protocol provisions.[10] The Final Decision concerned Croatia's calculation of its assigned amount, calculation of its commitment period reserve, and its compliance with the modalities for the accounting of assigned amounts. Croatia had argued that it should be allowed more flexibility in relation to the above stated issues because of

contractual conceptualisation which sees international organisations as part of the international legal order (permeable), and a constitutionalist conceptualisation, which sees international organisations as autonomous legal orders (impermeable), but regarding the law of international organisations as a reconciliation between the two).

[6] Herbert LA Hart, *The Concept of Law* (OUP, 1961).

[7] Kingsbury, 'The Concept of "Law" in GAL', 30. Echoed in Lorenzo Casini and Benedict Kingsbury, 'Global Administrative Law Dimensions of International Organizations Law' (2009) 6 *International Organizations Law Review* 319, 354. For the expectation that new rules of recognition will spread to new manifestations of public authority, see also Jean d'Aspremont, *Formalism and the Sources of International Law: A Theory of the Ascertainment of Legal Rules* (OUP, 2011), ch 9.

[8] Casini and Kingsbury, 'GAL Dimensions of International Organizations Law', 354.

[9] Kyoto Protocol Compliance Enforcement Branch, CC-2009-1-8/Croatia/EB, 26 November 2009.

[10] ibid.

the content of several decisions *taken by the COP to the UNFCCC* – not the Kyoto COP/MOP – and argued that the EB should defer to those COP decisions in the interpretation of what the Kyoto Protocol requires. The EB disagreed, in particular deciding that Croatia could not rely on Decision 7/CP.12 of the COP to the UNFCCC for the determination of its base year. It reasoned that:

> The application of decision 7/CP.12 under the Kyoto Protocol *does not follow from any of the provisions of the Kyoto Protocol or from [COP/MOP] decisions*. Since the COP and the [COP/MOP] are *two distinct decision-making bodies*, the fact that all Parties to the Kyoto Protocol are also Parties to the United Nations Framework Convention on Climate Change does not provide a sufficient basis for establishing the application of COP decisions under the Kyoto Protocol.[11]

From this reasoning of the Enforcement Branch, it can be plausibly inferred *a contrario* that the authority of Kyoto Protocol COP/MOP decisions in compliance assessments is that the Kyoto Protocol's decision-making body has adopted them, rather than a body outside that treaty order.

This reasoning by the Enforcement Branch suggests that the '*internality*' of COP/MOP decisions and decisions of its subsidiary bodies is what makes them applicable to assessing the compliance of parties with the treaty under which they operate. Just like Dutch legislation is applied by the courts of the Netherlands, EU regulations and directives are applied by the CJEU, and international law is applied by the ICJ, the PTRs of a particular international environmental regime are applied in the treaty bodies, including the compliance mechanisms, of that regime. The internal normative order of the Kyoto Protocol treaty bodies is thus surprisingly closed off from other normative orders, even from the order closest to it, the UNFCCC normative order.[12]

That the internal normative orders treat different norms as authoritative is not to say that these orders are completely impermeable. In the international and domestic legal orders, courts do not reason that *because* PTRs originate in another legal order, they cannot affect legal obligations elsewhere at all.[13] For instance, in the arguments it brought forward in the *Whaling in the Antarctic* case, Australia relied on *CITES* PTRs to suggest conflicting interpretations of the term 'commercial purposes' as opposed to the term 'scientific purposes' in Article VIII *ICRW*, pointing to Article 31.3(c) VCLT (principle of systemic integration).[14] Moreover, the authority of a PTR in the internal normative order from which it originates can certainly have an impact on its authority in the international and domestic legal orders. For instance, in the Australian *Greentree* case, discussed in the case studies

[11] ibid, para 3(c).

[12] It is not uncommon, however, that PTRs incorporate the content of PTRs from other MEAs.

[13] However, also for courts in the international and domestic legal orders it is quite unusual to rely on PTRs from one treaty regime to interpret the treaty provisions of another treaty regime.

[14] *Whaling in the Antarctic (Australia v Japan: New Zealand intervening)* (Memorial of Australia) [2011] ICJ Rep 262.

below, the Australian Federal Courts observed the low authority of a number of Ramsar Convention PTRs within the Ramsar normative order. This weighed heavily in their decision that these PTRs did not preclude the listing of the wetland on the List of Wetlands of International Importance, contrary to what a farmer, Mr Greentree, had argued.[15]

Apart from having many of the *characteristics* of a separate normative order, the question remains whether states, as treaty parties, have the *power* to create such orders. As Klabbers has noted, the creation of new normative orders is premised on the 'thoroughly subjectivist conception'[16] that they can create a space governed by a (partly) different rule of recognition. In practice, however, it seems to be accepted that states can. In any case, the approach of this study is to take the phenomenon that the treaty parties act as if they have created such a new normative order at face value, and only criticise it insofar as it has repercussions for the authority of PTRs and the interests of those affected by them (see chapters five and six).

Having established the existence of the internal normative orders, the question remains whether they should be called *legal* orders. Obviously, the international legal order and the domestic legal orders are not just 'ordinary' normative orders. There is presently little disagreement that these are legal orders, notwithstanding differences between the concepts of law in both types of order. However, there are reasons to withhold this term from the internal normative orders of the international environmental regimes.

To begin with, in these internal normative orders, the language of law is almost entirely absent. The MEA, the text of the PTRs, the meetings in which they are adopted: in none of these texts do the treaty parties discuss PTRs in legal terms. When applied in the operation of the treaty meetings, PTRs are never referred to as legal instruments.[17] In the context of compliance control, the compliance bodies of international environmental regimes never speak of 'breach of treaty' or 'legal violation', but always of 'non-compliance'.[18] Moreover, the compliance bodies never invoke the language of treaty interpretation. It would be strange to call a normative order that so effusively eschews the use of legal terminology a 'legal' order.

Furthermore, using the term normative rather than legal when noting that new normative orders develop, side-steps the difficulty of having to engage with questions about the concept of law beyond the scope of this study. What matters here is that international environmental regimes constitute some kind of normative order, so that the authority of instruments of global governance within these orders can be examined. It is not uncommon for scholars engaging with issues of

[15] See below, section B.1.
[16] Jan Klabbers, 'The Redundancy of Soft Law' (1996) 65 *Nordic Journal of International Law* 167, 170.
[17] See ch 3.
[18] Jan Klabbers, 'Compliance Procedures' in Daniel Bodansky, Jutta Brunnée and Ellen Hey (eds), *The Oxford Handbook of International Environmental Law* (OUP, 2007), 995; Martti Koskenniemi, 'Breach of Treaty or Non-Compliance? Reflections on the Enforcement of the Montreal Protocol' (1992) 3 *Yearbook of International Environmental Law* 123.

global governance to discuss the advent of new normative orders and systems, a plurality of normative orders, without calling them 'legal' orders. Klabbers, for instance, talks of 'different normative systems';[19] Shaffer and Pollack of 'the interaction between distinct normative orders – state and non-state'.[20] This choice does not signal an implication on their side, or on the side of this study, that these new normative orders are certainly *not* legal orders.

2. Relevance of the Three Orders for International Environmental Law

Each of the three normative orders has its own importance in the development and implementation of international environmental law, and environmental PTRs in particular. The authority of PTRs in the *internal normative* orders is obviously the most important for the implementation of internal PTRs, those PTRs addressed at the operation of treaty meetings, and their subsidiaries. Prominent examples are the CITES *Listing Criteria* or the Montreal Protocol *Critical-Use Criteria*. Such PTRs are to be collectively implemented within the regime in the shape of particular decisions and recommendations, like the listing of species on the CITES Appendices or the setting of yearly exemptions for the critical use of methyl bromide. Without authority here, these internal PTRs cannot operate, and risk being meaningless for the development of international environmental law.

But the internal normative orders also have a role to play for external PTRs, the numerous PTRs directly aimed at the environmental conduct of the treaty parties and their domestic regulation of the environmental conduct of private actors. The plenary treaty meetings and the compliance bodies of the regime are the only instances in which the parties collectively have the opportunity to control the compliance of treaty parties with their treaty obligations, and the PTRs that interpret and supplement them.[21] The CITES COP, for example, is in a position to determine whether CITES parties have failed to comply with their obligations to such an extent that a suspension of trade with these parties is justified. It is therefore crucial that they include adherence to CITES PTRs, such as those prescribing the adoption of domestic legislation making international trade in endangered species

[19] Jan Klabbers, 'The Commodification of International Law' in Hélène Ruiz Fabri, Emmanuelle Jouannet and Vincent Tomkiewicz (eds), *Select Proceedings of the European Society of International Law* (Hart Publishing, 2008) 341, 342–43.

[20] Gregory C Shaffer and Mark A Pollack, 'Hard vs Soft Law: Alternatives, Complements, and Antagonists in International Governance' (2010) 94 *Minnesota Law Review* 706, 740.

[21] In this vein, Handl submits that the 'perhaps most significant' reason why compliance control is a matter of special concern in the context of international environmental law, is that 'compliance control serves not just verification of a state's abidance by its obligations, but also – preliminarily – ascertainment of the existence of the norm(s) potentially in dispute'. Günther Handl, 'Compliance Control Mechanisms and International Environmental Obligations' (1997) 5 *Tulane Journal of International and Comparative Law* 29, 30–32.

punishable by criminal law. Likewise, the Kyoto Protocol Compliance Committee is the one forum where adherence to PTRs that prescribe how the treaty parties can achieve compliance with their emissions reduction targets can be controlled.

The *international legal order* is witnessing a growing number of disputes relating to environmental treaty obligations. Considering the globalisation of trade with (potential) environmentally degrading consequences (endangered species, GMO contamination), the continuing transboundary character of pollution (heavy industry,[22] aerosols, forest fires,[23] nuclear facilities)[24] and disagreements over the use of shared resources (for example, Japanese whaling versus Australian whaling tourism),[25] states are more likely than ever to become involved in international disputes caused by environmentally degrading activities.[26] Moreover, environmental aspects are increasingly part of disputes arising in other areas of international law, such as trade and investment law or the law of the sea.[27] Other environmental problems, particularly those with difficult-to-establish causation such as ozone depletion and climate change, do not lend themselves particularly well to (bilateral) dispute settlement. The last two decades have certainly shown an accelerating increase in cross-border disputes with at least some environmental aspect actually going to international dispute settlement.[28]

While a number of these disputes are primarily based on bilateral treaties, even in such cases, the parties try to sustain their interpretation of the bilateral treaty by references to MEAs, such as the Biological Diversity Convention or the Ramsar Convention, as well as (mostly external) PTRs adopted on their basis.[29] Others, such as the *Whaling in the Antarctic* case, arise directly from MEAs such as the International Convention on the Regulation of Whaling (ICRW). In its memorial in *Whaling*, Australia also relied on CITES PTRs to suggest conflicting interpretations of the term 'commercial purposes' as opposed to the term 'scientific purposes' in Article VIII ICRW, pointing to Article 31.3(c) VCLT (principle of systemic integration).[30] It is therefore an increasingly important question whether parties to international environmental disputes can rely on PTRs to win their arguments before international tribunals. Or, phrased differently, whether treaty parties involved in such disputes can or cannot escape PTRs as reference points.

[22] *Pulp Mills on the River Uruguay (Argentina v Uruguay)* (Judgment) [2010] ICJ Rep 14.

[23] Referring to the Indonesia–Malaysia dispute over forest fires. See John Vidal, 'Indonesia's forest fire smoke blows deeper into Malaysia' *Guardian* (London 24 June 2013) www.theguardian.com/environment/2013/jun/24/indonesia-forest-fire-malaysia-singapore, accessed 26 August 2018.

[24] Referring to the *MOX Plant* cases (*Ireland v United Kingdom*) brought in various forums in 2001.

[25] Referring to *Whaling in the Antarctic (Australia v Japan: New Zealand intervening)* (Judgment) [2014] ICJ Rep 226.

[26] *cf* Cesare P Romano, 'International Dispute Settlement' in Daniel Bodansky, Jutta Brunnée and Ellen Hey (eds), *Oxford Handbook of International Environmental Law* (OUP, 2007), 1036.

[27] Examples are *Shrimp/Turtle*, *Tuna* and *Seals* (WTO Appellate Body), *Methanex v US* (investment arbitration) and *Southern Bluefin Tuna* and *Swordfish* (law of the sea).

[28] Including cases at the ICJ, the ITLOS, the WTO and various arbitration procedures.

[29] As Argentina argued in *Pulp Mills on the River Uruguay*, para 191.

[30] *Whaling in the Antarctic* (Memorial of Australia), p 262.

Despite these developments, the relevance of the international legal order for the effective implementation of PTRs remains limited due to the horizontal nature of dispute settlement in international law and the nature of the environmental issues addressed through MEAs. Environmental issues addressed through MEAs are often not suitable to traditional dispute settlement. International dispute settlement works best in cases where an environmental dispute is localised.[31] The internalisation of dispute settlement through non-compliance procedures has further reduced recourse to traditional means.[32] On the rare occasions that a dispute is brought to the ICJ, the applicant is not (and cannot be) the COP, COP/MOP or MOP, but a single state.[33]

Finally, the effective implementation of external PTRs depends on their authority in *domestic legal orders* to a large extent.[34] External PTRs are those addressed at the environmental conduct of states, and the regulation by states of the environmental conduct of private actors on their territories. Most IEL ultimately deals with the conduct of private actors.[35] The Montreal Protocol deals with domestic regulation of national consumption and production of ozone-depleting substances; the Kyoto Protocol deals with national energy policies regulating domestic production and consumption of energy; CITES deals with export and import restrictions by domestic agencies of trade in endangered species; the Ramsar Convention deals with wise use of wetlands located within one or several national jurisdictions. Although compliance bodies check overall compliance by the parties, including with a number of PTRs insofar as these are mandatorily phrased, they rarely check compliance of states with situations concerning particular individuals, areas, industries, etc. As Redgwell concludes, at most '[t]hrough reporting, it is possible to obtain a snapshot of overall implementation and enforcement patterns'.[36] Only if international environmental law is implemented through domestic regulation and enforcement can it become effective.[37]

National implementation of obligations would be very minimal if it excluded PTRs. As discussed, MEAs contain marginal or very broadly formulated obligations. National implementation of MEAs becomes far more meaningful if it has to include the specific requirements and guidelines found in numerous post-treaty rules.[38] A particularly important role here is reserved to domestic courts.

[31] Romano, 'International Dispute Settlement', 1042.

[32] ibid, 1041.

[33] Or, rarely, one applicant state and one intervening state, as in *Whaling in the Antarctic*.

[34] Making this argument for international law generally early on is Benedetto Conforti, *International Law and the Role of Domestic Legal Systems* (Springer, 1993).

[35] Daniel Bodansky, Jutta Brunnée and Ellen Hey, 'International Environmental Law: Mapping the Field' in Daniel Bodansky, Jutta Brunné and Ellen Hey (eds), *Oxford Handbook of International Environmental Law* (OUP, 2007), 16.

[36] Catherine Redgwell, 'National Implementation' in Daniel Bodansky, Jutta Brunnée and Ellen Hey (eds), *The Oxford Handbook of International Environmental Law* (OUP, 2007), 922, 942.

[37] André Nollkaemper, 'Compliance Control in International Environmental Law: Traversing the Limits of the National Legal Order' (2002) 13 *Yearbook of International Environmental Law* 167.

[38] *cf* Carl Bruch, 'Is International Environmental Law Really Law? An Analysis of Application in Domestic Courts' (2006) 23 *Pace Environmental Law Review* 423, 458: 'When the decisions of the COPs

Although legislation and administrative action are the primary tools to achieve implementation of PTRs, it is possible that compliance by reluctant or unwilling governments can only be enforced through the courts.[39] Moreover, the courts may be the only place where individuals, companies and civil society have an opportunity to successfully challenge the national implementation of PTRs.[40]

3. Observing the Authority of PTRs in the Three Orders

How to observe the degree to which a PTR is a reference point in the development of environmental treaty norms that is difficult to escape for law appliers and legal subjects? The place to observe the authority of PTRs is in the practice of their application.[41] Practice includes the treatment of an instrument by the actor that adopted it in the first place, the attempts that actors make to apply the instrument to others, the reaction of actors affected by the instrument when others try to declare it applicable to them, and the extent to which courts find such an instrument difficult to escape in reaching judgment. The places to observe this practice are future decisions of the body adopting the instrument, opinions voiced by actors addressed by the instrument, of actors who defend their actions pointing to the instrument, or call out the behaviour of others, and decisions of courts and quasi-judicial bodies. The following practices in the three normative orders are particularly relevant for these observations.

In the *internal normative orders*, the work of the plenary meetings and their subsidiaries, including the compliance bodies, and sometimes the Secretariat, constitutes the crucial practice for revealing the authority of PTRs. For internal PTRs, which concern the operation of the plenary meetings and their subsidiaries, the practice of the plenary meetings and their subsidiaries is of foremost importance. For external PTRs, the practice of those subsidiaries of the plenary meetings that are concerned with review and control of compliance of the parties with their treaty obligations are most relevant.

are taken into account, international environmental treaties take on a character that is much more legislative with regulatory clarifications (through COP decisions), administrative guidance (from the Secretariat), and (quasi-)judicial interpretation and enforcement (through the compliance committee decisions and findings).'

[39] Well explained in Daniel Bodansky and Jutta Brunnée, 'Introduction: The Role of National Courts in the Field of International Environmental Law' in Michael Anderson and Paolo Galizzi (eds), *International Environmental Law in National Courts* (BIICL 2002), 15. See generally Eyal Benvenisti, 'Reclaiming Democracy: The Strategic Uses of Foreign and International Law by National Courts' (2008) 102 *American Journal of International Law* 241.

[40] Michael Bowman, Peter Davies and Catherine Redgwell, *Lyster's International Wildlife Law* 2nd edn (CUP, 2010), 92, 102 ('plaintiffs' only recourse may be national judicial implementation and enforcement measures').

[41] As Marmor submits, '[w]e can only identify the existence of [practical authority] by observing the norms that actually prevail in a given context'. Andrei Marmor, 'An Institutional Conception of Authority' (2011) 39 *Philosophy & Public Affairs* 238, 247.

In each of the regimes under consideration in this study, the parties have developed one or more mechanisms for the review of implementation and compliance.[42] For the purpose of examining the applicability of PTRs in the context of these compliance procedures, the variations need not stand in the way of a comparative overview. CITES has its Standing Committee,[43] the Montreal Protocol its Implementation Committee (better known as the 'Non-Compliance Procedure'),[44] and the Kyoto Protocol its Compliance Committee with a Facilitative and an Enforcement Branch.[45] The exception is the Ramsar Convention, for which the review powers are rather weak.[46] Particularly in CITES and the Ramsar Convention, the Secretariat also plays an important role as initiator of the procedure or information supplier.[47] Regardless of the numerous variations in the precise tasks and powers of these bodies, they are all, in some way, tasked with 'the international monitoring and supervision of states parties' implementation of and compliance with international treaty-based obligations'.[48] They usually control compliance with reporting obligations as well as substantive obligations.[49] All these mechanisms report back to the treaty's plenary meeting, which may make a final decision about the taking of actual measures to induce compliance.

It is all the more remarkable, then, that – so far – the extensive literature on compliance with IEL has hardly addressed the particular question of whether the assessment of parties' compliance is specifically based on parties' compliance *with PTRs* as well.[50] Two large comparative studies on compliance procedures of MEAs do not pay the subject the slightest attention.[51]

In the *international legal order*, the obvious places to look for practice from which the degree of authority of PTRs can be deduced are the decisions of international courts and tribunals that deal with cases involving international environmental law. These courts and tribunals, first and foremost, include the

[42] In some regimes, the division of implementation review and compliance control is not so rigid. The broader view taken by Raustiala is to refer to compliance mechanisms and review mechanisms together as 'review institutions'. See Kal Raustiala, *Reporting and Review Institutions in Ten Multilateral Environmental Agreements* (UNEP 2001).

[43] www.cites.org/eng/disc/sc.php.

[44] http://ozone.unep.org/en/handbook-montreal-protocol-substances-deplete-ozone-layer/2117.

[45] http://unfccc.int/kyoto_protocol/compliance/items/3024.php.

[46] Bowman, Davies and Redgwell, '*Lyster's International Wildlife Law*', 435–36.

[47] Frank Biermann and Bernd Siebenhüner, *Managers of Global Change: The Influence of International Environmental Bureaucracies* (MIT Press, 2011).

[48] Handl, 'Compliance Control Mechanisms', 30.

[49] Tuomas Kuokkanen, 'Putting Gentle Pressure on Parties: Recent Trends in the Practice of the Implementation Committee under the Convention on Long-Range Transboundary Air Pollution' in Martti Koskenniemi (ed), *Nordic cosmopolitanism: essays in international law for Martti Koskenniemi* (2003), 315; Duncan Brack, 'Monitoring the Montreal Protocol' (2003) *Verification Yearbook* 209, 217.

[50] An exception is Peter H Sand, 'Institution-Building Compliance with International Environmental Law: Perspectives' (1996) 56 *Zeitschrift für ausländisches öffentliches Recht und Volkerrecht (ZaöRV)* 774.

[51] Raustiala, '*Reporting and Review Institutions*', 3 (stating only that 'these decisions may also be the focus of review institutions'); UNEP, *Compliance Mechanisms under Selected Multilateral Environmental Agreements* (2007). Studies on the effectiveness of international environmental law also rarely touch on the particular effectiveness of PTRs.

International Court of Justice and the UN Tribunal on the Law of the Sea, but could also include arbitral tribunals and the WTO Appellate Body, insofar as international environmental treaties are relevant to their decisions. Any judicial decision to which environmental PTRs have relevance in terms of subject matter could provide information about the authority of PTRs. These decisions include the ICJ judgments and individual opinions in *Whaling in the Antarctic* and *Pulp Mills*, in which the degree of authority of PTRs proved decisive for the outcome of the case.

In the *national legal orders*, national courts particularly constitute an important arena for observing the authority of PTRs. For effective national implementation, legislation and administrative action are obviously the primary tools. The role of courts in implementation is supplemental.[52] However, there are compelling reasons to look to domestic courts when attempting to establish the degree of authority of PTRs in the national legal order.

First, courts are compelled to provide legal reasoning, more than legislators or administrative authorities. Legislators and executives may act in accordance with PTRs for various reasons, only one amongst which is their authority.[53] They may also choose to do so because they think a PTR sets out the best policy, in other words, for reasons of persuasion. As Friedrich remarks, 'nonbinding instruments cannot guarantee that domestic implementation will take place, since nonbinding instruments do not trigger domestic legislative implementation efforts automatically. Even though the adoption of nonbinding instruments can thus not guarantee that domestic processes of implementation will be put into motion, nonbinding instruments may and often do lead to legislative implementation efforts'.[54] To some extent, whether legislators and executives were motivated by the authority of PTRs or other considerations may be gleaned from debates within these institutions. However, the picture becomes more complete when a government organ's act or omission is challenged before a court. In a judicial procedure, the question of the degree of authority of PTRs comes to the fore much more explicitly, and is thus easier to observe.

Second, because the domestic authority of international non-binding instruments is an issue that is in development and not yet part of settled law in most jurisdictions, the practice of courts takes on special importance. Applications of PTRs are part of a practice that sustains and increases (or decreases) the domestic authority of PTRs on future occasions. In this respect, there is not much difference between monist and dualist states. Whether a treaty is valid in the national legal order (monism) or a treaty has to be transposed into national legislation (dualism); in both cases, the question remains to what extent PTRs become

[52] *cf* Redgwell, 'National Implementation', 932 ('the courts play a role supplemental to the state's political organs, with whom the principal implementation obligation resides'). Bowman, Davies and Redgwell, '*Lyster's International Wildlife Law*, 101.

[53] See the Introduction, section D.

[54] Jürgen Friedrich, *International Environmental 'Soft Law': The Functions and Limits of Nonbinding Instruments in International Environmental Governance and Law* (Springer, 2013), 289.

reference points, of either the treaty or the transposing statute, that are difficult to escape. After all, PTRs are ordinarily neither valid law in monist states, nor transposed into national legislation in dualist states (see chapter three).

The application of environmental post-treaty rules by national courts has never received systematic attention in the literature. There has been some attention to landmark cases by legal scholars from the jurisdiction where they were issued,[55] or it has been addressed as a small aspect of the national implementation of international environmental law or global administrative law that need only be noted in passing.[56] Most accounts, however, leave PTRs undiscussed in their treatment of the invocation of treaties before national courts.

The following two sections use the aforementioned sources and methods of observation to gain insight into the authority of a number of PTRs from the Ramsar Convention, CITES, the Montreal Protocol and the Kyoto Protocol. The selected PTRs have in common that their authority can be shown in as many as possible different normative orders (the Ramsar COP *Identification Criteria* and *Designation Conditions*, the CITES COP *Primarily Commercial Purposes Resolution* and the *Reason to Believe Paragraph*, and the Montreal MOP *Critical Use Criteria* and *Exemption Decisions*), or that it can be shown particularly well in one normative order (the Kyoto COP/MOP *Accounting Modalities* and *LULUCF Decision*). In this manner, the internal and national normative orders receive their share of attention, while, at the same time, a picture forms of the authority of particular PTRs throughout various stages of their existence, and, as a result, the role that they play in the development of international environmental law.

B. Eternal Interpretation: The Ramsar Convention and CITES

In the 1970s, two environmental treaties were adopted that did not just address key environmental issues, but also became experiments in international law making

[55] Alice L Bodnar, 'NRDC v EPA: Testing the Waters of the Constitutionality of Delegation to International Organizations' (2007) 34 *Ecology Law Quarterly* 895; John H Knox, 'Natural Resources Defense Council v Environmental Protection Agency 464 F.3d 1' (2007) 101 *American Journal of International Law* 471; Jonathan Verschuuren, 'Ramsar Soft Law Is Not Soft at All – Discussion of the 2007 Decision by the Netherlands Crown on the Lac Ramsar Site on the Island of Bonaire [Translation of a Case Law Annotation in Dutch]' (2008) 35 *Milieu en Recht* 28. An exception is the valuable article by Annecoos Wiersema, 'The New International Law-Makers? Conferences of the Parties to Multilateral Environmental Agreements' (2009) 31 *Michigan Journal of International Law* 231 (including a comparison between the US case *NRDC v EPA* and the Dutch case *Lac Sorobon*).

[56] Bruch, 'Is International Environmental Law Really Law?', 436–37 (discussing briefly the *Castlewood Products* cases); Ellen Hey, 'The European Community's Courts and International Environmental Agreements' in Michael Anderson and Paolo Galizzi (eds), *International Environmental Law in National Courts* (BIICL 2002), 65 (discussing briefly the jurisprudence of the European courts in this regard); Benedict Kingsbury, 'Weighing Global Regulatory Rules and Decisions in National Courts' (2009) 9 *Acta Juridica* 90.

that were successful enough to remain with us until this day: The Ramsar Convention on Wetlands and the Washington Convention on Endangered Species, better known as CITES. The foresight of their drafters, drawn from decades of previously adopted – and failed – treaties aimed at nature conservation, was to include two key elements in their architecture: phrasing the key substantive provisions such that they could be adapted to changing circumstances; and setting up a Conference of the Parties to do the adaptation, in the form of resolutions and recommendations.

This section looks at what happens when international environmental norms in key areas of the Ramsar Convention and CITES are developed through resolutions and recommendations over a period of 30–40 years and counting. On the one hand, a picture emerges of an eternal process of interpretation towards more and more crystallised norms, taking on board lessons from the functioning of the norms in practice. Finding more than a dozen resolutions on one single term or phrase in one treaty article is not uncommon. On the other hand, the central question of this chapter – what is the authority of these resolutions in the practice of both the internal normative orders as well as the international and national legal orders – has a disappointing answer.

The Ramsar Convention resolutions on the identification and designation of wetlands have been applied haphazardly in the meetings and subsidiary bodies of the treaty, so that treaty parties could for a long time get away with designating wetlands of international importance on the list of protected wetlands, without providing even their exact location on a map. This practice has lowered the authority of the Ramsar resolutions to such an extent that Australian courts pushed them aside when a local farmer alleged that Australia's failure to abide by the resolutions had prevented the wetland on which part of his farm was located from getting on to the list of protected wetlands. The same fate is met by numerous CITES resolutions, which phrase crucial paragraphs – paragraphs that can make the difference between allowing or prohibiting the importation of heavily endangered species – in such a recommendatory fashion that national courts stand powerless when faced with governmental authorities ignoring them.

1. The Ramsar Convention: *Identification Criteria* and *Designating Conditions* for 'Wetlands of International Importance'

Wetland ecosystems (including lakes, rivers, marshes, and coastal regions to a depth of 6 metres at low tide) are estimated to cover more than 1,280 million hectares of the earth's surface, and probably much more than that in reality.[57] They perform enormously important functions for human well-being, such as

[57] 'Ecosystems and Human Well-being: Wetlands and Water *Synthesis*', in *Millennium Ecosystem Assessment*, 2005, World Resources Institute, Washington, DC, p 3.

providing flood, coastal and climate protection, and filtering water. They harbour a disproportionate wealth of biodiversity, including many economically valuable resources. The *Millennium Assessment Report* states that '[w]hen both the marketed and nonmarketed economic benefits of wetland are included, the total economic value of unconverted wetlands is often greater than that of converted wetland'.[58]

In spite of their value, and because of it, wetlands are deteriorating very fast,[59] for instance through exploration of fossil fuels in mangrove areas and forest clearing on peatlands. In Indonesia, which harbours 70 per cent of the world's tropical peat swamp forest, a particular type of wetland, the total area of peatland went from 25 to 17 million hectares between 1990 and 2000, mostly due to land conversion.[60] Wetland conservation will become increasingly crucial in the twenty-first century to provide basic living conditions in developing countries in particular.

The primary justification of international cooperation on wetlands was initially considered to be their function as habitat for migratory waterfowl (migratory birds dependent on wetlands). Although the title of the Ramsar Convention gave prominence to this aspect – 'Convention on Wetlands of International Importance, especially as Waterfowl Habitat'[61] – the text already reflected a broader ambition.[62] The preamble mentions the importance of the fundamental ecological functions of wetlands with regard to water regimes, and the many resources that wetlands possess, objectives in which the international component is less obvious than the immediate local concern.

The Ramsar Convention is one of the clearest examples of a regime for which the conventional text did not prescribe a particular course of action or behaviour for the parties, except for some 'ancillary obligations'[63] such as listing one wetland upon ratification or accession, and establishing nature reserves. The convention sets hortatory conservation standards and further responsibilities ('so as to promote', 'as far as possible', 'wise use'). Apart from the preferred presence of migratory waterfowl, the text of the convention is rather unspecific about what qualifies a wetland for 'listing', which is important because different standards of protection apply to 'Listed' and 'non-Listed' wetlands respectively.

[58] ibid, ii.

[59] ibid, ii. 'The primary direct drivers of degradation and loss include infrastructure development, land conversion, water withdrawal, eutrophication and pollution, overharvesting and overexploitation, and the introduction of invasive alien species'.

[60] Jack Rieley, 'Kalimantan's peatland disaster', in 65 *Inside Indonesia* 2001, at www.insideindonesia.org/feature-editions/kalimantans-peatland-disaster.

[61] Convention on Wetlands of International Importance especially as Waterfowl Habitat (adopted 2 February 1971, entered into force 21 December 1975) 996 UNTS 245 (Ramsar Convention).

[62] *cf*, eg, Art 2.2 to Art 2.6. The Ramsar Convention was signed in Ramsar, Iran, in 1971. With currently 170 parties that joined incrementally over four decades, it is now a widely ratified treaty, although still quite some way from universality. On 19 August 2018, these 170 parties had listed 2,323 wetlands of international importance, with a total surface area of 248,533,302 hectares, see www.ramsar.org/. This coverage is only a fraction of the total wetland areas in the world.

[63] Bowman, Davies and Redgwell, '*Lyster's International Wildlife Law*', 426.

In other words, the Ramsar Convention is full of open-ended treaty provisions with the potential to serve as implicit enabling clauses. Post-treaty rules are therefore incredibly important for the success of wetlands conservation. The Ramsar Convention was the first MEA to provide a 'Conference of the Parties'[64] to this hortatory framework. From its first meeting onwards, over the last three decades, almost all important issues within the scope of the convention, and some previously outside of it, have become the subject of extensive decision making by the Ramsar COP: the definition of 'suitable wetlands' for listing; how and under which conditions listed wetlands may be deleted or restricted because of 'urgent national interests', and how this must be compensated; what standards of conservation and 'wise use' are required for listed and non-listed wetlands; and what a change in the 'ecological character' of a wetland amounts to. In 2011, the Ramsar Secretariat counted 186 resolutions and 96 recommendations, adopted during the first 10 Ramsar COPs.[65]

The centrality of COP decisions to the development of the Ramsar regime is unequivocal for scholars specialising in international wetland protection.[66] Most importantly, 'the apparent demarcation between conservation of listed and wise use of unlisted wetlands is undergoing a significant metamorphosis'.[67] Furthermore, the COP addresses a wide range of issues beyond the initial preoccupations of the Convention, such as human health, poverty eradication, food security and climate change.[68] The current 'holistic' approach to the conservation of nature also 'contrasts markedly' with the segmented approach which appears on the face of the Ramsar Convention.[69]

The Ramsar *Listing Criteria* and *Designation Conditions* are interesting cases to discuss in more detail for various reasons. As opposed to the CITES species listing criteria, they are not only aimed at the Ramsar COP, but also at the treaty parties and the Secretariat. Primarily, they address the Parties' unilateral selection and designation of wetlands for listing. The Ramsar COP exhorts treaty parties regularly that they should list certain wetlands that meet the criteria and deserve priority from an international perspective. Yet, since recently, the Ramsar COP's newest version assigns the Ramsar Secretariat the ultimate decision of whether or not to turn a unilateral designation into an actual listing. Moreover, these PTRs concern both the internal decision making within the Ramsar regime (internal PTRs), and the conduct of governmental and private actors in their own national legal orders (external PTRs).

[64] Art 6. *cf* ibid, 404.

[65] See http://archive.ramsar.org/cda/en/ramsar-documents-guidelines-concept-index/main/ramsar/1-31-105%5E22144_4000_0__, 23 February 2011.

[66] David Farrier and Linda Tucker, 'Wise Use of Wetlands Under the Ramsar Convention: A Challenge for Meaningful Implementation of International Law' (2000) 12 *Journal of International Environmental Law* 21, 41. Also Wiersema, 'The New International Law-Makers', 238, 240.

[67] Farrier and Tucker, 'Wise Use of Wetlands', 25.

[68] Peter Herkenrath, 'Ramsar Convention on Wetlands: 10th Conference of the Parties' (2009) 43 *Oryx* 170.

[69] Farrier and Tucker, 'Wise Use of Wetlands', 41.

To what extent do the series of listing criteria and designation conditions adopted over the past decades exert authority over the listing process, and the question of whether a site is successfully listed or not? In the Ramsar normative order, can parties designate wetlands not satisfying the *Criteria*, and/or without fulfilling the *Conditions*, according to the content of COP recommendations and resolution, as well as according to the legal status of those resolutions and recommendations? For the national legal orders, the question is what happens to the national legal status of a wetland that the Ramsar Secretariat has allowed to be listed, but which fails to satisfy the *Criteria* or the *Conditions*.

a. Resolutions on the Identification and Designation of Wetlands of International Importance

An important characteristic of the Ramsar Convention is that becoming a party to the Convention does not automatically bring all of that party's wetlands under the highest standard of protection.[70] The designation of wetlands to the List of Wetlands of International Importance[71] is a unilateral, voluntary act. Only 'Listed' wetlands are subject to a standard of 'conservation' rather than 'wise use' (which applies to all other wetlands). Although consecutive Ramsar PTRs have conflated the notions of 'conservation' and 'wise use' more and more – see the discussion in chapter one, section E – there are additional differences in the standard of protection. These variances include: the requirement to keep the Ramsar COP informed of changes in the ecological character of wetlands only applies to Listed wetlands (Article 3.2); the wise use of all wetlands is only required 'as far as possible', while the parties 'shall … promote' the conservation of Listed wetlands (Article 3.1); and for Listed sites that have undergone ecological changes, there is a possibility to add them – again through a voluntary, unilateral act of the party on whose territory the site is located – to the Montreux Record, a special list of wetlands receiving heightened attention from the COP (Ramsar COP Recommendation 4.8).[72]

The heightened protection for listed sites makes the identification, designation, restriction and deletion of wetlands a significant affair. Article 2 of the Ramsar Convention sets out basic obligations relating to the identification, designation, restriction and deletion of wetlands. It obliges Ramsar parties to list at least one wetland when ratifying or acceding to the Convention (Article 2.4), determines that only suitable wetlands are to be designated (Article 2.1), which at the least means that they must be of 'international significance' (Article 2.2), and sets out that wetlands 'shall be precisely described and also delimited on a map' (Article 2.1). However, '[t]he inclusion of a wetland in the List does not prejudice the exclusive sovereign rights of the Contracting Party in whose territory the wetland is

[70] Bowman, Davies and Redgwell, '*Lyster's International Wildlife Law*', 420.
[71] See www.ramsar.org/sites/default/files/documents/library/sitelist.pdf.
[72] Ramsar COP Recommendation 4.8, *Change in ecological character of Ramsar sites.*

situated' (Article 2.3), and the parties remain free to delete or restrict the boundaries of wetlands already included in the List because of 'urgent national interests' (Article 2.5). Finally, Article 2.6 vaguely speaks of 'international responsibilities' that the parties shall consider 'both when designating entries for the List and when exercising its right to change entries in the List'.

Evidently, the various provisions of Article 2 leave undecided a number of important issues, such as how 'significant' a wetland has to be in order to be acceptable for listing, and which criteria matter for this 'significance' in addition to the wetland's international importance for 'waterfowl' (Article 2.2). Insofar as basic criteria are mentioned in Article 2.2, these are set out using the verb 'should': 'Wetlands should be selected for the List on account of their international significance in terms of ecology, botany, zoology, linology or hydrology'. It remains entirely unclear if a party's 'international responsibilities for the conservation, management and wise use of migratory stocks of waterfowl' would, in any way, oblige that party to list more than one wetland. The different parts of Article 2 itself are such that they ultimately leave it to the parties' discretion to decide *which* wetlands to suggest for listing, and *how many* (with a minimum of one).[73] Various terms and phrases in these provisions are sufficiently open-ended so as to allow for extensive further detailing, such as which are 'wetlands of international importance' and 'suitable wetlands', and what are a party's 'international responsibilities … when designating entries for the List'.

The Ramsar COP has adopted PTRs on all of these issues, approaching these provisions as implicit enabling clauses. Even before the entry into force of the Ramsar Convention, it was obvious that Article 2 did not provide sufficiently precise criteria for the identification and designation of wetlands to the List. Moreover, awareness grew that the emphasis on 'waterfowl' in the Convention threatened to exclude wetlands with other kinds of endangered species. In response, over time, the Conference of the Parties adopted numerous resolutions on identification of suitable wetlands and on the more procedural issues relating to the actual designation: the *Criteria for Identifying Wetlands of International Importance*. The first official version of these *Criteria*, Recommendation 1.4, was adopted in 1980.[74] They were revised at almost every subsequent Ramsar COP. At present, the revised versions of these criteria are part of the wider *Strategic Framework and Guidelines for the Future Development of the List of Wetlands of International Importance*.[75] The most recent versions of the *Identification Criteria*

[73] Art 2.4 Ramsar Convention: 'Each Contracting Party shall designate at least one wetland to be included in the List when signing this Convention or when depositing its instrument of ratification or accession, as provided in Article 9'.

[74] Ramsar COP Recommendation 1.4, *Criteria for identifying Wetlands of International Importance*.

[75] Ramsar COP Res XI.8, *Streamlining procedures for describing Ramsar Sites at the time of designation and subsequent updates*, Annex 2, *Strategic Framework and guidelines for the future development of the List of Wetlands of International Importance of the Convention on Wetlands (Ramsar, Iran, 1971) – 2012 revision*.

and the *Designation Conditions* are incorporated as Appendices into the *Strategic Framework* of 2012.[76]

Ramsar COP resolutions are normally adopted by consensus or by acclaim. For instance, the *Strategic Framework* was adopted 'by acclaim'. Resolutions VI.13 and VI.16 were also adopted 'by acclaim' or 'by acclamation'.[77] Acclaim requires more than the mere absence of objections (consensus), but less than a unanimous vote. Some form of approval must have been shown by the COP as a whole. The formulation 'by consensus' is, however, found in many later Conference Reports, for instance in relation to the adoption of Resolution VIII.11, *Additional guidance for identifying and designating under-represented wetland types as Wetlands of International Importance*.[78]

b. The 'Identification Criteria' and 'Designation Requirements' in the Internal Order of the Ramsar Regime

The rules for the listing of new wetlands can be divided into, on the one hand, criteria for identifying wetlands of international importance ('the identification criteria') (a) and, on the other hand, the conditions relating to information that should accompany the designation ('the designation requirements') (b). A recent addition is the gatekeeper role of the Ramsar Secretariat (c).

i. The 'Identification Criteria'

Over time, the *Criteria*, later encompassed by the *Strategic Frameworks*, have specified the criteria that should be had in mind in the decision to list a wetland in considerable detail, but have also expanded the reasons for listing wetlands.

On the one hand, an increasing level of detail can be found in the nine detailed ecological criteria that make a wetland qualify as a site of international importance. The main criterion is that '[a] wetland should be considered internationally important if it contains a representative, rare, or unique example of a natural or near-natural wetland type found within the appropriate biogeographic region', but each of the nine criteria on its own is in principle sufficient to identify a wetland as having international importance.[79] The most current criteria relate to water birds, fish, other species, or the maintenance of ecological communities or biodiversity

[76] Ramsar COP Res XI.8, Annex 2, respectively in Appendix D; and in paras 5, 7 and 9, and Appendices C and E. On top of that, there are many more Ramsar COP Resolutions addressing specific problems of identification and designation.

[77] *Proceedings of the 6th Meeting of the Conference of the Contracting Parties*, Brisbane, Australia, 19–27 March 1996.

[78] *Report of the 8th Meeting of the Conference of the Contracting Parties*, Valencia, Spain, 18–26 November 2002, Notes on the Sixth Plenary Session, 25 November 2002, 09.30–13.00, Agenda Item XVIII: Adoption of Conference Resolutions and Recommendations, para 73.

[79] *Strategic Framework*, para 101.

in a certain biogeographic area.[80] The *Strategic Framework* further works out these criteria in detailed guidelines,[81] other considerations that may guide the parties in designating wetlands,[82] and considerations regarding a number of specific wetland types.[83] This specification clarifies which wetlands should be included, but has also the opposite function of preventing listing of unqualified sites, for example if the wetland is not a 'representative example of a (near)-natural wetland type found within the appropriate biogeographical region'.[84]

On the other hand, in response to disappointing numbers of listed wetlands, the *Strategic Frameworks* and other Ramsar COP resolutions now also emphasise the social and economic value of wetlands as reasons for listing. They explain the roles that wetlands play 'for sustaining human life',[85] such as water supply and fishery resources,[86] human health[87] or poverty reduction.[88] Most explicit is the greater emphasis on the cultural value of wetlands as a listing factor.[89] These criteria may have an impact on which and how many wetlands developing parties propose for listing, because cultural and socio-economic reasons may

be more legitimate and attractive to developing countries and their populations.[90] The correlation between socio-economic importance and wetlands-listing is however crafted in rather less specific language than the ecological criteria. Considering that Article 2 only mentions 'ecology, botany, zoology, limnology or hydrology' as relevant to the international significance of wetlands, socio-economic reasons only count as additional reasons for listing, not as independent criteria.

The *Criteria* and *Framework* are ambiguous as regards the authority of the identification criteria. First of all, nothing in these PTRs suggests a change to the central premise of voluntary, unilateral designation by the parties. States still determine *whether* they want to propose a site for listing in the first place. There is no *obligation* to designate.[91] That is not surprising, as it would have amounted to a modification of the Convention, requiring a formal amendment procedure.

[80] *Strategic Framework*, Appendix D, *Criteria for Identifying Wetlands of International Importance.*

[81] *Section V.* Criteria for identifying Wetlands of International Importance, guidelines for their application, and long-term targets.

[82] *Section IV.* Guidelines for adopting a systematic approach to identifying priority wetlands for designation under the Ramsar Convention.

[83] *Section VI.* Guidelines for identifying and designating specific wetland types (karst and other subterranean hydrological systems; peatlands; wet grasslands; mangroves; coral reefs; temporary pools; artificial wetlands).

[84] Bowman, Davies and Redgwell, '*Lyster's International Wildlife Law*', 408.

[85] *Strategic Framework*, para 6.

[86] *Strategic Framework*, para 87, p 22.

[87] Ramsar Secretariat, Ramsar Technical Report No 6, *Healthy wetlands, healthy people: a review of wetlands and human health interactions.*

[88] Ramsar COP Res IX.14. *Wetlands and poverty reduction.*

[89] *Strategic Framework*, Annex 2, section 5.10, p 24.

[90] Bowman, Davies and Redgwell, '*Lyster's International Wildlife Law*', 409.

[91] *cf* Bowman, Davies and Redgwell, '*Lyster's International Wildlife Law*', 407. See Resolution IX.1, Annex B: *Revised Strategic Framework and guidelines for the future development of the List of Wetlands of International Importance*, and Resolution VII.11: *Strategic framework and guidelines for the future development of the List of Wetlands of International Importance.*

The *Strategic Framework* does state that 'Contracting Parties are urged to consider all of the Criteria fully',[92] and 'Contracting Parties are encouraged to identify priority candidate sites'.[93] This makes it clear that the Ramsar COP is quite convinced that only wetlands qualifying under the *Criteria* should be included in the List. But the language does not go beyond these hortatory encouragements and urgings. They remain 'guidelines', 'guidance' and 'criteria'. Is the listing of a wetland which fails to satisfy the specified number of criteria still successful in light of each treaty party's national discretion to list? That is difficult to say from the text of the *Criteria* alone, but depends on their usage in practice.

ii. The 'Designation Conditions'

Article 2.1 Ramsar Convention prescribes that '[t]he boundaries of each wetland *shall* be precisely described and also delimited on a map'. This sentence in Article 2.1 is difficult to read otherwise than that precise boundary description and delimitation on a map are obligatory, at least at some point in time. As was the case for the listing criteria, the question is whether failure to fulfil that condition precludes a successful listing.

A long series of Ramsar COP resolutions and recommendations repeatedly underlined the importance of boundary description when listing a wetland. Yet, there are also numerous indications that the Ramsar COP did not intend that failure to do so precluded a successful listing. Moreover, the Ramsar COP resolutions addressing the information that should accompany a party's designation of a wetland are formulated as guidelines, even if in the most urgent of tones sometimes.

The policy considerations behind both interpretations are obvious. On the one hand, making the onerous task of description and delimitation obligatory for a successful listing could well have put off or postponed the listing of many now-listed wetlands by developing states lacking the resources for 'precise' boundary description. On the other hand, without such precise descriptions and delimitations, difficult legal issues can arise with regard to areas that may be either inside or outside the site and the scope of the Ramsar Convention.

Resolution 4.5 (1990) already recommended that any Contracting Party that had not, when signing the Ramsar Convention or depositing its instrument of ratification, 'provided the Depositary with a precise description and map of the boundaries of the wetland or wetlands *so designated*, provide such documentation to the Bureau of the Secretariat as early as possible thereafter' (emphasis added).[94] So, the listing was not precluded by failing to meet those conditions. Annex 2A to Recommendation 4.7 (1990) introduced the Ramsar Information Sheet (RIS) still

[92] *Strategic Framework and guidelines for the future development of the List of Wetlands of International Importance* 3rd edn, as adopted by Resolution VII.11 (COP 7, 1999) and amended by Resolutions VII.13 (1999), VIII.11 and VIII.33 (COP 8, 2002), IX.1, Annexes A and B (COP 9, 2005), and X.20 (COP 10, 2008)), para 46.

[93] *Strategic Framework*, para 48.

[94] Ramsar COP Recommendation 4.2, *Criteria for Identifying Wetlands of International Importance.*

in use, which calls for the inclusion of geographical coordinates and an outline map of the site '(to be appended)'.[95] These urgent requests and recommendations were repeated at the 5th COP (1993)[96] and the 6th COP (1996).[97] During the 1996 meeting, the COP decided 'that the boundaries of each additional site, designated subsequently by States for the List of Wetlands of International Importance, shall be precisely described and also delimited on a map'.[98] That is simply a repetition of Article 2.1, and fails to mention an exact point in time at which the information must have been provided in order to have the listing succeed.

From a number of COP meetings and documents in the 1990s, it becomes clear that the parties did not consider a listing failed if not accompanied by this information during this period. For instance, in the RIS sheet, the option is created to tick a 'No' box in response to the question of 'whether or not a map accompanies the Information Sheet', and introduces a differentiation between 'ideal' and other Ramsar sites: 'The 'ideal' Ramsar site will clearly show the boundaries of the Ramsar site'.[99] During the 7th COP (1999), the parties expressed profound concern 'that there remain a number of Ramsar sites for which an official description has not been provided or updated',[100] clearly indicating that these omissions had not prevented the wetlands from becoming Ramsar sites. In other words, not providing a boundary description and delimitation on a map at the moment of listing did not have immediate consequences for those sites: the sites were listed nonetheless.

Is the treaty obligation in Article 2.1 an obligation at all, according to these Ramsar PTRs? To hold otherwise would be a direct contradiction of the text of Article 2.1 of the Ramsar Convention, even if the absence of a clear time limit makes it difficult to state *when* the obligation has been breached. In practice, however, the COP kept urging treaty parties to submit the information, rather than removing these sites from the list.

iii. Gatekeeper Role of the Secretariat

However, the situation has changed recently to increase the authority of the *Identification Criteria* and the *Designation Conditions* alike. The criteria and

[95] Ramsar COP Recommendation 4.7, Annex 2, part A: *Information Sheet on Ramsar Sites*, Ramsar COP Recommendation 4.7, *Mechanisms for improved application of the Ramsar Convention*, points 7 and 32.

[96] Ramsar COP Res 5.3, *Procedure for initial designation of sites for the List of Wetlands of International Importance.*

[97] Ramsar COP Res VI.13, *Submission of information on sites designated for the Ramsar List of Wetlands of International Importance.*

[98] Ramsar COP Res VI.16, *Accession procedures.*

[99] Ramsar Convention Scientific and Technical Review Panel (STRP) and Ramsar Secretariat, *Measures Taken for Improving Data on Ramsar* Sites, 29 June 1997.

[100] Ramsar COP Res VII.12, *Sites in the Ramsar List of Wetlands of International Importance: official descriptions, conservation status, and management plans, including the situation of particular sites in the territories of specific Contracting Parties.*

conditions continue to be phrased in hortatory terms ('should', 'urgently requests', etc.). But a new Ramsar COP resolution – the revised *Strategic Framework* (2012) – now instructs the Secretariat to list no longer designated wetlands that fail to meet the *Criteria* or the *Conditions*. Thus, the Secretariat is in effect instructed, in mandatory language, to ignore the hortatory language of the resolutions, *and* the imprecise language of the Convention in terms of the exact moment that detailed information on the site is required.

It occurs from the revised *Strategic Framework* that *designation* and *listing* have now clearly become two separate acts, the first of which is performed by the treaty party, while the second is performed by the Secretariat – including a check against the identification criteria for wetlands of international importance and the designation conditions:[101]

> The Ramsar Secretariat is responsible for checking and confirming that the RIS and its map(s) confirm that the site qualifies for designation under the Ramsar Criteria, and that the RIS and its map(s) have been correctly completed in line with the adopted guidance for this, and then for placing the designated site on the Ramsar List.[102] … [V]ery importantly, the information provided in the RIS concerning the Criteria for the site's international importance and the justifications for each Criterion applied confirm that *a) the site does qualify for designation as internationally important, and b) each Criterion has been correctly applied.*[103] … Once the Secretariat confirms that the RIS meets the above requirements, the Secretary General approves the Site to be formally placed on the List of Wetlands of International Importance.[104]

The new *Framework* also requires the Secretariat to refuse the listing of an improperly described and delimited site: '[T]he Ramsar Secretariat is required to review the RIS (including maps) to confirm that: … iii) RIS maps have been prepared and provided in conformity with the specific guidance adopted for map preparation (see Appendix C)'.[105] In other words, this last strengthening of the check performed by the Secretariat should now make it no longer possible for wetlands to be listed that do not conform to the *Designation Conditions*, as happened in the past. The new *Framework* arguably constitutes a modification of the Convention, because it prohibits the listing of wetlands until they have fulfilled the identification criteria and designation requirements, something that cannot be inferred from the Convention.

The designation and listing of new Ramsar sites indeed functions in the way prescribed in the *Framework*. In the latest *Report of the Secretary General concerning the List of Wetlands of International Importance*, the Ramsar Secretariat confirms that it only places new wetland sites on the List when it is satisfied that the designation is accompanied by the information required by the relevant Ramsar

[101] *Strategic Framework*, para 405.
[102] *Strategic Framework*, para 406.
[103] *Strategic Framework*, para 418.
[104] *Strategic Framework*, para 420.
[105] *Strategic Framework*, para 418.

COP resolutions.[106] The authority of the designation requirements in the internal normative order of the Ramsar regime has increased over time, up to the point where the requirements are highly authoritative in practice.

c. *The* Designation Conditions *before the Australian Federal Courts: A Designated Wetland?*

The *Designation Conditions* also have an external component. A successfully listed site often falls within a higher standard of protection under national law, and this can make the cost of conservation for the owners of the land higher as well. If the listing has failed, the obligations do not apply. This makes their authority in the national legal orders relevant as well.

The Australian *Greentree* case dealt exactly with this problem, and is a clear example of the lack of authority of PTRs in the national legal orders when they are worded and treated as recommendations rather than obligations. The case went all the way up to the Full Court of the Federal Court of Australia. The dispute arose before the recent strengthening of the Ramsar Secretariat's gatekeeper role. The judges decided on the understanding that it was still Ramsar practice to allow listing of a site if the designation was unaccompanied by a clear description and a designation on a map. The judgment even contrasted the situation under the Ramsar Convention with the situation under the World Heritage Convention, considering the latter to possess a 'gateway function' for designations but not the former. Absent this 'gateway function', the limited mandatory quality of the resolutions took centre stage. *Greentree* clearly shows that the weight which the wording carries for national courts should not be easily dismissed. It also underlines the importance of the authority of the relevant PTRs in the practice of the internal normative orders.

The *Greentree* case received its name from Mr Ronald Greentree, a landholder, clearing, ploughing and sowing wheat in what the Australian authorities considered to be part of the Windella Ramsar site in New South Wales, Australia. To defend these activities, Mr Greentree and his fellow respondents submitted amongst others:

> [T]hat the Windella Ramsar site had never been 'designated by the Commonwealth under Article 2 of the Ramsar Convention' within the meaning of s17(1) of the [Australian] [Environment Protection and Biodiversity Conservation] Act. This was so, they argued, because the purported designation neither described precisely the boundaries of the relevant wetland, nor delimited it on a map, as required by Art 2 of the Ramsar Convention. At no time had the Commonwealth remedied this deficiency, with the consequence that the affected landholders could not ascertain the boundaries of the Ramsar sites on their land. Thus the Windella Ramsar site was not a 'declared

[106] *Report of the Secretary General pursuant to Article 8.2 concerning the List of Wetlands of International Importance*, Ramsar COP 11, DOC. 8, 2012, para 4.

> Ramsar wetland' as defined in s17(1) of the EPBC Act. It followed that the respondents could not have contravened s16(1) of the EPBC Act, since their actions did not affect a 'declared Ramsar wetland'.[107]

The case was first decided by the Federal Court of Australia (FCA), and subsequently on appeal by the FCA's Full Court ('Full Court'), which confirmed the findings of the FCA insofar as relevant to the present inquiry.

The Australian Federal Courts in *Greentree* concluded that the Australian Environment Protection and Biodiversity Conservation Act 1999 (EPBC Act) had to be interpreted in accordance with the Ramsar Convention, and that, in turn, the Ramsar Convention had to be interpreted in accordance with Article 31 VCLT:

> It is also necessary to take into account any subsequent agreement between the parties regarding the interpretation of the treaty and any subsequent practice in the application of the treaty which establishes the agreement of the parties regarding its interpretation: Art 31(3) of the Vienna Convention.[108]

On appeal, the Full Court agreed that 'regard may be had to the terms of a Convention where there is ambiguity in the domestic legislation',[109] and that this should be done 'in accordance with the requirements of the Vienna Convention on the Law of Treaties Article 31', including subsequent practices and agreements.[110]

When it came to the Ramsar resolutions in question, however, their recommendatory nature, as well as the Ramsar COP's treatment of them as recommendatory, proved crucial for the FCA's judgment:

> It is true, as the respondents pointed out, that successive Conferences have repeatedly urged Contracting Parties to submit complete maps and descriptions of wetlands at the time of designation, or as soon as possible thereafter. But as shown earlier in this judgment, there has never been any suggestion at the Conferences that a failure of the Contracting Party to provide a precise description of the boundaries of a designated wetland will result in the wetland being denied a place on the List or in the Contracting Party being relieved of its obligations under Art 3 of the Ramsar Convention. In short, the practice of the Contracting Parties is consistent with them regarding the obligation to provide precise boundary descriptions as important, but not going to the validity or effectiveness of a designation of a wetland for inclusion in the List.[111]

On appeal, the 'Full Court' confirmed these findings. The Full Court agreed also that while

> [t]he history of the meetings of the Contracting Parties discloses a concern to have the information required by Article 2(1), and more, provided[, a]t no point however has it

[107] *Minister for the Environment and Heritage v Greentree (No 2)*, [2004] FCA 741, 11 June 2004, para 47.

[108] *Greentree* (FCA), para 133.

[109] *Greentree v Minister for the Environment and Heritage*, [2005] FCAFC 128 (Full Court), 13 July 2005, para 29.

[110] *Greentree* (Full Court), paras 37 and 38.

[111] *Greentree* (FCA), para 135.

> ever been suggested that if it were not done at the time of designation, that designation is taken not to have occurred or that a listing would be regarded as invalid.[112]

The two courts can certainly not be faulted for their interpretation of the wording of the Ramsar PTRs, which, at the time of the *Greentree* proceedings, indeed remained hortatory. Moreover, various Ramsar resolutions confirm that successful listings were not precluded by failing to provide the delimitation on the map and the description of the boundaries. With the new 'gatekeeper' function of the Secretariat, the assessment might well have turned out differently.

In the *Greentree* case, the FCA furthermore sought to justify its overall conclusion that minor problems in a wetland designation would not prevent a successful listing by pointing out that the object and purpose of the Convention of slowing down progressive encroachment of wetlands would not be served by withholding the Ramsar conservation regime from a wetland that was not designated entirely correctly.[113] The Full Court agreed that the object and purpose prevented an alternative view.[114] The reliance on object and purpose is less convincing from the perspective of the recent introduction of a 'gateway function' for the Secretariat. Following the Australian courts' line of argument, the new 'gateway function' would be in contravention of the object and purpose of the Ramsar Convention, because it withholds protection from a failure to designate properly. Yet, the opposite could easily be argued: that proper description and delimitation better enables accurate conservation measures, and prevents farmers from accidentally harming parts of a wetland. Moreover, under the old practice, it often happened that, once listed, the necessary information was never provided at a later date, including for the Windella site. The Australian Federal Courts thus used a doubtful teleological reasoning to support its judgment in favour of the Australian federal government's stance on what the resolutions required from it.

2. CITES: *The 'Primarily Commercial Purposes' Resolution* and the *Reason to Believe Paragraph*

Biologists like to point out that, among the many threats to global biodiversity, international trade in endangered species is, surprisingly, a relatively minor one. This is true even for internationally traded endangered species.[115] Arguably the most serious threats include habitat change, pollution and invasive alien species.[116]

[112] *Greentree* (Full Court), para 43.
[113] *Greentree* (FCA), para 134.
[114] *Greentree* (Full Court), para 40.
[115] For instance, to large felids [cats] across Africa, habitat loss and retaliatory killing are the primary threats. See Craig Packer and others, 'Effects of Trophy Hunting on Lion and Leopard Populations in Tanzania' (2011) 25 *Conservation Biology* 142, 142.
[116] *Millennium Assessment Report, Ecosystems and Human Well-being: Biodiversity Synthesis*, 2005, World Resources Institute, Washington, DC, Key Messages.

This does not mean that 'trade' – or when it is penalised: smuggling – is a negligible threat. For species like elephants, rhinoceros, tigers and turtles, as well as commonly traded 'natural resources' such as tropical timber[117] and numerous marine species, cross-border supply and demand is a major danger. The world is experiencing a recent surge in export of dead and living specimens to the emerging economies, Asian and Middle-Eastern in particular, where many traditional uses for such specimens as medicine and art are still alive, and people now have the money for it.[118] Other causes include an increasing demand for fashion accessories, and a growing pool of affluent hunters from all parts of the world seeking trophy species. The rising demand has attracted a growing involvement of major international crime syndicates, who have picked up this lucrative business,[119] and rebel groups in need of cash.[120] Depending on whether or not fish and timber are included, the value of illegal international trade in species is estimated at between hundreds of millions of dollars and 20 billion dollars yearly, ranking it alongside illicit arms trade and human trafficking.[121]

Illegal international trade is one of the few threats to biodiversity for which a specific conventional regime with a near-global membership exists: the Convention on International Trade in Endangered Species (CITES), adopted in 1973 in Washington, DC. Apart from being a threat to biodiversity, trade in endangered species also jeopardises the use of, and trade in, resources in the future.[122] CITES was aimed at conserving species as a natural resource, and maintaining a level playing field for traders worldwide.[123] To the present day, resource conservation to safeguard future human use continues to play an important role next to conservation of biodiversity, evidenced for example by the CITES quota systems for some Appendix I species, and the possibility to downlist species once they are generally accepted to be out of the danger zone.

In short, CITES regulates international trade in specimens of species of wild fauna and flora, including export, re-export and import of live and dead animals and plants, and of parts and derivatives thereof, through a system of permits and certificates. Permits may only be issued if certain conditions are met, which have to be presented before consignments of specimens are allowed to leave or enter a country, depending on the Appendix on which the species is listed. Appendix I

[117] *cf* Peter H Sand, 'Whither CITES? The Evolution of a Treaty Regime in the Borderland of Trade and Environment' (1997) 8 *European Journal of International Law* 29, 56.

[118] Bryan Walsh, 'Traffic: Why It's Time to Get Serious About the Bloody Illegal Wildlife Trade', 5 March 2013, at http://science.time.com/2013/03/05/traffic-why-its-time-to-get-serious-about-the-bloody-illegal-wildlife-trade/#ixzz2ZP7Fxpos, accessed 17 September 2018.

[119] Walsh, 'Traffic: Why It's Time to Get Serious About the Bloody Illegal Wildlife Trade'.

[120] Patience Akumu, 'Joseph Kony's child army and the ivory trade that pays its bills' *Independent* (London 8 January 2014) www.independent.co.uk/voices/comment/joseph-kony-s-child-army-and-the-ivory-trade-that-pays-its-bills-9047525.html, accessed 26 August 2018.

[121] www.traffic.org/trade/.

[122] Sand, 'Whither CITES?', 34.

[123] Sand, 'Whither CITES?', 55.

species are subject to the strictest conditions. Each Party must designate a Management Authority responsible for issuing these permits and certificates, subject to the advice from a Scientific Authority.[124]

CITES currently has 175 parties, and roughly 35,000 species within its remit (of which about 29,000 are plants, of which – in turn – the great majority are orchids; and only around 800 are mammals).[125] Many possibly endangered species remain unlisted, for several reasons, important ones being a lack of information and resources to gather it,[126] as well as strong national interests in continuing import or export of certain species.

The Conference of the Parties to CITES has, by way of adopting COP decisions, shaped the most important rules of the regime, thus developing very broadly formulated convention provisions – i.e. implicit enabling clauses – into more specific rules. The importance of COP decisions to the development of the rules of the CITES regime are well understood in the specialised literature. As Favre already concluded in 1987, a number of phrases in CITES 'represent "tension points" within the Convention in that, due to their inherent vagueness, they have become a focal point for disagreement between the parties'.[127] Most of these 'tension points' are now addressed by resolutions. Issues illustrating the central importance of post-treaty rules for CITES include the criteria for listing species on the Appendices; definitions of hunting trophies, farming, introduction from the sea and many more terms; the standards for national authorities to make findings of non-detriment, including quota systems; and how national authorities should treat confiscated specimens. On all these issues, an extensive body of COP resolutions greatly influences the operation of the convention. Around[128] 30 CITES resolutions setting general rules are currently operative, most of which have been adjusted or replaced several times.

a. Resolutions on the Import and Export of Protected Species

Two CITES resolutions (and their predecessors) relating to the tasks of the importing and exporting Authorities are particularly interesting for the question of the authority of PTRs in the national legal orders, because they concern the operation of the national 'Scientific Authorities' and 'Management Authorities' that

[124] Willem Wijnstekers, *The Evolution of CITES* (2011), 47.

[125] http://www.cites.org/eng/disc/species.php.

[126] Shaun A Goho, 'The CITES Fort Lauderdale Criteria: The Uses and Limits of Science in International Conservation Decisionmaking' (2001) 114 *Harvard Law Review* 1769, 1784.

[127] David S Favre, 'Tension Points Within the Language of the CITES Treaty' (1987) 5 *Boston University International Law Journal* 247, 247.

[128] An exact number would require very precise criteria on what 'specific decisions' are and on what 'general rules' are. For this calculation, rules for specific species or groups of species, such as sharks or elephants, were left out.

the parties to CITES must establish after becoming a party to the Convention.[129] Resolution 5.10 on '*primarily commercial purposes*' sets out to define that complex term as part of the three-tier test which importing Authorities must perform before granting an import permit for Appendix I species (Article III CITES). Resolution 12.3 on *Permits and Certificates* recommends various procedural innovations and improvements to Article VI on Permits and Certificates, but thereby also adjusts some important aspects of the substantive export and import tests laid down in Article III, IV and V, such as the definition of 'hunting trophy', and foremost the role of the importing authority in controlling that a specimen was legally required in the country of origin.[130] Being aimed at the national Authorities, these resolutions are clearly external PTRs. The practice of national courts in relation to the application by national Management Authorities of these CITES resolutions is the most extensive available practice of national courts in relation to PTRs as a whole.

The conditions for granting export and import permits as laid down in Articles III (Appendix I species), IV (Appendix II species) and V (Appendix III species)[131] leave unanswered considerable questions, and have become the subject of numerous CITES COP resolutions over the last decades. These Articles set out the following differentiated tests for the granting of export permits, import permits, and the actual importation of species from the three Appendices.

The *granting of an export permit* for Appendix I and II is subject to a three-tier test: the export is non-detrimental to the survival of the species (non-detriment test); the specimen is not obtained in contravention of the conservation laws of the exporting state (legality test); and preparation and shipment do minimal harm to the specimen (minimal harm test). For Appendix I species, an additional requirement for granting an export permit is that an import permit has already been granted.[132] For Appendix III species, the non-detriment test is not required, only the latter two.

The *import of specimens* is also subject to tests of descending rigidity for species from the three Appendices, whereby a separate import permit is required for Appendix I species, whereas no import permit is required for Appendix II and III species, and the presentation of an export permit suffices. Hence, in relation of Appendix II and III species, one can only speak of the requirements for the *actual* importation. For Appendix I species, the Authorities of the state of import must again perform the non-detriment test, must ascertain that the proposed recipient is suitably equipped to house and care for the specimen, and that the specimen is not to be used for primarily commercial purposes. For Appendix II species,

[129] Art IX Convention on International Trade in Endangered Species of Wild Fauna and Flora (adopted 3 March 1973, entered into force 1 July 1975) 993 UNTS 243 (CITES).

[130] CITES COP Res 12.3 substituted CITES COP Res 10.2, *Permits and Certificates*, to which it made various changes.

[131] Appendix III species are species voluntarily listed by one or more treaty parties, and are limited to specimens on the territory of these treaty parties only.

[132] *cf* the analysis in Bowman, Davies and Redgwell, '*Lyster's International Wildlife Law*', 500.

only the presentation of an export (or, as the case may be, a re-export) permit is required. The test for Appendix III species is lighter still, requiring the presentation of an export permit when the specimen in question is imported from a state that has included the species on Appendix III, and otherwise merely a certificate of origin (showing, in other words, that the specimen is not currently protected by CITES).

Article VI on Permits and Certificates contains the formal requirements for permits and certificates, which particularly aim to prevent imitation and guarantee authenticity, and also to prevent the use of a single permit for several specimens. Every export and import permit 'shall be in accordance with the provisions of this Article'.

Articles III–VI CITES leave unanswered important questions to be addressed by the CITES COP or local Authorities. For the granting of export permits for Appendix I and II species, the primary questions are: Under what circumstances is an export (not) detrimental to the survival of a species, and does it concern the population in that state or all populations in the region or worldwide? For the granting of import permits for Appendix I species, primary unanswered questions are: What purposes of import should be thought of that are detrimental to the survival of the species, and what are uses that are primarily for commercial purposes?

For Appendix II and III species, the scope and depth of review by the importing authorities of the validity of the export permit, and what they may do to prohibit the actual importation of a specimen accompanied by a valid export permit, is surrounded by difficult issues. The text of the convention does not assign the importing Authorities their own substantive test for Appendix II and III species. The terms of the treaty point in the direction of accepting an export permit at face value if it conforms to the formal requirements of Article VI. However, is an export permit 'complete' and valid if it has not dealt with the three- or two-tier substantive tests for granting an export permit for Appendix II and III species respectively, for instance the condition that the exported specimen 'was not obtained in contravention of the laws of that State for the protection of fauna and flora'?[133] Are the importing Authorities obliged to check this substantive validity under certain circumstances?

On several of these issues, the CITES COP has adopted extensive resolutions, and has revised most of them regularly. On export and import permits and certificates generally, the parties adopted Res Conf 12.3 on *Permits and Certificates* (revised again at COP 15),[134] which succeeded the earlier adopted Res Conf 10.2. It was 'adopted' by the plenary.[135] Res Conf 11.3 on *Compliance and Enforcement*,

[133] Art III.2(c) CITES.

[134] CITES COP Res 12.3 (Rev CoP 15), *Permits and Certificates*.

[135] See IISD Reporting Services, ENB Volume 21, no 30, Monday, 18 November 2002, *Summary of the twelfth conference of the parties to the convention on international trade in endangered species of wild fauna and flora: 3–15 November 2002*, at www.iisd.ca/vol21/enb2130e.html.

a topic that partly overlaps with permits and certificates, was 'adopted without objection'.[136] On 'primarily commercial purposes', the parties adopted Res Conf 5.10.[137]

Here, the analysis of the text of these resolutions is limited to two of the issues left unresolved in the CITES treaty provisions on *import* permits and import authorisation: the term 'primarily commercial purposes' (Res Conf 5.10) and the question of whether import Authorities may not, have to, or may check the 'completeness' of an exporting Authority's grant of an export permit, or must defer to the export permit if it satisfies the formal requirements for permits in Article VI (Res Conf 10.2, 11.3 and 12.3).

b. The 'Primarily Commercial Purposes' Resolution

Resolution 5.10 engages with the question of what '*primarily commercial purposes*' are in view of Article III.3(c) CITES, reading 'a Management Authority of the State of import is satisfied that the specimen is not to be used for primarily commercial purposes'. With Res Conf 5.10 (Rev CoP15), the COP issued a few core principles, and a list of examples of 'transactions in which the non-commercial aspects may or may not be predominant, depending upon the facts of each situation'. This Resolution is, for example, relevant to the debate on whether Japan's whaling activities are 'for commercial purposes', and whether Japan is bound by that definition and/or can base itself on it in its own defence.[138] It is also relevant for imports of specimens of Appendix I species by zoos, the subject of the Australian and US court cases discussed below.

According to Resolution 5.10, an activity can generally be described as commercial if 'its purpose is to obtain economic benefit … and is directed toward resale, exchange, provision of a service or any other form of economic use or benefit'.[139] Most pertinently, General Principle 2 states that '[t]he term "commercial purposes" should be defined by the country of import as broadly as possible so that any transaction which is not wholly "non-commercial" will be regarded as "commercial"'.[140] However, the treaty criterion is not commercial purposes versus non-commercial purposes, but 'primarily commercial purposes':

> In transposing [General Principle 2] to the term 'primarily commercial purposes', it is agreed that all uses whose non-commercial aspects do not clearly predominate shall

[136] 11th meeting of the Conference of the Parties, Gigiri (Kenya), 10–20 April 2000, *Summary Report of the Plenary*, p 14, at www.cites.org/sites/default/files/eng/cop/11/other/Plen.pdf. The draft consolidated resolutions in Annexes 2B, regarding enforcement and compliance, and 3B, regarding exchanges of specimens, were adopted without objection.

[137] It was not possible to retrieve the mode of adoption of CITES Res Conf 5.10 from the documentation available online relating to COP 5 in Buenos Aires.

[138] *Whaling in the Antarctic* (Memorial of Japan), p 297; *Whaling in the Antarctic* (Memorial of Australia), p 262.

[139] CITES COP Res 5.10 (Rev CoP 15), *Definition of 'primarily commercial purposes'*, General principle 2.

[140] CITES COP Res 5.10, General principle 3.

> be considered to be primarily commercial in nature, with the result that the import of specimens of Appendix-I species should not be permitted.[141]

In other words, non-commercial aspects should clearly predominate over any form of economic use or benefit, in order for the importing Authority to grant a permit. Thereby, the focus should be on the intended use in the country of import, not on the nature of the transaction between seller and buyer.[142] The examples then listed in the resolutions all concern activities 'in which the non-commercial aspects may or may not be predominant, depending upon the facts of each situation', to which the General Principles should be applied.

The Resolution clearly reads as recommended guidance for national Authorities to be able to distinguish commercial from non-commercial purposes as well as possible. Note the use of the wording *should* and *as possible*, the designation of the operative part of the Resolution as general *principles*, and the inclusion of *examples* that provide *guidance* in the Annex to the Resolution. The definition leaves quite some room for subjective differences of understanding: when do non-commercial purposes 'clearly predominate'? Nonetheless, the depth of detail provided in the examples, which focus precisely on categories for which doubts could arise, at least achieves some more clarity on a matter which is inherently subject to dispute.

i. The 'Primarily Commercial Purposes' Resolution in the Memorials of the *Whaling* Case

The term 'commercial purposes' is also used in Article VIII of the International Convention on the Regulation of Whaling (ICRW) and Paragraph 10(e) of the ICRW Schedule. In their memorials (written pleadings) in the *Whaling* case before the International Court of Justice, Japan and Australia therefore both referred to the CITES definition in Res 5.10 of the term 'commercial purposes': Australia in order to confirm, Japan to deny, the commercial nature of Japan's scientific whaling operations. Both Parties acknowledge that CITES was not the basis for the adjudication between them, so that the legal relevance of CITES as a whole is dependent on Article 31.3(c) VCLT (principle of systemic integration providing a connection to all relevant rules of international environmental law).[143]

Australia's argumentation regarding the legal relevance of Res 5.10 indicates the resemblance between Res 5.10's definition and the definition of 'commerce' in various ICJ judgments (*Oil Platforms*, *Costa Rica v Nicaragua*) as well as WTO panel reports.[144] In other words, Australia appears to be hinting at a customary law definition of 'commercial purposes' reflected in and supported by Res 5.10, although no express reference to customary law is made in the memorial. It is

[141] CITES COP Res 5.10, General principle 3.
[142] CITES COP Res 5.10, General principle 4.
[143] *Whaling in the Antarctic* (Memorial of Australia), para 4.81–4.86; *Whaling in the Antarctic* (Memorial of Japan), Section III.2.
[144] *Whaling in the Antarctic* (Memorial of Australia), para 6.8, p 262.

rather doubtful that the mentioned ICJ judgments can be considered together with the Res 5.10 definition, as the latter is very specifically aimed at the issuance of import permits for trade in specimens of highly endangered Appendix I species. Indeed, Japan points to Res 5.10 in support of the fact that even highly endangered species may nonetheless be traded under CITES, as long as the specimen is not to be used for primarily commercial purposes.[145]

ii. The 'Primary Commercial Purposes' Resolution in the Australian and United States Courts: Import of Elephants

In the case *Animal Welfare v Australia*, dealing with a question about the legality of import of a number of Appendix I specimens by Australian zoos,[146] the Australian Administrative Appeals Tribunal did not find Res 5.10 very helpful in interpreting Australia's treaty obligations, due to its lack of specificity in relation to the issue in front of that Court:

> We will bear these provisions in mind but they do not seem to us to resolve the most difficult issue in the present case. What the explanatory resolutions say is that both 'commercial' and 'commercial purpose' should be widely construed. Where they do not assist is with respect to the activities of not for profit organisations, which do not produce a surplus from these activities.[147]

The Court then continued to do its own common-sense analysis: is the fact that zoos charge an entrance fee more predominant than its educational purposes? It emphasised the fact that the zoos were not making an overall profit, an aspect that is not especially central in the Resolution. Although the Tribunal was unable to find sufficiently specific guidance to find an answer to the question before it, it did not state that it did not follow the Resolution on account of its recommendatory nature.

The Tribunal's US counterpart went so far as to ignore the recommendatory nature of the Resolution. The US District Court case of *Born Free USA v Norton*[148] concerned the importation of African elephants, which is an Appendix I species, from Swaziland to a couple of US zoos. While the Court, on the one hand, 'find[s] the language in example (e) to be confusing',[149] and concluded that the imports under consideration did 'not fit cleanly into any of the non-exhaustive list of examples in Resolution Conf 5.10', on the other hand, it found that 'under the

[145] *Whaling in the Antarctic* (Memorial of Australia), para 6.29.

[146] *The International Fund for Animal Welfare (Australia) Pty Ltd and Ors and Minister for Environment and Heritage and Ors*, [2005] AATA 1210 (Administrative Appeals Tribunal of Australia), 7 December 2005. The case concerned the importation of Asian elephants, which is an Appendix I species, from Thailand to a couple of Australian zoos.

[147] *Animal Welfare*, para 108.

[148] *Born Free USA v Norton*, 278 F.Supp.2d 5 (D.D.C.), 8 August 2003.

[149] *Born Free USA*, p 15. Example (e) in CITES COP Res Conf 5.10 relates to 'Captive-breeding programmes'.

guidance of Res Conf 5.10, it is reasonable for [the US Fish and Wildlife Service] to conclude that this is not a setting in which commercial aspects of the zoos' purposes predominate over non-commercial aspects'.[150] The Court does not show any signs that it is bothered by the recommendatory (i.e. non-mandatory) nature of the Resolution, and is therefore not inclined to study any other sources that could clarify the term 'primarily commercial purposes'.

To summarise, while the Australian administrative tribunal concluded that the resolutions were too unspecific to have any authority, the US District Court first concluded that the Resolution gave no guidance, only to decide that the Fish and Wildlife Service's decision was reasonable 'under the guidance' of the Resolution. This is a clear demonstration of the ambiguous authority of this PTR in the national legal orders.

c. *The* Reason to Believe Paragraph

The set-up of the case of the mahogany traders is a central story in the introduction to the book, because it contains all the ambiguities surrounding the authority of PTRs in the national legal orders, the extent to which courts are mostly improvising what to do with them, and usually end up following the view of the government. Here we pick up the story again.

i. Interpretation or Modification?

Resolution 12.3's Paragraph II(j)[151] states that the Conference of the Parties:

> RECOMMENDS that … (j) Parties not authorize the import of any specimen if they have reason to believe that it was not legally acquired in the country of origin.

Likewise, Resolution 11.3 on *Compliance and enforcement* recommends that:

> [I]f an importing country has reason to believe that specimens of an Appendix-II or -III species are traded in contravention of the laws of any country involved in the transaction, it: i) immediately inform the country whose laws were thought to have been violated and, to the extent possible, provide that country with copies of all documentation relating to the transaction; and ii) where possible, apply stricter domestic measures to that transaction as provided for in Article XIV of the Convention.

Furthermore, Resolution 12.3 also recommends that:

> [T]he Parties refuse to accept any permit or certificate that is *invalid*, including authentic documents that do not contain all the *required* information … or that contain information that brings into question the validity of the permit or certificate (emphasis added).[152]

[150] *Born Free USA*, p 16.
[151] Formerly CITES Res Conf 10.2, *Permits and Certificates*, para II(h).
[152] CITES COP Res Conf 12.3, para XIV(d).

These *Reason to Believe Paragraphs* cast considerable doubt on two of the impressions the text of the Convention, as reviewed above, leaves about the respective roles of exporting and importing Authorities. One, the impression that to check if the specimen in question was not obtained in contravention of the laws for the protection of fauna and flora of the exporting state is part of the test to be performed by the *exporting* state alone (Article III.2(b), Article IV.2(b) and Article V.2(b)). Two, the impression that, except for the particular tests to be performed by the importing Authorities in case of a specimen of an Appendix I species, the import of a specimen of any listed species requires only 'the presentation of an (re-)export permit', which 'shall be in accordance with the formal requirements of [Article VI]'.[153] At the very least, importing Authorities are not explicitly tasked by the Convention to check the validity of the export permit in terms of the substantive test performed by the exporting Authorities. Added up, it is questionable that paragraphs such as II(j) and XIV(d) of Res 12.3 can be fitted in with the scheme set up by Articles III–VI CITES. The argument can be advanced that these provisions do not enable such a recommendation, and that this Paragraph should be considered to be a *modification* of the Convention – it is contradicting clear treaty language.

That contention, however, might be rebuttable by means of Article XIV.1(a), CITES' acceptance of stricter domestic measures than the Convention prescribes. Article XIV.1 states that '[t]he provisions of the present Convention shall in no way affect the right of Parties to adopt (a) stricter domestic measures regarding the conditions for trade, taking, possession or transport of specimens of species included in Appendices I, II and III, or the complete prohibition thereof'.[154] This provision might be understood, amongst others, to allow for stricter export and import conditions than those required by Articles III–V CITES. The understanding of Article XIV.1 in the thick guidebook called *The Evolution of CITES*, written by a former Secretary-General of CITES, is that 'the great many resolutions adopted by the parties' which 'call for measures that go further than the provisions of the Convention' are intended to be covered by the Article.[155]

Is the *Reason to Believe Paragraph* simply *stricter* than the Convention, or does it go *against* the Convention's division of labour in the implementation phase, which places the emphasis of the controlling task with the exporting Authorities? Stricter domestic measures are not the same as that the importing Authorities can go so far as to intervene with a test that the treaty assigns to the exporting Authorities. This is clearly a difficult question of interpretation of a potential contradiction between Articles III–V, XIV.1(a), and the resolutions.

[153] The import Authorities' check of these formal requirements is also recommended in CITES COP Res Conf 12.3, in para XIV(d), which recommends that 'the Parties refuse to accept any permit or certificate that is invalid, including authentic documents that do not contain all the required information … or that contain information that brings into question the validity of the permit or certificate'.

[154] Art XIV CITES, titled 'Effect on Domestic Legislation and International Conventions'.

[155] Wijnstekers, '*The Evolution of CITES*', 431.

Looking at the wording of the Paragraph, it shows evidence of a consensus among the parties in support of, at least, a partial review of the export Authorities' correct performance of one of the three tests for granting an export permit (the legality test) by the import Authorities. Then again, the use of the phrase 'reason to believe' is rather unspecific. When should import Authorities have 'reason to believe,' and how much of an effort should they make to find out whether they *should* have a 'reason to believe'? Paragraph XIV(d) of Res 12.3 fails to clarify what it means by 'invalid' in relation to an export permit: only regarding formal requirements or also fulfilment of the substantive export tests? Furthermore, the use of the verb 'recommend' does little to boost these Paragraphs' mandatory character, i.e. whether authorities are merely *allowed* to look behind the formal requirements of Article VI CITES or are *obliged* to do so.

ii. The *Reason to Believe Paragraph* in United Kingdom and United States Courts: Shipments of Mahogany

What authority does this decidedly external PTR have in the jurisdictions where it is to be implemented? In most domestic legal orders, legislation is adopted to implement CITES, and sometimes particular CITES resolutions. For instance, the European Union's 'CITES Regulation' (EC Regulation 338/97) Article 14.1(b) partially incorporates the *Reason to Believe Paragraph*, or at least contains a similar clause: 'If, at any time, the competent authorities have reason to believe that these provisions [the provisions of the EC Regulation incorporating CITES] are being infringed, they shall take the appropriate steps to ensure compliance or to instigate legal action'. The 'provisions' here referred to clearly mean the test to be performed by the exporting Authorities. They are therefore even broader than the *Reason to Believe Paragraph*, which only relates to one of the conditions in the test, that 'the specimen was not obtained in contravention of the laws' of the exporting state (Article III.2(b) CITES).

In the *Mahogany Cases*, two US courts and one UK court have issued judgments, all relating to the same *problématique*: the treatment of shipments of a certain species of mahogany from Brazil (a species Brazil had unilaterally listed in Appendix III) by importing Management Authorities. The Brazilian Management Authority (IBAMA) had, against its own assessment that such shipments were illegal under Brazilian conservation laws, nonetheless granted export permits, following an injunction to do so from a Brazilian federal court. This took place at a time when the Brazilian central government tried to stop illegal logging, but other (domestic) forces attempted to prevent this through the courts – with some success. In relation to both the US and UK shipments, IBAMA had communicated this state of affairs, its own assessment as well as the reason why it had nonetheless been forced to grant export permits, to the respective importing Authorities.[156]

[156] See *R (on the application of Greenpeace Ltd) v Secretary of State for the Environment, Food and Rural Affairs*, EWCA Civ 1036 (Civil Division), 25 July 2002, paras 8–18.

The one significant difference was that the US Management Authorities (the Animal and Plant Health Inspection Service, 'APHIS', and the Fish and Wildlife Service, 'FWS') subsequently *refused* entry to the shipments, whereas the UK Management Authority (Commissioners of Customs and Excise, CCE) *allowed* them entry. As a result, plaintiffs in the US case were the companies that had purchased the shipments, while the UK case was brought by Greenpeace.

The questions before both courts were very similar. In short, the dilemma for the US courts was whether it was unlawful for the FWS, in possession of knowledge that the Brazilian Authority was not satisfied that the mahogany was legally obtained, to conclude that the export permits were invalid, and refuse entry for that reason.[157] The dilemma the UK court was faced with was whether it was unlawful for the UK Commissioners *not* to conclude the invalidity of the export permits considering its comparable knowledge that the Brazilian Authority was not satisfied that the mahogany was legally obtained, and refuse entry for that reason.[158]

In short, were the Authorities *prohibited*, *obliged* or *allowed* to act in accordance with the relevant CITES resolutions? The facts of these cases are unequivocally within the scope of the *Reason to Believe Paragraph* in Resolutions 10.2, 11.3 and 12.3: where importing Authorities have *reason to believe* that the specimen was not acquired legally in accordance with the laws of the exporting state, they should not authorise importation. Did the Paragraph have authority in the national legal orders? The following paragraphs trace the treatment of the issue by respectively the UK Court of Appeal (Civil Division) in the case of *Greenpeace v Secretary of State for the Environment*,[159] and in the US District Court and US Court of Appeals in the case of *Castlewood Products v Norton (Secretary of U.S. Department of Interior)*.[160]

In the *Greenpeace v Secretary of State* case, minority judge Laws formulated the question before the Court as follows:

> Where an export permit to which the Regulation applies, being valid on its face, is presented to the competent authorities of a Member State to support the importation into that State of flora or fauna covered by Annex C to the Regulation (Appendix III to the Convention), *are the authorities obliged to accept the permit, and allow the import, even though they know that the management authority which issued the permit in the exporting State was not 'satisfied that the specimen was not obtained in contravention of the laws of that State for the protection of fauna and flora'* within Article V(2)(a) of the Convention?[161]

Despite this question being directly addressed in the *Reason to Believe Paragraph*, the two majority opinions in the UK *Greenpeace* case completely ignore it.

[157] *Castlewood Products* (District Court); *Castlewood Products* (Court of Appeals).
[158] *Greenpeace*, Lord Justice Laws, para 27.
[159] *R (on the application of Greenpeace Ltd) v Secretary of State for the Environment, Food and Rural Affairs*, EWCA Civ 1036 (Civil Division), 25 July 2002.
[160] *Castlewood Products v Norton*, 264 F.Supp.2d 9 (D.D.C.), 16 April 2003; *Castlewood Products Llc v A Norton*, 365 F3d 1076 (DC Cir), 30 April 2004.
[161] *Greenpeace*, Lord Justice Laws, para 22.

The majority did not even refer to the *existence* of the relevant PTRs (Res Conf 10.2, the predecessor of Res Conf 12.3). This is not because they were unaware of the Paragraph's existence, as it was mentioned extensively in the pleadings of Greenpeace and in the opinion of the minority judge. Instead, only looking at the text of the Convention, one majority judge concluded that:

> [T]he importing authorities are *entitled* to treat [the permit] as a valid and subsisting permit. I can see nothing unlawful in the import authority accepting it as documentary evidence having the effect that it purports to have and in acting upon it. *It is not required* to check the correctness or validity of the decision of the management authority of the state of export that the stipulated conditions have been met for the grant of an export permit(emphasis added).[162]

Implicitly, though, the majority's strong emphasis on the textual interpretation of the Convention can be understood as the majority's conviction that the treaty text should prevail over the resolutions, and that this justifies ignoring the resolutions. Unfortunately, the majority does not say whether they would have considered it *equally lawful* had the Management Authority acted in accordance with the *Reason to Believe Paragraph*, or that they still would have considered that a violation of the prevalence of the treaty text. The emphasised parts of the quote ('entitled', 'It is not required') seem to indicate that the Commissioners could also have refused the import permit.

Minority judge Laws comes to an opposite conclusion, following the course of action recommended in the *Reason to Believe Paragraph* word for word:[163]

> [T]he authorities in the importing State knew (at the time the export permit was presented) that the management authority of the exporting State was not satisfied as required by Article V(2)(a) when it issued the permit, they should have rejected the permit for failure to comply with Article 4(3)(a) of the Regulation. The permits in this case were accordingly unlawful.[164]

The minority judge also makes a strong appeal to what, in his perception, should be considered the primary purpose of CITES:

> The Convention, though certainly it seeks to support viable international trade, is first and foremost intended as a legal antidote to some of the damage done by man's exploitation of nature's resources. That purpose must, in my judgment, serve as the most influential factor in the interpretation of the [EU] Regulation [incorporating CITES] … For these reasons I prefer the construction advanced in Greenpeace's modified argument.[165]

Even in one single case, judges could easily reach two completely opposite outcomes. The majority completely ignored the PTR in question, while the

[162] *Greenpeace*, Lord Justice Mummery, para 59.
[163] At the time of the *Greenpeace* case, the *Reason to Believe Paragraph* was laid down in Resolution 10.2, para II(h) – also incorporated into Art 14.1(b) of the EC CITES Regulation.
[164] *Greenpeace*, Lord Justice Laws, para 35.
[165] *Greenpeace*, para 34.

minority judge followed it to the letter, neither really arguing why they should or should not defer to it.

In the *Castlewood Products* case, the District Court held that CITES Resolutions 10.2 and 11.3 'clearly evince a "postratification understanding" of the parties to CITES'.[166] The US Supreme Court has held previously that such postratification understandings of the contracting parties must be considered aids to the underlying treaty's interpretation.[167] Having established their interpretive relevance, in the *Castlewood* case, the District Court interpreted the Resolutions not as mere recommendations to the parties, but states that 'the parties to CITES have adopted "resolutions" thereunder *instructing* one another to refuse imports of specimens for which there is "reason to believe it was not legally acquired"' (emphasis added).[168] Therefore, it concluded, the Resolutions clearly expect the parties to render 'mutual assistance in the enforcement of their respective environmental laws'.[169] This reading lends a mandatory quality to the Resolutions, going beyond what the *Reason to Believe Paragraph* in fact states ('recommends').

On appeal, the US Court of Appeals took a more careful approach. It builds a step-by-step argumentation to reconcile the approach recommended by the *Reason to Believe Paragraph* with the text of CITES (as incorporated by the US statute incorporating CITES).[170] The Court of Appeals first notes that CITES:

> merely requires a valid foreign export permit, but it does not specify the conditions that a foreign export permit must meet in order for U.S. officials to regard the permit as valid.[171]

The Court then pointedly observes that CITES:

> does not say that these requirements are the only conditions that an agency may lawfully require before accepting a permit.[172]

In other words, it follows the interpretation discussed above, that the checking of formal requirements is the minimum that the importing Authorities should do, but not the maximum permissible. The Court puts much emphasis on the fact that IBAMA (the Brazilian Management Authority):

> confirmed that although it had issued the CITES export permits for the shipments, it had done so under court injunctions which it was appealing. IBAMA indicated it had not determined whether the mahogany had been legally acquired, which is a prerequisite to the issuance of a CITES export permit for this species.[173]

[166] *Castlewood Products* (District Court), p 12.
[167] *Zicherman v Korean Air Lines Co*, 516 U.S. 217, 116 S.Ct. 629 (1996), 16 January 1996, p 226.
[168] *Castlewood Products* (District Court), p 1210.
[169] *Castlewood Products* (District Court), p 1210.
[170] Title 50 Code of Federal Regulations, Part 23, *Convention on International Trade in Endangered Species of Wild Fauna and Flora*.
[171] 50 C.F.R. §§ 23.12(a) and 23.14(a). *Castlewood Products* (Court of Appeals), para 39.
[172] *Castlewood Products* (Court of Appeals), para 39.
[173] *Castlewood Products* (Court of Appeals), para 27.

Finally, the Court of Appeals points to the CITES Resolutions which urge that:

> [T]he Parties refuse to accept any permit or certificate that is invalid, including authentic documents that do not contain all the required information … or that contain information that brings into question the validity of the permit or certificate.[174]

The Court of Appeals takes the position that it is surely *reasonable* to rely on Resolution 12.3 as *embodying the agreement of the parties*. It acknowledges that the CITES Resolutions 'are not binding on the United States'.[175] However, it nonetheless relies on the Resolutions to an important extent, concluding that the US Management Authority's refusal to accept Brazilian export permits was perfectly reasonable:

> This does not render the resolutions meaningless, however. There would be no point in the contracting states agreeing on resolutions only to then completely ignore them. Therefore, while not binding, it was surely reasonable for [the US Management Authorities] to look to the CITES resolutions for guidance in interpreting the regulations implementing CITES.[176]

As in the *Greenpeace* case, the question arises of how the Circuit Court would have decided if the FWS had *not* acted in accordance with the Resolutions. Would that have been equally lawful?

While Article XIV.1(a) CITES indeed allows for more stringent domestic measures, it is questionable that this would go so far as warranting the importing Authorities' evaluation of the exporting Authority's decision to grant export permits. That would seem to be quite an inroad into the sovereign decision of the exporting state. However, in these particular cases, it was the Brazilian Authority that informed the importing Authorities that the shipments had been logged in contravention of Brazilian conservation laws, in other words, urged the UK and US Authorities to ignore its sovereign but not so freely made decision.

The quite astonishing conclusion of *Greenpeace* and *Castlewood*, viewed together, is that both national Management Authorities acting in accordance with the Resolution's recommendations and ones not acting in accordance with the Resolution's recommendations, are likely to be found lawful by domestic courts. In connection with that observation, there is the contrasting finding between the two cases that, according to the *Castlewood* judgments, 'there would be no point in the contracting states agreeing on resolutions only to then completely ignore them',[177] while, according to the *Greenpeace* majority decision, '[n]o such obligation is expressly or impliedly imposed by the export permit scheme in the Convention or in the [EU] Regulation'.[178] Before courts, government agencies get away with both acting in accordance with, and acting against, CITES resolutions.

[174] *Castlewood Products* (Court of Appeals), para 42.
[175] *Castlewood Products* (Court of Appeals), para 44.
[176] *Castlewood Products* (Court of Appeals), para 44.
[177] *Castlewood Products* (Court of Appeals), para 44.
[178] *Greenpeace*, para 56.

C. Closing the Gap: The Montreal and Kyoto Protocols

Compared to the Ramsar Convention and CITES, the Montreal and Kyoto Protocols are very detailed and few key terms are not defined. However, these Protocols do leave open many explicit gaps in the treaty, assigning their Meetings the task to subsequently try to fill these gaps. This has led to equally extensive series of, in this case, not resolutions and recommendations, but 'decisions', 'guidelines', 'modalities' and 'principles'. The architecture of norm development under the Montreal and Kyoto Protocols and other protocols like them is, as a result, more purposeful and specific about which issues can and cannot be subject to further rulemaking.

This is reflected directly in the higher and clearer authority of Montreal and Kyoto PTRs in their respective internal orders, compared to the PTRs of the Ramsar Convention and CITES. It is obviously more difficult to escape PTRs in the operation of regime meetings and bodies when the treaty has explicitly commanded the adoption of those PTRs. Both the Montreal Protocol Critical Use Exemptions for Methyl Bromide and the Kyoto Protocol Accounting Modalities are cases in point. Regime bodies simply operate in accordance with those decisions, and do not try to work around them, like we saw in the context of the Ramsar Convention. This has, however, remarkably little effect on the degree of authority of the very same decisions in national court proceedings, which turns out to be equally ambiguous.

1. The Montreal Protocol: *Critical Use Exemptions for Methyl Bromide*

As game theorist Scott Barret explains, the depletion of the ozone layer is a very atypical environmental public 'bad' in a very good way.[179] Western countries, the US on the frontlines, perceived ozone layer depletion as dangerous (the famous removal of skin cancer from Reagan's nose), while many other global environmental problems primarily endanger developed countries; there were no serious consequences, financial or otherwise, to switching to alternative substances, at least for most industries (certain agricultural uses of methyl bromide proved to be one of the temporary exceptions); and the monetary cost of not acting far outweighed that of acting, including the cost of assisting developing countries to make the transition.[180] Because of this atypicality, delivering the public 'good' of stopping further degradation, and thereby laying the groundwork for recovery, led to what is considered to be the most successful global environmental cooperative effort of modern times: the Montreal Protocol on Substances that Deplete the Ozone Layer (Montreal, 1987).

[179] Scott Barrett, *Why Cooperate? Incentives to Supply Global Public Goods* (OUP 2007), ch 3.
[180] Barrett, '*Why Cooperate?*', 74–84.

Adopted as a follow-up to the framework-type Vienna Convention for the Protection of the Ozone Layer, the Montreal Protocol sets out the ultimate objective to eliminate the emission of a number of substances that deplete ozone in the atmosphere.[181] Currently, it has 197 Parties. The Protocol makes a clear differentiation between the obligations of developed countries' industrialised parties and the so-called 'Article 5, paragraph 1' parties, 148 developing country parties which fulfilled the lower than 0.3 kilograms emissions per capita condition. However, in contrast to the climate change negotiations, there is much less controversy about the fact that these Article 5 parties must *also* phase out the controlled ozone-depleting substances, albeit at a more relaxed pace – reaching zero use of CFCs in 1996 and 2010 respectively. Near-complete phasing out for all controlled substances is not projected before 2040 (Article 5 Parties' production of HCFCs).[182]

The Montreal Protocol is much more detailed on its main substantive issues than the Kyoto Protocol. For example, Article 2H on methyl bromide, the subject of this case study, prescribed a meticulous phase-out of that controlled substance, providing clear percentages of reduction in consumption and production for the years 1995, 1999, 2001, 2003, and 2005, with that last year reaching zero consumption and production.[183] Moreover, the parties have formally amended the Protocol on matters of substance to a far greater degree than under any other protocols and conventions, and with high ratification rates. The innovative 'adjustments' technique of decision making, discussed in chapter one, section A, played a major role in efficiently developing the obligations under the Montreal Protocol.

That generally no insurmountable obstacles existed to reach global consensus on eliminating substances depleting the ozone layer, however, does not imply that there was no disagreement about many important details. Explicit enabling clauses inserted into the Protocol led to smaller and larger battles being fought through Montreal MOP PTRs: critical use exemptions with regard to methyl bromide; essential use exemptions with regard to other controlled substances such as CFCs; addition of new substances to the Annexes; defining the 'basic domestic needs' of developing countries;[184] trade restrictions with non-parties; and so on. Through to the 22nd MOP in 2010, the parties had already adopted more than 720 post-treaty instruments. On the ozone-depleting substance methyl bromide alone – a central example in this study – seven Montreal MOP decisions containing rules[185] and 14 decisions applying those rules were adopted over the years.

[181] Arts 2A to 2I of the Montreal Protocol on Substances that Deplete the Ozone Layer (adopted 16 September 1987, entered into force 1 January 1989) 1522 UNTS 3 (Montreal Protocol).

[182] 'Summary of control measures under the Montreal Protocol', http://ozone.unep.org/montreal-protocol-substances-deplete-ozone-layer/79744/44, accessed 17 September 2018.

[183] In practice, however, critical use exemptions for a number of Parties have extended far into the 2010s.

[184] Montreal MOP Decision VII/9, *Basic Domestic Needs*.

[185] Montreal MOP Decisions VIII/16: *Critical agricultural uses of methyl bromide*; IX/7, *Emergency methyl-bromide use*; XIII/11, *Procedures for applying for a critical-use exemption for methyl bromide*; XV/54, *Categories of assessment to be used by the Technology and Economic Assessment Panel when*

a. Resolutions Concerning Methyl Bromide

Methyl bromide (MB) is an ozone-depleting substance phased out by the Montreal Protocol, used primarily in intensive agriculture. The MOP decision on *Critical-use exemptions for methyl bromide* (the '*Critical Use Criteria*') and the yearly *Exemption Decisions* based on these criteria, make an interesting case study, because their authority in the internal normative order of the Montreal regime, and in the national legal orders, matters for their implementation. First of all, the *Criteria* for the adoption of country-specific critical-use exemptions address the MOP's yearly decision making in this respect. Do they, in fact, constitute the dominant reference point in this respect? Second of all, the Montreal Protocol Implementing Committee, in controlling compliance with the Protocol, must determine if compliance includes compliance with the *Exemption Decisions*. Third of all, the *Exemption Decisions* are clearly directed at implementation in the national legal order. Does that mean that persons affected by the *Decisions* – farmers or anyone affected by the hole in the ozone layer – can contest domestic implementation before domestic courts?

Article 2H.5 of the Montreal Protocol creates the possibility of exemptions for critical uses of methyl bromide up to 30 per cent of 1991 levels:

> [2H.]5. … This paragraph will apply save to the extent that the Parties decide to permit the level of production or consumption that is necessary to satisfy uses agreed by them to be critical uses.

This explicit enabling clause formed the basis for a set of criteria for critical use exemptions as well as a series of yearly decisions that allocate amounts for critical use to individual treaty parties. The use of the verb 'decide' in the Protocol text gives some indication of the rather high authority that the prospective 'decision' is intended to have. There is something about the term 'decision' that makes it stand firm and indisputable. At the very least, it should be clear that this 'decision' ought to be more than just a recommendation. This makes it one of the strongest examples of delegation of regulatory authority to plenary treaty meetings.

At MOP IX, the parties adopted Decision IX/6 containing criteria to apply to parties' requests for critical use exemptions.[186] In Decision Ex.1/3, the MOP approved a first *Exemption Decision* with country-by-country exemptions in 2005, on the basis of Decision IX/6.[187] The Report of this meeting states that a 'compromise text' for which 'the deliberations had been both long and arduous'

assessing critical uses of methyl bromide; Ex.I/4, *Conditions for granting and reporting critical-use exemptions for methyl bromide*; XVI/3, *Duration of critical-use nominations of methyl bromide*; XVI/6, *Accounting framework*.

[186] The report of the 9th meeting of the Montreal MOP does not state the mode of decision making by which the decision was adopted.

[187] Montreal MOP Decision Ex.I/3, *Critical-use exemptions for methyl bromide for 2005*, and Annexes to the *Report of the First Extraordinary Meeting of the Parties to the Montreal Protocol*.

'was adopted as decision Ex.1/3', warranting the conclusion that the Decision was adopted by consensus, albeit one that was difficult to reach.[188]

In Decision IX/6, the parties decided that 'use' of methyl bromide should qualify as 'critical' only if 'the lack of availability of methyl bromide for that use would result in a significant market disruption' and '[t]here are no technically and economically feasible alternatives or substitutes'.[189] Furthermore, production or consumption of methyl bromide would be permitted only if it was 'not available in sufficient quantity and quality from existing stocks of banked or recycled methyl bromide'.[190] A consolidated list of alternative substances was also set up, together with a Handbook on Critical Use Nominations for methyl bromide.[191] MOP Decision XV/54 later established that exemptions 'are intended to be limited, temporary derogations from the phase-out of methyl bromide',[192] a narrowing of the scope of the exemption that does not necessarily follow from Article 2H.5 of the protocol.

b. *Authority of the* Criteria *and the* Exemption Decisions *in the Montreal Normative Order*

The *Critical Use Criteria* is the type of PTR that is aimed at future collective decision making in the MOP about individual treaty party obligations (internal PTRs). These criteria were to be applied by the COP to nominations by parties, upon recommendations of a special panel, the Technology and Economic Assessment Panel (TEAP).

With the criteria in place, the Montreal MOP approved a first *Exemption Decision* in 2005 on the basis of the criteria of Decision IX/6.[193] The United States was allowed the largest exemption by far (7,659 tonnes), with the EU coming in second (3,910 tonnes). This figure placed the US exemption close to the maximum of 30 per cent of the US's 'baseline value' allowed by Article 2H.5, with some commentators even measuring 35 per cent.[194] In other words, the MOP's acceptance of this figure for the United States defined 'critical use' as allowing at least a temporary continuance of a level of production and consumption at, or slightly above, the maximum level allowed in the treaty. The *Exemption Decisions* employed the broadest discretion that the Protocol left to

[188] *Report of the First Extraordinary Meeting of the Parties to the Montreal Protocol on Substances that Deplete the Ozone Layer*, Montreal, 24–26 March 2004, p 11. See http://ozone.unep.org/sites/default/files/Meeting_Docs/Meeting_Documents/mop/Ex_mop/1ex_mop-3.e.pdf, accessed 17 September 2018.

[189] Montreal MOP Decision IX/6, *Critical-use exemptions for methyl bromide*, paras 1.a.i and ii.

[190] Montreal MOP Decision IX/6, para 1.b.ii.

[191] Montreal MOP Decision XIII/11, *Procedures for applying for a critical-use exemption for methyl bromide*, paras 2 and 3.

[192] Montreal MOP Decisions XV/54 and Ex.1/3.

[193] Montreal MOP Decision Ex.I/3 and Annexes to the report of the *First Extraordinary Meeting of the Parties to the Montreal Protocol.*

[194] See www.gpnmag.com/montreal-protocol-approves-methyl-bromide-exemptions-after-phase-out-deadline.

them, and may have even slightly violated the Protocol. Afterwards, the level of the exemptions was brought down gradually, with the EU and its member states no longer having submitted any requests for MB critical-use exemptions after 2008,[195] and the remaining exemptions of the US, Canada and Australia down to less than 500 tonnes by 2014 (with the US still accounting for the largest relative share).[196]

The precise relation between production, consumption and existing stocks turned out to be subject to interpretive disagreement. The United States had argued for some time that existing stocks should not be counted because it was privately owned, and therefore there was no guarantee that these stocks could be directed towards US farmers for which the US critical-use exemption was demanded.[197] Consecutive *Exemption Decisions* of the MOP clearly indicate that they are taken in accordance with the *Criteria*'s central statement that 'the production and consumption of methyl bromide for critical uses should be permitted only if methyl bromide is not available in sufficient quantity and quality from existing stocks of banked or recycled methyl bromide'.[198] The *Exemption Decisions* expressly indicate that the amount they allocate for production by the United States is the amount indicated in the decision *minus available stocks*. The authority of the *Criteria* thus withstood political pressure from the US for an interpretation more in its favour.

Another arena to examine the authority of the *Criteria* and the *Exemption Decisions* in the Montreal normative order is the operation of the Montreal 'Non-Compliance Procedure' (NCP). The Montreal Protocol Implementation Committee has no express legal basis for checking compliance with MOP decisions. Article 8 of the Protocol speaks only of non-compliance 'with the provisions of this Protocol'. Likewise, the revised NCP of 1998 gives no indication that Montreal MOP decisions are to be applied in compliance assessment. In other words, the Montreal Protocol and the MOP decision establishing the Montreal Protocol NCP do not give any indication that PTRs are to be reference points in the Implementation Committee's control of compliance.

However, looking at the practice of the Implementation Committee, there is no question that it considers the *Exemption Decisions* equally relevant to findings of (non-)compliance as the Montreal Protocol itself. This Implementation Committee Report from 2008 leaves little doubt:

> 15. With regard to deviations from the control schedules, [the Secretary General] explained the exemptions, allowances and special cases permitted under the Montreal Protocol. These included essential use exemptions for CFCs, *critical use exemptions for methyl bromide*, the global exemption for laboratory and analytical uses, and allowances for production to meet the basic domestic needs of Article 5 Parties. …

[195] Montreal MOP Decision XX/5, *Critical-use exemptions for methyl bromide for 2009 and 2010*, Annex (no exemptions for EU member states).

[196] Montreal MOP Decision XXIV/5, *Critical-use exemptions for methyl bromide for 2014*, Annex.

[197] US delegation, *Report of the 24th OEWG 2004*, Geneva, 13–16 July 2004, paras 137–44.

[198] eg Montreal MOP Decision XXII/6: *Critical-use exemptions for methyl bromide for 2011 and 2012.*

> 16. Bearing in mind all these permitted deviations, no non-Article 5 Party was in non-compliance with its production or consumption requirements for 2006 or, on the basis of data reported to date, for 2007. Similarly, no Article 5 Party was in non-compliance with its production requirements for 2006 or, on the basis of data reported to date, for 2007 (emphasis added).[199]

In the Implementation Committee, treaty parties exceeding their critical use exemption will have a hard time trying to challenge control of their compliance against the *Exemption Decisions*.[200]

c. *The* Exemption Decisions *in United States Courts: The Natural Resources Defense Council's Challenge to US Methyl Bromide Policy*

Considering that by far the highest yearly exemptions for critical use of methyl bromide have been granted to the United States over the years, the authority of the *Exemption Decisions* (interpreted in light of the *Criteria*) in the US legal order is crucial for the effective implementation of the worldwide methyl bromide phase-out. A much-discussed case before a US Court of Appeals between the Natural Resources Defense Council (NRDC) and the federal Environmental Protection Agency (EPA) concerned precisely the authority of the *Exemption Decisions* over US environmental policy making regarding the production and consumption of methyl bromide. It is the most high-profile domestic court case involving environmental PTRs to date, because it involved a challenge of policy making not being in accordance with PTRs, not just one individual coming up against a decision in a specific case.[201]

The Natural Resources Defense Council, an influential US-based environmental NGO, had claimed that the US Environmental Protection Agency's yearly 'Rule' concerning the production and consumption of MB[202] was at odds with MOP Decision Ex.1/3, the very first of the *Exemption Decisions*.[203] The NGO made a number of arguments, all relying heavily on the various Montreal MOP PTRs. It argued, first, that the EPA's Rule did not offset the new production of MB against existing stocks, which were at least as large as the United States' critical use allocation for 2005. Recall that the *Criteria* and the *Decisions* stated that national implementation of the exemptions must 'take into account available stocks',

[199] *Report of the Implementation Committee under the Non-Compliance Procedure for the Montreal Protocol on the work of its fortieth meeting*, Bangkok, 2–4 July 2008, Section III. Report of the Secretariat on data under Art 7 of the Montreal Protocol.

[200] Brack, 'Monitoring the Montreal Protocol', 217.

[201] Standing of NRDC to bring the case rested on expert testimony that '[t]he lifetime risk that an individual will develop nonfatal skin cancer as a result of EPA's rule' increased by between 1 in 129,000 and 200,000 individuals, and that therefore two to four of NRDC's half a million members would statistically develop skin cancer. *Natural Resources Defense Council v Environmental Protection Agency (Judgment after rehearing)*, 464 F3d 1 (DC Cir), 29 August 2006, p 10.

[202] See *Final Rule*, 69 Fed. Reg. at 76,989.

[203] *NRDC v EPA*, p 11.

authorising new production and consumption of MB only if it 'is not available in sufficient quantity and quality from existing stocks'.[204] Second, NRDC argued that the EPA's Rule allowed non-critical users to reduce existing stocks, while this is implicitly prohibited by the *Decisions*. Third, NRDC argued that the EPA's Rule did not explain why it had to approve uses up to the maximum for which the US had received an exemption, even though Decision Ex.1/3 states '[t]hat Parties should endeavour to allocate the quantities of methyl bromide recommended by the Technology and Economic Assessment Panel'.[205] However, the Court never examined if the *Decisions* in substance required what the NRDC argued. In its judgment, the focus lies solely on denying the domestic legal relevance of the *Decisions*.

The Court of Appeals in *NRDC v EPA* must be applauded for being one of the few domestic courts actually confronting the question of the domestic legal status of PTRs directly, even though there is much to disagree with in the answers it settled on. Although describing the *Decisions* as 'subsequent consensus agreements of the Parties that address the interpretation and application of the critical use provision',[206] hinting at a qualification of the *Decisions* as interpretive agreements between the parties, the Court concluded that '[n]owhere does the Protocol suggest that the Parties' postratification consensus agreements about how to implement the critical-use exemption are binding in domestic courts'.[207] Likewise, the United States Clean Air Act, which implements the Protocol into US law, merely states that the Environmental Protection Agency may exempt critical uses '[t]o the extent consistent *with the Montreal Protocol*' (emphasis added).[208] The Court took this quite literally, and decided that Montreal MOP decisions were not (part of) the Protocol.[209]

This line of reasoning is too simple insofar as it argues that the *Decisions* are not binding in domestic courts *because the Protocol does not say so*. International agreements rarely stipulate that they are binding in the domestic legal order. Sometimes, they might stipulate whether treaty provisions are intended to be directly applicable in national courts or not, but even then the domestic legal status of international instruments and their applicability before domestic courts is ultimately a question for the domestic legal order. What the judges may have meant is that the Montreal Protocol does not even stipulate that the *Decisions* are binding in the *international* legal order.[210] Instruments that are not legally binding in the international legal order tend to not be considered legally binding in national legal orders either.

[204] Montreal MOP Decision IX/6, para 1(b)(ii).
[205] Montreal MOP Decision Ex.1/3, para 4.
[206] *Final Rule*, 69 Fed. Reg. at 76,985.
[207] *NRDC v EPA*, p 14.
[208] 42 U.S.C. § 7671c(d)(6).
[209] *NRDC v EPA*, p 14.
[210] *cf* Andrew D Finkelman, 'Agreements of the Parties to the Montreal Protocol: Law or Politics? An Analysis of Natural Resources Defense Council v EPA' (2007) 93 *Iowa Law Review* 665, 688.

The Court subsequently decided that, because the *Decisions* did not interpret terms in the treaty text, but constituted agreements between the parties to 'fill gaps' in the treaty text, the *Decisions* were 'international political commitments rather than judicially enforceable domestic law'.[211] The Court is right that this is a 'gap-filling' PTR rather than an 'interpretive' PTR. Whether 'gap-filling' PTRs fall outside the scope of Article 31.3(a) is more extensively discussed in chapter four. In short: the *travaux préparatoires* of Article 31 VCLT illustrate that not just 'agreements on interpretation', but also 'agreements on application' (that would include 'gap-filling') fall within the scope of Article 31.3(a).[212] The Court's position leads it to the extremely binary understanding that international agreements are either treaties or have no domestic legal relevance at all. Since 'there is no doubt that the "decisions" are not treaties', they must be (international) 'political commitments'. The Court failed to recognise the in-between option that gap-filling agreements can also have some degree of authority.[213] As a result, it did not even take into account the *Exemption Decisions* in its determination of the EPA's 'Rule'.

The judges in the *NRDC v EPA* case also criticised the legitimacy of the *Decisions* in light of the US Constitution's authorisations of international law making. This legitimacy critique seems to have been their main reason for refusing to consider the *Exemption Decisions* as reference points difficult to escape, and instead to construe them as legally irrelevant and mere 'political commitments':

> If the 'decisions' are 'law' – enforceable in federal court like statutes or legislative rules – then Congress either has delegated lawmaking authority to an international body or authorized amendments to a treaty without presidential signature or Senate ratification, in violation of Article II of the Constitution.[214]

Here, the Court sharply perceives that, in a court judgment, there is little room between giving effect to the *Decisions* and not giving effect to them, and that to give effect to them would mean to treat them as if they were law. The Court presents the problem in US constitutional terms, an argumentation unlikely to hold according to US international and constitutional lawyers.[215] However, the viewpoint of the Court is understandable. As Klabbers points out, when courts are faced with a decision on whether or not to apply non-legal instruments, the outcome is that they either apply it as hard law, or they apply it not at all.[216] Once the Court had opened the door to any authority of these PTRs, how could it still have decided differently than what is prescribed in those PTRs? The PTRs would have gone from nothing to being decisive – quite a jump for instruments that are

[211] *NRDC v EPA*, p 15.
[212] See ch 4, section A.1.
[213] *cf* Kingsbury, 'Weighing Global Regulatory Rules'.
[214] *NRDC v EPA*, p 13.
[215] Knox, 'Natural Resources Defense Council'.
[216] Klabbers, 'The Commodification of International Law', 347 (stating that 'whenever judges apply [soft law], they typically apply it as hard law, indistinguishable from a treaty').

not an express delegation of international *law*-making, and not made in accordance with formal amendment procedures.

2. The Kyoto Protocol: *The Land Use and Forestry Decisions (LULUCF)* and *Accounting Modalities*

The complexity and daunting nature of addressing climate change can hardly be overstated. The uncertainty and strong disagreements have cast a dark shadow over what has so far been adopted in terms of intergovernmental agreements: a stand-off between interests that are still not sufficiently aligned to make tough changes in our economies and way of living. In fact, after the adoption of the UNFCCC, and the disappointment of the Kyoto Protocol, hopes of coming to a solution diminished instead of increased for a long time. Now, some hope is back with the 2015 Paris Agreement,[217] although it still falls far short of the 1.5 degree Celsius temperature increase considered safe by scientists, and the 2 degree Celsius temperature increase politically agreed upon as sufficiently safe.[218] Of course, that is assuming that the Agreement is fully implemented.

The Kyoto Protocol's importance for the future mitigation and adaptation to climate change is now overshadowed by the Paris Agreement. It remains very relevant for the purposes of this study, however, because of its extensive use of explicit enabling clauses, which left undecided enormously important aspects of how reduction targets were to be measured, and the actions through which the targets were to be achieved. The discussion in this section therefore focuses principally on the Kyoto Protocol and the COP decisions filling its many gaps. The UNFCCC's principles and objectives are only playing a role in the background.[219]

The Kyoto Protocol was adopted in Kyoto, Japan, on 11 December 1997, and entered into force on 16 February 2005. The Protocol's 'major achievement' was that developed countries entered quantifiable targets and clearly defined timetables for their reduction commitments. The average reduction target was 5 per cent below 1990 levels, and the period within which these reductions were to be realised was 2008–2012 (the 'first commitment period'). However, the major developed country emitter, the United States, did not ratify the Treaty. In 2012, Kyoto has been haphazardly extended, but with fewer parties (Japan, Canada, Russia and New Zealand dropped out).[220] The European Union added an extra 12 per cent

[217] *Paris Agreement*, Conference of the Parties, Twenty-first session, Paris, 30 November to 11 December 2015.

[218] Joeri Rogelj et al, 'Paris Agreement Climate Proposals Need a Boost to Keep Warming Well below 2 C' (2016) 534 *Nature* 631.

[219] A valuable reference to the UNFCCC is still Daniel Bodansky, 'The United Nations Framework Convention on Climate Change: A Commentary' (1993) 1 *Yale Journal of International Law* 451.

[220] Decision 1/CMP.8, *Amendment to the Kyoto Protocol pursuant to its Article 3, paragraph 9 (the Doha Amendment).*

reduction by 2020 to its first period target of an 8 per cent reduction compared to the base year of 1990.[221]

Article 3.1 Kyoto Protocol – together with Annex B which contains the individual targets of the Annex I developed country parties – is the basic provision on emissions reduction or limitation commitments:

> The Parties included in Annex I shall, individually or jointly, ensure that their aggregate anthropogenic carbon dioxide equivalent emissions of the greenhouse gases listed in Annex A do not exceed their assigned amounts, calculated pursuant to their quantified emission limitation and reduction commitments inscribed in Annex B and in accordance with the provisions of this Article, with a view to reducing their overall emissions of such gases by at least 5 percent below 1990 levels in the commitment period 2008–2012.

Article 2 of the protocol then appears to suggest that the primary means of reaching the mentioned targets is through domestic 'policies and measures' aiming to decrease emission patterns. However, there is no obligation in the protocol to undertake the specific reduction activities listed here to reach the targets. Kyoto offered a relatively cheap way out for this undertaking, in the shape of several flexibility mechanisms that aim at an 'efficient' market-based solution: emissions trading (Article 17), joint implementation (JI, Article 6) and the clean development mechanism (CDM, Article 12). These mechanisms allowed parties to reach their targets, in part, by buying up emission rights from other parties, or helping other parties with targets (JI) or without them (CDM) to achieve emission reductions. In other words, they did so by partly reaching their targets without changing their emissions patterns. Moreover, Kyoto left considerable room for reaching the target through carbon sinks in addition to emissions limitations (Article 3.3). Because the Protocol focuses on emissions reduction or limitation targets, the accounting and reporting of emissions and sinks (Article 3.4, 7 and 8) as well as the measuring of existing levels at the base year (Article 3.4) also took on a crucial role.

What all these mechanisms and calculations would look like exactly and to what actual reduction result they would lead, however, was left essentially undefined in the Protocol's provisions. The Protocol did not determine the relative weight of Article 2-type 'domestic actions' on the one hand, and of the flexibility mechanisms and sinks on the other, except Article 17's minimal stipulation that emissions trading 'shall be supplemental to domestic actions for the purpose of meeting quantified emission limitation and reduction commitments'.

The COP resolutions and decisions containing the 'modalities', 'principles', 'rules', 'guidelines' and 'procedures' addressing these and other crucial elements were thus allowed to have an enormous influence on the ways in which parties could reach their targets without changing behavioural patterns.[222] All in all, eight

[221] Kyoto COP/MOP Decision 1/CMP.8.

[222] Michel G den Elzen and André P de Moor, 'Analyzing the Kyoto Protocol under the Marrakesh Accords: Economic Efficiency and Environmental Effectiveness' (2002) 43 *Ecological Economics* 141; Ian Fry, 'Twists and Turns in the Jungle: Exploring the Evolution of Land Use, Land-Use Change and

of the Kyoto Protocol's articles – together representing the core of its approach to mitigation – explicitly depended on rules to be agreed upon later for their meaningful implementation. As Brunnée and Toope rightly suggest:

> The Kyoto Protocol too is in some respects a framework agreement. … [T]he protocol contains a series of provisions that anchor the outlines of key elements …. But it was left to the plenary bodies of the convention and the protocol, respectively, to approve the rules, guidelines, and procedures required to transform broad concepts into regimes that are sufficiently detailed to allow implementation and that enable states to decide whether or not to ratify the protocol.[223]

Most of the relevant resolutions are part of what came to be called the Marrakech Accords, a book as thick as a thumb, which was adopted shortly before parties ratified the Protocol. The Accords were the *sine qua non* for a successful ratification. It is one of the most explicit showings of the importance of PTRs: without them, parties had no clue what the extent of their obligations would be, or whether they would be willing and able to comply with them.[224]

a. Resolutions Concerning Forestry and Accounting

A central role in the Marrakech Accords was occupied by the *Definitions, modalities, rules and guidelines relating to land use, land-use change and forestry activities* (*LULUCF Decisions*) and the *Modalities for the accounting of assigned amounts* (*Accounting Modalities*).[225] These two Decisions, and the later Decisions that developed them further, are crucial to the Kyoto Protocol's approach to emissions reduction. They are closely related to each other, because of the need to agree on accounting methods for, amongst others, Land Use, Land Use Change and Forestry (LULUCF) as sources and sinks of emissions, before it could be calculated what land use and forestry activities may subtract from the assigned emissions reductions amounts. In addition, the *LULUCF Decisions* are important because they define what qualifies as LULUCF activities; the *Accounting Modalities* matter a great deal for calculating the initial levels of carbon levels in 1990, which have a direct relation to the reduction targets.

Forestry Decisions within the Kyoto Protocol' (2002) 11 *RECIEL* 159; Christoph Böhringer, 'Climate Politics From Kyoto to Bonn: From Little to Nothing?!?' (2001) *Zentrum für Europäische Wirtschaftsforschung Discussion Papers* 49.

[223] Jutta Brunnée and Stephen J Toope, *Legitimacy and Legality in International Law* (CUP, 2010), 135.

[224] ibid, 186 ('the actual scope and impact of these commitments … was ascertainable only once the supplementary decisions had been adopted'). Also Jutta Brunnée, 'Reweaving the Fabric of International Law? Patterns of Consent in Environmental Framework Agreements' in Rüdiger Wolfrum and Volker Röben (eds), *Developments of International Law in Treaty Making* (Springer, 2005) 101; Gerhard Loibl, 'Conferences of Parties and the Modification of Obligations', in Matthew CR Craven and Malgosia Fitzmaurice, *Interrogating the Treaty: Essays in the contemporary law of treaties* (2005), 103.

[225] The LULUCF activities were primarily addressed in Decision 17/CMP.1 and its successor Decision 2/CMP.7; the accounting modalities were primarily addressed in Decision 13/CMP.1.

The authority of these Decisions in the Kyoto normative order is of primary interest. Violation of the Decisions by a number of treaty parties was invoked as one reason for non-compliance in a number of compliance decisions of the Enforcement Branch of the Kyoto Protocol. Contrary to what we have seen so far, these Decisions tend to be given full effect by domestic courts, except for paragraphs that are phrased as recommendations.

Article 3.3 and 3.4 Kyoto Protocol indicate that removals by sinks, i.e. 'the uptake of greenhouse gases by forest soils', are relevant to the determination of a party's baseline emissions as well as in the calculation of whether they reach their assigned reduction amounts. Strictly speaking, Article 3.3 is not an explicit but an implicit enabling clause, because it does not specifically call for further guidelines, or rule on what constitute land-use and forestry activities, but leaves these terms vague and thus subject to extensive interpretation. The later definition of these terms by the Kyoto COP/MOP is thus based on the COP/MOP's general implementing powers. By contrast, Article 3.4 explicitly calls for 'modalities, rules and guidelines as to how, and which, *additional* human-induced activities related to changes in greenhouse gas emissions by sources and removals by sinks in the agricultural soils and the land-use change and forestry categories shall be added to, or subtracted from, the assigned amounts' (emphasis added).[226]

Like in the case of flexibility mechanisms, the Kyoto Protocol did not indicate a cap on the extent to which sinks could be used for reaching the targets. To complete the ambiguity, Article 7.4 also postponed the 'modalities for the accounting of assigned amounts' to the post-treaty stage, including modalities for accounting for LULUCF activities. Article 3.7 had only provided the main factors determining the assigned amount for the first commitment period, from 2008 to 2012. In particular, Article 3.7 left open the possibility that LULUCF circumstances and activities would impact on the assigned amount.[227] Multiple questions were left unanswered, the answers to which could make a world of difference for the obligations of the parties, and to what extent these would impact on domestic societies or would mostly come down to smart forest management. The answers had significant repercussions for the calculation of the assigned amounts as well as for whether there was a limit on the amount of sinks that could be used in achieving the assigned amounts.[228]

As opposed to the term 'decision' in Article 2H.5 Montreal Protocol, Article 3.4 Kyoto Protocol calls for 'modalities, rules and guidelines' and Article 7.4 Kyoto

[226] Article 3.4 Kyoto Protocol to the United Nations Framework Convention on Climate Change (adopted 11 December 1997, entered into force 16 February 2005) 2303 UNTS 162 (Kyoto Protocol).

[227] See Art 3.7 Kyoto Protocol 'Those Parties included in Annex I for whom land-use change and forestry constituted a net source of greenhouse gas emissions in 1990 shall include in their 1990 emissions base year or period the aggregate anthropogenic carbon dioxide equivalent emissions by sources minus removals by sinks in 1990 from land-use change for the purposes of calculating their assigned amount'.

[228] Fry, 'Twists and Turns in the Jungle', 160.

Protocol calls for 'modalities'. Ulfstein has argued that the use of the term 'rules' in Article 17 of the Kyoto Protocol would point to the binding nature of decisions taken on its basis.[229] Yet, rules can just as well be non-binding. Use of the term 'rules' does not imply that they are binding rules.[230] The term 'modalities' is obviously even more open-ended. It projects a certain matter-of-factness, and is very technocratic. The term 'guidance' is downright recommendatory.

The 'Bonn Agreements' that would form the basis for the eventual Marrakech Accord were 'approved by the ministers in Plenary late Monday morning, and formally adopted by the COP'.[231] The Marrakech Agreements, including the Decisions relating to LULUCF and the accounting of assigned amounts, were also 'adopted by the COP'.[232] The Kyoto COP/MOP then 'adopted the package without further amendment' during its first meeting in 2005.[233] Although the reports of these meetings do not show the mode of decision making for the adoption of the decisions, this language is sufficient indication that the decisions were adopted by some form of consensus. The Cancun Agreements – which partly revises and complements LULUCF – were formally adopted by consensus, but in the face of opposition from a small number of developing states.[234]

The significance of the *LULUCF Decision* can hardly be overstated. It contains a very broad definition of 'forest', and definitions of 'afforestation', 'reforestation' and 'deforestation'.[235] It introduces and defines the 'additional human-induced activities' mentioned in Article 3.4, including 'revegetation', 'forest management', 'cropland management' and 'grazing land management', as all being activities relevant for the calculation of achieving the assigned amounts.[236] 'Rewetting' and 'wetland drainage' were added to this list later.[237] Most of these activities were defined to encompass a wide range of activities,[238] as advocated by countries of the Umbrella Group,[239] a group of developed country parties that would benefit from lowering the burden to achieve their assigned amounts. The decisions leave it up to individual parties to elect which of the activities to include in the calculation of their assigned amounts.[240] Particular clauses were inserted for numerous Annex I

[229] Geir Ulfstein, 'Reweaving the Fabric of International Law? Patterns of Consent in Environmental Framework Agreements, Comment by Geir Ulfstein', in Rüdiger Wolfrum and Volker Röben (eds), *Developments of International Law in Treaty Making* (Springer, 2005), 145, 148.

[230] *cf* Brunnée, 'Reweaving the Fabric of International Law?', 112.

[231] IISD Reporting Services, ENB Volume 12 Number 189, *Summary of UNFCCC COP-7, 12 November 2001, Marrakech, Morocco*, p 2.

[232] ibid, pp 4 and 6.

[233] IISD Reporting Services, ENB Volume 12 Number 291, *Summary of UNFCCC COP 11 and COP/MOP 1, 28 November – 9 December 2005, Montréal, Canada*, p 10.

[234] See ch 7.

[235] Kyoto COP/MOP Decision 16/CMP.1, *Land use, land-use change and forestry*, Annex, para A.1(a).

[236] Kyoto COP/MOP Decision 16/CMP.1, Annex, paras. A.1(b)–(d).

[237] Kyoto COP/MOP Decision 2/CMP.7, *Land use, land-use change and forestry* (Durban, 2011), para C.6.

[238] Kyoto COP/MOP Decision 16/CMP.1, paras A.1(e)–(h).

[239] *cf* Fry, 'Twists and Turns in the Jungle', 159, 160, 164.

[240] Kyoto COP/MOP Decision 16/CMP.1, para C.7.

Parties, such as for Russia, which was allowed to keep its allowable forest management tonnages flexible, and Australia, which was allowed to maximise its base year emissions from land clearing for agriculture.[241]

The Accounting Modalities introduced new accounting units, the so-called Removal Units (RMUs), specifically designed for the accounting of LULUCF activities.[242] The Modalities also set out how the assigned amount is to be calculated, although it follows Article 3.7 quite closely in this regard.[243] Furthermore, they set out which additions to, and subtractions from, the assigned amount shall be made with regard to the issuing or cancelling of Removal Units in accordance with its forestry activities in the various commitment periods.[244] As a final significant point, the Modalities state that RMUs shall be part of the assessment of the parties' compliance with the Kyoto Protocol. While the Paragraph does not say that such compliance assessment shall include a party's compliance with the *LULUCF Decision*, it is difficult to envisage another scenario for assessing compliance in light of RMUs, since the very activities through which parties can acquire RMUs are defined in that Decision. This will certainly make it difficult to escape the Modalities and the Decision as reference points in the interpretation of what is required to comply with the Kyoto Protocol.

This whole range of post-treaty rules was used to set up an entire structure for the scope, eligibility, definitions, maximal allowable tonnages, accounting, reporting and verification for LULUCF, developing Articles 3.3, 3.4 and 7.4. Taking into account the additional human-induced forestry and land-use activities is not obligatory, but because this greatly facilitates the achievement of targets for some parties, and would thus be used extensively, it makes the mandatory conditions sticking to each option substantively authoritative indeed. In other words, when a party elected to account for the *removals by sinks* achieved through one of the additional activities added by the COP/MOP in pursuance of Article 3.4,[245] such a party also had to account for the *emissions by sources* through those activities.[246] On the one hand, this created leeway for parties to choose to account for activities that have a positive balance towards removals by sinks. On the other hand, however, this came with conditions attached: the choice is fixed for an entire commitment period,[247] the party must prove that the activities are human-induced,[248] and the impact of LULUCF is limited to a maximum amount.[249]

[241] Fry, 'Twists and Turns in the Jungle', 165–68. Reporting and verification of all the relevant activities was regulated in separate guidelines.

[242] Kyoto COP/MOP Decision 13/CMP.1, *Modalities for the accounting of assigned amounts under Article 7, paragraph 4, of the Kyoto Protocol*, para A.4.

[243] Kyoto COP/MOP Decision 13/CMP.1, paras. B.5–B.8.

[244] Kyoto COP/MOP Decision 13/CMP.1, para D.

[245] Revegetation, forest management, cropland management and grazing land management.

[246] Kyoto COP/MOP Decision 16/CMP.1, para 6.

[247] Kyoto COP/MOP Decision 16/CMP.1, para 7.

[248] Kyoto COP/MOP Decision 16/CMP.1, para 8.

[249] Kyoto COP/MOP Decision 16/CMP.1, paras 10, 11 and 12.

The LULUCF definitions, modalities, rules and guidelines have been renewed over time. For example, Decision 2/CMP.7 on 'Land use, land-use change and forestry' added wetland drainage and rewetting to the list of human-induced activities eligible for accounting assigned amounts.[250] The same decision introduced the exoneration that emissions from 'natural disturbances' such as forest fires can, under certain conditions, be excluded from the accounting.[251]

b. Authority of the LULUCF *and* Accounting Modalities *in the Kyoto Normative Order*

The decisions of the Kyoto Compliance Committee's Enforcement Branch show not a shred of doubt that the *Accounting Modalities* and the *LULUCF Decisions* need be complied with by a Kyoto Protocol Party in order to achieve compliance with the Protocol. In particular, non-compliance with these and other PTRs also constitutes non-compliance with the eligibility requirements to participate in the three flexibility mechanisms.[252] The earlier quoted Enforcement Branch *Final Decision* with regard to the compliance of Croatia, is a good illustration. The Enforcement Branch takes the Accounting Modalities as the standard against which Croatia's compliance must be assessed. 'In particular,' it writes, 'the expert review team considered that the addition of 3.5 million tonnes (Mt) carbon dioxide equivalent (CO_2 eq) by Croatia to its base year level following decision 7/CP.12 is not in accordance with Article 3, paragraphs 7 and 8, of the Kyoto Protocol *and the modalities for the accounting of assigned amounts*' (emphasis added).[253]

In the 'Question of Implementation' concerning Ukraine, that country's non-compliance was in part founded on the Expert Review Team's conclusion that Ukraine's national system of reporting 'was not able to ensure that areas of land subject to LULUCF activities under Article 3, paragraphs 3 and 4, of the Kyoto Protocol … are identifiable in accordance with paragraph 20 of the [*LULUCF Decision*]'.[254] Other examples of the authority of Kyoto COP/MOP decisions in findings of non-compliance include the 'Questions of Implementation' concerning Greece (*Guidelines for national systems* and *Guidelines for the preparation of the information required under Article 7 of the Kyoto Protocol*);[255] Bulgaria (*Guidelines for national systems for the estimation of anthropogenic greenhouse gas emissions*

[250] Decision 2/CMP.7, para C.6.
[251] Decision 2/CMP.7, para 1(a). See for the exact extent of exclusion of emissions from natural disturbances, para 33 ff.
[252] Kyoto COP/MOP Decisions 3, 9 and 11/CMP.1.
[253] Kyoto Protocol Compliance Committee Enforcement Branch, CC-2009-1-6/Croatia/EB (Preliminary Finding), 13 October 2009, para 5.
[254] Kyoto Protocol Compliance Committee Enforcement Branch, CC-2011-2-6/Ukraine/EB (Preliminary Finding), 25 August 2011, para 5. See also paras 14 and 17.
[255] Kyoto COP/MOP Decisions 15 and 19/CMP.1. See Kyoto Protocol Compliance Committee Enforcement Branch, CC-2007-1-8/Greece/EB (Preliminary Finding), 17 April 2008, para 5.

by sources and removals by sinks);[256] and Romania (*Guidelines for the preparation of the information required under Article 7 of the Kyoto Protocol* and the *LULUCF Decision*).[257]

c. Authority of Kyoto COP/MOP Decisions in the EU and the Netherlands

In most national legal orders of treaty parties with targets under the Kyoto Protocol, the Protocol is incorporated into domestic statutory law, often including (dynamic) references to Kyoto COP/MOP decisions. For the Member States of the European Union, the EU legislator adopted Directive 2003/87/EC[258] establishing a scheme for greenhouse gas emission allowance trading within the (former) Community. Various provisions in that Directive made extensive references to 'the decisions adopted pursuant to the UNFCCC or the Kyoto Protocol' in defining the various types of emissions units relevant to emissions trading. Such an indirect incorporation of the Kyoto COP/MOP decisions relating to emissions trading essentially makes the content of those decisions binding in the EU legal order. Going one step further, Decision 529/2013/EU of the EU Parliament, and the Council of 21 May 2013, directly incorporates many of the definitions, rules, modalities and guidelines from Decisions 13 and 16/CMP.1. These EU Directives and Decisions, and the references they make, are binding on the Member States. EU Directives usually have direct effect in the national legal orders of the EU member states. Since EU Decision 529/2013/EU addresses all the Member States,[259] it may also be invoked by persons before national courts against a government decision allegedly in conflict with that EU Decision (vertical direct effect).[260]

In the single case in this study's repertoire of cases in which the authority of a Kyoto COP/MOP decision was directly at stake, the vulnerability of parts of these decisions that are not incorporated into national or EU law shows immediately. In the Netherlands, the recommendatory wording of Paragraph 33 of the Accounting Modalities played an important role in a lower Administrative Court decision on a dispute between private reforestation enterprise Face the Future and the State

[256] Kyoto COP/MOP Decision 19/CMP.1. See Kyoto Protocol Compliance Committee Enforcement Branch, CC-2010-1-8/Bulgaria/EB (Preliminary Finding), 28 June 2010, paras 5–6.

[257] Kyoto Protocol Compliance Committee Enforcement Branch, CC-2011-1-8/Romania/EB (Preliminary Finding), 27 August 2011, paras 5–6.

[258] Directive 2003/87/EC of the European Parliament and of the Council of 13 October 2003 *establishing a scheme for greenhouse gas emission allowance trading within the Community and amending Council Directive 96/61/EC.*

[259] Decision 529/2013/EU, of the European Parliament and of the Council of 21 May 2013 *on accounting rules on greenhouse gas emissions and removals resulting from activities relating to land use, land-use change and forestry and on information concerning actions relating to those activities*, Art 1.

[260] See the judgments Case C-9/70 *Franz Grad v Finanzamt Traunstein*, Judgment of the Court of 6 October 1970 and Case C-80/06 *Carp Snc di L. Moleri e V Corsi v Ecorad Srl.*, Judgment of the Court of 7 June 2007.

of the Netherlands.[261] In short, Face the Future argued that the Dutch State was not allowed to count Assigned Amount Units resulting from forests that Face the Future had privately planted. The administrative court stated that 'the State of the Netherlands on the basis of para 33's clear terms has the *competence*, not the *duty*, to annul Assigned Amount Units. Even apart from the question of direct applicability art. 33 of 13/CMP.1 and its invocability by Face the Future, *considering this freedom of choice*, the State can impossibly have acted in contravention of a legal duty' (emphasis added).[262]

D. Conclusion

The case studies in this chapter show differences in the authority of PTRs along three lines, which, to some extent, roughly correspond with the differences between PTRs of the Conventions-Annex MEAs and the Convention-Protocol MEAs: between recommendatory and mandatory language; between internal and external PTRs; and between interpretive PTRs (including those arguably of a modifying character) and gap-filling PTRs.

The differences between the mandatory quality of PTRs from the Kyoto Protocol and the Montreal Protocol on the one hand, and from the Ramsar Convention and CITES on the other hand, surfaced clearly in these close-up examinations. PTRs, or parts of PTRs that are of a clearly recommendatory nature, lack authority in *both* the internal and national orders (*Greentree*, *Face the Future*, *Animal Welfare*), and the PTRs adopted under the two Conventions tend to be phrased in much more recommendatory language than PTRs adopted under the two Protocols. However, in some national court cases, this recommendatory nature was strangely ignored (*Castlewood Products* District Court), or somehow found to be compensated for by other factors (*Born Free*). In the Ramsar normative order, the recent assignment to the Secretariat to list only wetlands that fulfil the identification criteria and designation conditions ignores the recommendatory nature of the resolutions setting out those criteria. PTRs that lack specificity also tend to lack authority before domestic courts, but again, there are exceptions. In two almost

[261] *Accounting Modalities*, para 33: 'Each Party included in Annex I may cancel ERUs, CERs, AAUs and/or RMUs so they cannot be used in fulfilment of commitments under Art 3, paragraph 1, in accordance with paragraph 12(f) above, by transferring ERUs, CERs, AAUs and/or RMUs to a cancellation account in its national registry. Legal entities, where authorised by the Party, may also transfer ERUs, CERs, AAUs and RMUs into a cancellation account.'

[262] *Face the Future B.V. v De Staat der Nederlanden*, LJN: BX1737 (Rb.' s Gravenhage), 6 June 2012. [Translation of: 'De Staat heeft op grond van art. 33 13/CMP.1, zoals uit de bewoordingen van dit artikel duidelijk blijkt (zie hierboven onder 2.11), de bevoegdheid, en niet de plicht, AAU's te annuleren. Nog daargelaten de vraag of Face the Future een direct beroep toekomt op art. 33 13/CMP.1, handelt de Staat, gezien de keuzevrijheid die hij hierin heeft, niet in strijd met een wettelijke plicht door geen AAU's te annuleren op basis van deze bepaling.']

identical cases concerning the importation of elephants to zoos, a US District Court considered CITES Resolution 5.10 (Primarily Commercial Purposes) sufficiently specific to direct it toward a solution (*Born Free*), whereas an Australian Administrative Court failed to find any helpful direction in it (*Animal Welfare*).

The language of the PTRs of the Montreal Protocol and the Kyoto Protocol, the *Critical Use Criteria* and *Exemptions*, *LULUCF*, and the *Accounting Modalities*, is almost devoid of recommendatory words such as 'should,' 'urges' or 'recommends'. Indeed, these Decisions all have a high degree of authority – indistinguishable from their underlying Protocols – in the Montreal and Kyoto normative orders. In the national legal orders, the character of their wording is hardly ever an issue in the determination of their authority, except when, as in *Face the Future*, the paragraph of the PTR at issue is recommendatory.

A second difference is the one between internal and external PTRs. Internal PTRs, such as the Montreal *Critical Use Criteria*, are primarily aimed at further specific decision making within Kyoto and Montreal orders. External PTRs, such as the CITES *Reason to Believe Paragraphs* and the *Primarily Commercial Purposes* Resolution, are aimed at the conduct of the parties individually. However, this a rather weak correlation. Most of the Kyoto Protocol PTRs are external, but have high authority, while the Ramsar *Identification Criteria* and *Designation Conditions*, aimed at further decision making in the Ramsar COP, had limited authority over the process of designating new wetlands for a long time, until the Secretariat in 2012 was prohibited from listing wetlands not complying with the *Criteria* and the *Conditions*.

Third, in the national legal orders, no significant differences could be observed between the authority of interpretive PTRs on the one hand, and gap-filling PTRs on the other hand. With regard to PTRs of a gap-filling, supplemental character in relation to the underlying treaty, based on an explicit enabling clause, the US Court of Appeals raised questions about their authority from two perspectives in *NRDC v EPA*. First, can gap-filling PTRs such as the *Exemption Criteria* and *Decisions* still be brought under the rubric of 'interpretive aids', and claim authority from it, if they clearly do not interpret terms in the treaty? Second, the Court argued that the explicit enabling clause in the treaty constituted 'agreements to agree', and wondered how they could have a high degree of authority if nothing in the Protocol text suggested that these were legally binding agreements. More than with interpretive PTRs, the question arises of why a national court should consider PTRs as authoritative when their *explicit* basis in the treaty does not say that they are binding. At the very least, these arguments represent a way out for national courts seeking to avoid PTRs as reference points, thus making them easier to escape.[263]

[263] By contrast, in *One Etched Tusk*, a US District Court refused to take into account a CITES COP resolution of a clearly interpretive character. *U.S. v One Etched Ivory Tusk of African Elephant (Loxodonta Africana)*, No 10-CV-308, 871 F.Supp.2d 128, 17 May 2012, p 136. And various domestic court cases relating to the Kyoto Protocol extensively took into account Kyoto COP/MOP decisions based

Finally, did the arguably modifying character of some of the PTRs in these case studies limit their authority? Quite some of the PTRs in the case studies straddle the edge between interpretation and modification. For instance, the Ramsar *Strategic Framework* now makes obligatory precise boundary description and delimitation on a map at the time of designation, failing which the Secretariat will not place the designated wetland on the List. The Ramsar Convention does not connect successful listing to submitting the information. Secondly, the *Reason to Believe Paragraph* in CITES Resolutions 10.2, 11.3 and 12.3 can be questioned from a substantive validity standpoint for recommending a level of scrutiny of export permits for Appendix II and III species to importing Authorities that contradicts the division of competences set out in Articles III–VI CITES. Lastly, the *LULUCF Decisions* taken in the aftermath of the Kyoto Protocol lowered the need for 'domestic actions' in the sense of the Protocol by according a large role to greenhouse gas sinks (forests, and forest planting). However, the case studies provided no evidence that the arguably modifying character of these PTRs was a problem for their authority in either the internal normative or the national legal orders. This is clearly something that parties to the relevant disputes should have brought forward in order for it to be addressed. Absent such protest, the modifying character of PTRs is no obstacle to their authority in any of the orders.

The most constant factor in the case studies, however, is the enormous difference between the authority of PTRs in their own normative orders and national legal orders. In other words, the picture that forms is one of 'compartmentalised authority'. The authority of PTRs in their own normative orders, and the authority they have in the national legal orders, are not just different, but also hardly connected.

The authority in the internal normative orders of none of the PTRs reviewed here was questioned in further decision making of the plenary treaty meetings, or in the context of non-compliance procedures. The Kyoto Protocol Compliance Committee and the Montreal Protocol Implementation Committee find it entirely evident that their compliance control includes compliance with PTRs. The Kyoto Protocol PTRs are *the* reference point in determining the eligibility of the parties for the flexibility mechanisms. The Montreal Protocol MOP has been allowing exemptions from the phasing out of methyl bromide, based on its own *Critical Use Criteria*, for more than a decade now. As Gehring summarises, the one solid conclusion is that, '[i]f provisions for the assessment of production and consumption figures under the Montreal Protocol, criteria for the classification of endangered species under CITES, or the rules of the clean development mechanism under the Kyoto Protocol are formulated in a particular way that has been agreed upon within the relevant COP or MOP, the treaty systems will simply

on explicit enabling clauses such as Arts 3.4 and 7.4 Kyoto Protocol. See *Spencer v Commonwealth of Australia*, [2008] FCA 1256 (Federal Court of Australia), 26 August 2008; *Deutsche Bank AG v Total Global Steel Ltd*, EWHC 1201 (England and Wales Commercial Court), 11 May 2012.

operate accordingly'.[264] Even the Ramsar *Identification Criteria* and *Designation Conditions*, which are phrased as recommendations, achieved high authority in the internal normative order in recent years by prohibiting the Secretariat from listing any further wetlands not fulfilling the *Criteria* and the *Conditions*.

In the domestic courts, a much more diffuse picture emerges. PTRs have very little authority in national legal orders. Some domestic courts in these case studies understand their national laws on the applicability of international law before domestic courts to provide some legal relevance to PTRs, as interpretive agreements: Sometimes on the basis of Article 31 of the Vienna Convention on the Law of Treaties (Ramsar resolutions in *Greentree*), sometimes on the basis of a longstanding domestic doctrine on treaty interpretation (CITES Resolutions in *Castlewood Products* District Court). The US Court of Appeals dismissed the interpretive character of Montreal MOP decisions in *NRDC v EPA*, and placed them outside of the scope of interpretation. Other judgments, such as in *Face the Future*, or the majority in *Greenpeace*, circumvent the issue of legal relevance, or leave it entirely out of the discussion. When PTRs are incorporated into domestic statutory law in some more or less direct or indirect manner, the problem of domestic authority shifts to the authority of domestic legislation and status, which is unquestioned. Incorporation of Kyoto Protocol PTRs into EU law, for instance, removes the issue of their domestic authority. However, the limitations of authority due to the recommendatory or unspecific nature of CITES (*Reason to Believe Paragraph*) and Ramsar resolutions (Identification Criteria and Designation Conditions) persists if the same formulation is kept in the domestic statute, such as the incorporation of CITES into US law.

Those judgments in domestic court cases that do rely extensively on PTRs to reach a decision, do not allow for simple conclusions about the authority of these PTRs in the national legal orders. Did these courts apply the PTRs because they were difficult to escape as reference points in the interpretation of the underlying PTR, or did the judges have other reasons to apply them? The justifications for application found in the judgments give reason to think that non-application of the PTRs would have been equally possible. The justifications are very divergent: the 'logic' of respecting the agreement of the parties (*Castlewood*); contributing to the object and purpose of the underlying MEA (*Greentree*, *Greenpeace*); primacy of the treaty over the subsequent agreement (*NRDC v EPA*, *Greenpeace*); non-interference with international trade (*Greenpeace*); the process of adoption of PTRs goes contrary to the national constitutional separation of powers (*NRDC*). Whether a PTR is applied by a domestic court relies strongly on the discretion and thus the perceptions and preferences of the judges. This is a strong indication that the authority of PTRs before domestic courts is limited. Of course, the volume of case law used for these case studies is limited. However, the consistency

[264] Thomas Gehring, 'Treaty-Making and Treaty-Evolution' in Daniel Bodansky, Jutta Brunnée and Ellen Hey (eds), *The Oxford Handbook of International Environmental Law* (OUP, 2007), 467, 493.

with which the high authority in the internal normative orders contrasts with their ambiguous authority in the national legal orders is no coincidence.

How do domestic courts handle their large discretion? Remarkably, the case studies show that courts have a strong tendency to decide the application of PTRs in favour of government agencies, regardless of whether the government agency does or does not act in accordance with the terms of the relevant PTRs. This was illustrated most clearly by the *Mahogany Cases*, where two national courts were dealing with almost the exact same facts but came out with opposite conclusions regarding the application of PTRs – but both in favour of the State. In *Castlewood*, both Courts supported the Fish and Wildlife Service acting in accordance with the *Reason to Believe Paragraph*. In *Greenpeace*, the Court supported the UK Government *not* acting in accordance with the *Reason to Believe Paragraph*. In court, government agencies are thus likely to get away with giving effect to a PTR as well as with not giving effect to that same PTR. The language used by the majority in *Greenpeace* is telling in this respect. According to the Lord Justices, the Commissioners were *entitled* not to look beyond the validity of the export permit, creating the presumption that the Commissioners could also have looked beyond the valid permit, and still acted lawfully. In the *NRDC* case, had the plaintiffs been strawberry farmers suing the EPA *because of* relying on the Montreal *Exemption Decisions*, the Court may have said that, while 'not enforceable in federal court' as 'ongoing international political commitment[s],' the EPA would have been free to act in accordance with them, even if not obliged to do so. That is the wonderful thing about PTRs for states and governments: courts will leave them alone in deciding whether or not to act in accordance with them.

This finding of strongly compartmentalised authority raises further questions, the first of which is addressed in the following Part's chapters: what *causes* the authority of PTRs to be so different in the three relevant normative orders? Is it the terms in which PTRs are drafted, is it their ambiguous legal status, the vagueness in the enabling clauses in respect of their authority? In other words, this finding calls for an investigation into the *sources* of the different authority of PTRs. There is a need for a better understanding of the sources explaining the authority of PTRs in the internal normative orders, and the lack of it in the international and national legal orders.

PART II

The Sources of the Authority of Environmental Post-Treaty Rules

3

The Silence of the Enabling Clauses: Delegated Authority and the Doctrine of Sources

The wide variety in the authority of PTRs transpiring from the case studies in the previous chapter raises important questions. What are the sources of this (lack of) authority? What could explain the variety across different regimes, types of PTR, and normative orders? This and the following chapters attempt to answer these questions.

The current chapter begins by briefly looking at delegation *per se* as a source of authority. The terms in which the adoption of PTRs is delegated might in theory hold the key to the degree of authority that the treaty parties wished to imbue PTRs with. The mere act of delegation is, however, discarded as sufficient to explain the *degree* of authority of PTRs in the various normative orders.

Closely related to delegation as a source of authority are the formal sources of international law, or the doctrine of sources. Assuming that the treaty parties are knowledgeable of the sources of international law, when delegating the adoption of PTRs they have the option to choose to require the treaty meetings to do or not do so in conformity with the conditions an international instrument needs to meet in order to qualify as legally binding international law. Discussing the various sources of international law, it is concluded that treaty parties have in most cases deliberately not chosen a legal form for their delegation of rule making. The treaty parties have not precisely prohibited a legal form either, but the treaty meetings themselves have generally not used that wiggle room to decide for a legal form after all. In other words, as international and national case law confirms, PTRs are seldom legally binding. The source of such authority they possess must be looked for elsewhere.

Yet even apart from *legal* authority, enabling clauses also lack other terminology implicating that the PTRs based on them are obligation. Regime bodies control compliance by parties with PTRs without citing a basis in the treaty for it.

A. PTRs as International Delegated Acts

Bradley and Kelley provide the following definition of international delegation: 'a grant of authority by two or more states to an international body to make decisions or take actions.'[1] In the light of chapter one's observation of the lack of autonomy of COPs and MOPs from their composite states, it makes sense to start with this second element of international delegation, to conclude that we are dealing with a special kind of delegation: delegation to a collective of state representatives. A second element of 'delegation' is a 'grant of authority'.[2] The main vehicles for international delegation and other forms of international power conferral are treaties.[3] For PTRs, the grant of authority to adopt them can indeed be found in the MEA, in the form of open-ended clauses and explicit enabling clauses.

International delegation theory recognises two main possibilities: (1) delegations of competences to an international 'body', or (2) 'ordinary' international cooperation between states whereby states commit to an international agreement 'but implementation is through strictly national laws or regulations'.[4] However, PTRs show that reality is more complicated. Considering the argumentation in chapter one concerning the lack of autonomy of treaty meetings, evidently they are not a standard case of international delegation to an international body. But they are not 'ordinary' stand-alone commitments either.

The weak autonomy of the COPs, COP/MOPs and MOPs illustrated above makes PTRs a very peculiar case of international delegation. At first glance, the near-identity between the members of the diplomatic conference adopting the MEA and of the parties in the COPs, COP/MOPs and MOPs seems to conceptually preclude the possibility of delegation between the two. The same states that adopt the agreement which *delegates* authority, after all, also make up the body to which authority *is* delegated.[5] The plenary meetings consist of representatives of

[1] Curtis A Bradley and Judith G Kelley, 'The Concept of International Delegation' (2008) 71 *Law and Contemporary Problems* 1, 2–3. Slightly different, with more focus on the principal–agent relationship and therefore possibly excluding conferences of parties, are Darren G Hawkins et al, *Delegation and Agency in International Organizations* (CUP, 2006), 7 ('Delegation is a conditional grant of authority from a principal to an agent that empowers the latter to act on behalf of the former'). Also Dan Sarooshi, *International Organizations and Their Exercise of Sovereign Powers* (OUP, 2007), 18 (speaks of 'conferral of powers', distinguishing three types of conferral to international organisations: agency, delegation and transfer). His distinction between delegation and transfer seems hard to maintain in practice. Further, his understanding of the concept of delegation as entailing that states are not bound by an international body's exercise of it is awkward.

[2] Such a grant can be *de facto* or *de jure*. Henrik Enroth, 'The Concept of Authority Transnationalised' (2013) 4 *Transnational Legal Theory* 336, 342.

[3] Sarooshi, '*International Organizations*', 18 ff.

[4] Hawkins et al, '*Delegation in International Organizations*', 11.

[5] In the definition of Hawkins et al, with its focus on a principal–agent relationship, grants of authority to the COPs, COP/MOPs and MOPs would arguably be outside that definition. Hawkins et al, '*Delegation in International Organizations*', 7 ('Delegation is a conditional grant of authority from a principal to an agent that empowers the latter to act on behalf of the former'). The far-reaching identity between principal and agent in the case of COPs and PTRs presses this definition to its limits.

the same parties that have ratified or acceded to the Protocol.[6] Decisions adopted in the treaty meetings are then simply a new round of diplomatically agreed upon international commitments by the states themselves.

A pragmatic solution is to consider PTRs as a form of delegation, but a very peculiar one, by not interpreting the phrasing in the definition – 'an international *body*' – too rigidly. Bradley and Kelley do exactly that by putting delegation to COPs, COP/MOPs and MOPs in their category 'delegation to collective bodies'.[7] As Hawkins et al's definition allows, the autonomy of the agent to which authority is delegated can vary strongly;[8] even when the agent has but little autonomy, this does not preclude that delegation has taken place.

Moreover, regardless of the near-identity between delegator and delegatee, there are changes in the *dynamics of decision making and the power distribution* in the COP, COP/MOP and MOP, even if these are not in the nature of more autonomy for an international body, compared to ordinary 'international cooperation' through a single treaty that is only implemented at a national level.[9] In contrast to the entry into force of the MEA, no individual state consent is required for PTRs to become 'operative' (to use the expression 'enter into force' for the latter would be confusing).[10] States that are unable to prevent the emergence of consensus on a particular PTR, which is fairly common in COP decision making, no longer have the option to withhold their consent or opt-out,[11] as they would have been able to do in the case of treaty making, amendments or annex amendments.

In other words, assigning rule-making tasks to the COP, COP/MOP or MOP is an – admittedly peculiar – form of international delegation, albeit not to an *autonomous international entity*.[12] It is a delegation to a *collective of state representatives* that, for most of the individual states making up the collective, decreases

[6] Art 11 Montreal Protocol on Substances that Deplete the Ozone Layer (adopted 16 September 1987, entered into force 1 January 1989) 1522 UNTS 3 (Montreal Protocol) ('The *parties* shall hold meetings at regular intervals').

[7] Bradley and Kelley, 'The Concept of International Delegation', 6, 8–9.

[8] Hawkins et al, '*Delegation in International Organizations*', 8.

[9] ibid, 11.

[10] The *mode* of decision making is in itself not different: both the adoption of a treaty text and the adoption of a PTR are done by consensus. It is the subsequent requirement of individual state consent in order for a treaty to enter into force and become binding for those states that have consented to it which sets the adoption of PTRs apart from the adoption of MEAs and other treaties, and which qualifies the adoption of PTRs as a delegated activity.

[11] Notably, however, most MEAs prohibit prospective parties to enter reservations. See, eg, Art 18 Montreal Protocol and Art XIII Convention on International Trade in Endangered Species of Wild Fauna and Flora (adopted 3 March 1973, entered into force 1 July 1975) 993 UNTS 243 (CITES).

[12] *Contra* Robin R Churchill and Geir Ulfstein, 'Autonomous Institutional Arrangements in Multilateral Environmental Agreements: A Little-Noticed Phenomenon in International Law' (2000) 94 *American Journal of International Law* 623; Jessica F Green and Jeff Colgan, 'Protecting Sovereignty, Protecting the Planet: State Delegation to International Organizations and Private Actors in Environmental Politics' (2013) 26 *Governance* 473, 479 ('The agent must be an actor other than the entire group of states, but the agent could be a subgroup of those states').

the possibility to continue to determine their own course of action in accordance with their preferences.

B. PTRs' Delegated Authority According to the Sources of International Law

In searching for the sources of authority of PTRs, that they are products of delegation as such brings us not even halfway. In accordance with the general definition of authority, delegated authority should be defined as the degree to which *the act of delegation* makes it difficult for the treaty parties to escape PTRs as reference points in the interpretation of the underlying MEA. The questions then are, *how much* authority is delegated, in *which legal order*, and *over whom*?

As with many state-based global governance arrangements, at first glance it makes sense to explain the authority of PTRs through the link that delegation makes between the consent of the treaty parties and PTRs.[13] The treaty assigns or allows for the adoption of PTRs; hence, they must have authority.[14] But once one starts perusing the terms of MEAs and enabling clauses, they turn out to be devoid of terminology that helps determine the resulting PTRs' degree of authority, whether in terms of international law, national law, or even regardless of legal categories. This section makes this point for international law, the following sections do the same for the internal orders of the treaty meetings (the regimes) and for the national legal orders.

1. Treaties or Treaty Amendments?

What does the doctrine of sources make of PTRs? To begin with the sources mentioned in the ICJ Statute, PTRs are not treaties in their own right. It is not plausible that they would amount to 'simplified treaties' that require no ratification,[15] since the articles on formal amendment found in each MEA do not dispense with formal consent requirements.[16]

[13] Scott Cooper, Darren Hawkins, Wade Jacoby and Daniel Nielson, 'Yielding Sovereignty to International Institutions: Bringing System Structure Back In' (2008) 10 *International Studies Review* 501; and Liesbeth Hooghe and Gary Marks, 'Delegation and Pooling in International Organizations' (2013) 10 *The Review of International Organizations* 1.

[14] Chittharanjan F Amerasinghe, *Principles of the Institutional Law of International Organizations* 2nd edn (CUP, 2005), 163 (stating that '[t]his is so even if subsequent practice is invoked to interpret constitutional provisions'). As Amerasinghe notes for international organisations, 'no resolution can have a greater effect than the [treaty] permits'; ibid, 163.

[15] As argued in Churchill and Ulfstein, 'Autonomous Institutional Arrangements', 640.

[16] Jutta Brunnée, 'Reweaving the Fabric of International Law? Patterns of Consent in Environmental Framework Agreements' in Rüdiger Wolfrum and Volker Röben (eds), *Developments of International Law in Treaty Making* (Springer, 2005) 101, 112.

Nor are PTRs formal amendments of treaties. Perhaps this becomes most evident from the one available counter-example: the Montreal Protocol *Adjustment Mechanism*. Article 2.9 of the Montreal Protocol states: 'the decisions shall be binding on all Parties'. The same Article 2.9 also uses the language of 'entry into force',[17] parallel to the language used in relation to formal treaty amendments. What this clause makes abundantly clear is that the treaty parties no doubt have the capacity to provide information on the authority of decision making in the plenary meetings if they wish. They can state that PTRs will be binding or that they will not be binding. But we find no such language in any other (true) enabling clause (the *Adjustment Mechanism* is really a mechanism to amend annexes to the Montreal Protocol). None of them confers authority on PTRs as high as Article 2.9 Montreal Protocol does, simply by the terms of the delegation.

Enabling clauses also contain no conclusive language revealing an implicit intention to create legally binding instruments. Explicit enabling clauses often stipulate legally meaningless denominations under which PTRs are to be adopted, such as 'rules', 'decisions' or 'modalities'. Churchill and Ulfstein have argued that the use of the term 'rules' in the enabling clause in Article 17 of the Kyoto Protocol, enabling the adoption of 'rules' for emissions trading, would indicate the binding nature of decisions taken on its basis.[18] However, while the terms 'binding' and 'entry into force' provide legally meaningful information about the status of an instrument, the term 'rules' is much more ambiguous.[19] 'Rules' need not necessarily be binding, let alone legally binding; they can just as well be non-binding rules. The term 'rules' at most says something about the relatively high specificity and mandatory quality one would expect to find in the resulting PTR. However, an authoritative rule formulation alone is not sufficient to indicate an instrument's legally binding status.

Moreover, Article 17 speaks of 'principles, modalities, rules and guidelines'.[20] So how does one distinguish between these four in the eventual PTRs? Which are the rules, and which are the guidelines? Kyoto COP/MOP 'Decision' 11 CMP/1 – adopted on the basis of Article 17 – simply repeats almost the same collection of denominations – 'rules, modalities and guidelines' – for emissions trading.[21]

[17] Art 2.9(d) Montreal Protocol: 'The decisions, which *shall be binding* on all Parties, shall forthwith be communicated to the Parties by the Depositary. Unless otherwise provided in the decisions, they shall *enter into force* on the expiry of six months from the date of the circulation of the communication by the Depositary.'

[18] Geir Ulfstein, 'Reweaving the Fabric of International Law? Patterns of Consent in Environmental Framework Agreements, Comment by Geir Ulfstein' in Rüdiger Wolfrum and Volker Röben (eds), *Developments of International Law in Treaty Making* (Springer, 2005), 145, 148; Churchill and Ulfstein, 'Autonomous Institutional Arrangements', 639 ('The use of the word 'rules' suggests that such a measure is intended to be legally binding').

[19] *cf* Brunnée, 'Reweaving the Fabric of International Law?', 112.

[20] 'The Conference of the Parties shall define the relevant principles, modalities, rules and guidelines, in particular for verification, reporting and accountability for emissions trading.'

[21] Decision 11/CMP.1 on *Modalities, rules and guidelines for emissions trading under Article 17 of the Kyoto Protocol*.

In practice, the Kyoto COP/MOP decisions contain rules with high mandatory quality *as well as* low mandatory quality.[22] And why is this PTR called a 'Decision'; what degree of authority does that convey? 'Decision' is a rather neutral term, signalling neither high nor low authority. The same applies to the term 'decision' in Article 2H.5 Montreal Protocol on *Critical Use Exemptions*.

2. (Binding) Decisions of International Organisations?

That PTRs are not binding decisions of international organisations (IOs) does of course also follow logically from the conclusion in chapter one that COPs, COP/MOPs and MOPs are not IOs because they are lacking a distinct will and international legal personality. But even if they were IOs, decisions of IOs are only binding if this follows from the constituent instrument,[23] which is not the case for PTRs. Arguing that PTRs are decisions of IOs therefore would not make them legally binding.[24] One could even go a step further: since MEAs do not state the possibility that the COP adopts 'binding' or 'legally binding' decisions or other instruments, the COP is arguably even *prevented* from issuing internationally legally binding instruments.[25] To suggest otherwise would require far-reaching reliance on either implied or inherent powers, and that for a semi-institutionalised gathering of the parties. The Montreal Protocol Adjustment Mechanism again can be referred to: when states want to insert the power to adopt binding decisions, they can and need to do so.

3. Customary Law or Soft Law?

PTRs may perhaps very sparingly contribute to the formation of customary law.[26] In such rare circumstances they amount to *evidence* of customary law. Where they do, the PTRs are obviously not themselves customary law, but either a reflection of existing customary law or a contribution to the formation thereof. Moreover, to reiterate, neither most PTRs, nor the treaty provisions on which they are based, give any indication that the parties believe that they are under a *legal* obligation to comply with them, putting the *opinio juris* element in jeopardy.

[22] See ch 4, section C.

[23] The primary example is Art 25 Charter of the United Nations (adopted 26 June 1945, entered into force 24 October 1945) (UN Charter).

[24] *cf* Annecoos Wiersema, 'The New International Law-Makers? Conferences of the Parties to Multilateral Environmental Agreements' (2009) 31 *Michigan Journal of International Law* 231, 246.

[25] Amerasinghe, '*Principles of the Insitutional Law*', 163 (stating that 'no resolution can have a greater effect than the [treaty] permits').

[26] The arguments of Australia and Japan in the *Whaling* case relating to the CITES resolution's definition of 'primarily commercial purposes' can be regarded as an attempt to argue a customary definition of those terms. See *Whaling in the Antarctic (Australia v Japan: New Zealand intervening)* (Memorial of Australia) [2011] ICJ Rep 262, and *Whaling in the Antarctic* (Counter-Memorial of Japan) [2012], para 628.

This already brings us to the end of the relevant sources of international law. The concept of *soft law* is not overly helpful in establishing any kind of international legal status either.[27] Several commentators mention PTRs as one of the many forms of soft law.[28] Granted, the concept of soft law is a starting point in acknowledging that instruments can have legal relevance to some degree, even if they are not a formal source of international law. The concept 'is designed to acknowledge the powerful practical significance of measures'.[29] Yet, the statement that an instrument is 'soft law' tells us very little about what kind of 'significance',[30] only that it may have *some* degree of influence in practice. Soft law is more effect-based than that it signifies what the source of that 'effect' is. A description of PTRs as 'soft law' is thus uninformative for a more precise understanding of the role played by legal status or legal obligation in that 'significance'.[31] Authors using this term rarely go beyond it to explore what the *exact* relevance of the instrument is: they only mention the phenomenon in a general way. Apart from this lack of information, the concept of 'soft law' is also overly broad. Since 'soft law' is used to describe such a wide array of instruments from the Rio Declaration to UNEP *Guidelines* to PTRs,[32] it is only logical that it would not provide accurate information about the type of legal obligation of one of its particular sub-categories.

To conclude, PTRs exist in what Bodansky has appropriately described – for the entire body of environmental soft law – a kind of legal 'purgatory'.[33]

C. PTRs' Delegated Authority in the Internal Normative Orders of MEAs

Regardless of the absence of indications in MEAs at large or in specific enabling clauses that PTRs are internationally legally binding, MEAs might still be expected to indicate in other, non-legal terms the authority of PTRs within the internal

[27] *cf* Wiersema, 'The New International Law-Makers', 259–64.

[28] Including Alan Boyle, 'Some Reflections on the Relationship of Treaties and Soft Law' (1999) 48 *International and Comparative Law Quarterly* 901; Michael Bowman, Peter Davies and Catherine Redgwell, *Lyster's International Wildlife Law* 2nd edn (CUP, 2010), 38; Jürgen Friedrich, *International Environmental 'soft Law': The Functions and Limits of Nonbinding Instruments in International Environmental Governance and Law* (Springer, 2013), 45–46.

[29] Bowman, Davies and Redgwell, '*Lyster's International Wildlife Law*', 37.

[30] Matthias Goldmann, 'Inside Relative Normativity: From Sources to Standard Instruments for the Exercise of International Public Authority' in Armin Von Bogdandy et al (ed), *The Exercise of Public Authority by International Institutions* (Springer, 2010), 667–68.

[31] See Harri Kalimo and Tim Staal, ''Softness' in International Instruments – the Case of Transnational Corporations' (2014) 41 *Syracuse Journal of International Law and Commerce* 257.

[32] See, eg, Christine M Chinkin, 'The Challenge of Soft Law: Development and Change in International Law' (1989) 38 *International & Comparative Law Quarterly* 850; Pierre-Marie Dupuy, 'Soft Law and the International Law of the Environment' (1991) 12 *Michigan Journal of International Law* 420.

[33] Daniel Bodansky, *The Art and Craft of International Environmental Law* (Harvard University Press, 2010), 99.

normative orders where they have been adopted. After all, the previous chapter found that the authority of PTRs is at its highest in the treaty meetings and other regime bodies. However, an exploration of the four MEAs central to this study reveals few signs that PTRs must be applied in treaty meetings and other treaty bodies.

1. Correspondence between Delegation and Delegated Act?

The primary addressees of enabling clauses are the treaty parties in their capacity as collective treaty meetings. To address the extent to which the authority of PTRs derives from the enabling clauses as acts of delegation, it therefore makes sense to see if the treaty meetings provide PTRs with a wording that is characterised by the same authority as envisaged by the enabling clause on which it is based. In short, if the enabling clause contains mandatory wording, do the PTRs also contain mandatory wording? And if the enabling clause contains recommendatory wording, is that also true for the PTRs based on it?

What is clear is that the underlying treaty provision's mandatory quality is a cap to the *maximum* mandatory quality of subsequent PTRs. Examining the PTRs themselves discloses some important correlations between how the Parties are willing to phrase PTRs and the text of a treaty provision, or of the treaty as a whole. A number of examples from the Ramsar Convention regime confirm this proposition. If Article 3.1 of the Ramsar Convention uses the qualified phrase '[t]he Contracting Parties shall formulate and implement their planning so as to promote … as far as possible the wise use of wetlands in their territory', this indicates an objectified intention of the parties that a subsequent PTR is prohibited from requiring that, in the formulation and implementation of their planning, the parties must go further than 'to promote … as far as possible', at pains of amounting to a contradiction, and thus a modification of the terms of the treaty. The various Ramsar *Guidelines* on wise use based on this Article use the equally modest terms 'so as to promote' and 'as far as possible'.

Yet the language of enabling clauses in MEAs discloses very little to no information on what *necessarily should be* the kind of wording in subsequent PTRs. Mandatory treaty terms do not automatically lead to mandatory PTR terms, as testified by various examples from CITES. For instance, according to Article VIII.4 of CITES, treaty parties are obliged to return irregularly imported specimens to the wild, or to place them in a rescue centre or another appropriate place (captivity). The CITES resolution on *Disposal of Specimens*, by contrast, is phrased entirely in the language of urgings and recommendations.[34] A potential for PTRs with obligatory language does not *have to* be banked by the treaty parties.

[34] CITES COP Res Conf 9.10 (Rev CoP15), *Disposal of confiscated and accumulated specimens* (consolidating seven earlier resolutions on the topic), and CITES COP Res Conf 10.7 (Rev CoP15), *Disposal of confiscated live specimens of species included in the Appendices.*

Under the Montreal Protocol, however, the language of PTRs does tend to align closely with the underlying enabling clauses. Large parts of the Montreal Protocol text are already worded in mandatory and specific terms, and this is reflected in the PTRs adopted in its wake.

However, what really determines the wording of PTRs, and the differences between the PTRs of CITES and the Montreal Protocol in this respect, is the level of political agreement. All MEAs deal with issues on which political disagreement exists and on which states foremost agree that they wish to retain national sovereignty; for some, this is even truer than for others. The Kyoto Protocol is a good example of the continued visibility of a treaty's highly politicised character in the subsequent PTRs. The choice for several options that its PTRs leave open to the parties, whether in relation to the flexibility mechanisms or LULUCF, is a continuation of the decision made in the treaty to use controversial market mechanisms such as the Clean Development Mechanism in reaching economically efficient emissions reduction. In the Ramsar Convention, national sovereignty plays a large role in the sense that most wetlands are located in one or more parties' territories, and contain valuable natural resources. These parties wish to retain a large measure of freedom in deciding how to explore the economic possibilities of their wetlands, which explains the voluntary language used in Ramsar resolutions.

By contrast, it is precisely the fact that those parties of CITES home to species most threatened by international trade are loath to see these valuable resources disappear with the revenue flowing to illegal trafficking operations rather than to government funds, that made them willing to agree on a rather precise and mandatory system of regulating international trade in endangered species, in the text of CITES and in its PTRs. That also means that, when political agreement on an issue increases or decreases, this new level of political (dis)agreement may affect the wording of PTRs as much as the wording of the underlying treaty.

This point can be clearly demonstrated by the most extreme example of difference between the authority of an enabling clause and the subsequent PTR. Article 18 of the Cartagena Biosafety Protocol states that the COP/MOP '*shall* take a decision on the detailed requirements … *no later than two years after the date of entry into force of this Protocol*'. Here, the adoption of the PTR is, on the face of it, obligatory and time-bound, and is described as a 'decision', which – in the Montreal Protocol – led to the *Critical Use Criteria* with their high mandatory quality and specificity. Yet, Article 18 Cartagena Protocol still awaits the actual adoption of a PTR setting the assigned rules, confirming that even explicit enabling clauses are *obligations of conduct* rather than of result.[35] The COP/MOP to the Biosafety Protocol, rather than adopting detailed criteria for the identification

[35] *cf* René Lefeber's early prediction that Art 18.2(a) is '*an obligation of conduct* and absolutely no guarantee that such a decision will be taken, even though there will be strong political pressure to do so'. René Lefeber, 'Creative Legal Engineering' (2000) 13 *Leiden Journal of International Law* 1, 8.

of GMOs itself, established an 'open-ended technical expert-group'.[36] This expert group was assigned the task of assisting the COP/MOP in reaching such criteria, somewhat surprising in the light of the obvious political side to this agreement that had been exposed in the inability to agree on the requirements during the protocol negotiations.[37] At subsequent meetings of the expert group[38] and the COP/MOP, however, it was noted repeatedly that 'experience gained to date' was 'limited', so that – four meetings later – the COP/MOP 'decided to postpone until its seventh meeting further decision-taking on detailed information to be included in documentation accompanying LMOs-FFP'.[39]

The oft-made observation that the more specific a treaty provision is, the less room it leaves for further specification – and vice versa –[40] is not entirely reflected in the PTR practice. On the one hand, many of the Kyoto Protocol's numerous unspecified aspects were responded to by extremely detailed PTRs, and the very specific PTRs of the Montreal Protocol on critical use follow up on explicit enabling clauses that openly leave room for specification. Re-examining the various *Guidelines* adopted on the basis of Article 3.1 Ramsar Convention, which is very open-ended, they contain very detailed 'best practices'. On the other hand, some very open-ended MEA provisions lead to equally open-ended PTRs, and some very specific ones are specified even further in PTRs. The CITES COP's decision on export quotas is only slightly more specific than Article III.3 CITES as regards what amounts to exports detrimental to the survival of a species. The 'supplementality' in Article 17 Kyoto Protocol remained 'supplementality' in the Kyoto COP/MOP decisions on the *Flexibility Mechanisms*. Some rather specific treaty provisions still apparently allow for yet more specific and elaborate supplements. An example is Article 3.4 Kyoto Protocol on (accounting for) LULUCF, which in itself already provided numerous detailed prescriptions, but was followed by the far more detailed *Accounting Modalities*.

This goes to prove that the actual adoption of a PTR, let alone the precise type of language of a PTR, as long as it does not modify the treaty, is mostly up to the treaty meeting. This all but negates the idea that the degree of authority of a PTR would be based on the degree of authority that the enabling clause delegates to the treaty meeting.

[36] Cartagena COP/MOP Decision BS-1/6, *Handling, transport, packaging and identification of living modified organisms (Article 18)*.

[37] Lefeber, 'Creative Legal Engineering', 8.

[38] Stanley W Burgiel, 'The Cartagena Protocol on Biosafety: Taking the Steps from Negotiation to Implementation' (2002) 11 *RECIEL* 53, 57 (noting that '[t]he ICCP-2's discussions on the topic, most particularly with regard to shipments of LMO-FFPs, were reminiscent of the final hours of negotiations at the resumed ExCOP, where the issue was the last outstanding matter').

[39] Cartagena COP/MOP Decision BS-V/8, *Handling, transport, packaging and identification of living modified organisms: paragraph 2(a) of Article 18*.

[40] Sean D Murphy, 'The Relevance of Subsequent Agreement and Subsequent Practice for the Interpretation of Treaties' in Georg Nolte (ed), *Treaties and Subsequent Practice* (OUP, 2013) 82, 91.

2. Is Compliance with PTRs Obligatory?

MEAs shine no light on how PTRs affect the obligations of the parties – legal or otherwise. But what about those MEA provisions that determine the scope of compliance control? Do they oblige the compliance mechanisms to include PTRs in their assessment of compliance? To be sure, even if that would be the case, this would at most be an obligation on the part of the compliance committees, and only indirectly on the part of the treaty parties, having committed themselves to these systems of compliance control. Yet MEAs do not even do that. With few exceptions, they merely stipulate that compliance bodies and other implementing bodies check compliance with the *treaty*. Rarely do they stipulate if that includes compliance with PTRs. This mere assignment to check compliance with the treaty is insufficient to imply that this includes operating in accordance with and checking compliance with PTRs.

The same is true for what could be labelled 'procedural PTRs', PTRs that flesh out the rules for the operation of compliance procedures and other review procedures. In chapter two, we saw that the Montreal Protocol Implementation Committee includes the *Critical Use Exemptions* in their control of compliance. Yet, the *Non-Compliance Procedure* of the Montreal Protocol, which has become the model for many subsequent NCPs, is completely silent on Montreal MOP decisions. Article 8 of the Protocol speaks only of non-compliance 'with the provisions of this Protocol'. Likewise, the revised NCP of 1998 gives no indication that Montreal MOP decisions are to be applied in compliance assessment.[41] About the scope of non-compliance determinations, the procedures only state on several occasions that this concerns 'compliance with the provisions of the Protocol'.[42]

Similarly, in the text of the Kyoto Protocol, there is no explicit indication that the Compliance Committee's Facilitative and Enforcement Branches should check compliance with Kyoto COP/MOP decisions.[43] The *Procedures and Mechanisms Relating to Compliance under the Kyoto Protocol* (Decision 27/CMP.1) mention the Protocol articles with which the Enforcement Branch must assess compliance, but not the various decisions adopted on the basis of those articles containing further guidance.[44] Only with regard to the *Accounting Modalities*

[41] See Montreal MOP Decision X/10 (revising Decision IV/5), Annex II, *Non-Compliance Procedure.*

[42] See Montreal MOP *Non-Compliance Procedure*, paras 1, 2, 3, 4 and 7(b).

[43] Art 18 Kyoto Protocol to the United Nations Framework Convention on Climate Change (adopted 11 December 1997, entered into force 16 February 2005) 2303 UNTS 162 (Kyoto Protocol) speaks of 'procedures and mechanisms to determine and to address cases of non-compliance *with the provisions of the Protocol*'.

[44] See Kyoto COP/MOP Decision 27/CMP.1, Annex, *Procedures and mechanisms relating to compliance under the Kyoto Protocol*, para V.4: 'The enforcement branch shall be responsible for determining whether a Party included in Annex I is not in compliance with:

(a) Its quantified emission limitation or reduction commitment under Article 3, paragraph 1, of the Protocol;

does Decision 27/CMP.1 state that a determination that the emissions of a Party have exceeded its assigned amount is also to be made pursuant to those modalities.[45] The *Modalities* themselves state that compliance must be assessed *inter alia* on the basis of comparing various types of 'units' earned through forestry activities, joint implementation, and the Clean Development Mechanisms, to its actual emissions.[46] Considering that these activities and units are defined and limited by various Kyoto COP/MOP decisions, in a very indirect way, one can conclude that compliance with the Protocol can only be assessed by consulting these decisions as well. Obviously, all this is not exactly an express statement that this or all Kyoto PTRs create some kind of (legal) obligation in the Kyoto internal normative order.

Several 'procedural' CITES PTRs state that relevant resolutions and decisions must be taken into account in assessing compliance and taking implementing measures. Article XIII of CITES on *International Measures* is no different from the other MEAs: it requires the Secretariat to monitor and communicate whether 'the provisions of the present Convention are not being effectively implemented,' with no specific mention of implementation of COP resolutions and decisions. This is markedly different in the two most important COP resolutions on compliance and enforcement, Resolution 14.3 containing the *Guide to CITES Compliance Procedures*, and Resolution 11.3 (Rev CoP 16) on *Compliance and Enforcement*. The *Guide to CITES Compliance Procedures* states that '[t]his Guide addresses compliance matters relating to the obligations under the Convention, taking into account relevant Resolutions and Decisions'.[47]

On the scope of the CITES Standing Committee's[48] mandate, however, Paragraph 12 of the *Guide to CITES Compliance Procedures* takes a step back, merely stating that '[t]he Standing Committee … handles general and specific compliance matters, including: a) monitoring and assessing overall compliance

(b) The methodological and reporting requirements under Article 5, paragraphs 1 and 2, and Article 7, paragraphs 1 and 4, of the Protocol; and
(c) The eligibility requirements under Articles 6, 12 and 17 of the Protocol.'

[45] Kyoto COP/MOP Decision 27/CMP.1, Annex, para XV.5. 'Where the enforcement branch has determined that the emissions of a Party have exceeded its assigned amount, calculated pursuant to its quantified emission limitation or reduction commitment inscribed in Annex B to the Protocol and in accordance with the provisions of Article 3 of the Protocol as well as the modalities for the accounting of assigned amounts under Article 7, paragraph 4, of the Protocol, taking into account emission reduction units, certified emission reductions, assigned amount units and removal units the Party has acquired in accordance with section XIII, it shall declare that that Party is not in compliance with its commitments under Article 3, paragraph 1, of the Protocol.'

[46] Kyoto COP/MOP Decision 13/CMP.1, Annex, paras 11–13.

[47] CITES COP Res Conf 14.3, Annex, *Guide to CITES compliance procedures*, para 2.

[48] 'The Standing Committee provides policy guidance to the Secretariat concerning the implementation of the Convention and oversees the management of the Secretariat's budget. Beyond these key roles, it coordinates and oversees, where required, the work of other committees and working groups; carries out tasks given to it by the Conference of the Parties; and drafts resolutions for consideration by the Conference of the Parties [see Resolution Conf 11.1 (Rev CoP16) Annex 1].' See https://cites.org/eng/disc/sc.php.

with obligations *under the Convention*' (emphasis added).[49] Moreover, as the denomination '*Guide*' implies already, this Resolution expressly notes its *own* non-legally binding status – '[t]his Guide is not legally binding'[50] – and its recommendatory nature – 'RECOMMENDS that the Guide be referred to, when dealing with compliance matters'[51] – seriously questioning whether it actually creates obligations in itself.

In the context of issuing trade suspensions – the most powerful stick in the enforcement toolbox of the CITES COP – non-compliance with 'resolutions and decisions' is clearly included again: 'Such a recommendation [to suspend trade] is always specifically and explicitly based on the Convention *and on any applicable Resolutions and Decisions of the Conference of the Parties*' (emphasis added).[52] A footnote specifically mentions a number of applicable resolutions on national reporting, national implementing legislation, review of significant trade and compliance and enforcement, on which recommendations to suspend trade should be based.[53]

Under the Ramsar Convention, there is little direct assessment of country-by-country compliance, although there are other implementation mechanisms such as Ramsar Advisory Missions and National Reports, and the Montreux Record, which records changes in the ecological character of listed sites.[54] Its international implementation is therefore better characterised as supervision and assistance than as compliance control,[55] and it is underutilised at that.[56] Resolutions of the COP certainly play a significant role in this gentle supervision, although they are hardly ever recited directly.[57] However, nowhere is it expressly stated that parties

[49] *Guide to CITES compliance procedures*, para 12.

[50] CITES COP Res Conf 14.3, Annex, para 1.

[51] CITES COP Res Conf 14.3, *CITES compliance procedures*, Preamble.

[52] CITES COP Res Conf 14.3, Annex, para 30.

[53] According to this footnote, 'These currently include:

- Resolution Conf. 11.17 (Rev. CoP14) (National reports);
- Resolution Conf. 8.4 (Rev. CoP15) (National laws for implementation of the Convention);
- Decision 14.29 (National laws for implementation of the Convention);
- Resolution Conf. 12.8 (Rev. CoP13) (Review of Significant trade in specimens of Appendix-II species);
- Convention Article XIII and Resolution Conf. 11.3 (Rev. CoP15) (Compliance and enforcement); and
- Resolution Conf 11.1 (Rev. CoP15) (Establishment of committees).'
- In the context of the monitoring to achieve compliance of a party with measures taken against it, specific mention is again made of resolutions and decisions of being part of the relevant framework for this monitoring process. CITES COP Res Conf 14.3, Annex, para 35.

[54] Ramsar COP Recommendation 4.8, Change in Ecological Character of Ramsar Sites. See for discussion Ornella Ferrajolo, 'State Obligations and Non-Compliance in the Ramsar System' (2011) 14 *Journal of International Wildlife Law & Policy* 243, 253–54. Bowman, Davies and Redgwell, '*Lyster's International Wildlife Law*', 443–45.

[55] ibid, 435–36.

[56] Ferrajolo, 'State Obligations and Non-Compliance', 253–54.

[57] See, eg, *Report of the Secretary General on the implementation of the Convention at the global level*, COP10, Changwon, 2008, Agenda item XI, Ramsar COP10 DOC. 6.

are expected to comply with or take into account COP resolutions, or that the various implementing institutions are expected to take into account COP resolutions in their reports. There is one act of treaty parties that is expressly governed by Ramsar resolutions, and that is the designation of new wetland sites to the Ramsar List. In Annex 2 to Resolution XI.8, it is stated clearly that the Secretariat reviews wetlands designated by treaty parties against the criteria for identifying wetlands of international importance before adding them to the List.[58]

In other words, the MEA or PTR provisions that compel bodies involved in implementation and compliance control to base their compliance control and recommendation of measures on PTRs, can be counted on one hand. The same goes for the applicability of PTRs to the operation of COPs, COP/MOPs and MOPs.

The silence about the origins of the authority of PTRs in the internal normative orders continues all the way to the practice of compliance bodies and plenary treaty meetings. In their records, no reference can be found at all to doctrines or case law relating to the type of legal obligation that PTRs create in the international legal order. When compliance bodies discuss a party's compliance with some PTR, they do not support this action on their part with a reference to, for instance, formal treaty amendments, the binding nature of some decisions of IOs, or the theory of soft law. None of that is invoked. The authority of PTRs is simply assumed.

Remarkably, the Kyoto Protocol Compliance Committee's Enforcement Branch *does require* an explicit basis in the Kyoto Protocol where it concerns the applicability of PTRs originating in other regimes than its own. (Recall that the Enforcement Branch denied Croatia's attempt to argue that it was in compliance with the Protocol on the basis of a PTR from the UNFCCC COP.) For Kyoto COP/MOP decisions, however, this applicability is apparently 'implied,' and needs no such basis in the Kyoto Protocol. At least, there is no decision of the Branch in which it states such a corresponding need, or points to the Kyoto Protocol or PTR provision that would form such a basis.

One interesting exception is a decision of the Montreal Implementation Committee, finding Israel to be in non-compliance with several MOP decisions on the use of ozone-depleting substances as process agents.[59] The Implementation Committee stated that '[r]eporting of process agent uses was *regulated* by three decisions of meetings of the parties' (emphasis added).[60] If the parties are 'regulated' by MOP decisions, it could imply that the NCP understands them to be

[58] Ramsar COP Res XI.8, Annex 2.

[59] Montreal Protocol, Implementation Committee under the Non-Compliance Procedure for the Montreal Protocol, Fiftieth meeting, Bangkok, 21 and 22 June 2013, UNEP/OzL.Pro/ImpCom/50/4, pp 14–15, '*Recalling* decision X/14, which defined the conditions under which parties could treat certain uses of ozone-depleting substances as process agents, *Recalling* also decision XVII/6, which provided that Parties with process agent applications should report annually, in accordance with decisions X/14 and XV/7'.

[60] Montreal Protocol Implementation Committee, ibid, 14.

binding for what constitutes compliance. But the Montreal NCP does not regularly employ such language, so it could have been a 'slip of the pen'.

D. National Legal Orders

This section of chapter three investigates to what extent PTRs are considered legally binding in the national legal orders of monist states and to what extent they become part of binding national law in other ways, primarily through transposition and (dynamic) referencing. In the latter case, it is of course important to signal that it is not the PTR that possesses authority but the national law into which it is transposed or in which it is referenced. The reason for the transposition or referencing having taken place may or may not have been the authority of the PTR or other considerations.

There certainly are no MEA provisions that exhort national authorities to comply specifically *with COP resolutions and decisions* in ensuring 'strict [domestic] compliance and control in respect of all mechanisms and provisions *of the Convention*'.[61] Domestic compliance with PTRs remains a question left to the discretion of each particular domestic legal order. The normal tests that national legal orders use to determine the domestic legal status of international instruments differ between dualist and monist states. However, this difference plays a relatively minor role with regard to environmental PTRs. Most MEAs are transposed into national legislation, not just in dualist states, but also in monist states. This legislation must then be interpreted in accordance with the MEA it implements. The question, for both monist and dualist states, is subsequently *which version of the MEA* the domestic legislation must be consistently interpreted with: the version according to the PTR or the version according to other means of interpretation – such as grammatical or teleological methods, etc? On those few occasions on which an MEA has not been implemented into national law by a monist state, the question is not much different.[62] In that scenario, the question is: with the help of which interpretive aids is the MEA to be interpreted?

[61] CITES COP Res Conf 11.3, *Compliance and Enforcement*, for instance, 'recommends that:

a) all parties …

v) ensure strict compliance and control in respect of all mechanisms and provisions of the Convention relating to the regulation of trade in animal and plant species listed in Appendix II, and of all provisions ensuring protection against illegal traffic for the species included in the Appendices;

vi) in case of violation of the above-mentioned provisions, immediately take appropriate measures pursuant to Article VIII, paragraph 1, of the Convention in order to penalise such violation and to take appropriate remedial action'.

[62] André Nollkaemper and Gerrit Betlem, 'Giving Effect to Public International Law and European Community Law before Domestic Courts. A Comparative Analysis of the Practice of Consistent Interpretation' (2003) 14 *European Journal of International Law* 569, 571.

The following section examines the situation regarding the transposition of MEAs and PTRs into national legislation and administrative regulation, and 'references' to PTRs in such instruments. The next section looks into the arguments in favour and against the validity of PTRs in monist legal orders, and the direct applicability of MEAs in domestic courts, in those few instances in which they have not been transposed into national legislation.

1. Transposition of and 'References' to MEAs and PTRs

To begin with transposition, there are many examples of *domestic and EU legislative acts* incorporating the content of MEAs, a number of which were also at issue in court proceedings discussed below. For instance, the obligations arising under the Montreal Protocol, CITES, and the Kyoto Protocol have been implemented in the EU legal order by EU regulations[63] and directives.[64] These EU instruments are also relevant in the national legal orders of the EU member states, although the national legal order may retain supplementary legislation.[65] In Australia, the Ramsar Convention has been incorporated into the Environment Protection and Biodiversity Conservation Act 1999 (EPBC), in particular in Sub-division B of Division 1 of Part 3.[66] In the United States, CITES is implemented through the Endangered Species Act,[67] and the Montreal Protocol through the Clean Air Act.[68] The majority of domestic court cases deal with PTRs adopted on the basis of MEAs that have indeed been implemented through the above-mentioned and many other domestic legislative acts.

In addition, there are often various further implementing instruments of MEAs in the shape of *administrative or executive acts*. In some of the court cases discussed below, the legality of executive acts from the perspective of relevant PTRs is precisely what is at issue. For example, in *NRDC v EPA*, the legality of the Final Rules of the EPA concerning production and consumption of ozone-depleting substances was at issue.[69] On other occasions, executive acts are part of the relevant domestic instrumentarium possibly subject to interpretation in accordance

[63] Regulation (EC) No 2037/2000 of the European Parliament and of the Council of 29 June 2000 *on substances that deplete the ozone layer* (OJ 2000 L 244, p 1); EC Council Regulation No 338/97 of 9 December 1996 *on the protection of species of wild fauna and flora by regulating trade therein* (OJ L 61, 3.3.1997).

[64] Directive of the European Parliament and of the Council, 2003/87/EC of 13 October 2003 *establishing a scheme for greenhouse gas emission allowance trading within the Community and amending Council Directive 96/61/EC* (OJ L 275/32, 25.10.2003).

[65] eg, the Dutch *Flora en Fauna Wet* supplements CITES implementing regulation 338/97. *Wet van 25 mei 1998, houdende regels ter bescherming van in het wild levende planten- en diersoorten* (Flora- en faunawet).

[66] Entered into force 16 July 2000.

[67] 16 USC § 1531 et seq.

[68] *Clean Air Act*, Title VI – *Stratospheric Ozone Protection* (CAA § 601–618; USC § 7671–7671q).

[69] *Final Rule* 69 Fed Reg at 76,989.

with PTRs, just like legislative acts. Important examples are EU Commission Regulation 1808/2001 (CITES) and EU Commission Decision 2005/625/EC of 23 August 2005 (Montreal Protocol),[70] and the US Fish and Wildlife Service's (CITES) regulations.[71]

Some of these legislative and executive acts contain direct references to PTRs. The existence of such a reference is a reason for courts to treat the referenced resolution as part of the applicable law.[72] For instance, Commission Regulation 1808/2001 (which further implements the EC CITES Regulation) contains a (dynamic) reference to any resolutions the CITES COP might adopt on approved or recommended methods of marking specimens, including specifically of containers of caviar.[73] A CITES COP Resolution on *Conservation of and trade in sturgeons and paddlefish*, including labelling methods for caviar, indeed exists.[74] In a case concerning the import of caviar, i.e. sturgeon eggs, a lower court in the Netherlands concluded that it had to review the legality of these imports in the light of this CITES COP Resolution prescribing labelling methods for caviar.[75] Similarly, EU Directive 2003/87/EC, which establishes a scheme for greenhouse gas emission allowance trading within the Community, extensively references 'the decisions adopted pursuant to the UNFCCC or the Kyoto Protocol' in defining the various types of emissions units relevant to emissions trading. In *Deutsche Bank AG v Total Global Steel Ltd*, a UK Commercial Court relied on these references in the EU Directive. Finally, the EU's Montreal Protocol implementing regulation provides:

> In the light of the proposals made by Member States, the Commission shall …
>
> apply the criteria set out in Decision IX/6 of the Parties, together with any other relevant criteria agreed by the Parties, in order to determine every year any critical uses for which the production, importation and use of methyl bromide may be permitted in the Community after 31 December 2004, the quantities and uses to be permitted and those users who may take advantage of the critical exemption.[76]

In the case *Mebrom v Commission*, both parties – as well as the (now) General Court of the EU – accepted that the Commission was under an obligation to apply the criteria of Decision IX/6 of the Montreal MOP.[77]

[70] OJ 2005 L 219, p 47 (determining the quantities of methyl bromide permitted to be used for critical uses in the European Community from 1 January to 31 December 2005 pursuant to the Regulation).

[71] 50 CFR §§ 23.1–23.92.

[72] For the phenomenon of (dynamic) references to international environmental instruments generally, see Jürgen Friedrich and Eva Julia Lohse, "Spaces of Normativity' – Revisiting the Junctures of International and Domestic Administration in Times of New Forms of Governance: Modes of Implementing Standards for Sustainable Development and Their Legitimacy Challenges' (2008) 2 *European Journal of Legal Studies* 49, 61–62.

[73] Art 34.2(g) and (h), and Art 36.4 of Commission Regulation 1808/2001.

[74] CITES COP Res Conf 12.7 (Rev CoP16).

[75] *X tegen de Staat (Import Kaviaar)*, LJN: AX8598 (Rb. Haarlem), 11 May 2006.

[76] Art 3(2)(ii) of EC Regulation No 2037/2000.

[77] Court of First Instance of the European Union, Case T-216/05 *Mebrom NV v Commission*, Judgment of the Court of 22 May 2007.

Some implementing acts even directly incorporate parts of the content of PTRs, rather than referring to them. US implementing acts of CITES include parts of various resolutions and decisions adopted by consecutive CITES COPs, and are regularly amended in this respect.[78] There is at least one known case, involving the importation of a protected species of hardwood, in which a court relied on such an incorporation to include Resolution 13.7 of the CITES COP in its analysis.[79]

2. Particular Issues Concerning Monist States: Validity and Direct Applicability

PTRs are not among the category of instruments that monist states tend to accord domestic *validity*, which is a condition to achieve the status of law in monist domestic legal orders. Monist states tend to look to *international* legal validity in according domestic legal validity. As a result, MEAs, being international conventions, will in principle be valid law within monist states. However, as it was concluded above that PTRs are not a formal source of international law, neither are they domestic law in monist legal orders. Some voices in US legal scholarship have argued that a domestic legal status for PTRs would moreover be barred by a constitutional limit to international delegations.[80] However, several other US legal scholars reacted with surprise[81] when the Court of Appeals in the *NRDC v EPA* case reflected, in a dictum, that '[a] holding that the Parties' postratification side agreements were "law" would raise serious constitutional questions in light of the nondelegation doctrine, numerous constitutional procedural requirements for making law, and the separation of powers'.[82] Most commentators to the

[78] See regular amendments to the *Federal Regulations Implementing the Convention on International Trade in Endangered Species of Wild Fauna and Flora (CITES)* 50 CFR § 23, eg by 72 Fed Reg 48,402 (23 August 2007).

[79] See *US v 1866.75 Board Feet and 11 Doors and Casings, More or Less, of Dipteryx Panamensis Imported from Nicaragua*, 587 F.Supp.2d 740 (E.D.Va.), 24 November 2008, pp 745–46 ('the Court recognises that both parties cited Conference Resolution 13.7 as providing guidance regarding the household effect exception, and the FWS indicates that *the provisions of Conference 13 were included in this revised version of the statute. Therefore* in the section of this analysis where the Court discusses the application of the exception for household effects to the facts of this case, *the Court finds it appropriate to consult the amended statute in order to glean further insight into the intended application of the exception*') (emphasis added).

[80] Julian G Ku, 'The Delegation of Federal Power to International Organizations: New Problems with Old Solutions' (2000) 313 *Minnesota Law Review* 71; Alice L Bodnar, 'NRDC v. EPA: Testing the Waters of the Constitutionality of Delegation to International Organizations' (2007) 34 *Ecology Law Quarterly* 895.

[81] John H Knox, 'Natural Resources Defense Council v. Environmental Protection Agency 464 F.3d 1' (2007) 101 *American Journal of International Law* 471, 477; Duncan Hollis, 'NRDC v. EPA: Are IO Decisions Really Only Political Commitments?', *Opinio Juris*, 5 September 2006; Andrew D Finkelman, 'Agreements of the Parties to the Montreal Protocol: Law or Politics? An Analysis of Natural Resources Defense Council v. EPA' (2007) 93 *Iowa Law Review* 665.

[82] *NRDC v EPA*, p 9.

NRDC case dismissed the Court's dictum that a US domestic court's application of PTRs would violate the non-delegation doctrine.[83]

The route to applicability of PTRs *via* the validity of MEAs is theoretically blocked by a further barrier: the requirement that treaty provisions need to be 'self-executive'[84] or 'directly applicable',[85] or a comparable requirement, such as the EU's doctrine of the 'nature and broad logic' of a provision.[86] Most monist (leaning) states have some such constitutional rule or doctrine in place to prevent application by their courts of treaty provisions that are insufficiently specific or insufficiently mandatorily formulated to function as 'objective law' without further law making by the legislator or administrative agencies,[87] or that were not intended by the parties or other relevant actors to function as law before legislative implementation.[88] *Prima facie*, this poses a difficult hurdle, because most MEA provisions on which PTRs are based do not conform to the usual tests for direct applicability (objective intent, precision, nature and broad logic, etc). However, in practice, this has turned out to be rarely problematic, in large part because also in monist states, as we have seen above, MEAs are often incorporated into domestic legislative acts. Therefore, it is not necessary to go into detail as regards the precise scope of direct applicability in various domestic jurisdictions.

In fact, this study found only one domestic court case in which direct applicability was raised as an issue. In the previously discussed case *Lac Sorobon*, the Dutch Crown Court (Council of State) surprisingly declared that the requirement of direct applicability did not prevent Article 3.1 of the Ramsar Convention, certainly a prime example of a treaty provision that is not directly applicable, from constituting the basis for the Court's judgment of the legality of the Governor's revocation of a licence to build a resort within 500 metres of the Lac Sorobon wetland.[89] The mere *validity* of the Ramsar Convention in the Netherlands' legal

[83] Knox, 'Natural Resources Defense Council'; Finkelman, 'An Analysis of NRDC v. EPA'. More open to the argument is Bodnar, 'NRDC v. EPA: Testing the Waters'.

[84] For a definition of the US law concept of 'self-executive', see Carlos Manuel Vázquez, 'The Four Doctrines of Self-Executing Treaties' (1995) 89 *American Journal of International Law* 695, 695 ('At a general level, a self-executing treaty may be defined as a treaty that may be enforced in the courts without prior legislation by Congress').

[85] In international law, the first important reference to 'direct applicability' is *Jurisdiction of the Courts of Danzig* (Advisory Opinion) PCIJ Rep Series B No 15.

[86] European Court of Justice, Joined Cases C-21/72 to 24/72 *International Fruit Co v Produktschap voor Groenten en Fruit (No. 3)*, Judgment of the Court of 12 December 1972; Joined Cases C-120/06 P and C-121/06 P *Fabbrica italiana accumulatori motocarri Montecchio SpA (FIAMM) and Fedon v Council and Others*, Judgment of the Court of 9 September 2008; Case C-308/06 *Intertanko and Others*, Judgment of the Court of 3 June 2008.

[87] David Sloss, 'Domestic Application of Treaties' in: Duncan B Hollis (ed), *The Oxford Guide to Treaties* (OUP, 2012) 367, 387, citing André Nollkaemper, 'The Netherlands' in David Sloss (ed), *The Role of Domestic Courts in Treaty Enforcement: A Comparative Study* (CUP, 2009), 333.

[88] The US doctrine of self-executive/non-self-executive treaties initially focused on this intent element. See Vázquez, 'The Four Doctrines of Self-Executing Treaties' 710–11.

[89] *Lac Sorobon*, para 2.2.3.5. On the absence of the requirements of direct applicability and invocability when courts in the Netherlands have to judge the exercise of discretionary powers by the executive branch against international environmental law, see André Nollkaemper, 'Compliance Control in

order was deemed sufficient.[90] Since there are no other known cases in which this issue arose in such a direct way,[91] it is difficult to say anything more general on the subject. Nonetheless, considering the large number of MEA provisions that are phrased in language which normally stands in the way of direct applicability, this remains a point to which attention must be paid in monist (leaning) states.[92]

When direct applicability is refused, there is still indirect applicability of treaties to turn to. According to surveys, 'indirect application' of international treaties through treaty-conforming interpretation of national law (including implementing legislation) makes up the greatest number of cases in which international environmental law plays a role in national courts.[93] In most domestic jurisdictions, it is normal practice that judges assume that the legislator, in implementing international (environmental) treaties as well as in legislating generally, 'is not presumed to intend a violation of international law. … Given that legislators will rarely legislate in explicit contradiction to international law, courts have considerable room to use international environmental law as interpretive aid'.[94] The advantages of treaty-consistent interpretation, from the point of view of effective implementation of IEL, are that the validity, direct applicability, and invocability by or against private persons of the relevant treaty provisions are no longer a requirement.[95] Indirect applicability allows for the interpretation of national environmental legislation in the light of MEAs. But indirect applicability is limited to (legally binding) international law. It does not extend to PTRs.

E. Conclusion

After this exposé of the limited extent to which the authority of PTRs can be traced back to an intention in the act of delegation, the environmental treaty, most would agree with the following statement by Wiersema: asking whether PTRs can be categorised within the formal sources of international law, law in the

International Environmental Law: Traversing the Limits of the National Legal Order' (2002) 13 *Yearbook of International Environmental Law* 167, 180.

[90] *Lac Sorobon*, para 2.2.3.5. See for analysis Verschuuren, 'Ramsar Soft Law Is Not Soft at All'.

[91] In *Face the Future*, para 4.2.1., a Netherlands administrative court did not preclude that the private claimant might have been barred from basing its claim on the Kyoto Protocol and the relevant COP/MOP decisions.

[92] Voicing this concern in relation to domestic judicial application is Carl Bruch, 'Is International Environmental Law Really Law? An Analysis of Application in Domestic Courts' (2006) 23 *Pace Environmental Law Review* 423, 424. Also Daniel Bodansky and Jutta Brunnée, 'Introduction: The Role of National Courts in the Field of International Environmental Law' in Michael Anderson and Paolo Galizzi (eds), *International Environmental Law in National Courts* (BIICL, 2002), 12; Catherine Redgwell, 'National Implementation' in Daniel Bodansky, Jutta Brunnée and Ellen Hey (eds), *The Oxford Handbook of International Environmental Law* (OUP, 2007), 933.

[93] Bodansky and Brunnée, 'Introduction: The Role of National Courts', 13.

[94] ibid.

[95] Nollkaemper, 'Compliance Control in International Environmental Law', 180.

international legal order, 'is asking the wrong question'.[96] And the same can be said for the internal normative orders: one searches in vain for signs in the MEAs, in procedural PTRs, in the practice of the treaty meetings and subsidiary bodies, that the degree of authority that PTRs have in practice, whether high or low, has a clear origin in the delegation to adopt PTRs as such. In the national legal orders, finally, the story is no different, since these have to work with the same material, the doctrine of the sources and the text of the MEAs, and their own doctrines for the domestic validity of international law, into which PTRs clearly do not fit. The initial delegation thus tells us little about the *degree or extent* of a PTR's authority. Perhaps more information can be found in the product of the exercise of the act of delegation: in the interpretive authority of PTRs according to the doctrine of interpretation.

[96] Wiersema calls this the search for a qualification of PTRs as 'stand-alone legal obligations that can be assessed independently of the original treaty': Wiersema, 'The New International Law-Makers', 250, 266. Wiersema further notes, at 258, 264, that 'attempts to analyse COP activity according to conventional standards for finding legal obligation are fraught with difficulty', and that 'a one-size-fits-all determination of their legal status or relationship to underlying treaty obligations is impossible'.

4

'Taking into Account': Interpretive Authority and Wording

Can an instrument that does not have the status of binding law still affect legal obligations in other ways, and could this explain the authority of PTRs? Theoretically, that would be an option most international lawyers accept by now. Even instruments that do not have the status of law can create or affect legal obligations in ways not captured by the concept of 'legally binding'. The binary nature of 'law' or 'not law' does not exclude that there are more than two shades of legal *obligation*. In debates among international legal theorists, that notion is called relative legal normativity.[1] The search for the sources of the authority of PTRs takes much more from this relative legal normativity than from the binary question of legal status, which the previous chapter found did not provide satisfying answers. But what do these different degrees of legal normativity look like?

An instrument may be an 'ordinary' legal obligation with which the addressee has to 'act in accordance', such as a treaty, a unilateral promise, or a domestic statute, i.e. what international lawyers usually call 'legally binding', or simply 'law'. The addressee or applier has to follow the instrument's development of the norm in question,[2] except for the existence of conflicting instruments that carry a comparable or peremptory legal obligation.[3] The previous chapter searched in vain for indications that PTRs are in this category.

Yet even instruments emerging from the international activities of states that do not have the status of law can still be accorded a certain *effect* on other legal obligations. Such an effect must inevitably be considered a *legal* effect, as it changes the content of the law. Classic examples of this are the contributions of non-legally

[1] The term was coined in Prosper Weil, 'Towards Relative Normativity in International Law?' (1983) 77 *American Journal of International Law* 413. See also Matthias Goldmann, 'Inside Relative Normativity: From Sources to Standard Instruments for the Exercise of International Public Authority' in Armin Von Bogdandy et al (ed), *The Exercise of Public Authority by International Institutions* (Springer, 2010), 671 ('Relative positions, however, assume that different grades of legal normativity are conceivable. In the case of international law, some relativists suggest a continuum ranging from non-law to ius cogens.').

[2] Federick Schauer, *Thinking Like a Lawyer: A New Introduction to Legal Reasoning* (Harvard University Press, 2009), 69 ('They are mandatory in the sense that they must be used and in the sense that they must be followed.').

[3] ibid, 62 ('When a rule (or a command, an order, or an instruction) is authoritative, its subjects are expected to obey regardless of their own opinions of its wisdom.').

binding instruments to the formation of customary law,[4] such as various principles from the Rio Declaration on Environment and Development or various articles in the ILC Articles on the Responsibility of International Organizations. Another example is the legal effect of subsequent agreements and subsequent practice, which include, as this chapter sets out to show, environmental post-treaty rules. A breach of such 'ancillary' instruments, as others have called them, is in fact not really a breach of the ancillary instrument, but of the obligation that it has affected. In the case of interpretive instruments, then, not complying with the interpretive instrument might constitute a breach of the underlying treaty. So too, in the case of non-binding declarations that affect the formation of customary law it is the latter that is capable of being breached, not the former.

The distinction between legally binding instruments and instruments that affect legal obligation, although not themselves being legally binding, can also be viewed as a distinction between delegated authority and interpretive authority. D'Aspremont calls instruments with merely legal effects 'legal *facts*' rather than 'legal *acts*', arguing that it is the secondary rules of the legal system, not the intention of the parties, that creates the legal effect of this category.[5] In the case of 'legal acts', he maintains, states are directly 'willing' to create an instrument with legal effect.[6] D'Aspremont's statement is perhaps too strong. Treaty parties are aware of how they must show their intention to conclude a binding treaty, but they are also aware of the existence of secondary rules of the international legal system concerning the formation of customary law of the interpretation of treaties. Nonetheless, it is no doubt true that states have more direct influence over the legal obligations they create by concluding a treaty than by adopting all sorts of other instruments that the legal system might in some way attach weight to. The legal effect of non-legally binding instruments may only materialise years later, in ways not foreseen at the time of their adoption. The search for the authority of PTRs not as legally binding but as non-legally binding instruments is therefore a search for their *interpretive authority*.

Since the internal normative orders completely eschew any discussion of PTRs as having an effect on the legal obligations of the parties, this chapter concentrates on the international legal order and the national legal orders. Since the low threshold of both for recognising the activities of treaty parties as *to some extent* relevant for the interpretation of treaty obligations, the chapter quickly

[4] Goldmann, 'Inside Relative Normativity', 672 ('non-binding instruments are seen as important evidence of the existence of opinio iuris').

[5] Jean d'Aspremont, 'Softness in International Law: A Self-Serving Quest for New Legal Materials' (2008) 19 *European Journal of International Law* 1075, 1079 ('those acts which yield legal effects but which are not a direct consequence of the will of legal persons cannot be considered legal acts. Their legal effects originate in the legal system itself, which provides for such an effect prior to the adoption of the act.').

[6] d'Aspremont, 'Softness in International Law', 1078 ('To enable it to qualify as a legal act, the legal effect of the act in question must directly originate in the will of the legal subject to whom the behaviour is attributed and not to any pre-existing rule in the system.').

finds itself walking down a by now familiar pattern. Just as the qualification of PTRs as delegated acts was as unproblematic as the issue of the *degree of authority* this resulted in was problematic, the qualification of PTRs as interpretive acts in the sense of the Vienna Convention on the Law of Treaties is the easiest part. Most PTRs do indeed qualify as subsequent agreements. However, what that means exactly for the obligations of treaty parties, whether in the international or national legal orders, is much less straightforward. Yet again, the causal effect between the legal qualifications of PTRs as official means of interpretation and their authority in practice appears to be thin. Why would a subsequent agreement prevail over an interpretation in accordance with the practice of the treaty parties, or with the object and purpose of the treaty? The law of treaties does not provide a clear answer.

Of course, one might riposte, the exact obligation that an instrument, whether legally binding or not, creates for its addressees depends on its content, on its wording. The wording may turn the scales in favour of the subsequent agreement over other means of interpretation. The final section of this chapter indeed finds some correlation between the mandatory or recommendatory nature of a PTR's wording and its authority in practice. Nonetheless, there are numerous counterexamples of PTRs with recommendatory wording that still turn out to be decisive for judgments of international and national courts, and vice versa. Although interpretive authority is able to explain much more convincingly than delegated authority the authority of PTRs in practice, the gaps between the prescribed interpretive weight of PTRs and their actual weight in practice remain glaring.

A. PTRs as Interpretive Agreements in the International Legal Order

1. PTRs as 'Subsequent Agreements'

In the past decade, the issue of subsequent agreements and practice has received growing attention not only from scholarship, but also in the International Law Commission's reports by Special Rapporteur Georg Nolte.[7] These reports, which appeared in the period between 2013 and 2018, include detailed attention to the position of environmental post-treaty rules as special kinds of subsequent agreements and practice.[8]

[7] For a collection of all documents relating to this project, officially named *Subsequent agreements and subsequent practice in relation to interpretation of treaties*, visit http://legal.un.org/ilc/guide/1_11.shtml.

[8] Particularly in A/CN.4/660, *Second report on subsequent agreements and subsequent practice in relation to treaty interpretation, of the Special Rapporteur, Mr. Georg Nolte* (65th session of the ILC (2014)), pp 36–48.

The authoritative definitions of subsequent agreements and subsequent practice can be found in Article 31 of the Vienna Convention on the Law of Treaties. Article 31.2, 31.3(a) and (b) of the VCLT, as relevant, respectively recognise as means of treaty interpretation:

> 2. The context for the purpose of the interpretation of a treaty shall comprise, in addition to the text, including its preamble and annexes:
>
> (a) any agreement relating to the treaty which was made between all the parties in connection with the conclusion of the treaty;
>
> ...
>
> 3. There shall be taken into account, together with the context:
>
> (a) any subsequent agreement between the parties regarding the interpretation of the treaty or the application of its provisions;
>
> (b) any subsequent practice in the application of the treaty which establishes the agreement of the parties regarding its interpretation;[9]

Most PTRs come closest to the 'subsequent agreements' of paragraph 3(a). However, the numerous decisions adopted under the Kyoto Protocol, preceding the ratification of that protocol by the parties, better fit the description of 2(a): agreements 'adopted in connection with the conclusion of the treaty'.[10] The practice of the parties collectively or their combined individual practices with regard to the *implementation* of PTRs falls within the 'subsequent practice' under 3(b).

As a preliminary matter, it is important to establish whether (the majority of) PTRs *qualify* as subsequent agreements and/or practice on interpretation or application at all.[11] The main conditions for an instrument to qualify as a 'subsequent agreement' are: 1) that it constitutes an 'agreement'; 2) that it is an agreement 'between the parties'; and 3) that it concerns 'the interpretation of the treaty or the application of its provisions' (Article 31.3(a) VCLT). In light of these conditions, a number of objections can and have been raised against the qualification of PTRs as 'subsequent agreements', but with regard to the majority of PTRs, these objections can be countered. As submitted by Special Rapporteur Nolte's reports, however, decisions of Conferences of the Parties 'do not automatically constitute a subsequent agreement under article 31(3)(a) since it must always be specifically established'.[12]

[9] Vienna Convention on the Law of Treaties (adopted 23 May 1969, entered into force 27 January 1980) 1155 UNTS 331 (VCLT).

[10] Art 31.2 VCLT.

[11] Annecoos Wiersema, 'The New International Law-Makers? Conferences of the Parties to Multilateral Environmental Agreements' (2009) 31 *Michigan Journal of International Law* 231, 247, 276–79; Jutta Brunnée, 'COPing with Consent: Law-Making Under Multilateral Environmental Agreements' (2002) 15 *Leiden Journal of International Law* 1, 31; Churchill and Ulfstein, 'Autonomous Institutional Arrangements', 641; Patricia Birnie, Alan Boyle and Patricia Redgwell, *International Law and the Environment* 3rd edn (OUP, 2009); Alan Boyle, 'Some Reflections on the Relationship of Treaties and Soft Law' (1999) 48 *International and Comparative Law Quarterly* 901.

[12] Nolte, *Second Report*, p 43.

Nolte also mentions a fourth requirement – or a more demanding first requirement – that in order to create a subsequent agreement, the treaty parties must intend that their agreement has legal, not just political significance: 'Such an intention is identifiable in particular by the specificity and the clarity of the terms chosen in the light of the text of the Conference of the States Parties decision as a whole.'[13] With all due respect to the Special Rapporteur, the problem with considering this to be a *sine qua non* for the existence of a subsequent agreement is that it requires interpretation itself, and raises the issue of where to draw the line. Moreover, as Nolte himself admits, PTRs are adopted by consensus, which 'is not a concept which necessarily indicates any degree of agreement on substance'.[14] And more fundamentally, it seems odd to equate the specificity and the clarity of the terms of a PTR with the intention to create an agreement. Why would it not be possible to agree on unspecified or unclear rules? Treaties are full of unspecified and unclear rules, and no-one would deny them the qualification 'treaty'. This is not to say that the wording of a PTR does not matter for its interpretive authority, but it is part of a later step in the interpretive process: what the weight of a particular PTR in the interpretive process should be (section C).

a. 'Agreement'

To begin with the more narrow condition of an *agreement*, then, the fact that PTRs are not *formal* agreements, i.e. are not themselves treaties, does not stand in the way of their qualification as subsequent agreements under Article 31 VCLT. As one authority on the subject states unequivocally: the '"agreement" does not have to be in treaty form but must be such as to show that the parties intended their understanding to be the basis for an agreed interpretation'.[15] In its *travaux préparatoires*, the ILC speaks simply of an 'agreement':

> Similarly, an agreement as to the interpretation of a provision reached after the conclusion of the treaty represents an authentic interpretation by the parties which must be read into the treaty for purposes of its interpretation.[16]

The very rationale behind Article 31.3(a) was that informal – i.e. non-treaty – agreements could be used to develop the meaning of treaty provisions, as long as they would not outright contradict clear treaty terms.

b. 'Between the Parties'

A second point to be raised in the qualification of PTRs as subsequent agreements is whether PTRs fulfil the requirement that there should be an agreement *between*

[13] ibid.
[14] Nolte, *Second Report*, p 46.
[15] Richard K Gardiner, *Treaty Interpretation* (OUP, 2007), 217–18. See also Anthony Aust, *Modern Treaty Law and Practice* 2nd edn (CUP, 2007), 191 ('[p]rovided the purpose is clear, the agreement can take various forms, including a decision adopted by a meeting of the parties').
[16] *Yearbook of the International Law Commission*, 1966, Vol II, p 221, para 14.

the parties. To what extent does it have to be established that *all* parties collectively, or even *each* party individually, expressed their agreement to the adoption of a PTR, so that it qualifies under Article 31.3(a)? Does consensus in the plenary meeting, the absence of formal objection, imply that the parties have 'reached a firm agreement'?[17] Does adoption of a PTR by (qualified) majority vote in the plenary meeting also suffice, as the ICJ has accepted in the past for QMV resolutions of the General Assembly?[18] The standard treatises on treaty interpretation all highlight this element, but defend quite different views. Villiger rather categorically takes the position that the means of interpretation listed in Article 31 paras 2 and 3(a) and (b) 'can only be invoked if all the parties to the treaty have been involved', 'whereby all parties themselves agree on (or at least tacitly accept) the interpretation of treaty terms'.[19] Gardiner more cautiously submits that the agreement 'must be such as to show that the parties intended their understanding to be the basis for an agreed interpretation'.[20] Elsewhere, he states that if a 'resolution was adopted by consensus, it seems clear that it is to be taken as part of the context of the treaty for purposes of interpretation', but does not exclude that non-consensual subsequent agreements may also have to be taken into account to some (possibly more limited) degree.[21]

The ICJ's long-time jurisprudence on the decisions of international organisations accepted that subsequent *practice* (Article 31.3(b) VCLT) included the decisions of organs of international organisations, and even included majority decisions. In *Certain Expenses*, the ICJ found the consistent practice of the General Assembly to be an authentic and appropriate guide to the meaning of the UN Charter.[22] The series of UNGA resolutions on which the Court relied were 'adopted by the requisite two-thirds majority', not by consensus.[23] In the *Wall* Opinion, the Court also relied on qualified majority resolutions of the UNGA in its interpretation of Article 12 UN Charter, adopted in the face of substantial negative votes.[24]

There are, however, four important differences between this ICJ jurisprudence and the question of whether the limited number of non-consensual (i.e. majoritarian) PTRs would qualify as being 'between the parties' in the definition of

[17] Gardiner, '*Treaty Interpretation*', 217. Also Georg Schwarzenberger, 'Myths and Realities of Treaty Interpretation: Arts 27–29 of the Vienna Draft Convention on the Law of Treaties' (1968) 9 *Virginia Journal of International Law* 1, 11.

[18] *Certain Expenses of the United Nations (Article 17, paragraph 2, of the Charter)* (Advisory Opinion) [1962] ICJ Rep 151, p 174; *Legal Consequences of the Construction of a Wall in the Occupied Palestinian Territory* (Advisory Opinion) [2004] ICJ Rep 136, para 27. For analysis, see Julian Arato, 'Treaty Interpretation and Constitutional Transformation: Informal Change in International Organizations' (2012) 38 *Yale Journal of International Law* 289, 320, 325.

[19] Mark E Villiger, 'The 1969 Vienna Convention on the Law of Treaties – 40 Years After' (2009) 344 *RdC* 9, 119–20.

[20] Gardiner, '*Treaty Interpretation*', 217–18.

[21] ibid, 81.

[22] *Certain Expenses*, pp 157–65; Arato, 'Treaty Interpretation and Constitutional Transformation', 219.

[23] *Certain Expenses*, p 174.

[24] *Construction of a Wall*, para 27.

'subsequent agreements'. First, in *Certain Expenses* and *Construction of a Wall*, the ICJ considered large volumes of consecutive resolutions and actions taken on the same issue (peacekeeping budgets, involvement of the UNGA in issues the SC is dealing with), and viewed them *together* as subsequent *practice*. The present section, however, is dealing with the question whether *single* post-treaty rules can qualify as subsequent *agreements*. Second, *Certain Expenses* and *Construction of a Wall* were dealing with the United Nations, a formal international organisation with organs with a will of their own.[25] By contrast, PTRs are adopted in loosely institutionalised frameworks for inter-state cooperation. Third, for the UNGA, it is well established in the Charter that it can adopt resolutions by qualified majority,[26] while with the exception of the Montreal Protocol Rules of Procedure, all MEA Rules of Procedure state that the Parties should strive for consensus. Moreover, as opposed to the UNGA, environmental plenary meetings have no solidified practice of majority decisions. Fourth, *Certain Expenses* and *Construction of a Wall* approach the UNGA resolutions as subsequent practice ('the practice of the United Nations')[27] more than as subsequent agreements. Here, we are examining whether PTRs are subsequent agreements in the first place, not whether their implementation constitutes subsequent practice. The conditions in the VCLT are not identical for both. Finally, the ICJ is the officially designated judicial entity to give Advisory Opinions about the UN Charter and to the UN organs.[28] MEAs and their plenary meetings are further at the periphery of the UN system. This line of jurisprudence is therefore only indirectly relevant to determine what the phrase 'between the parties' in Article 31.3(a) means in the context of environmental PTRs.

Recently, in the case of *Whaling in the Antarctic*, the ICJ has specifically adopted a position on the meaning of the phrase 'between the parties' with regard to the resolutions of an international plenary meeting, the International Whaling Committee (IWC). The *Whaling* case concerned a dispute between Australia and Japan (New Zealand intervening) regarding the interpretation of the International Convention on the Regulation of Whaling (ICRW). The ICRW is normally grouped with the environmental regimes and MEAs, rather than seen as a formal international organisation, even though its plenary meeting was set up with legal personality.[29]

For the international regulation of whaling, 1982 was an important year. The International Whaling Committee (IWC), the plenary meeting to the ICRW,

[25] Julian Arato, 'Subsequent Practice in the Whaling Case, and What the ICJ Implies about Treaty Interpretation in International Organizations', *EJIL: Talk!*, 31 March 2014, at www.ejiltalk.org/subsequent-practice-in-the-whaling-case-and-what-the-icj-implies-about-treaty-interpretation-in-international-organizations/#more-10605.

[26] Art 18.2 Charter of the United Nations (adopted 26 June 1945, entered into force 24 October 1945) (UN Charter).

[27] *Construction of a Wall*, paras 27–28.

[28] ibid.

[29] Nolte, *Second Report* p 37 calls the ICW 'a borderline case' of a Conference of the Parties.

adopted a 'moratorium on commercial whaling'.[30] But this moratorium was not complete in one important respect. The exception for 'scientific whaling' in Article VIII of the International Convention for the Regulation of Whaling:

> Notwithstanding anything contained in the Convention any Contracting Government may grant to any of its nationals a special permit authorizing that national to kill, take and treat whales for purposes of scientific research subject to such other conditions as the Contracting Government thinks fit, and the killing, taking, and treating of whales in accordance with the provisions of this Article shall be exempt from the operation of this Convention.

In order to safeguard that Article VIII ICRW would not be used to circumvent the moratorium, but only for genuine scientific research, the IWC adopted a set of recommendations, through Resolution 1986-2.[31] Most importantly, Resolution 1986-2:

> Recommends that Contracting Governments when considering proposed research permits and the Scientific Committee when reviewing such permits and when reviewing the results of research from permits previously issued in accordance with the procedures of the Convention should take into account whether:
>
> (1) the objectives of the research are not practically and scientifically feasible through non-lethal research techniques.

Furthermore, since the mid-1980s, the Scientific Committee of the ICRW has conducted its review of special permit Research Plans – which member states are obligated to submit in advance of granting actual permits to whalers in accordance with Paragraph 30 of the Schedule – also on the basis of 'Guidelines' issued or endorsed by the Commission.[32]

Immediately after the moratorium entered into force, Japan commenced the issuing of special permits: the Japanese Whale Research Program under Special Permit in the Antarctic (JARPA).[33] In its Application to the International Court of Justice two decades later, Australia argued that Japan's scientific

[30] Paragraph 10(e) of the *Schedule*: 'Notwithstanding the other provisions of paragraph 10, catch limits for the killing for commercial purposes of whales from all stocks for the 1986 coastal and the 1985/86 pelagic seasons and thereafter shall be zero. This provision will be kept under review, based upon the best scientific advice, and by 1990 at the latest the Commission will undertake a comprehensive assessment of the effects of this decision on whale stocks and consider modification of this provision and the establishment of other catch limits'.

[31] IWC Resolution 1986-2, 38th Annual Meeting, 1986 (*Rep. int. Whal. Commn 37*). Art VI of the International Convention for the Regulation of Whaling (adopted 2 December 1946, entered into force 10 November 1948) 161 UNTS 72 (ICRW) states that '[t]he Commission may from time to time make recommendations to any or all Contracting Governments on any matters which relate to whales or whaling and to the objectives and purposes of this Convention'.

[32] These are collected in the 'Annex Y: Guidelines for the Review of Scientific Permit Proposals'. The most current Guidelines are set forth in a document entitled 'Annex P: Process for the Review of Special Permit Proposals and Research Results from Existing and Completed Permits'.

[33] *Whaling in the Antarctic (Australia v Japan: New Zealand intervening)* (Judgment) [2014] ICJ Rep 226, paras 98–125.

whaling programme (by now called JARPA II) was 'not for purposes of scientific research' in the sense of Article VIII ICRW, as such amounted to commercial whaling 'in disguise', and therefore violated a number of important prohibitions in the so-called Schedule, such as the zero-catch limit (moratorium on commercial whaling) and the Southern Ocean Sanctuary. For an important part, this position was based on Resolution 1986-2. Australia even went so far as to argue that Article VIII, when read in accordance with Resolution 1986-2, 'authorises the granting of special permits to kill, take and treat whales only when non-lethal methods are not available',[34] a reading that goes beyond what is stated in the Resolution – i.e. that the availability of other methods 'should be taken into account'.

The majority view of the ICJ regarding the authority of Resolution 1986-2 was that Japan '*should give due regard to recommendations* calling for an assessment of the feasibility of non-lethal alternatives'. This is of course very abstract: what does it mean to 'give due regard' to a recommendation that 'should be taken into account'? Later in the judgment, however, it becomes clear that the Court really takes the view that Japan is under an obligation to do exactly as the Resolution recommended:

> The Court concludes that the papers to which Japan directed it reveal little analysis of the feasibility of using non-lethal methods to achieve the JARPA II research objectives. *Nor do they point to consideration of the possibility of making more extensive use of non-lethal methods in order to reduce or eliminate the need for lethal sampling*, either when JARPA II was proposed or in subsequent years. Given the expanded use of lethal methods in JARPA II, as compared to JARPA, this is difficult to reconcile with Japan's *obligation* to give due regard to IWC resolutions and Guidelines and its statement that JARPA II uses lethal methods only to the extent necessary to meet its scientific objectives.[35] (Emphasis added.)

In other words, although the Resolution is worded as a recommendation, the majority of the Court considers it obligatory for Japan to have actually, meaningfully considered the availability of non-lethal methods.

But on the basis of what legal argumentation did the ICJ come to this conclusion regarding the authority of the IWC PTRs over the parties? The Court started from the position that recommendations and guidelines, which take the form of resolutions, 'are not binding. However, *when they are adopted by consensus or by a unanimous vote*, they may be relevant for the interpretation of the Convention or its Schedule.'[36] The Court thus establishes point blank that *only* resolutions adopted by consensus or unanimous vote may be relevant for the interpretation of the Convention. Other recommendations and resolutions are not relevant for the interpretation of the ICRW *at all*: non-consensual IWC resolutions do not

[34] *Whaling in the Antarctic*, para 78.
[35] *Whaling in the Antarctic*, para 144.
[36] *Whaling in the Antarctic*, para 46.

constitute subsequent practice either. In paragraph 83, the Court applies this position to the case:

> Australia and New Zealand overstate the legal significance of the recommendatory resolutions and Guidelines on which they rely. First, many IWC resolutions were *adopted without the support of all States parties* to the Convention and, in particular, *without the concurrence of Japan*. Thus, such instruments cannot be regarded as subsequent agreement to an interpretation of Article VIII, nor as subsequent practice establishing an agreement of the parties regarding the interpretation of the treaty within the meaning of subparagraphs (a) and (b), respectively, of paragraph (3) of Article 31 of the Vienna Convention on the Law of Treaties.[37] (Emphasis added.)

Unfortunately, the Court does not entirely clarify whether this requirement is based on the ICRW's voting rules and other ICRW rules on the validity of its PTRs, or whether this requirement is based on Article 31 VCLT directly. It appears that the Court indicates the latter, however, so that even if an MEA's voting rules *allow* for QMV or simple majority adoption of PTRs, PTRs adopted in that way would at the very least not be relevant to the interpretation of the underlying MEA in which a treaty party voting against the PTR is involved. The judgment may even go one step further, that is to strike down majoritarian PTRs altogether, regardless of whether one or more of the parties before it were in the minority or not.

For most future disputes involving environmental PTRs, the impact of this part of the *Whaling* case will, however, be limited. Most environmental post-treaty instruments *are* adopted by consensus, even if the respective Rules of Procedure of the different MEAs allow for majority or qualified majority adoption in theory. That is, unless one takes seriously the rather strict description of consensus the Court uses – 'the support of all States parties to the Convention'[38] – a description closer to the accepted definition of unanimity than of consensus. What level of 'support' would this require? Most of the time, consensual PTRs are adopted by tacit acquiescence rather than through explicit acclaim. In exceptional cases, PTRs are even adopted in the face of objection by one or more parties, such as happened in the case of the Bolivian objection against the Kyoto Protocol Cancun Agreements.[39]

c. *'Regarding the Interpretation of the Treaty or the Application of its Provisions'*

A third condition for PTRs to qualify as 'subsequent agreements' is that they *concern the interpretation of the treaty or the application of its provisions*. Three possible obstacles have been raised in accordance with this final condition: 1) that gap-filling or supplementing PTRs fall outside the definition of 'subsequent

[37] *Whaling in the Antarctic*, para 83.
[38] ibid.
[39] See ch 7, section A.2.

agreements'; 2) that 'subsequent agreements' do not extend to modifying PTRs; and 3) that even PTRs of an interpretive character may only make slight changes so as to qualify as subsequent agreements.

Some commentators have argued that PTRs based on explicit enabling clauses are not 'subsequent agreements' in the sense of Article 31.3(a), because they are gap-filling agreements, not 'agreements on interpretation'. Brunnée, for instance, discusses the relevance of Article 31.3(a) and (b) VCLT only with regard to PTRs of an interpretive character,[40] and in the already discussed *NRDC v EPA* case, the US District Court refused to construct PTRs based on explicit enabling clauses as interpretive agreements.[41] This is a serious challenge, since gap-filling agreements include the Kyoto Protocol *Flexibility Mechanisms* Decisions, *Accounting Modalities* and *LULUCF* Decisions, as well as the Montreal Protocol *Critical Use Criteria* and *Exemption Decisions*. And technically it is true, as this study argues as well, that the filling of gaps that have been explicitly left in the treaty is not an act of interpretation.

Yet based on textual analysis of Article 31.3(a) and consultation of the proceedings of the Vienna Conference on the Law of Treaties, the view that this places them outside the purview of subsequent agreements is not correct. Initially, the draft version of paragraph (a) was indeed limited to agreements 'regarding the *interpretation* of the treaty' (emphasis added).[42] However, during the diplomatic conference that was held on the draft text – formally known as the Meetings of the Committee of the Whole – Pakistan submitted an amendment that could count on broad support, proposing to add 'or *implementation* of the treaty'[43] to the draft provision. Pakistan's delegate argued, in support of this amendment, that:

> [A]part from the case of subsequent agreements between the parties regarding the interpretation of the treaty, there were cases where the parties entered into subsequent agreements concerning the implementation of the treaty, which might shed light on their intentions.[44]

The Pakistan amendment was referred to the Drafting Committee, which decided to amend paragraph (a) using slightly different terms than suggested by Pakistan, but with largely the same implication, adding the words 'or the application of its

[40] Brunnée, 'COPing with Consent', 33.

[41] *NRDC v EPA*, p 9: 'Like any interpretive tool, however, the "decisions" are useful only to the extent they shed light on ambiguous terms in the Protocol. But the details of the critical-use exemption are not ambiguous. They are nonexistent. The "decisions" do not interpret treaty language. They fill in treaty gaps'.

[42] Draft Art 27, *Draft Articles on the Law of Treaties*, Yearbook of the International Law Commission, 1966, Vol II, p 217.

[43] A/CONF.39/14 *Report of the Committee of the Whole on its work at the first session of the Conference* (A/CONF.39/C.1/L.182), p 150.

[44] Mr Samaad, delegate of Pakistan, *31st Meeting of the Committee of the Whole*, 19 April 1968, para 53, p 168.

provisions' at the end of paragraph (a).[45] As a result, although PTRs based on explicit enabling clauses could be said to fall outside the scope of agreements on *interpretation*, they certainly fall within the scope of agreements on the *application* of the treaty, and thus within the scope of Article 31.3(a).[46]

Another issue is whether *modification* of the meaning of treaty provisions is allowed through subsequent agreements,[47] rather than through formal amendments.[48] Commentaries on the law of treaties and the VCLT object to modification by way of subsequent agreements in light of the deletion of Draft Article 38 VCLT at the Vienna Conference on the Law of Treaties.[49] That once prospective article allowed for treaty modification through informal means. Because it was deleted, it is implausible that Article 31.3(a) and (b) are to be understood as having *reintroduced* the possibility of informal modification.

Some confirmation of this point, in regard to PTRs specifically, can be found in the ICJ's *Pulp Mills* judgment. The *Pulp Mills* case did not arise out of a multilateral environmental agreement, but out of a dispute over a bilateral watercourse agreement, the 1975 Statute of the River Uruguay. It involved the consequences of the discharge of effluent by pulp mills located on the Uruguayan side of the river for the Argentine environment. Under the 1975 Statute, the so-called 'CARU Digests' adopted by the Administrative Commission of the River Uruguay (CARU) perform a very similar role to COP, COP/MOP and MOP decisions. But apart from the CARU, the two states also created, by later agreement, a negotiating framework called GTAN,[50] 'in order to study, analyse and exchange information on the effects that the operation of the cellulose plants that were being constructed in the Eastern Republic of Uruguay could have on the ecosystem of the shared Uruguay River'.[51] The two parties disputed whether this agreement suspended certain procedural obligations in the CARU, especially the obligation of Uruguay to consult with Argentina before taking further steps in the construction of its

[45] Stating that 'that addition was based on the Pakistan amendment'. *74th Meeting of the Committee of the Whole*, 16 May 1968, p 442, para 29.

[46] Gardiner, '*Treaty Interpretation*', 219–20 (noting that the text of paragraph 3 includes not only agreements explicitly on interpretation but also those that have implications for the interpretation of the treaty).

[47] See, eg, the questions raised in Gerhard Hafner, 'Subsequent Agreements and Practice: Between Interpretation, Informal Modification, and Formal Amendment' in Georg Nolte (ed), *Treaties and Subsequent Practice* (OUP, 2013) 105; José E Alvarez, 'Limits of Change by Way of Subsequent Agreements and Practice' in Georg Nolte (ed), *Treaties and Subsequent Practice* (OUP, 2013) 123.

[48] Note the difference between the present discussion and the discussion in ch 1, section E.4, on the legal validity of informal treaty modification *per se*.

[49] United Nations Conference on the Law of Treaties (First session, 26 March to 24 May 1968), A/CONF.39/C.1/SR.38, '38th meeting of the Committee of the Whole', 207; ibid (First and Second sessions 26 March to 24 May 1968 and 9 April to 22 May 1969), A/CONF.39/14, 'Report of the Committee of the Whole on its work at the first session of the Conference', 158; ILC, Yearbook, Vol II (1966), p 236. For a discussion, see Ingo Venzke, *How Interpretation Makes International Law: On Semantic Change and Normative Twists* (OUP, 2012), ch V.

[50] Spanish acronym of 'High-Level Technical Group'.

[51] *Pulp Mills on the River Uruguay (Argentina v Uruguay)* (Judgment) [2010] ICJ Rep 14, para 136.

pulp mills. The Court dismissed Uruguay's position, considering that an agreement set up by Argentina and Uruguay within the framework of a bilateral treaty between them:

> [W]hile indeed creating a negotiating body capable of enabling the Parties to pursue the same objective as that laid down in Article 12 of the 1975 Statute, cannot be interpreted as expressing the agreement of the Parties *to derogate from other procedural obligations laid down by the Statute*.[52] (Emphasis added.)

Thus, a subsequent agreement cannot run counter to, may not depart from, procedural rights provided by the underlying treaty. Although the majority of PTRs do not contradict the terms of the enabling clause, working within the often considerable margins of these terms instead, chapter two, section E showed that there are exceptions. When a PTR contradicts the underlying treaty provisions, there is a good chance that the ICJ would not accept its modification of the treaty should a dispute arise.

Finally, some scholars take an even stricter viewpoint on the scope of the changes in an agreement between treaty parties, in order for it to qualify as a subsequent agreement. Some make this point in a normative sense, debating whether subsequent agreements *should be allowed* to be used for bringing about such far-reaching changes to the international obligations of the parties as some PTRs would do.[53] Others – predominantly writers of commentaries on the law of treaties[54] – assert, from a doctrinal point of view, that subsequent agreements may only amount to slight changes of pre-existing meanings of treaty provisions. They even venture that 'subsequent interpretive agreements … seem more in the order of *confirmation* rather than assertion'.[55] There are several problems with this position. It is difficult to ascribe any determinate 'original' or 'existing' meaning to MEA provisions that lends itself to being 'confirmed' or 'slightly changed'; it is difficult to draw an objective line between slight changes and more than slight changes; and it is unclear what legal source this limitation is based on.

[52] *Pulp Mills*, para 140; para 141 ('Consequently, the Court finds that Argentina, in accepting the creation of the GTAN, did not give up, as Uruguay claims, the other procedural rights belonging to it by virtue of the 1975 Statute, nor the possibility of invoking Uruguay's responsibility for any breach of those rights'. See also James Crawford, 'A Consensualist Interpretation of Article 31(3) of the Vienna Convention on the Law of Treaties' in Georg Nolte (ed), *Treaties and Subsequent Practice* (OUP, 2013), 32.

[53] Marcelo Kohen, 'Keeping Subsequent Agreements and Practice in Their Right Limits' in Georg Nolte (ed), *Treaties and Subsequent Practice* (OUP, 2013) 34, 34 (insisting 'upon the importance of relying on formal agreements' and that 'caution must be exercised when identifying subsequent practice'). See also *Whaling in the Antarctic* (Separate Opinion of Judge Greenwood) para 7.

[54] Including those discussed in Christian Djeffal, 'Commentaries on the Law of Treaties: A Review Essay Reflecting on the Genre of Commentaries' (2013) 24 *European Journal of International Law* 12, 23.

[55] Jean-Marc Sorel and Valérie Boré-Eveno, 'Article 31 (1969)' in Olivier Corten and Pierre Klein (eds), *The Vienna Convention on the Law of Treaties, A Commentary (Volume I)* (OUP, 2011) 8, 26. In the same vein Villiger, 'The VCLT – 40 Years After', 122.

To conclude, no convincing arguments exist for why a very large majority of PTRs would not at least *qualify* as subsequent agreements under Article 31.3(a), or in some cases, when they are adopted before the entry into force of the MEA, as agreements adopted in immediate connection with the adoption of the treaty (Article 31.2). But what follows from this qualification as subsequent agreements for the kind of legal effect that PTRs have on treaty obligations?

2. The Riddle of 'Taking into Account'

Even if PTRs qualify as interpretive agreements in the sense of Article 31, it is not so clear what this means for the obligations of the treaty parties in the international legal order.[56] Confusion arises in this respect upon a closer look at Article 31.3's wording, as well as at how Article 31 as a whole, and the nature of the act of interpreting in general, is to be construed. The *Whaling* and *Pulp Mills* cases show a serious level of disagreement and uncertainty.

First, the simple but crucial point that Article 31.3(a) and (b) VCLT merely state that subsequent agreements and practice 'shall be *taken into account*' is often overlooked. Crawford recently submitted in this regard that 'lawyers can take things into account in a variety of ways. They can take things into account by giving them effect, such as you might take a statute into account. Alternatively, things might be taken into account in the sense of "we take this into account, but we do not give it much attention".'[57] Accordingly, the phrase 'shall be taken into account' is itself strongly dependent on further interpretation. This interpretive process has not yet reached the point of crystallisation into a less ambiguous notion, and perhaps never will.

The ambiguity in what it means to 'take into account' becomes readily apparent in reading the judgments and individual judicial opinions in the *Whaling* case. Having dismissed any legal relevance for non-consensual IWC resolutions, the Court turns to what the *consensual* ICRW resolutions require from Japan exactly. The difficulties immediately begin with the substance of Resolution 1986-2. The Court concludes that the Resolution's language of 'should take into account' falls short of 'establishing a requirement that lethal methods be used only when other methods are not available'.[58] In other words, Article VIII ICRW must be interpreted as such that Japan is under an obligation to 'take into account' that 'it should take into account' the feasibility of non-legal methods. To complicate things further, the Court takes a leap, seemingly out of nowhere, from the law of treaties towards international institutional law:

> The Court however observes that the States parties to the ICRW have a duty to co-operate with the IWC and the Scientific Committee and thus should give due

[56] *cf* Wiersema, 'The New International Law-Makers', 278.
[57] Crawford, 'A Consensualist Interpretation', 29–30.
[58] *Whaling in the Antarctic*, para 83.

> regard to recommendations calling for an assessment of the feasibility of non-lethal alternatives.

Other than that it refers to the recognition by the Parties in the course of the proceedings that such a duty exists,[59] the Court does not point at any legal source for it, not even its own jurisprudence. It later repeats the point in relation to Japan's alleged non-compliance with Paragraph 30 of the Schedule (review of permits for scientific research), stating that this obligation:

> must be appreciated in light of the duty of co-operation with the IWC and its Scientific Committee that is incumbent upon all States parties to the Convention, *which was recognized by both Parties and the intervening State.*[60]

The Court fails to explain why the duty to cooperate – originating in international institutional law – would be applicable to a recommendation of an international plenary body, which is surprising considering that there is considerable debate on whether international institutional law applies to it,[61] and that a few sentences above it the judgment was still steeped in the language of the law of treaties.[62]

[59] In para 137, the Court states that '*Japan has accepted* that it is under an obligation to give due regard to such recommendations'.

[60] *Whaling in the Antarctic*, para 240.

[61] See the discussion in ch 1, section B.

[62] There is little dispute that a general 'duty to cooperate' or even a 'duty to cooperate in good faith' exists in the UN Charter (Art 1(3)), in international institutional law. Chittharanjan F Amerasinghe, *Principles of the Institutional Law of International Organizations* 2nd edn (CUP, 2005), 178–80; Armin Von Bogdandy, 'General Principles of International Public Authority: Sketching a Research Field' (2008) 9 *German Law Journal* 1909. But there is little agreement about what the duty requires specifically. It has certainly never before been found by an international court to render all consensual output of international bodies more or less legally binding. The Court may well have looked back to Judge Lauterpacht's Dissenting Opinion in the *Voting Procedures Opinion* (1954), where he argued that '[t]he State in question, while not bound to accept the recommendation, is bound to give it due consideration in good faith'. *Voting Procedure on Questions relating to Reports and Petitions concerning the Territory of South West Africa* (Dissenting Opinion of Judge Lauterpacht) [1955] ICJ Rep 67, p 118–19. The duty of cooperation was also recognised in *Interpretation of the Agreement of 25 March 1951 between the WHO and Egypt* (Advisory Opinion) [1980] ICJ Rep 73, para 93: 'The very fact of … membership in the Organization entails certain mutual obligations of co-operation and good faith'. Referring to *WHO/Egypt* (paras 95, 97), Amerasinghe takes the view that while the duty to cooperate 'cannot leave a member state free simply to disregard the recommendation' and 'certainly involves the obligation to *consider* the recommendation in good faith and "to consult together in good faith"', the duty to cooperate 'should not be confused with co-operation in *carrying out* the recommendations which is not an obligation'. Amerasinghe, '*Principles of the Institutional Law*', 178–80 ('While there may be a duty to consider in good faith recommendations and a duty of co-operation, there generally is no duty to comply with recommendations as such') (citing Separate Opinion of Judges Lauterpacht and Klaestad in the *Voting Procedures Opinion*).

A similar duty is recognised in international environmental law. Principle 7 of the Rio Declaration: 'States shall cooperate in a spirit of global partnership to conserve, protect and restore the health and integrity of the Earth's ecosystem'. In that context, it also remains one of the vaguer principles, '[a]part from suggesting that States co-operate in good faith and collaborate towards the achievement of certain communal goals'. Duncan French, 'Sustainable Development' in Malgosia Fitzmaurice, David M Ong and Panos Merkouris (eds), *Research Handbook on International Environmental Law* (Edward Elgar, 2010) 51, 61.

In any case, the Court's construction can be summed up as a 'duty to cooperate', constituting an obligation 'to give due regard' to an obligation 'to take into account' a *recommendation* 'to take into account'. A legal obligation to 'give due regard' (duty of cooperation) of course has a different effect on an obligation to 'take into account' (Resolution 1986-2) than on an obligation that a treaty party 'shall act' in a certain way. In the former – present – scenario, it is simply a repetition of the same degree of obligation: nothing changes in what is required. Carrying out the Resolution in question amounts to the *same activity* as giving it due consideration. In the latter scenario, a duty to give due consideration does have an effect: it *mellows* the obligation in the primary rule. It remains to be seen what the Court would have decided when confronted with an IWC resolution actually requiring the *use* of non-legal methods, rather than taking such use into account. The line of argument of the Court would leave room for a treaty party to justify merely to take into account such an obligation to use non-lethal methods, but not actually use non-lethal methods.

The ambiguity arising from the various judges' individual opinions is worse. Almost all – dissenting and concurring – opinions in *Whaling in the Antarctic* discuss the legal relevance of the IWC recommendations, and they are extremely divided on the issue. While half of the opinions take a view similar to the judgment, some give a different reasoning, some propose to accord more weight to the recommendations, and some deny them any legal relevance at all. To start with the opinions containing a plea for the highest type of effect on the obligations of the ICRW parties: Judge Sebutinde speaks of 'the *binding* resolutions of the IWC'[63] (emphasis added) and Judge Yusuf states that the resolutions and guidelines are 'part of the relevant legal criteria to be considered' and are part of the provisions that 'constitute the *law* applicable to the circumstances of the present dispute' (emphasis added).[64]

On the other side of the spectrum, Judge Xue notes that 'resolutions relating to scientific whaling are generally of a recommendatory nature' without explaining further.[65] Most adamant in his opposition is Judge Bennouna, who wonders how Japan can have been found in breach of Article VIII based on 'its failure to give due regard to IWC resolutions and Guidelines, despite the fact that, by their nature, these are *not* binding upon that State'.[66] According to Bennouna, resolutions carry no degree of legal obligation at all: 'We may well ask ourselves how a legal obligation can derive … from a failure to have regard to acts of international bodies which carry *no* normative force in relation to those to whom they are addressed' (emphasis added).[67]

The judges in agreement with the judgment's finding that Japan had to 'give due regard', but nonetheless submitted a separate opinion, provide various reasons

[63] *Whaling in the Antarctic* (Separate Opinion of Judge Sebutinde), para 10.
[64] *Whaling in the Antarctic* (Dissenting Opinion of Judge Yusuf), para 11.
[65] *Whaling in the Antarctic* (Separate Opinion of Judge Xue), para 6.
[66] *Whaling in the Antarctic* (Dissenting Opinion of Judge Bennouna), p 4.
[67] *Whaling in the Antarctic* (Dissenting Opinion of Judge Bennouna), p 3.

for why this would be so, and what this amounts to. Judge *ad hoc* Charlesworth de-emphasises the judgment's differentiation between consensual and majority decision making: 'Resolutions adopted by the IWC under Article VI, *whether by consensus or by vote*, may also inform the duty of co-operation. The resolutions express the views of the IWC and, *when adopted by consensus or a large majority vote*, they represent an articulation of the shared interests at stake in the regulation of whaling. States parties to the ICRW are thus required to consider these resolutions in good faith.'[68]

Judge Greenwood provides a carefully argued analysis, capturing the essence of the difference between legally binding and taking into account. His point is essentially that resolutions and recommendations can never reach the same degree of legal obligation as a treaty or Schedule provision, considering the logic of international law making and the safeguards surrounding treaty making, both in general and in the particular case of the ICRW and its Schedule. '[A]ny assessment of the potential relevance of recommendations as an aid to the interpretation of the Convention must take into account the relationship between recommendations, which (as their name suggests) are not mandatory, and regulations, which are legally binding.'[69] Although Greenwood's objections are mostly aimed at non-consensual resolutions, according to him, resolutions are never more than an '*aid* to interpretation' that may 'be relied on to *sustain* an interpretation of the Convention'[70] (emphasis added), whether consensual or not. It implies that the degree of legal obligation of PTRs will always be at least *somewhat* limited compared to the underlying treaty.

Greenwood's point connects to an important second observation with regard to the question of what the legal obligation 'to take into account' means: that there is *no indication* in the text of Article 31 VCLT as a whole that the mere existence of a PTR *puts it at the top of the list of interpretive means.*[71] For Greenwood, subsequent agreements must connect to a plausible reading of the relevant treaty provision, in this case Article VIII ICRW, also in the light of other interpretive means. The existence of PTRs cannot eliminate the importance of rival means of interpretation. Quite the contrary, if any hierarchy would exist, the place of interpretive agreements in paragraph 3 of Article 31, the final paragraph of the Article, would indicate that they only gain weight 'in the absence of a clear solution based on the means of interpretation enunciated in the previous paragraphs.'[72]

[68] *Whaling in the Antarctic* (Separate Opinion of Judge *ad hoc* Charlesworth), para 13.

[69] *Whaling in the Antarctic* (Separate Opinion of Judge Greenwood), para 7.

[70] ibid.

[71] *cf* Nolte, *Second Report* p 45, restating the position of the VCLT Drafting Commission 'according to which a subsequent agreement under article 31(3)(a) is only one of several different means of interpretation which shall be taken into account in the process of interpretation.'

[72] Sorel and Boré-Eveno, 'Article 31 (1969)', 26. See also Wiersema, 'The New International Law-Makers', 267 ('It is not hard to see that a tribunal faced with the question in this way would place the original treaty obligation on a higher hierarchical level than the subsequent modification agreed to by consensus of the parties.').

According to many accounts of interpretation, it is still the ordinary meaning of a treaty provision that is the starting point from which the interpreter should not easily diverge. Ordinary meaning, of course, does not reach very far in the case of most MEA provisions under which PTRs are adopted. But also the other means of interpretation are inserted into Article 31 before paragraph 3, and are not qualified by the phrase 'shall be taken into account'. Paragraph 1 states that a treaty 'shall be interpreted in good faith in accordance with the ordinary meaning to be given to the terms of the treaty in their context and in the light of its object and purpose'. Paragraph 2 states what the context 'shall comprise'.[73]

If no such hierarchy is accepted,[74] and subsequent agreements are therefore neither at the top nor at the bottom of a supposed hierarchy, all means of interpretation require equal consideration. In that scenario, it remains for the interpreter – be it a state, a treaty body or a dispute resolution body – to decide the respective weight that should be accorded to the different means of interpretation of Article 31. Besides subsequent agreements, they are good faith, object and purpose, the wording and the intentions of the drafters, as well as 'the context', subsequent practice, and any other relevant rules of international law applicable in the relations between the parties. If the (auto) interpreter relies solely on PTRs, and not on the other interpretive means, that is a choice not prescribed by Article 31 VCLT (which is not to say that it is an entirely free choice). The recent ICJ case *Costa Rica v Nicaragua* exemplifies this.[75] The Court's majority argued that the term *comercio* in the Treaty of Limits between the two states was inherently evolutive; Judge Skotnikov argued in a separate opinion that the correct interpretation should be based on the subsequent practice of the parties.[76] Judge *ad hoc* Guillaume argued that the term *comercio* had always had the meaning it presently had.[77] It would be difficult to argue that any of these judges is legally 'wrong'.

The argument that, because PTRs are the most *detailed* source of information about the parties' preferred subjective interpretation of a treaty provision, that 'logically' makes it the primary means of interpretation, is also not convincing.

[73] This perhaps places PTRs that qualify under Art 31, paragraph 2 VCLT (mainly PTRs adopted in the context of the ratification of the Kyoto Protocol to the United Nations Framework Convention on Climate Change (adopted 11 December 1997, entered into force 16 February 2005) 2303 UNTS 162 (Kyoto Protocol)) in a comparatively slightly more preferential position.

[74] See to this effect the remarks of McDougal in his position as delegate at the Vienna Conference on the Law of Treaties, who already pointed at '[t]he overwhelming body of case-law of international courts and arbitral tribunals, and the practices of Foreign Affairs in the interpretation of treaties, bore out the right of the interpreter to take into account any circumstance affecting the common intern that the parties had sought to express in the text', and argued for 'removing all hierarchical weightings and obstacles to an unrestricted inquiry into all elements relevant to rational interpretation'. *Thirty-first Meeting of the Committee of the Whole*, pp 167–68, paras 38–50.

[75] See *Dispute Regarding Navigational and Related Rights (Costa Rica v Nicaragua)* (Judgment) General List No 133 [2009] ICJ 2, and the excellent analysis in Arato, 'Subsequent Practice and Evolutive Interpretation'.

[76] *Costa Rica v Nicaragua* (Separate Opinion of Judge Skotnikov).

[77] *Costa Rica v Nicaragua* (Declaration of Judge *ad hoc* Guillaume).

Admittedly, oftentimes, the means of interpretation of paragraph 1 and 2 of Article 31 VCLT will not provide a single, sufficiently clear meaning of a treaty provision. This is certainly to be expected with regard to the environmental treaty provisions on which PTRs are based. The ordinary meaning, if available, will be as broad and indeterminate as to only set the broad boundaries of meaning for interpretative purposes. The environmental treaty as a whole will be based on multiple, conflicting objects and purposes – such as sustainability *and* development, mitigation *and* cost effectiveness – so that the object and purpose as an interpretive technique can also at most help to establish broad boundaries of excluded meanings. Therefore, *if* a PTR exists, it will provide a relatively detailed indication of what the parties state that the treaty provision in question requires, which makes it very appealing for judges to hang on to. In the words of Simma, on subsequent agreements more generally, 'if there exists – and this is a matter of fact – subsequent practice or a subsequent agreement, there is, *lege artis*, simply no way to get around it'.[78] This might be called the 'pragmatic view': there is simply nothing else to go with.

Still, the mere lack of a clear answer being available through other interpretive means is in itself not sufficient to justify a subsequent agreement's precedence. Even if a PTR is the only means of interpretation available that might provide any clarification about the (subsequent) intentions of the parties with the underlying treaty provision, we can still not ignore the phrase 'to take into account'. If a treaty party has 'taken into account' the relevant PTR, but has decided to act differently, that is still a lawful course of action. Moreover, what exactly were the 'intentions' of the parties? They clearly did not have the intention to create a legally binding instrument. As Nolte's Second Report submits, 'consensus … is not a concept which necessarily indicates any degree of agreement on substance'.[79] The lack of meaningful interpretation provided by the ordinary meaning and the object and purpose leaves not only the option of going with the PTR's interpretation; the other option remaining is that there *is* no legal obligation.

Arguments based on the notion of 'good faith' share the same fate.[80] At first glance, it may seem contrary to good faith to ignore the very instrument in which parties have collectively adopted an interpretation of the treaty. Yet, there is no good reason why good faith should necessarily be coupled to one particular means of interpretation, i.e. subsequent agreements, or why good faith should mean that after taking into account a subsequent agreement, a treaty party actually has to act in accordance with it. Why should precisely subsequent agreements be relied upon

[78] Bruno Simma, 'Miscellaneous Thoughts on Subsequent Agreements and Practice' in Georg Nolte (ed), *Treaties and Subsequent Practice* (OUP, 2013) 46, 46.

[79] Nolte, *Second Report* p 46.

[80] Sam Foster Halabi, 'The World Health Organization's Framework Convention on Tobacco Control: An Analysis of Guidelines Adopted by the Conference of the Parties' (2010) 39 *Georgia Journal of International and Comparative Law* 121, 161–62. The good faith obligation is also found in Art 26 VCLT with regard to the parties' performance of their treaty obligations in good faith, and is regarded to be a general principle of international law.

in good faith? Should that be so merely because it is the most concrete statement the interpreter has at its disposition? Should the *treaty* as the primary instrument not take precedence, even if it is less specific?[81] Moreover, what does it mean to rely on good faith?

As Virally posited, 'if one persists and asks exactly what [good faith] means and precisely how good faith functions in the creation and performance of international obligations, one will obtain only vague explanations'.[82] One of his answers is that 'good faith is always presumed of actors in international legal life',[83] otherwise any trust in the system would collapse. This presumption is worked into Article 31 in the sense that, as long as one can explain one's interpretation in the light of one or more of Article 31's means of interpretation, one acts in good faith, because Article 31 as a whole is a specification of what it means to act in good faith.[84]

To conclude, if no conflict exists with other interpretations of the underlying treaty, the addressee is obliged to show that it has *considered* following the norm that the PTR states, not that it has actually *followed* it to the full extent of its substantive claim. Yet, in the *Whaling* case, starting from the duty to 'give due regard to' and 'take into account' the recommendation 'to take into account', the Court arrived at holding Japan to the exact letter of the Resolution. The Court decided that Japan did too little to show that it had taken into account *the feasibility of non-lethal methods*,[85] while the Court should have merely required Japan to show that it had taken into account *the Resolution*. In the end, one is thus left with the question, how is that final leap to decide what it takes to 'take into account' made? And why did *Special Permits* Resolution 1986-2 prevail over the other means of interpretation? International law does not provide the answers.

B. PTRs as Interpretive Agreements in National Courts

Just like in international law, in national legal orders the doctrine of interpretation is much more helpful than the doctrine of sources in gaining a better understanding of the authority that PTRs possess there. The practice of domestic courts

[81] In this vein, Kohen, 'Keeping Subsequent Agreements', 34.

[82] Michel Virally, 'Review Essay: Good Faith in Public International Law (Reviewing E Zoller, Good Faith in Public Internatonal Law)' (1983) 77 *American Journal of International Law* 130, 130.

[83] ibid, 132.

[84] ibid, 132–33.

[85] 'The Court concludes that the papers to which Japan directed it reveal little analysis of the feasibility of using non-lethal methods to achieve the JARPA II research objectives. Nor do they point to consideration of the possibility of making more extensive use of non-lethal methods in order to reduce or eliminate the need for lethal sampling, either when JARPA II was proposed or in subsequent years. Given the expanded use of lethal methods in JARPA II, as compared to JARPA, this is difficult to reconcile with Japan's obligation to give due regard to IWC resolutions and Guidelines and its statement that JARPA II uses lethal methods only to the extent necessary to meet its scientific objectives.'

constitutes the best source of information in this respect. In the repertoire of cases assembled for this study, different practices in relation to the domestic degree of legal obligations of PTRs can be found, and interpretation plays a key role in most of them: reliance on the international law rules of treaty interpretation; reliance on domestic rules of treaty interpretation very similar to those of international law; a much stricter understanding of what constitute interpretive agreements; outright denial of any degree of legal obligation; and, finally, no discussion of legal obligation at all.

First, in interpreting MEAs or interpreting legislation that implements MEAs, domestic courts – particularly in the Netherlands and Australia – sometimes state that they rely on Articles 31 and 32 of the VCLT. These courts look at PTRs through the lens of Article 31(3)(b) (subsequent practice), such as the Federal Court of Australia in the *Greentree* case,[86] or refer to Article 31(3)(a), such as in the *Lac Sorobon* case.[87] The mention of Article 31 VCLT does not necessarily imply that some *uniform* international understanding of what the VCLT rules require is applied.[88] A recent case study showed that the interpretation of the VCLT's interpretation rules diverges greatly among domestic courts as well as between domestic and international courts.[89] Nonetheless, most of the domestic courts that rely on Article 31.3(a) or (b) understand it to require formally to 'take into account' PTRs in the interpretation of the underlying MEA.

Some of the judgments in this category show a good understanding of what 'taking into account' means, when they rely on PTRs to reach a decision, because the PTR and the underlying MEA can be interpreted to sustain each other. When a court finds that a PTR sustains its interpretation of the underlying MEA provision, it is much more likely that that court is willing to rely on the PTR in reaching judgment. For instance, in *Cayman Turtle Farm v Andrus*, a US District Court held that '[t]he interpretation advocated by defendants and intervenor … is consistent with the protective policy of the Endangered Species Act of 1973. Moreover, the defendants' and intervenors' more strict definition of "closed-cycle" comports with the terms and underlying policy of the resolution adopted by the parties to the Convention.'[90] Likewise, in *Born Free* USA, a US District Court held, in relation to the plaintiff NGO's claim that the importation of CITES Appendix I species for zoos was contrary to the 'commercial purposes' prohibition, that '[n]either the language of CITES nor the Resolution indicates that the Treaty goes that far'.[91]

[86] *Greentree* (FCA), p 58 ('It is also necessary to take into account any subsequent agreement between the parties regarding the interpretation of the treaty and any subsequent practice in the application of the treaty which establishes the agreement of the parties regarding its interpretation: Art 31(3) of the Vienna Convention.'); *Greentree* (Full Court), paras 37 ('Treaties are interpreted in Australia in accordance with the requirements of the Vienna Convention on the Law of Treaties Article 31.') and 43.

[87] *Lac Sorobon*, para 2.2.3.5.

[88] Helmut Philipp Aust, Alejandro Rodiles and Peter Staubach, 'Unity or Uniformity? Domestic Courts and Treaty Interpretation' (2014) 27 *Leiden Journal of International Law* 75.

[89] ibid, 110–12.

[90] *Cayman Turtle Farm, Ltd v Andrus*, 478 F. Supp. 125 (D.D.C.), 29 May 1979, pp 133–34.

[91] *Born Free USA*, p 16.

Second, some domestic courts, particularly in the US, rely on domestic rules of interpretation that are very similar to Article 31(3)(a) and (b) VCLT in content. For instance, in *Castlewood Products v Norton*, the DC District Court relied on the US Supreme Court's holding in *Zicherman v Korean Airlines* that 'we have *traditionally* considered as aids to [treaty] interpretation the negotiating and drafting history … and the postratification understanding of the contracting parties' (emphasis added).[92] The District Court concluded on the basis of this jurisprudence that the CITES resolutions at issue in the dispute before it 'clearly evince a "postratification understanding" of the parties to CITES'.[93] Courts that rely on a rule of interpretation that echoes Article 31.3(a) or (b) VCLT likewise state that PTRs are 'aids to interpretation' or 'relevant to' the interpretation of the underlying MEA.

Third, at least two domestic courts did not consider PTRs to be interpretive agreements at all. In *NRDC v EPA*, the US Court of Appeals in charge of the case relied on an understanding of 'interpretive agreement' that is much narrower than that of Article 31(3)(a) VCLT, and which therefore excludes PTRs from its scope. Even though the US Environmental Protection Agency characterised the relevant Montreal MOP decisions as 'subsequent consensus agreements of the Parties that address the interpretation and application of the critical use provision',[94] the Court entirely ignored the above-cited Supreme Court case *Zicherman*.[95] The Court excluded the MOP decisions from the definition of interpretive agreements:

> Like any interpretive tool, however, the 'decisions' are useful only to the extent they shed light on ambiguous terms in the Protocol. But the details of the critical-use exemption are not ambiguous. They are nonexistent. The 'decisions' do not interpret treaty language. They fill in treaty gaps.[96]

The Court then applied domestic contract law jurisprudence to conclude that such gap-filling agreements are not 'enforceable' in US courts. As this study reconstructed in the section on *international* legal obligation, this is a narrower understanding of interpretive agreements than how they are defined in Article 31(3)(a), which also covers agreements on application and implementation.[97]

In the case of *One Etched Tusk*, a US District Court dismissed any domestic legal relevance of PTRs, without discussing the possibility of their relevance to treaty interpretation at all.[98] The claimant hunter in this case argued that a sport-hunted trophy should have been defined by the US Management Authority

[92] *Zicherman v Korean Air Lines Co*, 516 U.S. 217, p 226.
[93] *Castlewood Products* (District Court), p 12.
[94] *Final Rule*, 69 Fed. Reg. at 76,985.
[95] *Zicherman v Korean Air Lines Co*, 516 U.S. 217, p 226.
[96] *NRDC v EPA*, p 9.
[97] This view is sustained by the *travaux préparatoires* of Art 31.3.a VCLT and the Pakistan Amendment. See above, section A.1.
[98] *One Etched Tusk*, p 136.

(the Fish and Wildlife Service, 'FWS') in accordance with the definition of sport-hunted trophies in CITES Resolution 12.3.[99] The main – and for this dispute decisive – difference between Resolution 12.3's definition and the one adopted by the FWS is that the former includes 'raw, processed and manufactured' trophies,[100] while the latter only includes 'raw or tanned parts' and explicitly 'does not include articles made from a trophy'.[101] The elephant tusk in question had been inscribed with a scrimshawed scene of Africa's 'Big Five' game animals at the request of the hunter,[102] and therefore fitted the definition of sports-hunted trophy in the CITES Resolution, but not the FWS's definition. The US District Court plainly refused the claimant's request, and that had nothing to do with the Resolution's formulation as a recommendation. It simply did not consider the Resolution to have any domestic legal relevance at all (or even to have any international legal relevance):

> Claimant's citation to the resolution does not help his claim. Claimant does not provide authority to support the proposition that resolutions of parties to a treaty are binding on the parties even as a matter of international law (when those resolutions are not styled as amendments to the treaty and adopted through the treaty amendment procedure). … Therefore, the court will not apply its definition of sport-hunted trophy to this case.[103]

Fourth and finally, there are numerous cases dealing with MEAs and PTRs where the latter's legal relevance as interpretive agreements is not mentioned at all (and neither was any other justification for their application or non-application). This is not unique to the domestic application of PTRs; it is seen more generally in judgments concerning domestic application of international (environmental) law.[104] As Bruch submits, when 'the status of the legal provision might be unclear … courts might seek to avoid taking a position regarding the international legal status of a particular provision'.[105] This silence can be found in cases with very different result in terms of the eventual relevance of the PTR in question for the outcome of the case.

[99] CITES COP Res Conf 12.3 recommends to the parties to define the term 'hunting trophy', in relevant part, as a 'whole animal, or a readily recognizable part or derivative of an animal, specified on any accompanying CITES permit or certificate, that: i) is raw, processed or manufactured'. The only way in which CITES COP Res Conf 2.11, para (b) makes it easier for hunting trophies to pass the complementary export and import tests, is that the Scientific Authority of the import state should 'accept the finding of the Scientific Authority of the exporting country that the exportation of the hunting trophy is not detrimental to the survival of the species, unless there are scientific or management data to indicate otherwise'.

[100] CITES COP Res Conf 12.3, Recommendation I.(h).

[101] See 50 C.F.R. § 23.74(b).

[102] *One Etched Tusk*, p 130.

[103] *One Etched Tusk*, p 136.

[104] *cf* Carl Bruch, 'Is International Environmental Law Really Law? An Analysis of Application in Domestic Courts' (2006) 23 *Pace Environmental Law Review* 423, 428, 453 ('However, in many cases, the court refers to international environmental law without explaining the legal status of the specific norm within the context of the judicial decision.').

[105] ibid, 453.

On the one hand, various judgments apply PTRs as if they had a high authority, but without discussing the legal basis for this finding in any way.[106] For instance, in an interim judgment in the Dutch *Orka* case – concerning the lawfulness of a licence to transfer the Orca 'Morgan' to a marine park in Tenerife (Canary Islands) – the judge considered CITES COP Resolution 10.7 'important for the explanation of the licensing conditions' in the Dutch Flora and Fauna Law, 'because [it] clarifies the provisions of CITES'.[107] (In fact, the judgment resulted in transportation of Morgan to the Loro Parque in Tenerife, where she is – very much contrary to Article III CITES and its *Primarily Commercial Purposes* Resolution – being exploited for commercial purposes to this very day.)[108] Another important example is the *Nilsson* case before the then European Court of Justice (now CJEU). The ECJ interpreted Article VII(2) CITES on the basis of CITES COP Resolution 5.11(a)(i), to establish that 'the date on which a specimen is acquired is to be, for live and dead animals taken from the wild, the date of their initial removal from their habitat, but also, for parts and derivatives, that of their introduction to personal possession', and that therefore Nilsson's taking of the specimens into personal possession amounted to having 'acquired' them for the purposes of Article VII(2) CITES.[109] The judgment simply states that, from CITES COP Resolution 5.11, '[i]t follows that the concept of acquired for the purposes of Article 8(3)(b) of Regulation No 338/97 concerns any taking into possession with a view to personal possession'.[110]

On the other hand, there are also judgments that do *not* apply PTRs, without providing any legal basis for not doing so. The UK Court of Appeal's majority opinion in *Greenpeace* even entirely ignored the *existence* of the CITES COP's *Reason to Believe Paragraph*.[111]

The strong variation observed in the degree of legal obligation domestic courts accord to PTRs, and in the (lack of) legal reasoning on which it is based, should not come as a surprise. A recent study containing 11 country reports on domestic treaty interpretation 'd[id] not precisely portray the respective

[106] Judgments in at least two Australian cases also rely in part on PTRs without explanation of a legal basis for such reliance. See *And Jombi and Minister for the Environment and Heritage*, [2004] AATA 1380 (Administrative Appeals Tribunal of Australia), 20 December 2004: and *Spencer v Commonwealth of Australia*, [2008] FCA 1256 (Federal Court of Australia), 26 August 2008.

[107] *Orka*, para 4.6. [Translation from the Dutch: 'Ook de voorzieningenrechter acht de Resolutie 10.7 *bij de uitleg van de onderhavige vergunningsvoorwaarden van belang* … De resolutie *verduidelijkt* dat de bepalingen van de CITES niet zo moeten worden uitgelegd dat steeds uitzetting in de natuur moet volgen, maar dat dit slechts gewenst is onder heel specifieke omstandigheden.']

[108] See Hanna Gersmann, 'Rescued killer whale bound for amusement park following legal tussle' *Guardian* (London 22 November 2011) www.theguardian.com/environment/2011/nov/22/killer-whale-morgan-tenerife-park accessed 27 August 2018 and www.loroparque.com/morgan/hoy/index_en.html.

[109] European Court of Justice, Case C-154/02 *Criminal proceedings against Jan Nilsson*, Judgment of the Court of 23 October 2003, para 40.

[110] *Nilsson*, para 40.

[111] *R (on the application of Greenpeace Ltd) v Secretary of State for the Environment, Food and Rural Affairs*, EWCA Civ 1036 (Civil Division), 25 July 2002, para 43.

jurisdictions as faithful followers of the Vienna Convention approach'.[112] As Nollkaemper remarks, 'there is ample practice whereby domestic courts apply principles of domestic (statutory) interpretation, apparently unguided by international principles of interpretation'.[113] Some have argued that common law countries show less interest in uniform international rules on interpretation in general,[114] and this pattern returns to some extent for cases involving PTRs: in the UK and US cases in the selection of cases, there are very few references to Article 31 VCLT. But the EU courts have also introduced a two-tier system in their WTO and UNCLOS case law that first appreciates the general nature of the international agreement in question, before applying the Vienna Convention rules.[115] Furthermore, among the court cases on PTRs *not* discussing the applicable rules of treaty interpretation at all, there is also a case (the *Orka* case) from a civil law country – the Netherlands.[116] The Australian *Greentree* case contains the most in-depth discussion of the characterisation of PTRs as subsequent agreements in the sense of Article 31.3(a) VCLT. The differences between common law and civil law countries in this respect are, in other words, negligible.

C. The Effect of Wording on PTRs' Interpretive Authority

The previous two sections established clearly that according to the ILC, the ICJ and most national courts, PTRs are agreements relevant to the interpretation of treaties in both the international and the national legal orders. However, interpretive relevance turned out not to be the same as interpretive primacy. How much interpretive weight a particular PTR will have in the interpretation of an environmental treaty's provisions, then, also depends on its wording. The idea is that the wording of a PTR, as Nolte's Second Report also suggests, would provide information of the intentions of the treaty parties to adopt an authoritative instrument.[117]

[112] This conclusion is reached in Aust, Rodiles and Staubach, 'Domestic Courts and Treaty Interpretation', 85. But see Michael P Van Alstine, 'The Role of Domestic Courts in Treaty Enforcement: Summary and Conclusion' in David Sloss (ed), *The Role of Domestic Courts in Treaty Enforcement* (CUP, 2009) 555, 588–89, (reaching the opposite conclusion, based on the same set of country reports, that 'substantial similarities exist on the influence of the VCLT almost irrespective of tradition and member-state status').

[113] André Nollkaemper, *National Courts and the International Rule of Law* (OUP, 2011), 219.

[114] Aust, Rodiles and Staubach, 'Domestic Courts and Treaty Interpretation', 107 ('Arguably this … reflects the deeper indifference of a common-law judiciary to the project of creating a single authoritative international methodology.').

[115] Case C-308/06 *Intertanko* and Case C-149/96 *Portugal v Council*, Judgment of the Court of 23 November 1999.

[116] *Orka*, para 4.6.

[117] Wiersema has also suggested that the 'level of obligation' contained in the language can assist in determining PTRs' authority because they reveal the intent of the treaty parties. Wiersema, 'The New International Law-Makers', 253–54.

However, as chapter two has amply demonstrated, correspondence between a PTR's wording on paper and its authority in practice is only found half of the time. On the one hand, even the clearest and strongest language cannot overcome the 'mere' status of PTRs as interpretive agreements, not law. And on the other hand, even the most recommendatory language cannot be neglected out of existence: it may 'just' be guidance, but, as the Dutch saying goes, in the land of the blind, the cyclops is king. If there is nothing else to guide the interpretation of the treaty, mere 'guidelines' may tip over the balance in favour of a particular interpretation. The following paragraphs explore the variations in wording of PTRs and the extent to which they do and do not represent the crucial bridge over the gap between 'taking into account' and 'acting in accordance with'.

1. Mandatory Quality and Specificity

Many scholarly projects have advanced conceptualisations of degrees or types of authority (or 'obligation' or 'normativity') of international instruments in which wording plays an important role. The two key ways in which wording can determine the authority of an instrument are what Bodansky calls *mandatory quality* and *precision or specificity*.[118] The importance of such distinctions for the authority of law is also recognised in general legal philosophy. The degree to which an instrument is authoritative tends to be influenced by the extent to which it contains a rule formulation that *requires* a certain behaviour from its addressee or applier in a reasonably *clear and determinate* manner.[119]

The ICJ has also stressed the importance of language for the 'binding effect' of instruments adopted by international organisations and their organs, for instance in the 1971 *Namibia* Advisory Opinion:[120]

> 114. … The language of a resolution of the Security Council should be carefully analysed before a conclusion can be made as to its binding effect. In view of the nature of the powers under Article 25, the question whether they have been in fact exercised is to be determined in each case, having regard to the terms of the resolution to be interpreted.

In this paragraph the Court specifically deals with Security Council resolutions, but there is no reason why the Court would consider the language used in decisions of other international bodies less relevant for the authority than they would have over the addressees of that body.

For the purposes of this study, wording is *the degree to which a PTR's wording and relevant actors' interpretation of it make it difficult for legal subjects and law*

[118] Daniel Bodansky, *The Art and Craft of International Environmental Law* (Harvard University Press, 2010), 102–06.

[119] Frederick Schauer, *Playing by the Rules: A Philosophical Examination of Rule-Based Decision-Making* (Clarendon Press, 1991), 62 ff.

[120] *Legal Consequences for States of the Continued Presence of South Africa in Namibia (South West Africa) notwithstanding Security Council Resolution 276 (1970)* (Advisory Opinion) [1971] ICJ Rep 16.

appliers to escape that PTR's interpretation, modification or supplementation of the underlying treaty. When the wording of a PTR is phrased in a relatively precise and/or a relatively mandatory fashion, this generally makes it more difficult not to defer to that PTR in the interpretation of the underlying treaty,[121] other variables being equal. By contrast, PTRs with low mandatory quality simply do not *require* behaviour and PTRs with low specificity simply do not specify *what behaviour* is required. This implies that state addressees can relatively easily escape such PTRs as reference points.

To determine the authority emanating from the wording of PTRs, this study follows Bodansky's account in suggesting two main indicators: mandatory quality and specificity. *Mandatory quality* ranges from hortatory at one end to mandatory at the other. A hortatory norm makes a much weaker attempt to guide the behaviour of those to whom it is directed than a mandatory norm.[122] Its nature can normally be ascertained by means of the use of certain verbs, such as 'to urge' or 'to promote', or adjectives such as 'appropriate' on the hortatory side of the spectrum, and verbs like 'shall' or 'decides that' at the mandatory end.[123] But the hortatory or mandatory character of a PTR can also be stated explicitly in the preamble, as is the case for a number of CITES COP decisions, on for example the disposal of confiscated specimens.[124] Occasionally, it can be, in part, apparent from a PTR's designation, such as 'Guidelines' or 'Recommendation'. Usually, however, a closer look is necessary, as with most designations of international instruments.[125]

Specificity ranges from indeterminate and vague to very specific and precise. Low specificity may be apparent from non-defined terms, while high specificity is characterised by detailed paragraphs on what is required in all possible scenarios. In legal philosophy, the terminology of 'rules' and 'standards' is often used to denote respectively norms with low and high specificity and precision.[126] Specificity has an impact on a norm's authority because it shifts the power to interpret the meaning of the norm to the addressee of the norm, away from the actor formulating the norm. To be clear, even specifically worded rules continue to allow for disagreements as to their proper interpretation. For instance, the methyl bromide *Critical Use Criteria* and exemptions under the Montreal Protocol are a clear example of authoritative rule formulations. Still, discussion remains possible about, for instance, the wording on how the use of existing stocks relates to production, and consumption of new methyl bromide does not

[121] Nico Krisch, 'The Structure of Postnational Authority' (2015), at http://papers.ssrn.com/sol3/papers.cfm?abstract_id=2564579, 10–11.

[122] Bodansky, '*Art and Craft*', 103.

[123] ibid, 103–04. These insights trace back to the foundational work of John Searle.

[124] Like many CITES guidelines, CITES COP Res 10.7 (Rev CoP15), *Disposal of confiscated live specimens of species included in the Appendices*, opens with the phrase: 'The Conference of the Parties to the Convention recommends that'.

[125] Goldmann, 'Inside Relative Normativity', 687–89.

[126] Schauer, '*Thinking Like a Lawyer*', 188–202.

negate this. Some room for further specification through interpretation will always remain.

An important question is whether the definition of 'wording' should encompass more than the written language alone, to include the dominant interpretation of it in practice. The mandatory quality and specificity of PTRs are not static but dynamic: they can be changed through the shared or common understandings of the parties.[127] It is always a combination of the text of the PTR and the common understanding the parties have of it, insofar as such a common understanding exists. A PTR may use mandatory verbs like 'shall', but in the regime's bodies still be treated as if its prescriptions are softer than that. It is the meaning of a PTR's wording in the light of its use in practice over time that ultimately comes to matter more than what is written on paper.

The Australian *Greentree* case from the previous chapter, involving a wetland that Australia had listed on the Ramsar List of Wetlands, is telling in this respect. The respondents, owners of land bordering the wetland in question, had pointed to Ramsar COP Resolution VI.16,[128] which repeats Article 2.1 of the Convention in stating that 'the boundaries of each listed wetland *shall* be precisely described and also delimited on a map by States' (emphasis added).[129] However, the Federal Court did not detect any more than a serious policy encouragement:

> [T]here has never been any suggestion at the Conferences that a failure of the Contracting Party to provide a precise description of the boundaries of a designated wetland will result in the wetland being denied a place on the List ... In short, *the practice of the Contracting Parties is consistent with them regarding* the obligation to provide precise boundary descriptions as important, but not going to the validity or effectiveness of a designation of a wetland for inclusion in the List.[130] (Emphasis added.)

Through this move, the Court could hold that the Contracting Parties regard 'the obligation to provide precise boundary descriptions as important, but not going to the validity or effectiveness of a designation of a wetland for inclusion in the List'.[131] While the practice of the Ramsar COP *lowered* the 'common understanding' of the *Identification Criteria* and *Designation Conditions*' authority at first, the COP later strengthened the Ramsar Secretariat's role in listing newly designated wetlands. By prescribing that it not list any wetlands that fail to fulfil the *Criteria* or the *Conditions*, and the Secretariat strictly performing this new role in practice, the Ramsar COP again *enhanced* that 'common understanding' towards more authority.[132]

[127] Brunnée, 'COPing with Consent'; Jutta Brunnée, 'Reweaving the Fabric of International Law? Patterns of Consent in Environmental Framework Agreements' in Rüdiger Wolfrum and Volker Röben (eds), *Developments of International Law in Treaty Making* (Springer, 2005) 101; Schauer, '*Playing by the Rules*', ch 4, s 4.

[128] Ramsar COP Res VI.16, *Accession Procedures.*

[129] Ramsar COP Res VI.16, para 5.

[130] *Greentree* (FCA), Reasoning, para 135.

[131] *Greentree* (FCA), para 135.

[132] See ch 2, section B.1(b).

But, viewed differently, this example also serves as a warning sign that there are serious limits to what the wording of PTRs can indicate about their authority. The common understanding thereof in practice tends to *override* the authority that the text seemingly expresses in isolation, raising the question of whether it is really the *wording* that makes for the authority of the PTR, or the *practice*. Another telling example of this is CITES COP Resolution 12.8 on the *Review of Significant Trade* procedure, in which the Animals and Plant Committees issue *recommendations* to 'range states' to limit export of heavily traded species. The term 'recommendations' seems to indicate low authority, yet the CITES Standing Committee may suspend trade with these 'range states' if they fail to successfully implement the recommendations. Here, the overall authority of the PTR far exceeds the mandatory quality that the term 'recommendation' normally connotes. The relevance of a particular verb or noun may be diminished by a subsequent practice that is more authoritative or less authoritative than that noun indicates.

2. Variations in Mandatory Quality and Specificity

The degree of mandatory quality of PTRs is very divergent. Expressly voluntary guidelines exist, such as a number of CITES COP resolutions and Ramsar COP resolutions, where the voluntary character is literally announced in the preamble or first operative paragraph. There are PTRs using hortatory verbs such as 'to urge' or 'to recommend', signalling that it is up to the parties to decide the extent to which they shape their policies in accordance with them, although they are advised to do so. There are also PTRs that are formulated in rather neutral language, just stating a number of criteria, such as the CITES *Listing Criteria* and the Ramsar *Identification Criteria*, without much indication of mandatory quality. At the high end of the spectrum of mandatory quality, a considerable number of PTRs, particularly under the Montreal Protocol and the Kyoto Protocol, is formulated in a decidedly mandatory fashion. However, even here there are variations in terms of how much room is left to the parties to decide on how to comply. Of course, even within a single PTR, it is possible to find provisions of differing mandatory quality.[133]

Generally, the specificity of PTRs is rather high, especially if compared to their underlying enabling clauses. Nonetheless, there are instances in which a term that is undefined in the enabling clause remains undefined in the PTR based on it – such as the relation between 'human activities' and 'wise use' in several Ramsar COP resolutions, and 'commercial' in the CITES *Primarily Commercial Purposes* Resolution. A lack of specificity can offset high mandatory quality, such as the Kyoto COP/MOP decisions on the flexibility mechanisms, which do

[133] One example is the hortatory paragraph 33 in the otherwise mostly mandatorily phrased Kyoto Protocol COP/MOP Decision 13/CMP.1, *Modalities for the accounting of assigned amounts under Article 7, paragraph 4, of the Kyoto Protocol.*

not specify the meaning of a term, such as 'supplementality', any further than the treaty did.[134]

The following sections discuss the highly varied mandatory quality and specificity in the PTRs of the Ramsar, CITES, Kyoto and Montreal regimes, in addition to the examples already explored in the case studies of chapter two. The variance is particularly striking between those PTRs aimed at the behaviour of the parties collectively within the regime's bodies on the one hand (internal PTRs) and those directly aimed at the environmental conduct of individual treaty parties (external PTRs). The differences between the levels of authority emanating from the wording of PTRs can thus be regarded as one important explanation of their compartmentalised authority.

a. *The Ramsar Convention*

Expressly voluntary or recommendatory guidelines are widely found among Ramsar Convention PTRs. The Ramsar Convention's many implicit enabling clauses are often formulated using terms such as 'appropriate', 'promoting', 'adequately', 'shall endeavour' and 'as far as possible'. With such hortatory terminology in the underlying treaty, it is not surprising that Ramsar PTRs tend to be formulated in comparably unobtrusive language, starting with the description of the voluntary character of resolutions in the title.

A good example of expressly voluntary guidelines under the Ramsar Convention is Resolution VIII.20, on 'urgent national interests'. How much discretion does a party lose after a wetland's designation to the list? Can it change the site's boundaries or size, or even eliminate it from the list? What constitute its 'urgent national interests'? The Convention goes very far in protecting the sovereign discretion of the treaty parties on this issue. According to Article 2.5, a party 'shall have the right … because of its urgent national interest, to delete or restrict the boundaries of wetlands already included by it in the List'. Article 4.2 of the Convention does require compensation for loss of (parts of) listed wetlands by protecting or creating alternative areas, preferably through establishing additional nature reserves.

Resolution VIII.20, called *General guidance for interpreting 'urgent national interests' under Article 2.5 of the Convention and considering compensation under Article 4.2*,[135] is overtly hortatory in stating that 'this [Resolution's] guidance may be used by Contracting Parties if they so wish'.[136] It confirms, in absolute terms, that 'the determination of "urgent national interests" lies solely with the Contracting Party'. The Resolution provides a number of key *considerations*

[134] Hermann E Ott, 'The Bonn Agreement to the Kyoto Protocol – Paving the Way for Ratification' (2001) 1 *International Environmental Agreements: Politics, Law and Economics* 469, 471.

[135] Ramsar COP Res VIII.20, Annex, *General guidance for interpreting 'urgent national interests' under Article 2.5 of the Convention and considering compensation under Article 4.2.*

[136] Ramsar COP Res VIII.20, Annex, para 1.

for parties to be borne in mind when considering delisting or boundary restriction.[137]

With regard to compensation, the *General Guidance* cautiously states that 'a Contracting Party should as far as possible compensate for any loss of wetland resources. When considering such compensation, a Contracting Party may take into account' an inexhaustible range of circumstances.[138] Equally hortatory is the suggestion that '[a] prior environmental assessment, taking into consideration the full range of functions, services, and benefits offered by the wetland, would normally be an appropriate first step'.[139] The title *Guidance for the consideration of the deletion or restriction of the boundaries of a listed Ramsar site*[140] is misleadingly gentle this time. This Resolution provides a number of procedural steps to be followed if restriction or deletion is contemplated in surprisingly strong terms.[141]

The *Wise Use Guidelines*, while also bearing a title with a strongly recommendatory flavour, are at times phrased rather commandingly. Article 3.1 Ramsar Convention, with its dual standard of conservation and wise use, was already discussed in the context of the modifying character of PTRs, because Ramsar PTRs no longer recognise this dual standard, moving to 'wise use' as a single standard. This makes all the more important how the parties specified what the obligation of 'wise use' requires. Recently, the Ramsar COP defined wise use as 'the maintenance of their ecological character, achieved through the implementation of ecosystem approaches, within the context of sustainable development'.[142] A 'change in ecological character' is defined as 'the human-induced adverse alteration of any ecosystem component, process and/or ecosystem benefit/service'.[143] These definitions on the general policy level create some clarity about the general orientation of the convention.

The COP has further fleshed out wise use in a number of 'practical' implementing guidelines.[144] The Secretariat has transformed these into a thick Wise Use Handbook.[145] They focus on such matters as wetland inventory, impact assessment, international cooperation, and the wetland management process.[146]

[137] Ramsar COP Res VIII.20, Annex, para 3.

[138] Ramsar COP Res VIII.20, Annex, para 4.

[139] Ramsar COP Res VIII.20, Annex, para 5.

[140] Ramsar COP Res IX.6, *Guidance for the consideration of the deletion or restriction of the boundaries of a listed Ramsar site.*

[141] Ramsar COP Res IX.6, Annex, s IV.

[142] Ramsar COP Res IX.1, Annex A, *A Conceptual Framework for the wise use of wetlands and the maintenance of their ecological character.*

[143] Ramsar COP Res IX.1, Annex A.

[144] See, most significantly, Ramsar COP Res V.6, Annex, *Additional Guidance for the Implementation of the Wise Use Concept*; Ramsar COP Recommendation IV.10, Annex, *Guidelines for the Implementation of the Wise Use Concept.*

[145] Ramsar Secretariat, *Wise use of wetlands: Concepts and approaches for the wise use of wetlands. Ramsar handbooks for the wise use of wetlands Vol. 1* 4th edn (2010).

[146] Michael Bowman, Peter Davies and Catherine Redgwell, *Lyster's International Wildlife Law* 2nd edn (CUP, 2010), 419. This guidance is not only a volume of strategies, it entails important choices.

When it comes to these practical matters, according to some commentators, the parties have turned the barebones foundation of Article 3.1 into 'an extremely comprehensive and sophisticated policy framework for the management of wetlands areas'.[147] However, the alleged 'sophistication' should not be exaggerated. For instance, Ramsar COP Resolution V.6's guidelines on 'human activities' remain very superficial and open-ended, stating that '[i]n order to achieve wise use of wetlands, it is necessary to attain a balance', that '[w]ise use activities therefore can be varied in nature, ranging from very little or no resource exploitation, to active resource exploitation as long as it is sustainable,' and therefore 'needs to be adapted to suit local conditions'.[148]

As is clear from the designations of all the instruments on implementing wise use, as well as from their language, these are expressly of a guiding character: they provide the parties with tools that – when used – should lead to better national wetland policies, knowledge building, and maintenance of particular wetland sites.[149] Some parts are formulated in a slightly stronger form: 'In order to achieve wise use of wetlands, it is necessary to' or '[i]t needs to', taking on a matter-of-fact tone that clearly dismisses conduct that deviates from these instructions as amounting to 'wise use' of wetlands.

A particularly elaborate part of the 'wise use' implementing guidelines are the various resolutions and recommendations on Environmental Impact Assessments.[150] As elaborate as they are, the language consistently suggests that these remain guidelines for the parties to cherry-pick from. An interesting exception is 'Appendix 1' of the EIA Guidelines which provides an '[i]ndicative set of screening criteria to be further elaborated at national level', of which Category A lists activities for which '[e]nvironmental impact assessment [are] *mandatory*', such as 1) activities in protected areas, and 2) activities in threatened ecosystems outside protected areas. It would seem to be difficult for a state to argue that when such activities are contemplated (even without any transboundary effects), an EIA with at least minimal features has to be conducted, according to these Resolutions.

b. CITES

The degree of authority in the wording of CITES resolutions can, on average, be characterised as higher than those of the Ramsar Convention regime, but it

Impact assessments, for instance, have been accorded a central role. See, eg, Ramsar COP Res X.17, *Environmental Impact Assessment and Strategic Environmental Assessment: updated scientific and technical guidance.*

[147] ibid.

[148] Ramsar COP Res V.6, *The wise use of wetlands*, Part III.2.

[149] Ramsar COP Res V.6, Parts I, II and III.

[150] Ramsar COP Res X.17, *Environmental Impact Assessment and Strategic Environmental Assessment: updated scientific and technical guidance.*

still presents a fairly diverse picture. There is a notable difference between the wordings of internal and external PTRs. External resolutions settle on less mandatory terms, such as *recommends*, *urges*, or *should*. Internal resolutions use more neutral, or sometimes even mandatory, language. In terms of specificity, many different degrees can be observed, with some resolutions simply echoing open-ended phrases from the convention, while others work out in great detail what should – preferably – be understood by such phrases.

A good example of quite specific and neutrally phrased internal PTRs are the *CITES Listing Criteria* for the listing of species on CITES Appendices I and II. Article II.1 CITES states that 'Appendix I shall include all species threatened with extinction which are or may be affected by trade', while Article II.2 states that 'Appendix II shall include … all species which although not necessarily now threatened with extinction may become so unless trade in specimens of such species is subject to strict regulation in order to avoid utilization incompatible with their survival' – mandatory but extremely undetermined language.

To deal with the ambiguity in these provisions, the parties have adopted more detailed *Listing Criteria* for listing species on and deleting species from Appendix I and also Appendix II through at least 12 COP resolutions over the four decades of CITES' existence. The current 'Fort Lauderdale' Criteria, adopted in 1994 but revised by every Conference of the Parties since,[151] contain much more detailed biological criteria to define 'threatened with extinction'.[152] They assign an important role to information on the biological status of a species, while previously there was room for alternative interpretations of Article II, such as allowing for wider political considerations about species protection, the economic importance of trade to range states, or the attractiveness of species to the public. Even in contentious cases, they provide sufficient specificity to suppress a great deal of disagreement as to whether a species should be listed,[153] at least when sufficient information is available.[154] It is difficult for opponents to oppose listings that clearly fall within the criteria without making it obvious that they do so for 'parochial reasons'.[155] For proponents, it would be equally difficult to successfully propose a listing that does *not* satisfy the criteria, or is not supported by sufficient information to support the claim that it does.

[151] CITES COP Res Conf 9.24 (Rev CoP16), *Criteria for amendment of Appendices I and II*.

[152] In one sense, the criteria are still quite broad, because 'it is impossible to give numerical values to all taxa [species and subspecies]'. CITES COP Res Conf 9.24, Annex 5. Willem Wijnstekers, *The Evolution of CITES* 9th edn (International Council for Game and Wildlife Conservation, 2011), 77. A taxon is any unit used in the science of biological classification, or taxonomy.

[153] Thomas Gehring and Eva Ruffing, 'When Arguments Prevail Over Power: The CITES Procedure for the Listing of Endangered Species' (2008) 8 *Global Environmental Politics* 123, 131.

[154] ibid, 143–44 (discussing the role that a lack of information played in the discussions preceding the decision not to list the Great White Shark).

[155] Thomas Gehring, 'How to Circumvent Parochial Interests without Excluding Stake-Holders: The Rationalizing Power of Functionally Differentiated Decision-Making' (2004) *BACES Discussion Paper* 3.

An even more clearly mandatory internal PTR is CITES Res Conf 8.4 on *National laws for implementation of the Convention.*[156] Addressing the Secretariat and the Standing Committee, it *directs* and *instructs* these bodies to identify the parties' compliance with the requirement in Article VIII CITES that their national laws prohibit and penalise trade, and allow for confiscation of illegally traded specimens, and if necessary make recommendations to suspend trade with non-compliant parties.

Moving to the external PTRs of CITES, a very different picture, of strictly recommendatory PTRs, emerges. Two good examples are the already extensively discussed *Reason to Believe Paragraphs* and the *Primarily Commercial Purposes* Resolution. Others are the *Disposal of Specimens* Resolutions,[157] which set out – in much detail – how parties should *preferably* decide on the method for disposal of confiscated live animals and plants. The convention text (Article VIII.4) gives two broad possibilities for living specimens: return to the wild, or placement in a rescue centre or another appropriate place (captivity). However, it gives neither priority to any of them, nor any guidance as to which method is preferred in which situation. The Resolution, by contrast, gives very detailed guidelines, containing a 'decision tree'[158] for how national Management Authorities should arrive at their decision. Since the confiscation of popular mammals such as Orcas (killer whales) or seals may stir lively debates about what is best for the animal, the authorities are likely to use the guidelines as a defence against NGOs or popular outrage when choosing a certain option. At least in terms of specificity, the Resolutions substantially decrease the treaty text's deferral to national assessment about what is 'appropriate and consistent with the purposes of the present Convention' (Article VIII.4(b) CITES). However, the operative part is entirely phrased in the language of recommendations and urgings.

c. *Kyoto Protocol*

The wording of many Kyoto Protocol PTRs is characterised by an '*if, then*' form. The parties are quite free in choosing to make use of one or more market mechanisms – hence the term 'flexibility mechanisms' – and which sources and sinks of greenhouse gas to account for. Once they do so, however, they subject themselves to an intricate system of predominantly specific and mandatory conditions. This makes Kyoto Protocol PTRs difficult to scale: how mandatory and specific is a PTR, if the addressee can choose between various options?

[156] CITES COP Res Conf 8.4 (Rev CoP15), *National laws for implementation of the Convention.*

[157] Most notably CITES COP Res Conf 9.10 (Rev CoP15), *Disposal of confiscated and accumulated specimens* (consolidating seven earlier resolutions on the topic), and CITES COP Res Conf 10.7 (Rev CoP15), *Disposal of confiscated live specimens of species included in the Appendices.* See Wijnstekers, '*The Evolution of CITES*', 263.

[158] ibid, 282–83.

The bare-bones set-up of the Kyoto Protocol flexibility mechanisms – Joint Implementation (JI), the Clean Development Mechanism (CDM) and Emissions Trading (ET) – left unanswered essential questions. Two of the most important ones were: 1) what is the maximum part or percentage of emissions reductions for which the flexibility mechanisms may be used compared to the part for which domestic measures should account?; 2) what accounting methods are to be used for the different types of reductions achieved through the flexibility mechanisms? As part of the Marrakech Accords, which resulted from a number of 'extraordinary' and 'ordinary' Conferences of the Parties, the parties adopted PTRs that addressed both of these questions.

In the negotiations, the decisions on the 'supplementarity' of measures taken under the flexibility mechanisms did very little to reduce the considerable interpretive space left by Article 17.[159] At COP 6*bis* in Bonn (2001), the parties almost reiterated the indeterminate formula of the Protocol: '[T]he use of the mechanisms *shall be supplemental* to domestic action and domestic action shall thus constitute *a significant element* of the effort made by each Party included in Annex I to meet its quantified emission limitation and reduction commitments under Article 3, paragraph 1.'[160] Rather than an absolute cap, the parties adopted a number of decisions trying to guarantee that activities undertaken under the flexibility mechanisms would amount to real reductions, and excluded some activities from their scope. Essentially, the parties were free to choose which mechanisms to use, and to what extent, as long as they used them in accordance with a very complex rulebook.[161] For instance, nuclear power was excluded as an option for CDM or JI activities, and the host country had to retain the exclusive say over the sustainability of such projects.[162] The decisions also made the use of the flexibility mechanisms dependent on compliance with methodological and reporting requirements.[163] Moreover, much detail was invested in specifying the parties' emissions baselines.[164] In addition, a voluminous set of modalities, rules, principles and guidelines was adopted for the Clean Development Mechanism in particular, such as participation requirements, the role of the COP and subsidiary bodies in providing additional guidance, validation and registration, and many more procedural and administrative issues. Substantive guidance was given in the shape of definitions of crucial terms, such as what constitutes 'renewable energy'

[159] Ott, 'Paving the Way for Ratification', 471.

[160] UNFCCC COP Decision 5/CP.6., *The Bonn Agreements on the implementation of the Buenos Aires Plan of Action* and Kyoto COP/MOP Decision 2/CMP.1, *Principles, nature and scope of the mechanisms pursuant to Articles 6, 12 and 17 of the Kyoto Protocol.*

[161] Due to this complex legal design, particularly CDM and emissions trading have evolved into legal and research fields of their own. See, eg, David Freestone and Charlotte Streck (eds), *Legal Aspects of Implementing the Kyoto Protocol Mechanisms: Making Kyoto Work* (OUP, 2005).

[162] For additionality of CDM-projects, see Kyoto COP/MOP Decision 3/CMP.1, *Modalities and procedures for a clean development mechanism as defined in Article 12 of the Kyoto Protocol*, paras 43–48.

[163] Kyoto COP/MOP Decision 2/CMP.1, para 5.

[164] Kyoto COP/MOP Decision 3/CMP.1, paras 37–38.

and 'energy efficiency improvement project activities',[165] and particular conditions for small-scale projects as well as afforestation and reforestation projects.[166] Similar, if somewhat less complex, sets of modalities and guidelines were adopted with regard to emissions trading[167] and joint implementation.[168]

In terms of denominations, the use of different titles such as rules, modalities or guidelines emphatically lacks a direct connection with the mandatory quality of the content of the instrument. Perhaps surprisingly, the '*guidance*' with regard to small-scale CDM projects is phrased no less mandatory than the '*modalities*' for the CDM, or the '*principles*' on the use of the flexibility mechanism.

Other important examples of the 'if, then' character of many UNFCCC COP and Kyoto COP/MOP decisions – the parties have a choice of options, but all with mandatory conditions attached – are the previously discussed *LULUCF* Decision and the *Accounting Modalities* discussed in chapter two.[169] The language of these two PTRs is without a doubt mandatory. Both the Accounting Modalities and the LULUCF state that 'anthropogenic greenhouse gas emissions by sources and removals by sinks *shall* be accounted for in accordance with the annex to the present decision'.[170] The language is also very specific. In terms of specificity, each of these decisions considerably diminished the capacity for parties to present information in a parochially advantageous manner, or to be reviewed with less scrutiny. For instance, the *LULUCF* Decision provides the following definition of what constitutes a 'forest':

> 'Forest' is a minimum area of land of 0.05–1.0 hectare with tree crown cover (or equivalent stocking level) of more than 10–30 per cent with trees with the potential to reach a minimum height of 2–5 metres at maturity in situ. A forest may consist either of closed forest formations where trees of various storeys and undergrowth cover a high proportion of the ground or open forest. Young natural stands and all plantations which have yet to reach a crown density of 10–30 per cent or tree height of 2–5 metres are included under forest, as are areas normally forming part of the forest area which are temporarily unstocked as a result of human intervention such as harvesting or natural causes but which are expected to revert to forest.

Just as with the Kyoto COP/MOP decisions on the *Flexibility Mechanisms*, despite the mandatory language, the parties retain much freedom in choosing the

[165] Kyoto COP/MOP Decision 4/CMP.1, *Guidance relating to the clean development mechanism*, Annex II.A.

[166] Kyoto COP/MOP Decision 5/CMP.1, *Modalities and procedures for afforestation and reforestation project activities under the clean development mechanism in the first commitment period of the Kyoto Protocol*, and Decision 6/CMP.1, *Simplified modalities and procedures for small-scale afforestation and reforestation project activities under the clean development mechanism in the first commitment period of the Kyoto Protocol and measures to facilitate their implementation.*

[167] Kyoto COP/MOP Decision 11/CMP.1, *Modalities, rules and guidelines for emissions trading under Article 17 of the Kyoto Protocol.*

[168] Kyoto COP/MOP Decisions 9/CMP.1, *Guidelines for the implementation of Article 6 of the Kyoto Protocol* and 10/CMP.1, *Implementation of Article 6 of the Kyoto Protocol.*

[169] Kyoto COP/MOP Decision 13/CMP.1.

[170] Kyoto COP/MOP Decision 13/CMP.1, Operative Part, para 3.

cheapest path to reaching their targets as long as they remain within the possibilities set out by the *LULUCF* Decision. The decisions largely leave it up to individual parties to elect *which* of the forestry and land-use related activities to include in the calculation of their assigned amounts.[171] Only once an option is chosen will the party have to comply with the criteria prescribed in the PTR for this option. This freedom is even greater for some parties, for which particular exceptions were included. Russia was allowed to keep its allowable forest management tonnages flexible, and Australia was allowed to maximise its base-year emissions from land clearing for agriculture.[172]

There also remained important lacunas in this intricate web of conditions. In relation to accounting, for instance, the parties agreed on some limitations regarding the transferability and bankability of credits.[173] A restriction on Removal Units (RMUs) was placed to the effect that they could not be banked for using them after the so-called 'first commitment period'. However, this restriction was then offset by allowing *non-bankable* RMUs to be exchanged with other Annex I-Parties' *bankable* units. 'As there is no formal hierarchy in the use of the various permit types for meeting the Kyoto targets,' climate experts worried, 'non-bankable units can be used first to save bankable units, for example, by exchanging RMUs for AAUs [Assigned Amount Units].'[174]

In addition, even after selecting a pathway, further sub-options remain available. The earlier discussed Paragraph 33 of the *Accounting Modalities* allows individual treaty parties to make the choice whether or not they shall cancel 'units': 'Each Party included in Annex I *may* cancel ERUs, CERs, AAUs and/or RMUs so they cannot be used in fulfilment of commitments under Article 3, paragraph 1' (emphasis added).[175]

d. *Montreal Protocol*

For the wording of Montreal Protocol PTRs, it suffices to return to the *Critical Use Criteria* and the *Exemption Decisions*, which are exemplary for many Montreal Protocol PTRs, both in terms of mandatory quality and specificity. As set out in chapter two, Article 2H.5 created the possibility of exemptions for critical use of methyl bromide up to 30 per cent of 1991 levels. The *Critical Use Criteria* set several clear and specific boundaries, using mandatory language. 'Use' should qualify as 'critical' only if 'the lack of availability of methyl bromide for that use would result in a significant market disruption' and '[t]here are no technically and economically

[171] Kyoto COP/MOP Decision 16/CMP.1, para C.7.

[172] Ian Fry, 'Twists and Turns in the Jungle: Exploring the Evolution of Land Use, Land-Use Change and Forestry Decisions within the Kyoto Protocol' (2002) 11 *RECIEL* 159, 165–68.

[173] Michel G den Elzen and André P de Moor, 'Analyzing the Kyoto Protocol under the Marrakesh Accords: Economic Efficiency and Environmental Effectiveness' (2002) 43 *Ecological Economics* 141, 143.

[174] ibid.

[175] Kyoto COP/MOP Decision 13/CMP.1, para 33.

feasible alternatives or substitutes'.[176] Furthermore, production or consumption of methyl bromide would be permitted only if, crucially, it was 'not available in sufficient quantity and quality from existing stocks of banked or recycled methyl bromide'.[177] These criteria were to be applied to nominations by parties, upon recommendations of a special panel.[178] A consolidated list of alternatives was also set up, together with a detailed Handbook on Critical Use Nominations for Methyl Bromide.[179] Decision XV/54 established that exemptions 'are intended to be limited, temporary derogations from the phase-out of methyl bromide',[180] amounting to a narrowing of the scope of the exemption that does not necessarily follow from Article 2H.5 of the protocol.

Consecutive *Exemptions Decisions* of the MOP also clearly indicate that 'the production and consumption of methyl bromide for critical uses should be permitted only if methyl bromide is not available in sufficient quantity and quality from existing stocks of banked or recycled methyl bromide'.[181] The United States had argued for some time that existing stocks should not be counted because they were privately owned, and therefore there was no guarantee that these stocks would end up with US farmers.[182] The consecutive exemption decisions, however, expressly indicate that the amount allocated to the United States is the amount indicated in the decision *minus available stocks*.

e. Comparative Observations

The discussed examples from the various regimes within the purview of this study show an extremely varied picture with regard to authority in the wording of environmental PTRs. This variance exists both between and within the several regimes, between internal and external PTRs, and depending on the wording of the underlying treaty provisions. There is surprisingly little variation between PTRs based on explicit and implicit enabling clauses. The examples show that wording at least goes some way in explaining the overall authority of PTRs.

The most consistent difference can be observed between those PTRs aimed at the collective behaviour of the parties within the regime's bodies on the one hand (internal PTRs), and those directly aimed at the environmental conduct

176 Montreal MOP Decision IX/6, *Critical-use exemptions for methyl bromide*, paras. 1.a.i and ii.

177 Montreal MOP Decision IX/6, para 1.b.ii.

178 The Montreal Protocol Technology and Economic Assessment Panel (TEAP), at http://ozone.unep.org/content/technology-and-economic-assessment-panel?language=en.

179 Montreal MOP Decision XIII/11, paras 2 and 3; Technology and Economic Assessment Panel and the Methyl Bromide Technical Options Committee, *Handbook on Critical Use Nominations for Methyl Bromide* (Version 6, December 2007).

180 Montreal MOP Decisions XV/54, *Categories of assessment to be used by the Technology and Economic Assessment Panel when assessing critical uses of methyl bromide*, and Ex.1/3, *Critical-use exemptions for methyl bromide for 2005*.

181 See, eg, Montreal MOP Decision XXII/6, *Critical-use exemptions for methyl bromide for 2011 and 2012*.

182 US Delegation to the 24th Open-Ended Working Group of the Montreal Protocol, 2004.

of individual treaty parties (external PTRs).[183] Internal PTRs are generally more authoritatively formulated, and thus leave less room for diverging interpretations than external PTRs. Of course, internal PTRs can indirectly affect the regulation of the treaty parties' environmental conduct by reducing the bandwidth within which treaty bodies can adopt PTRs.[184] For instance, the specificity and mandatory quality of the CITES *Listing Criteria* will also indirectly reduce the room for manoeuvre in individual treaty parties' environmental behaviour once the CITES COP has applied them to add or remove species from the Appendices. Still, it is telling that the parties are more hesitant in prescribing authoritatively phrased rules for domestic environmental policies directly, which is obviously seen as a greater incursion into sovereignty.

3. Significance of Wording as a Source of the Authority of PTRs

In what respect is the variety in the wording of PTRs really significant for the overall difficulty to escape PTRs as reference points? In addition to its significance for the likelihood that treaty parties *regard* PTRs as authoritative, in two respects: 1) for the likelihood that PTRs are included in compliance control at all; and 2) for the likelihood that compliance bodies and courts regard government actors as being able to escape a PTR as reference points or not. However, higher degrees of specificity or mandatory quality by no means *guarantee* the overall authority of a PTR, while lower degrees do not prevent that it can be very difficult for states and non-state actors to escape them. Practice thus shows important limitations to the extent to which authority can be gathered from wording.

First, as a rule, compliance and implementation committees only tend to check compliance with mandatorily phrased PTRs. For instance, the various CITES bodies tasked with compliance control concentrate much of their efforts on those CITES resolutions directing them to identify gaps in national implementing legislation, and recommend suspensions of trade if necessary. As Sand submits, surveys in 1993–94 indicated that only 12 CITES parties 'had completed the full range of legislative and administrative measures needed to give effect to all aspects of the Convention and related resolutions and decisions of the Conference of the Parties. Legislation in at least twenty-six countries was found not to meet the four *minimum requirements set by the Conference*. … The twenty-six serious "laggards" … were notified that the next Conference would consider sanctions, including trade bans, against all parties that had not introduced … the necessary

[183] *cf* Wiersema, 'The New International Law-Makers', 237–45 (distinguishing between 'COP activity' with effects on the external and internal obligations of the parties).

[184] *cf* Wiersema, 'The New International Law-Makers', 241 ('Even this internal activity can have significant effects on the way in which the treaty operates, and, indirectly therefore, on the substantive obligations of the parties.').

regulatory measures by the time of the meeting in June 1997' (emphasis added).[185] Where PTRs set mandatory and specific requirements, more compliance control generally tends to take place, violations are more easily established, and tend to be followed by some form of sanctions. There are exceptions to this observation. While the CITES Animals and Plants Committees, based on the COP Resolution on *Significant Trade*, may merely issue *recommendations* to parties to limit trade in Appendix II species, compliance with these recommendations is in fact reviewed by the Secretariat and the Standing Committee. If their review concludes that the recommendation has been insufficiently implemented, the Standing Committee may suspend trade on the basis of non-compliance with the *recommendation*.[186]

Second, the likelihood that compliance bodies and courts regard government actors as being able to escape a PTR as reference point is much greater for PTRs with recommendatory wording. In *Whaling in the Antarctic*, the ICJ showed itself to be sensitive to the lack of mandatory quality of a PTR. As discussed above, Resolution 1986-2 of the International Whaling Commission:

> Recommends that Contracting Governments when considering proposed research permits and the Scientific Committee when reviewing such permits and when reviewing the results of research from permits previously issued in accordance with the procedures of the Convention *should take into account* whether: (1) the objectives of the research are not practically and scientifically feasible through non-lethal research techniques.[187]

The *Whaling* judgment states in relation to this Resolution that:

> [A]s a matter of substance, the relevant resolutions and Guidelines … call upon States parties to take into account whether research objectives can practically and scientifically be achieved by using non-lethal research methods, *but they do not establish a requirement that lethal methods be used only when other methods are not available*.[188] (Emphasis added.)

The same point can be witnessed in various judgments of national courts. Private actors have occasionally tried to challenge government conduct in contravention of a PTR phrased in a hortatory manner before national courts. Most of the time, these courts have been quick to dismiss that such a PTR poses a requirement to the state organs in question. The importance of the lack of mandatory quality of the previously discussed Paragraph 33 of the *Accounting Modalities* of the Kyoto COP/MOP was underlined by a Dutch Administrative Court decision in a dispute between private reforestation enterprise Face the Future – jointly owned by Dutch

[185] Peter H Sand, 'Whither CITES? The Evolution of a Treaty Regime in the Borderland of Trade and Environment' (1997) 8 *European Journal of International Law* 29, 47–48.

[186] The procedure is described in detail in Bowman, Davies and Redgwell, '*Lyster's International Wildlife Law*', 522–25.

[187] IWC Resolution 1986-2, *Resolution on Special Permits for Scientific Research*, 38th Annual Meeting, 1986 (Rep. Int. Whal. Commn 37), at https://archive.iwc.int/pages/search.php?search=%21collection72&k.

[188] *Whaling in the Antarctic*, p 83.

energy companies – and the Dutch Government. The Court stated that 'the State of the Netherlands, on the basis of para. 33's clear terms, has the *competence*, not the *duty*, to annul Assigned Amount Units. Even apart from the question of direct applicability art. 33 13/CMP.1 and its invocability by Face the Future, considering this freedom of choice, the State can impossibly have acted in contravention of a legal duty' (emphasis added).[189] A similar conclusion was reached by the Australian Federal Courts in the *Greentree* case discussed earlier, albeit that here the low mandatory quality of the relevant resolutions was further confirmed by the common understandings evident from the practice of the Ramsar COP with regard to those resolutions. In this case, the government was also found not to have acted unlawfully considering the hortatory nature of the *Designation Conditions*.[190]

Overall, authority before national courts also tends to be lower when resolutions are not phrased sufficiently precisely. In the earlier discussed *Animal Welfare*, the Administrative Appeals Tribunal of Australia concluded that CITES Resolution 5.10 (on the definition of the term 'commercial purposes' in Article III.3 CITES) was rather unclear about what are 'uses whose non-commercial aspects do not clearly predominate', when applied to the question of whether zoos have predominantly commercial or non-commercial purposes.[191] The Tribunal concluded that the Resolution could therefore not be interpreted as a ban on importing Appendix I species by Australian zoos.[192]

However, the recommendatory or non-specific wording of PTRs on several occasions formed less of an obstacle to application by national courts when *government agencies* claimed that their behaviour was *excusable* because they acted *in accordance* with a PTR. The key idea behind this difference, based on the limited practice of national courts, seems to be that even if there is no *obligation* to act in accordance with a PTR because of its language, there is also no *prohibition* to act in accordance with it.[193] Support for this finding is found in the cases *Lac Sorobon*, *Orka* and *Born Free USA*.

[189] *Face the Future v Staat der Nederlanden*, para 4.2.1 [Translated, TS: 'De Staat heeft op grond van art. 33 13/CMP.1, zoals uit de bewoordingen van dit artikel duidelijk blijkt (zie hierboven onder 2.11), de bevoegdheid, en niet de plicht, AAU's te annuleren. Nog daargelaten de vraag of Face the Future een direct beroep toekomt op art. 33 13/CMP.1, handelt de Staat, gezien de keuzevrijheid die hij hierin heeft, niet in strijd met een wettelijke plicht door geen AAU's te annuleren op basis van deze bepaling'.].

[190] *Greentree* (FCA), para 135.

[191] CITES COP Res Conf 5.10, *Definition of 'primarily commercial purposes'*, states that: 'The term "commercial purposes" should be defined by the country of import as broadly as possible so that any transaction which is not wholly "non-commercial" will be regarded as "commercial". In transposing this principle to the term "primarily commercial purpose", it is agreed that all uses whose non-commercial aspects do not clearly predominate shall be considered to be primarily commercial in nature with the result that the importation of specimens of Appendix-I species should not be permitted.'

[192] *The International Fund for Animal Welfare (Australia) Pty Ltd and Ors and Minister for Environment and Heritage and Ors*, [2005] AATA 1210 (Administrative Appeals Tribunal of Australia), 7 December 2005, para 108.

[193] This form of authority is sometimes called 'permissive authority'. See, eg, Weil, 'Towards Relative Normativity', 413 (norms that 'dictate what its subjects … may do').

In the Netherlands Antilles case *Lac Sorobon*, the Dutch 'Crown' Court (Council of State)[194] agreed with the local Bonaire Governor's decision to suspend a licence for a resort in the vicinity of the Lac Sorobon wetland.[195] According to the Governor, in granting that licence, the Bonaire Governing Council (Bestuurscollege) had not acted in accordance with several hortatory Ramsar COP resolutions and recommendations. The Bonaire Governing Council had issued a licence for constructing a resort within 500 metres from the Lac Sorobon wetland, listed on the Ramsar List of wetlands.[196] According to the Governor, the decision to issue the licence should have been based on an Environmental Impact Assessment (EIA), performed in accordance with the guidelines for the performance of EIAs laid down in a number of Ramsar Resolutions and Recommendations.[197] Without such an EIA, the Governor argued, the Netherlands Antilles would fail to be in compliance with the 'wise use of wetlands' as required by Article 3.1 of the Ramsar Convention.[198] The Governing Council disagreed, taking the position that within the Netherlands Antilles' legal order, government authorities are only under an obligation to adopt policies generally supporting the 'wise use of wetlands', as provided in Article 3.1, but were not bound by the Ramsar Resolutions' interpretation of that obligation.[199] The judgment of the Dutch Council of State largely ignores the hortatory nature of these Ramsar COP Recommendations and Resolutions by stating that the obligation of wise use in light of these PTRs 'at least *amounts to the obligation* to thoroughly research the environmental effects of the activities for which a permit is requested, before permission is granted', and that 'an EIA, *as foreseen in the guidelines in Resolution VIII.9*, is performed before taking a decision about the grant of a permit' (emphasis added).[200]

[194] Formally, the decision in this case was made by Queen Beatrix, on the advice of the Council of State of the Kingdom of the Netherlands. In reality, the decision was taken by the Council of State. Incidentally, the name of the company requesting the licence to build the hotel was, confusingly, called Crown Court Estate N.V.

[195] *Besluit van 11 september 2007 op het beroep van het Bestuurscollege van het Eilandgebied Bonaire tegen het besluit van de Gouverneur van de Nederlandse Antillen van 3 januari 2007 tot vernietiging van de besluiten van het Bestuurscollege van 14 juni 2006, nr. 16 (260090760) tot uitgifte in erfpacht aan Crown Court Estate N.V. van een perceel grond, gelegen te Sorobon, kadastraal bekend als Afdeling 6, Sectie B, nummer 54, en van 14 augustus 2006 (26012797) tot verlening van bouwvergunning aan Crown Court Estate N.V. voor het oprichten van een zogenoemd ecologisch resort op vorenbedoeld perceel*, Staatsblad 347.

[196] *Lac Sorobon*, paras 1 and 2.2.

[197] In the *Lac Sorobon* case, reference is made to the following Ramsar Resolutions and Recommendations: Annex to Ramsar COP Recommendation 4.10 (1990): 'the following actions should be taken to promote wise use of the wetland'; Ramsar COP Recommendation 6.2 (1996): '(EIA) is a recognized field which should be applied', 'EIA should be undertaken'; Ramsar COP Res VII.16 (1999): 'CALLS UPON,' 'ENCOURAGES'; Ramsar COP Res VIII.9 (2002): 'URGES appropriate use'. For the *Orka* case, see CITES COP Res Conf 10.7 (Rev CoP15) *Disposal of confiscated live specimens of species included in the Appendices*: 'RECOMMENDS that', 'consult with', 'takes note of'.

[198] *Lac Sorobon*, para 2.2.1.

[199] *Lac Sorobon*, para 2.2.2.

[200] *Lac Sorobon*, para 2.2.3.5. In the original judgment in Dutch: 'maar *houdt in ieder geval de verplichting in* dat de milieueffecten van te ontplooien activiteiten in en rond aangewezen Ramsargebieden

In another case from the Netherlands (*Orka*), a lower court found no fault with the Dutch Government's decision of 'disposing' of a 'confiscated' killer whale, among other reasons because it had made the decision in accordance with the CITES COP guidelines on disposal of confiscated specimens.[201] The language of these CITES COP guidelines is again overtly non-mandatory, raising the question of why it would sustain the legal position of the government of the Netherlands.

In a third case, the already-discussed US District Court case of *Born Free USA v Norton*,[202] concerning the importation of African Elephants to US zoos, the Court did consider the recommendatory nature of the Primarily Commercial Purposes Resolution an impediment to following the Resolution as faithfully as possible. While the Court found 'the language in example (e) to be confusing',[203] and concluded that the imports under consideration did 'not fit cleanly into any of the non-exhaustive list of examples in Resolution Conf. 5.10,' it did find that, 'under the guidance of Res. Conf. 5.10, it is reasonable for [the US Fish and Wildlife Service] to conclude that this is not a setting in which commercial aspects of the zoos' purposes predominate over non-commercial aspects'.[204] In other words, although the low specificity presented an obstacle for the Court to really understand what the CITES Parties had wanted to prohibit, the low mandatory quality did not prevent it from using the Resolution as a central building block in its judgment that the FWS had acted lawfully. Wording clearly explains some, but by far not all, of the authority of environmental post-treaty rules.

D. Conclusion

Delegated and interpretive authority have narrowed but not closed the explanatory gap regarding variations in the authority of post-treaty rules. In the previous chapter, it was already concluded that MEAs are mostly silent about the degree of authority of PTRs. MEAs state nothing about PTRs' legal status, and the wording of enabling clauses is at most an indication of PTRs' maximum mandatory quality. In the international legal order, the doctrine of subsequent agreements makes a decent case of being at least *a* source of the authority of PTRs, which have to be

grondig worden onderzocht, alvorens daarvoor toestemming wordt verleend. Zoals ook met de door de Nederlandse Antillen gegeven uitvoering aan artikel 3 van het Verdrag van Ramsar wordt erkend, vloeit uit deze verplichting voort dat een MER, *als voorzien in de richtlijnen bij Resolutie VIII.9.*, wordt uitgevoerd, alvorens over het toestaan van de desbetreffende activiteit wordt beslist.'

[201] *Stichting The Black Fish c.s. tegen de staatssecretaris van Economische zaken, Landbouw en Innovatie (Orka)*, LJN: BU5150 (Rb. Amsterdam), Voorlopige Voorziening [provisional order], 21 November 2011.

[202] *Born Free USA v Norton*, 278 F.Supp.2d 5 (D.D.C.), 8 August 2003.

[203] *Born Free USA*, p 15. Example (e) in CITES COP Res Conf 5.10 relates to 'Captive-breeding programmes'.

[204] *Born Free USA*, p 16.

taken into account in the interpretation of the underlying MEA, but not necessarily *the* source. It was also found that the wording of PTRs varies across and within environmental regimes, and that these variations correlate to some extent with the variations in overall authority. PTRs with high mandatory quality are more often subject to, and difficult to escape in, compliance and other dispute settlement procedures.

However, the dynamic nature of authority also became clear in the examination and this dampened the conclusions regarding the importance of wording for authority. The adoption of a PTR does not mark the end of the development of that PTR's authority. The meaning of the wording of PTRs may undergo changes over time. The interpretation of the mandatory quality of a PTR may change in the practice evolving around it. Or different courts may come to different conclusions about whether some PTR contains a sufficiently precise wording to serve as a yardstick to assess the legality of a governmental policy or decision.[205] A PTR that is worded in mandatory terms may in practice be treated as a mere recommendation, as a result of which its authority is lowered. The scope of delegation may also be subject to change due to an expansive interpretation thereof by the delegatee and acquiescence of the delegator. The effect of PTRs as a class in the interpretation of treaties may also change over time. For instance, the International Court of Justice changed its interpretation of what subsequent agreements require from the treaty parties: from a duty to take them into account to a 'duty to cooperate'.[206] Likewise, the ICJ adopted the strict standard that, to qualify as a subsequent agreement, all parties to the treaty need to have participated in the consensus behind the adoption of a resolution, including the party (Japan) against whom the resolution is invoked before the Court. This changed overnight the authority of PTRs not adopted by consensus.

After having applied these traditionally assessed sources of international authority, there are still many lacunas unfilled in accounting for the authority of environmental PTRs. In the practice of compliance bodies and courts in all three normative orders, PTRs with a recommendatory wording sometimes attained high degrees of eventual authority. In the national legal orders, courts often applied PTRs or refused to apply them without reference to their degree of legal obligation. In the national and international legal orders, courts were seen to make a leap from an obligation 'to take into account' to the difference between lawful and unlawful conduct. Most vexingly perhaps, hardly a trace was found of any degree of legal obligation PTRs might possess in the internal normative orders, in which chapter two showed the authority of PTRs to be the highest. These findings trigger the question of what, if anything, can account for the remaining part of PTRs' authority.

[205] See the opposite conclusions regarding the same CITES Resolution in *Born Free USA* (United States) and *Animal Welfare* (Australia).
[206] *Whaling in the Antarctic*, para 83.

5

Invisible Authority: Social Legitimacy and Social Pressures

Considering the partial but limited explanatory value of both the doctrine of sources and the doctrine of interpretation for the actual authority of PTRs in practice, there must exist still other factors behind the authority of PTRs. Commentators of environmental post-treaty rules have come to this conclusion before. Gehring concluded that '[t]he precise legal status of secondary rules is of comparatively little importance for the practical operation of environmental treaty systems,'[1] and Brunnée concluded that a 'formal' perspective cannot provide an entirely satisfactory account of the '*de facto* law-making' of the COPs and MOPs.[2] This chapter seeks out the factors invisible to established legal doctrines that determine whether a PTR makes the jump from merely 'relevant' to 'authoritative'. These factors can best be bundled under the rubric of *social legitimacy*, which when it attaches to a PTR, creates *social pressures* that render that PTR more authoritative. The key to grasping the authority of PTRs (or lack of it) is in adopting a social understanding of authority. After defining social legitimacy and its relationship to authority, the chapter discusses the myriad ways in which social legitimacy can affect the authority of PTRs, and the myriad terms behind which this process takes place.

A. Social Legitimacy and Authority

With Brunnée and Gehring, and outside the field of international environmental law with Krisch,[3] Venzke,[4] Zürn[5] and Marmor,[6] one has to look beyond the

[1] Thomas Gehring, 'Treaty-Making and Treaty-Evolution' in Daniel Bodansky, Jutta Brunnée and Ellen Hey (eds), *The Oxford Handbook of International Environmental Law* (OUP, 2007), 492–93.

[2] Jutta Brunnée, 'COPing with Consent: Law-Making Under Multilateral Environmental Agreements' (2002) 15 *Leiden Journal of International Law* 1, 6.

[3] Nico Krisch, 'The Structure of Postnational Authority' (2015), at http://papers.ssrn.com/sol3/papers.cfm?abstract_id=2564579.

[4] Ingo Venzke, 'Between Power and Persuasion: On International Institutions' Authority in Making Law' (2013) 14 *Transnational Legal Theory* 354.

[5] Michael Zürn, 'From Rule to Authority – Why We Enter a Phase of Reflexive Legitimacy', Paper distributed for a presentation at the University of Amsterdam, 17 March 2014 (on file with author).

[6] Andrei Marmor, 'An Institutional Conception of Authority' (2011) 39 *Philosophy & Public Affairs* 238.

traditional (Krisch speaks of 'solid') dimensions of authority, towards factors that are less visible and more fluctuating (Krisch speaks of 'liquid').[7] As Enroth submits, authority does not 'have to be formal and codified in order to be recognizable and operable' but might also 'rest on something less formal such as norms and practices in a collectivity',[8] as long as this takes on a certain consistency.[9] As Krisch submits, authority 'can also be based on normative internalization or a mere acceptance as "normal" … and will often bear a social dimension'.[10] Without claiming to create legal obligations for their addressees, the authority of a PTR springs from less visible forms of content-independent recognition.[11] Thus, attention must be shifted to social pressures other than law, and to the origin of those social pressures: legitimacy.

Legitimacy is quite impossible to define generically, without referring to its normative or social (or sociological) conceptions. From a normative viewpoint, legitimacy is the right to exercise authority over others, from the viewpoint of one or more preferred or current political theories and philosophies.[12] Habermas has said that legitimacy 'means that there are *good arguments* for a political order's claim to be recognised as right and just; … a political order's *worthiness* to be recognised'.[13] From a normative perspective, the relevant question is therefore: 'What gives some institutions or individuals the *right* to rule?'[14] The social conception, which goes back to Weber, rather emphasises the (subjective) acceptance of authority's rightfulness by a certain community.[15] A political scientist such as Dahl defines legitimacy in this way: 'A government is said to be "legitimate" if the people to whom its orders are directed *believe* that the structure, procedures, acts, decisions, policies, officials or leaders of government possess the quality of "rightness," propriety or moral goodness.'[16] To study legitimacy from a social perspective is to ask: 'What do the relevant actors think about legitimacy?'[17]

[7] For Krisch's project on Liquid Authority, see http://nicokrisch.net/projects/liquid-authority/.

[8] Henrik Enroth, 'The Concept of Authority Transnationalised' (2013) 4 *Transnational Legal Theory* 336, 342.

[9] See also Michael Zürn and Matthew Stephen, 'The View of Old and New Powers on the Legitimacy of International Institutions' (2010) 30 *Politics* 91, 92.

[10] Krisch, 'The Structure of Postnational Authority', 10. To remain within the concept of authority, these additional sources must fall short of either pure rational persuasion or pure coercion. Hannah Arendt, *Between Past and Future: Eight Exercises in Political Thought* (Penguin 2006 [1968]), 93.

[11] Krisch, 'The Structure of Postnational Authority', 10–11.

[12] See, eg, Hanna Pitkin, 'Obligation and Consent-II' (1966) 60 *American Political Science Review* 39, 39 ('Legitimate authority is precisely that which ought to be obeyed, … to which rational men considering all relevant facts and issues would consent.') Not only institutions, but also rules or actions, such as PTRs, can be evaluated as to their normative legitimacy. Christopher A Thomas, 'The Uses and Abuses of Legitimacy in International Law' (2014) 34 *Oxford Journal of Legal Studies* 729, 738.

[13] Jürgen Habermas, *Communication and the Evolution of Society*, Thomas McCarthy tr (Beacon, 1979), 178.

[14] Daniel Bodansky, 'The Concept of Legitimacy in International Law' in Rüdiger Wolfrum and Volker Röben (eds), *Legitimacy in International Law* (Springer, 2010), 313.

[15] Max Weber, *Economy and Society* (University of California Press, 1978), 953. See further Steven Bernstein, 'Legitimacy in International Environmental Governance' (2005) 1 *Journal of International Law & International Relations* 139, 156; Bodansky, 'The Concept of Legitimacy', 313 ('[I]t is an empirical question.').

[16] Robert A Dahl, *Modern Political Analysis* 2nd edn (1970), 41.

[17] Bodansky, 'The Concept of Legitimacy', 313.

It is this social conception of legitimacy that is most directly relevant for understanding the authority of PTRs. The social understanding of authority prescribed by the various authors cited above would hold that individual treaty parties and other affected actors find it difficult to escape PTRs *because of their belief that the wider community expects them to do so*. As Marmor puts it, '[t]he suggestion I put forward is that the norms in play [that is, the norms inducing deference] must be actual social norms, followed by a certain community, forming part of a social practice or institution'.[18] Authority thus is not exactly a dyadic relationship between the actor adopting the PTR and the individual addressees of the PTR, but a triadic one. As Venzke translates Flathman to international authority, '[w]hat matters for the existence of authority is that there is an expectation to follow what the authority says. What sustains the [expectation] is not individual recognition in the specific case of its exercise, but its social recognition'.[19]

It must immediately be added that, of course, the authority of all *legal* obligations also ultimately rests on such a social recognition that the law is obligatory for everyone in the community. Social legitimacy is very much a 'supporting' source of authority for all instruments of global governance, including the formal sources of international law. But it plays much less of a *separate* role in the case of formal sources of international law, such as treaties, for which social legitimacy largely is merged into the requirements of legal validity, primarily the requirement of consent. State consent is a requirement for the legal validity of a treaty, but it is also traditionally its most important source of input for legitimacy.[20] Likewise, accordance of treaty interpretation with the object and purpose of a treaty is a requirement for a legally valid interpretation of a treaty, but also a source of legitimacy, because states are assumed to have consented to these methods of interpretation. This is sometimes called *legal legitimacy*,[21] whereby legality and legitimacy beliefs are, to some extent, in sync. Therefore, an international or domestic court will rarely expressly point to state consent as an additional reason to support its reliance on a treaty provision in reaching judgment, because the legitimating device of state consent is already incorporated in the test for the legal validity of the treaty.

The crucial point is, however, that communities of states also have such expectations with regard to norms that are *not* legally binding. In accordance with Johnstone, the expectations of the addressees of, for instance, MEAs extend to those interpretations supported by 'the community of professionals engaged in the enterprise of treaty interpretation and implementation' (the 'interpretive

[18] Marmor, 'An Institutional Conception of Authority', 246.

[19] Venzke, 'Between Power and Persuasion', 366, relying on Richard E Flathman, *The Practice of Political Authority: Authority and the Authoritative* (Chicago University Press, 1980), 26.

[20] See Daniel Bodansky, 'The Legitimacy of International Governance: A Coming Challenge for International Environmental Law?' 1999 *American Journal of International Law* 596, 604, 612.

[21] Bodansky, 'The Legitimacy of International Governance', 605 ('Legal legitimacy is what connects an institution's continuing authority to its original basis in state consent.').

community').[22] In that context the interpretive community's expectations have a much greater separate importance, because it is a lot less clear what (non-legal) conditions non-binding instruments must attain in order to have an effect on legal obligations.

Social legitimacy can become the crucial missing link *complementing* the traditional legal sources of authority (just) enough to tilt the balance in favour of a PTR's authority. A recommendatory instrument is more likely to be considered relevant for interpretation if a law applier believes himself to be constrained by its output legitimacy. A rule that has an ambiguous legal status is more likely to successfully claim interpretive relevance if the law applier believes its adoption to have been the result of a sufficiently inclusive process (input legitimacy). An instrument based on an act of delegation that is rather vague about the scope of what it delegates might be more likely to constrain its addressees when the actor adopting the instrument is believed to be an expert on the issue in question (rationality, comparable to epistemic authority). In all these scenarios, legitimacy beliefs have the potential to increase the instrument's authority to the extent that addressees and law appliers feel more constrained than in the absence of those beliefs.

This systemic or social view of authority is expressed for international environmental law by Bodansky in the following manner:

> [W]hat matters is *the state of mind of the actors that comprise the relevant community* – what we referred to earlier as the actor's internal point of view – *a sense that the norm represents an obligation* and that compliance is therefore required rather than optional.[23] (Emphasis added.)

What may be found in that state of mind of the actors comprising the relevant community that sustains this expectation, this social recognition? What influences this 'sense of obligation'? Why do communities of states, compliance officials, treaty secretariats and other expert committees exert social pressure on complying with PTRs in the internal normative orders?[24]

The expectations of at least two – overlapping – 'communities' are at play in the case of PTRs. First, the expectations of the community of state representatives involved in the practice with regard to PTRs at the level of the plenary treaty meetings, and in various types of compliance and implementation committees. The authority of PTRs is then grounded in the treaty parties' collective perception

[22] Ian Johnstone, 'Treaty Interpretation: The Authority of Interpretive Communities' (1991) 12 *Michigan Journal of International Law* 371, 372, 374, 377 (referring to the theories of Owen Fiss and Stanley Fish).

[23] Daniel Bodansky, *The Art and Craft of International Environmental Law* (Harvard University Press, 2010), 101.

[24] Krisch expects that we have to look more towards what he calls the 'substantive grounding' of authority: 'in order to establish itself and gain recognition, [authority] has recourse to more substantive sources: expertise, moral principles and values, or problem-solving capacity'. Krisch, 'The Structure of Postnational Authority', 12.

of the PTR practice as a generally legitimate practice in terms of input, procedures, outcomes, and values. Brunnée speaks of 'horizontal' perceptions of social legitimacy.[25] The social pressures exerted by the community of states as represented in the plenary treaty meetings and compliance bodies would then be a translation of the dominant beliefs of that community regarding the legitimacy of PTRs. For 'community' does not imply that all these representatives have the same expectations all the time, but that usually one view on which instruments should possess a high degree of authority becomes dominant among them. If authority is considered as a triadic rather than a dyadic relationship, it would suffice for a powerful part of actors in the relevant legitimacy circle to consider those rules legitimate.

Yet, the expectations of the state parties and their representatives need not be the same with regard to the authority of PTRs outside the internal orders of the treaty meetings. Moreover, in the international and national legal orders, additional communities' expectations become important. In the international legal orders, not just the court that has jurisdiction over a dispute involving PTRs, but the entire pool of judges of international courts, the community of states that sustain the international judicial system, and the famous 'invisible college of international [environmental] lawyers'.[26] In the national legal orders, the domestic judicial community and the other branches of government look over the shoulders of the deciding court. Somewhere in the back of their minds, the expectations of the actors in all these communities are likely to be informed by what they think are the expectations of (at least part of) the audience of their decisions. Ultimately, that audience involves everyone affected in some way by decisions involving the environmental issues to which PTRs relate.

As this chapter sets out to argue and show, the differences between the community expectations in the different normative orders are the missing puzzle piece in explaining the variation in the authority of PTRs.

B. Social Legitimacy and Social Pressures in the Three Normative Orders

1. Internal Normative Orders

As observed in chapters two and three, as long as a PTR (1) is validly adopted in accordance with the Rules of Procedure, and (2) has been adopted by the COP,

[25] Brunnée, 'COPing with Consent', 13 ('[W]e need to focus first on what we might think of as horizontal legitimacy factors. They operate, at least for the time being, primarily between the state parties to an MEA.').

[26] Oscar Schachter, 'The Invisible College of International Lawyers' (1977) 72 *Northwestern University Law Review* 217.

COP/MOP or MOP of the same MEA as where the question of its authority is at play, all actors within the regime at least *treat it from the beginning and consistently* equivalently *as if it had a high degree of authority*.[27] This treatment can only be explained by a large measure of social legitimacy[28] among at least a dominant part of the community of treaty parties, over time making PTRs very difficult to escape in the interpretation of what the treaty requires. In the vocabulary of Brunnée and Toope, there is a shared understanding of the parties[29] as to the required deference to PTRs in the 'community'.

To reiterate once again the strong authority of PTRs in the internal normative order:

> From time to time, the CITES Standing Committee suspends trade with a CITES party in one or more CITES-listed species on the basis that the party has failed to comply with reporting obligations recommended by the Animals or Plants Committees on the basis of Res. Conf. 12.8 (Rev. CoP 13).[30] In July 2005, the Standing Committee suspended all trade in CITES-listed species with Nigeria on the basis of a recommendation of the CITES *Secretariat* on the inadequacy of its legislation.[31] The recommendations were based on non-compliance with COP Decisions 13.79 to 13.83 on national laws for implementation of the Convention, which in turn were based on COP Resolution 8.4 (Rev. 15).
>
> At the Montreal Protocol's recent 50th Meeting of the Implementation Committee, the Committee assessed compliance of several parties with information submission requirements in relation to Decision XV/19, which sets out the methodology to be used to review requests for the revision of baseline data.[32]
>
> The enforcement branch of the Kyoto Protocol Compliance Committee, in its assessment of Greece's implementation of the Protocol, found Greece to be in non-compliance with the guidelines for national systems under Article 5, paragraph 1, of the Kyoto Protocol (decision 19/CMP.1), and the guidelines for the preparation of the information required under Article 7 of the Kyoto Protocol (decision 15/CMP.1).[33] The non-eligibility of Greece to participate in the flexibility mechanisms of Article 6, 12 and 17 Kyoto Protocol at that point was, in part, based on the requirements laid down in those COP/MOP guidelines.[34]

[27] *cf* Geir Ulfstein, 'Reweaving the Fabric of International Law? Patterns of Consent in Environmental Framework Agreements, Comment by Geir Ulfstein', in Rüdiger Wolfrum and Volker Röben (eds), *Developments of International Law in Treaty Making* (Springer, 2005).

[28] Paraphrasing the ICJ's Advisory Opinion in *Reparation for Injuries Suffered in the Service of the United Nations* (Advisory Opinion) [1949] ICJ Rep 174.

[29] Jutta Brunnée and Stephen J Toope, *Legitimacy and Legality in International Law* (CUP, 2010); Brunnée, 'COPing with Consent'.

[30] See, eg, CITES Standing Committee, Notification to the Parties No 2013/013, Geneva, 2 May 2013, *CONCERNING: Implementation of Resolution Conf. 12.8* (Rev. CoP13) (Review of Significant Trade in specimens of Appendix-II species).

[31] Michael Bowman, Peter Davies and Catherine Redgwell, *Lyster's International Wildlife Law* 2nd edn (CUP, 2010), 519.

[32] Montreal Protocol Implementation Committee, Fiftieth meeting, Bangkok, 21 and 22 June 2013, UNEP/OzL.Pro/ImpCom/50/4, 8–12.

[33] Kyoto Protocol Compliance Committee Enforcement Branch, CC-2007-1-6/Greece/EB, Preliminary Finding, 6 March 2008, para 5.

[34] ibid, para 17.

Now consider that, in the internal normative orders, the consistent practices of plenary treaty meetings to operate in accordance with PTRs and compliance bodies to control compliance with PTRs is *almost never challenged by treaty parties.* Sand had to go back all the way to the 1987 Ottawa meeting of the CITES COP to find the last example of a protesting government: the Austrian Government resisting the bindingness of a CITES Secretariat recommendation, and the CITES COP Resolution underpinning it.[35] The combination of PTRs not being legally binding with their bindingness within the regime hardly ever being challenged, cannot but point to an effective mix of social legitimacy among the treaty parties and social pressures on the treaty parties. The following sections examine where this near-collective belief in the legitimacy of PTRs might be coming from, and how it translates into expectations and pressures, that is, authority, on individual parties.

a. Social Legitimacy

Without extensive interviews with state representatives, it is difficult to know with reasonable certainty what induces the parties' lack of protest. With that *caveat* in mind, there are many factors in the MEAs and in the procedures of adopting PTRs in which one can find reasons for why the treaty parties' governmental representatives are likely to believe that PTRs are sufficiently legitimate to *expect* deference to them by each party.

First, it is possible that, while they have not expressed it in the treaty text, a large part of the treaty parties always agreed on a shared *intention* that post-treaty rules would become binding in the internal normative order. Chapter three dismissed that such an 'intention' or 'implication' can be derived from the MEA provisions and PTRs on non-compliance. This is always a difficult argument to build. It is almost impossible to point out conclusive evidence of intent on the part of the drafters[36] with regard to what they may have intended. But it is very well possible that many negotiators of MEAs, either for themselves or in exchanges with other negotiators, did in fact have such an intention or acceptance when they inserted enabling clauses, created the COPs and MOPs, and gave them the power to adopt recommendations. According to Johnstone, 'in entering into a treaty, the parties assent not only to the terms of the agreement but also to a process

[35] Peter H Sand, 'Das Washingtoner Artenschutzabkommen (WA)' (2016) 54 *Archiv des Völkerrechts* 561–589 ('noch auf der sechsten Vertragsstaatenkonferenz (Ottawa, 1987) bestritt die österreichische Regierung in Erwiderung eines Sekretariatsberichts über Verstöße gegen CoP-Embargos deren rechtliche Verbindlichkeit'). See CITES Doc 6.19 (1987), Case No A.1 and Valerie Karno, 'Protection of Endangered Gorillas and Chimpanzees in International Trade: Can CITES Help?' (1990) 14 *Hastings International & Comparative Law Review* 989, 1006.

[36] Ingo Venzke, *How Interpretation Makes International Law: On Semantic Change and Normative Twists* (OUP, 2012), 3 (also pointing out that the *travaux préparatoires* are a last resort of interpretation, after all other means of interpretation have failed).

of interpretation whose goal is an intersubjective understanding of the treaty terms',[37] even though this is not made explicit. If true, this would be a very strong explanation for why PTRs carry a high social legitimacy for the treaty parties. While studying the text of the MEA does not provide clarity as to what the treaty parties have consented to, the negotiators, in this scenario, did in fact agree behind closed doors that they consented to a high authority for PTRs in the internal normative orders.

Second, even if there was no such intention, the parties and their representatives might regard the process of adopting PTRs as a legitimate process. In a formal sense, because PTR adoption *adheres to procedural rules*. For instance, there is nothing in the MEAs or their respective Rules of Procedure indicating that when a new PTR's adoption complies with the Rules of Procedure, this endows it with binding character in the internal normative order. Yet, it is not in any way strange that compliance with the Rules of Procedure would increase the social legitimacy that a PTR carries among the community of treaty party representatives. The Rules of Procedure have been adopted by the plenary treaty meetings by consensus, or by large majority. Thus, a high number of the treaty parties has found the procedure for adopting PTRs prescribed in these Rules of Procedure sufficiently legitimate for such a rule-making process to vote in its favour or to not object to its adoption.

Apart from adherence to the rules of procedures lending legitimacy to the process, there is the question of the parties' beliefs regarding the legitimacy of the procedures as such. There is likely to be a dominant perception among the treaty party representatives and other participants in the treaty bodies that *the consensual process of adoption is a legitimate process* for the purpose of adopting PTRs. As Brunnée puts it, '[i]t appears that the firm grounding of international environmental law in consensual processes has helped shield it from the crisis of legitimacy that has afflicted other areas of international law'.[38] In order for such crises to be prevented, the plenary treaty meetings 'must ensure that relevant processes are inclusive'.[39] Most treaty parties indeed appear to perceive the process of adoption of PTRs as sufficiently inclusive, and therefore sufficiently legitimate to defer to them.[40] Gehring expects that 'the contracting parties in most environmental treaty systems seek to adopt important, if not all, secondary decisions by consensus so as to extend the consent-based binding force to all parties'.[41]

[37] Johnstone, 'Treaty Interpretation', 381.

[38] Brunnée, 'COPing with Consent', 10.

[39] ibid, 41.

[40] ibid, 14 ('a widely shared sense of legitimacy at the international level, generated through adherence of law-making to certain requirements').

[41] Gehring, 'Treaty-Making and Treaty-Evolution', 493; Brunnée, 'COPing with Consent', 11, 34. Even without buying into Brunnée's constructivist frame of mind, without 'shared interests' or understandings of the content of their obligations, a shared perception of the *legitimacy* of the PTR adoption process can still be at play. We also need not go so far, as not only Brunnée, but also Wiersema suggests,

A third factor is that treaty party representatives make a clear distinction between PTRs originating inside or outside a particular regime. Recall the decision of the Kyoto Protocol Compliance Committee's Enforcement Branch in relation to Questions of Implementation regarding Croatia. The decision excluded a PTR of the *UNFCCC* COP from the normative framework against which the compliance of Croatia had to be controlled:

> The application of decision 7/CP.12 under the Kyoto Protocol does not follow from any of the provisions of the Kyoto Protocol or from [COP/MOP] decisions. Since the COP and the COP/MOP] are two distinct decision-making bodies, the fact that all Parties to the Kyoto Protocol are also Parties to the United Nations Framework Convention on Climate Change does not provide a sufficient basis for establishing the application of COP decisions under the Kyoto Protocol.[42]

From this reasoning of the Enforcement Branch, it can be plausibly inferred *a contrario* that the rationale for the application of *Kyoto Protocol COP/MOP* decisions to compliance assessments is that the Kyoto Protocol's decision-making body has adopted them, rather than some outside body. The importance of this strict distinction between inside/outside should not be underestimated. The crucial difference lies in the control that the parties have over the adoption of PTRs within the regime, compared to the lack of control they have over the adoption of PTRs from other regimes, which – if applicable – could upset an entire, carefully negotiated and calibrated system. As will be seen in the evaluation of the social legitimacy of PTRs outside the internal normative order (in the international and national legal orders), the beliefs of states in the legitimacy of applying a PTR outside its regime of origin is totally different.

Fourth, it is not impossible that some PTRs would entertain a certain level of what some have called *epistemic authority*, which is closely related to *rationality*, a ground of social legitimacy regarded as important by the likes of Weber.[43] Zürn et al define epistemic authority as being 'based on having special knowledge or moral expertise. It implies that the views expressed by an individual or an institution are recognised as trustworthy (an authority)'.[44] This could especially apply to those PTRs that originate in expert bodies of the regime, and concern topics with highly technical components – despite the highly political nature of decision

that this sense of legitimacy among the parties transforms PTRs into *law*, let alone that it is a requirement of all law. ibid, 36–37 ('Only through an inclusive process can actors participate in the shared understandings that are crucial to the emergence of legal norms.'); Annecoos Wiersema, 'The New International Law-Makers? Conferences of the Parties to Multilateral Environmental Agreements' (2009) 31 *Michigan Journal of International Law* 231, 250–51.

[42] Kyoto Protocol Compliance Committee Enforcement Branch, CC-2009-1-8/Croatia/EB, 26 November 2009, Para 3(c).

[43] Martin Spencer, 'Weber on Legitimate Norms and Authority' (1970) 21 *The British Journal of Sociology* 123, 123–24.

[44] Michael Zürn, Martin Binder and Matthias Ecker-Ehrhardt, 'International Authority and Its Politicization' (2012) 4 *International Theory* 69, 86.

making also in expert bodies. It is certainly not excluded that the authority of PTRs adopted by the Ramsar and CITES COPs in part rests on the decades of experience and knowledge collection in relation to wetlands and trade in endangered species of their secretariats and specialist government representatives. However, most PTRs are adopted by state representatives, not by (independent) experts; most PTRs are not presented as the best norms from an expert point of view, but as the outcome of a political consensus. Epistemic authority is therefore unlikely to play more than a subsidiary role for most PTRs. Other research methods than documentary study would have to provide more precise insights in this respect.

The same is true for the potential role of that other Weberian ground for social legitimacy – *tradition* – for which there are few explicit indications in official documents. No clear shift can be discerned in the authority of PTRs within the internal normative orders of environmental regimes, from one period to the next. The authority of PTRs – *mutatis mutandis* their wording – appears to have been relatively stable from the beginning, up until the present. Examples, such as those provided by Sand, of challenges to the authority of PTRs still happening occasionally in the 1980s but not afterwards, would fit into a theory that tradition has stabilised the authority of PTRs over time. More certainty in this respect could be achieved by interviewing persons involved in the development of international environmental regimes from the beginning.

That said, the social legitimacy of PTRs in the internal normative orders may of course undergo changes, threatening the authority of PTRs if the legitimacy crisis persists for too long. For instance, in the 1980s and 1990s, CITES underwent a crisis of trust among the exporting countries of products made out of endangered species.[45] They considered that their interests were not sufficiently represented at regular meetings of the COP, where listing and de-listing decisions were made and the criteria for those listings were determined. Had the CITES COP not heeded those concerns and granted export quotas for a number of African species, initially African ivory and leopard skins,[46] some Southern-African states might well have stopped to perceive the CITES COP as a legitimate decision maker. Instead, with the introduction of more and more quotas during the 1990s,[47] and the modernisation of the listing criteria, the COP was able to regain the trust of the wildlife exporting countries. The PTRs relating to the relevant species could therefore continue to exert authority over those parties as well.

[45] Bowman, Davies and Redgwell, *'Lyster's International Wildlife Law'*, 498.

[46] CITES Res. Conf. 10.14 (Rev. CoP16), *Quotas for leopard hunting trophies and skins for personal use*; CITES Res. Conf. 10.9, *Consideration of proposals for the transfer of African elephant populations from Appendix I to Appendix II.*

[47] Amongst others CITES Res. Conf. 10.10 (Rev. CoP16), *Trade in elephant specimens*; CITES Res. Conf. 10.15 (Rev. CoP14), *Establishment of quotas for markhor hunting trophies*; CITES Res. Conf. 13.5 (Rev. CoP14), *Establishment of export quotas for black rhinoceros hunting trophies.*

b. Social Pressures

It is very unlikely that the belief in the legitimacy of PTRs of all treaty parties and their representatives would be equally high at all times. But if a dominant part of them has a sufficient belief, it can turn into social expectations and pressures for everyone. For example, as protests at various meetings of the UNFCCC COP and Kyoto COP/MOP regarding the actual existence of consensus have shown, by far the minority of treaty parties find the practice of consensual decision making in the climate change regimes sufficiently inclusive.[48] However, if a sufficient number of parties hold the perception that the consensual process and the outcomes reached are legitimate, it almost certainly supplements the resulting PTRs' authority, because of authority's triadic character: the majority's positive perception of legitimacy is likely to translate into social pressure on the minority. As social theorist Luhmann notes, authority 'does precisely not rest … on convictions for which one is personally responsible, but to the contrary on social climate'.[49] What starts as individual beliefs of legitimacy becomes 'a generally shared expectation to follow what the authority says',[50] becoming stronger the longer it lasts. Looking at how social legitimacy is translated into social pressures consequently means moving into the borderland between authority and coercion: the impossible choices that treaty parties face if they consider escaping PTRs as reference points.[51]

Gehring has suggested several such social pressures. The first he identifies is the fear of loss of reputation. Not deferring to a consensual PTR 'undermines a state's reputation because offenders appear as unreliable cooperators'.[52] After all, in case of consensually adopted PTRs, no party formally objected to these PTRs. As a minimum, they acquiesced to them. The consensus reflects a promise to honour mutual commitments.[53] To later challenge their authority could come across as flippant and unreliable.

Gehring's second observation is the magnitude of the choice to try to escape PTRs. Choosing between accepting the operation of the system as it is, including PTRs, and unilateral complete withdrawal from the system, is really a non-choice. The system either operates in accordance with the PTRs or it does not operate at all. 'If provisions for the assessment of production and consumption figures under the Montreal Protocol, criteria for the classification of endangered species under CITES, or the rules of the clean development mechanism under the Kyoto

[48] See ch 7.

[49] Niklas Luhmann, *Legitimation durch Verfahren* (Suhrkamp, 1983) 34.

[50] Venzke, 'Between Power and Persuasion', 366.

[51] ibid, 368. Also Krisch, 'The Structure of Postnational Authority', 11 ('For an individual actor, deference to an authority may well seem involuntary if the authority is based on a recognition by other social actors who impose costs (or withhold benefits) in cases of non-compliance.').

[52] Gehring, 'Treaty-Making and Treaty-Evolution', 493.

[53] ibid.

Protocol are formulated in a particular way that has been agreed upon within the relevant COP or MOP, the treaty systems will simply operate accordingly'.[54] Alternative interpretations are excluded. Unilateral rejection is not a viable option for most treaty parties. Related to this point is the package deal and tit-for-tat nature of PTRs: If a party wants other treaty parties to defer to certain PTRs, it will itself have to defer to those and other PTRs as well. '[*E*]*x post* withdrawal from undesired parts of the package may prompt the withdrawal of other parties from their obligations.'[55]

Third, to escape from PTRs does not merely mean to challenge the authority of PTRs, but also the legality and legitimacy of the actions of the plenary treaty meetings and compliance committees applying them. The treaty parties have granted the power to operate, implement, control, and sanction to the COPs, COP/MOPs and MOPs as well as to the NCPs and other implementing bodies. The threat that the COP hands out sanctions or withdraws privileges from parties found to be in non-compliance with PTRs, such as the privilege to participate in the Kyoto Protocol's flexibility mechanisms or to receive technological and financial assistance for the phasing out of ozone-depleting substances, is real.[56] As the decisions of the Kyoto Protocol Enforcement Branch testify, the PTR-based eligibility criteria to participate in the flexibility mechanisms are the basis for the Branch to suspend eligibility.

The powers of the plenary treaty bodies and compliance committees should, in an environment operating in accordance with the rule of law, not provide them with carte blanche to select *which instruments* they apply. But if a dominant majority or near-consensus agrees that PTRs be applied to a certain matter, the party subject to the measure taken will fight an uphill battle. In other words, even for those parties that are more critical of the legitimacy of PTRs, challenging their authority within the regime has little chance of success considering these social pressures. Whether the social legitimacy behind these pressures is justified from a normative standpoint is considered in chapter seven.

2. International Legal Order

For the international legal order, chapter four found that there is a legal obligation for states to *take into account* PTRs in the interpretation of their underlying MEAs, thus falling short of a legal obligation *to act in accordance* with PTRs.

[54] ibid.
[55] ibid.
[56] ibid, 494. See the decisions of the Kyoto Protocol Compliance Committee EB, which recommends such sanctions for non-compliance with PTRs, particularly in regard to the accounting of assigned amounts. Sebastian Oberthür and René Lefeber, 'Holding Countries to Account: The Kyoto Protocol's Compliance System Revisited after Four Years of Experience' (2010) 1 *Climate Law* 133, 152 ('the compliance system utilises the incentives and disincentives that the Protocol and its implementing decisions have generated').

Still, it was observed that the ICJ in the *Whaling* and *Pulp Mills* cases ended up assessing the *lawfulness* of the conduct of, respectively, Japan and Uruguay in the light of the interpretations of the underlying treaties advocated in relevant PTRs. In other words, according to the ICJ, these states did have to act in accordance with PTRs. The chapter thus concluded that there was a gap to be explained between the degree of legal obligation of the relevant PTRs in the international legal order, and the actual effect that the ICJ accorded them in their judgments. The question is: what explains the closing of this gap?

The answer to this question is sought by looking at two aspects. (1) The beliefs of the parties to these disputes with regard to PTRs relevant to the dispute. Parties accused of having acted unlawfully by not acting in accordance with a relevant PTR regularly challenge the authority of these PTRs over them. The extent to which they do so presents a truly remarkable contrast with the aforementioned absence of such challenges in the internal normative orders. (2) The reasoning of the ICJ and its separately writing judges with regard to the crossing of the gap between taking into account and acting in accordance with. The ICJ takes the crucial step from 'taking into account' towards ascertaining lawfulness on the basis of PTRs, on the basis of these PTRs' supposed normative legitimacy as consensual decisions (input legitimacy) or because they serve the object and purpose of the treaty (output legitimacy).

a. *Stance of Governments in International Dispute Settlement*

To begin with, what do states believe about the authority of PTRs in the international legal order? It should not come as a surprise that, in the *Whaling* case, Australia, in whose favour it was that the *Special Permits Resolution* should become decisive in the interpretation of Article VIII ICRW, argued that Japan acted unlawfully by not complying with the Resolution.[57] More interesting is that Japan, in clear contrast to anything observed within environmental regimes, adamantly denied that the *Special Permits* Resolution and other IWC resolutions and recommendations:

> create any legal obligation, nor establish criteria for the assessment of the legality of special permits. They simply suggest a course of action, which the Contracting Governments are not bound to follow.[58]
>
> ...
>
> [IWC Recommendations] are merely invitations addressed to the Contracting Governments to consider a particular course of action, the Contracting Governments remaining free to accept or reject those invitations.[59]

[57] *Whaling in the Antarctic (Australia v Japan: New Zealand intervening)* (Memorial of Australia) [2011] ICJ Rep 262, paras 4.20–4.31, 4.65–4.69.

[58] *Whaling in the Antarctic* (Counter-Memorial of Japan) [2012], paras 8.31–8.32. Japan also argued that the IWC Resolutions were not even subsequent agreements at all. *Whaling in the Antarctic* (Counter-Memorial of Japan), paras 55, 7.23.

[59] *Whaling in the Antarctic* (Counter-Memorial of Japan), paras 8.2, 8.38.

> Thus, when [Australia] bases itself on resolutions, which … deny a Contracting Government the use of lethal methods, it wrongly alleges that these rights (or even obligations) expressly granted to the Contracting Governments under Article VIII have been superseded by non-binding instruments adopted by the IWC.[60]

At most, 'Japan accepts that, even in the absence of binding effect, there is a duty on the part of the Contracting Governments to *consider* a recommendation in good faith and, if requested, to explain their action or inaction' (emphasis added).[61] Japan thus regards the *Special Permit* Resolution and other IWC PTRs as relatively easy to escape, and approaches them as your average non-binding soft law.

By contrast, in the case *Pulp Mills on the River Uruguay*,[62] Argentina and Uruguay found themselves to be in agreement as regards the high authority of the rules and regulations (called 'CARU Digests') adopted by the Administrative Commission of the River Uruguay (CARU).[63] The *Pulp Mills* case did not arise out of a multilateral environmental agreement, but out of a dispute over a bilateral watercourse agreement, the 1975 Statute of the River Uruguay. It involved the consequences for the Argentine environment of the discharge of effluent by pulp mills located on the Uruguayan side of the river. Exercising its rule-making power, in 1984, the Commission adopted a Digest on the uses of the waters of the River Uruguay, and has amended it since.[64]

Explanations for this difference between the stances of the parties with regard to the authority of PTRs could well be that, first, the CARU Digests were not so clearly in favour of one of the parties as the IWC Resolutions had been in favour of Australia's position and against Japan's position; and, second, that it is much easier for a court to establish the agreement of the two parties to a bilateral agreement as regards their consent to the adoption of the CARU Digests – there is no doubt that the CARU standards enjoyed 'unanimous' support of the parties. Japan could perhaps have been expected to use any argument that could help it escape from the unfavourable IWC Resolutions. Nonetheless, it remains striking that Japan's stance is so much different from what is encountered within the regimes.

b. The ICJ's Justifications for Applying PTRs

What considerations were behind the ICJ judges' decision not just to 'take into account' the respective PTRs, but make them a basis for determining the legality

[60] *Whaling in the Antarctic* (Counter-Memorial of Japan), paras 8.53, 8.60.

[61] *Whaling in the Antarctic* (Counter-Memorial of Japan), para 8.63.

[62] *Pulp Mills on the River Uruguay (Argentina v Uruguay)* (Judgment) [2010] ICJ Rep 14.

[63] *Pulp Mills on the River Uruguay* (Memorial of Argentina) [2007], paras. 3.147–3.152. ('This instrument constitutes the direct expression of the intention of the parties and the way in which they construe the provisions of the 1975 Statute.'); *Pulp Mills on the River Uruguay* (Counter-Memorial of Uruguay) [2007], paras 4.20–4.31. ('The Parties are thus in agreement that a determination of whether a Party has satisfied its substantive obligations under the 1975 Statute with respect to pollution is made by measuring the Party's action against the applicable CARU regulations.').

[64] *Pulp Mills*, para 201. The functions of CARU under Art 56(a) include the making of rules governing the prevention of pollution and the conservation and preservation of living resources.

of the conduct of Japan and Uruguay respectively? To be sure, an analysis of the Court's reasoning can at most lead to conclusions as to *the arguments it provided for applying the relevant PTRs* in this way. It is quite impossible to ascertain what exactly the Judges' motivations were for doing so. One important difference between compliance bodies and courts when their decisions defer to a PTR to a greater degree than its degree of legal obligation *per se* requires, is that courts need to find some justification for this that is legally acceptable to the judicial community and the legal system they are part of.[65]

Justifications in the nature of input legitimacy do indeed play a prominent role in the ICJ's judgment in the *Whaling* case. As discussed before, the *Whaling* case sets an important *sine qua non* condition for PTRs to qualify as subsequent agreements in the sense of Article 31.3(a): the PTRs must be adopted by consensus, between all the parties.[66] Only with these consensual PTRs, the treaty parties have a 'duty to cooperate'. The Court presented the consensus requirement as an issue of legal definition.[67] But, in fact, the Court is drawing a sharp line between which instruments it considers to possess enough input legitimacy to determine the lawfulness of an activity, and which instruments it considers to possess too little input legitimacy. The Court *internalises* a legitimacy test ('adoption by consensus') into a formal condition for a PTR to even qualify as a subsequent agreement. On the one hand, the Court's move kept a number of resolutions of the IWC from having any relevance at all (even less than having to be 'taken into account'), despite the Rules of Procedure of most MEAs explicitly allowing for majority decision making. On the other hand, it boosted the authority of the consensual *Special Permits* Resolution to a level equal to the underlying Article VIII ICRW. Legitimacy considerations were decisive in weakening the authority of one category of IWC resolutions, and strengthening the authority of another.

Judge *ad hoc* Charlesworth expressed herself against the judgment's differentiation between consensual and majority decision making, but using the same input legitimacy-oriented reasoning: 'The resolutions express the views of the IWC and, when adopted by consensus or a large majority vote, *they represent an articulation of the shared interests at stake in the regulation of whaling*. States parties to the ICRW are thus required to consider these resolutions in good faith.'[68]

[65] *cf*, eg, Tulio Treves, 'Aspects of Legitimacy of Decisions of International Courts and Tribunals' in Rüdiger Wolfrum and Volker Röben (eds), *Legitimacy in International Law* (2010) 169, 170 ('when the requirements of legitimacy … are satisfied, something is added to "legality"; when they are not satisfied ("illegitimacy") something is subtracted from it; this "something" being a perception of acceptability').

[66] '[W]hen they are adopted by consensus or by a unanimous vote, they may be relevant for the interpretation of the Convention or its Schedule.' *Whaling in the Antarctic*, para 46.

[67] '[non-consensual] instruments cannot be regarded as subsequent agreement to an interpretation of Article VIII, nor as subsequent practice establishing an agreement of the parties regarding the interpretation of the treaty within the meaning of subparagraphs (a) and (b), respectively, of paragraph (3) of Article 31 of the Vienna Convention on the Law of Treaties'. *Whaling in the Antarctic*, para 84.

[68] *Whaling in the Antarctic* (Separate Opinion of Judge *ad hoc* Charlesworth), para 13.

In *Pulp Mills*, just as in *Whaling*, instead of just 'taking into account' the CARU's water quality standards as laid down in the CARU Digests, the Court elevated them in effect to *the* standard for examining the lawfulness of the level of environmental pollution of Uruguay's pulp mills. The Court decided to:

> apply, in addition to the 1975 Statute, these two sets of rules to determine whether the obligations undertaken by the Parties have been *breached* in terms of the discharge of effluent by the mill as well as in respect of the impact of those discharges on the quality of the waters of the river, on its ecological balance and on its biodiversity.[69] (Emphasis added.)

In paragraph 214 ff of the judgment, the Court indeed proceeds to apply CARU water quality standards to the dispute:

> [I]n so far as it is not established that the discharges of effluent of the Orion (Botnia) mill *have exceeded the limits set by those standards*, in terms of the level of concentrations, the Court finds itself unable to conclude that Uruguay *has violated its obligations* under the 1975 Statute.[70] (Emphasis added.)

In other words, the water quality PTRs become leading in exculpating Uruguay. In paragraph 239, the Court also applied the CARU Digest to Argentina's allegation that one of the Uruguayan Pulp Mills would have caused too low a level of dissolved oxygen in the river, pointing out that the available evidence stayed above the minimum level indicated by the CARU Digest.[71]

The reasoning for relying so heavily on the CARU standards in its judgment has characteristics of both input and output legitimacy. In terms of input legitimacy, the Court argued that the CARU Digests represent 'coordinated rule-making action' that '*expresses the will of the Parties* and their interpretation of the provisions of the 1975 Statute'.[72]

In terms of output legitimacy, the *Pulp Mills* court took the position that the object and purpose of the enabling clauses in the 1975 Statute is to adopt rules that govern the behaviour of the parties.[73] Supposedly, this purpose of enabling clauses would be harmed should treaty parties not be obliged to act in accordance with them. According to the Court, Article 36 of the 1975 Statute on the River Uruguay:

> *reflects the common interest dimension of the 1975 Statute and expresses one of the purposes for the establishment of the joint machinery which is to co-ordinate the actions and measures taken by the Parties* for the sustainable management and environmental protection of the river. *The Parties have indeed adopted such measures through the promulgation of standards by CARU.*[74] (Emphasis added.)

[69] *Pulp Mills*, para 202.
[70] *Pulp Mills*, para 214.
[71] *Pulp Mills*, para 239.
[72] *Pulp Mills*, para 199.
[73] Curiously, at no point does the Court refer to Art 31(1) (object and purpose) or Art 31(3)(a) specifically as a basis for the authority of the CARU standards in determining whether Uruguay has violated the 1975 Statute.
[74] *Pulp Mills*, para 184.

To put it differently: *because* the purpose of an enabling clause and the establishment of a plenary treaty meeting is to adopt common standards, these standards *must* have a major role to play in the interpretation of the enabling clause. The *existence* of a rule-making competence implies that the rules resulting from the *exercise* of that competence must 'co-ordinate the actions and measures taken by the Parties'. This resembles a kind of *effet utile* argument: should the CARU be given a task to adopt standards, it cannot be that these do not become leading in determining or interpreting the obligations of the parties. Doctrinally this position is problematic, as was shown earlier.[75] However, here the point is not whether the Court is right or wrong; the point is that the Court credits the CARU standards with high authority, because that is supposedly the most effective interpretation of the *purpose* of Article 36 of the Statute, thus substituting output legitimacy considerations for legal obligation.

To return briefly to the *Whaling* case, similar considerations appeared in the Separate Opinion of Judge Cançado Trindade. In relation to the permit programme review procedure of paragraph 30 of the Schedule, he submitted that 'if States were to decide, at their free will, whether or not to take into account the comments and recommendations of the IWC and the Scientific Committee, *that provision* [that is, paragraph 30] *would be rendered meaningless, dead letter*' (emphasis added).[76] The effectiveness of the ICRW Schedule then becomes a major consideration for the degree of authority that IWC recommendations should have.

The ICJ's actual reliance on and application of an environmental norm as developed by a PTR may strengthen its authority for the future, regardless of whether the initial reliance and application were induced by authority. This is particularly the case when the 'rule of recognition' in a legal order is in flux, such as testified by the debate in the international legal order regarding the law of treaties in relation to the authority of subsequent agreements. But the *Whaling* and *Pulp Mills* cases present not enough evidence to predict: whether, in the next case involving PTRs from another international environmental regime, non-consensual PTRs would also be excluded from the definition of subsequent agreements and practice; or whether, in a future case involving a multilateral rather than a bilateral agreement, the Court would as easily find that it was the will of the parties to create environmental standards governing the lawfulness of river pollution.

What is clear, though, is that parties to international dispute settlement have much fewer qualms about challenging the authority of PTRs over such disputes than they display within the regimes, while the ICJ readily engages in legitimacy considerations to justify or refuse its determination of the lawfulness of conduct on the basis of PTRs.

[75] It disregards the absence of any stipulation by the parties that the standards would be binding, which they could have chosen to do. Moreover, the existence of the standards is not enough to explain their comparative relevance to other means of interpretation, a problem confirmed by the three equally defensible positions of various ICJ judges in the *Costa Rica v Nicaragua* case. *Dispute Regarding Navigational and Related Rights (Costa Rica v Nicaragua)* (Judgment) General List No 133 [2009] ICJ 2. See above ch 4, section A.2.

[76] *Whaling in the Antarctic* (Separate Opinion of Judge Cançado Trindade), para 17.

3. National Legal Orders

Like the International Court of Justice, a domestic court arriving at an initial qualification of PTRs as having to be taken into account in the interpretation of the treaty, will have to *justify* why it nonetheless accords decisive influence to the PTR in reaching a decision. Or, in a few cases, why it does not accord any influence to the PTR at all. Such supplemental justifications include the purported legitimacy or illegitimacy of the adoption of the PTR, the (in)effectiveness of the PTR in the light of the treaty's object and purpose, or the 'logic' of applying PTRs when nothing else is available to shed light on the proper interpretation of the treaty. Governments, meanwhile, take a position on the authority of PTRs in the domestic legal order when they take executive decisions based on PTRs, or are drawn into litigation. Both domestic court judgments and governmental statements provide insights into why there is so much variation in the authority of PTRs in the domestic legal orders, as was established in chapter two.

a. Stance of Governments in Domestic Legal Orders

Just as in international dispute settlement, the curious contrast between dogmatic resistance 'outside' and pragmatic acquiescence 'inside' treaty bodies continues in domestic dispute settlement.[77] In official government documents, or when drawn into litigation by NGOs, companies or citizens, governments consistently maintain that they are not *legally bound* by PTRs. For instance, the US Environmental Protection Agency regularly expresses its stance that it is not legally bound by the Montreal MOP *Critical Use Exemptions* in the domestic legal order.[78] In the *Lac Sorobon* case, the Bonaire Governing Council argued that resolutions to the Ramsar Convention are no more than non-binding recommendations, and therefore have no legal force in the national legal order.[79] In *Bolivian Wildcats (Commission v France)*, the French Government maintained that the Commission was 'accusing it … of failing to implement the recommendation of the CITES Conference, whereas it has not been established that it was bound by that recommendation.'[80]

[77] Thanks to Peter Sand for putting it this way in our e-mail conversation of 18 July 2016.

[78] Note the stance of the US Government filed in the proceedings of *NRDC v EPA*, Supplemental Brief for the Respondent and Final Rule 69 Fed. Reg. at 76,989. The EPA repeats this stance in its yearly *Final Rules* on the use of methyl bromide, eg for the year 2013 see *Proposed Rule* 77 Fed. Reg. 74435, by pointing at the Supplemental Brief and the ruling in *NRDC v EPA*.

[79] *Lac Sorobon (Bestuurscollege van het Eilandgebied Bonaire tegen de Gouverneur van de Nederlandse Antillen), Staatsblad* 347, Kroonberoep Raad van State van het Koninkrijk der Nederlanden, 11 September 2007 ('De annexen bij resoluties hebben volgens het Bestuurscollege geen werking in de nationale rechtsorde; zij bevatten slechts aanbevelingen voor het beheer van aangewezen wetlands.').

[80] ECJ, Case C-182/89 *Commission v France* (Bolivian Wildcats), Opinion of Advocate-General Mischo, delivered on 18 October 1990.

At other times, the same governments have taken the position that they should be *permitted* to rely on PTRs to confiscate shipments of wood,[81] to allow zoos to import elephants,[82] or to dispose of an Orca in a certain manner.[83] In *Lac Sorobon*, the island of Bonaire's Governor found himself diametrically opposed to the Bonaire Governing Council, arguing that he had lawfully revoked the latter's granting of a licence because of the Environmental Impact Assessments recommended in Ramsar COP PTRs. Yet, even at such times, governments never argue that they are under an *obligation* to do so; merely that they are *permitted* to do so.

b. Domestic Courts' Justifications for Applying PTRs

In deciding whether to review the lawfulness of government actions or decisions on the basis of post-treaty rules, domestic courts have, in different instances, downplayed and exaggerated the required deference to PTRs compared to the legal obligation to take them into account. To defend decisions about PTRs, courts have relied on a number of justifications: the perceived (il)legitimacy of the process of adoption of PTRs; the perceived ineffectiveness of the MEA when not interpreted in accordance with the PTR in the light of what they conclude to be the object and purpose of the underlying MEA; or mere 'logic' and 'reason' in the light of the absence of anything else that might clarify the meaning of the underlying MEA. Often, two or more of these justifications are used together.

These justifications forwarded by courts are either based on their actual perceptions of legitimacy, effectiveness, object and purpose, logic and reasonableness, etc, that is, their perception that they should defer to PTRs for these reasons, or on their expectation that the parties to the dispute, the public at large and/or the legal discipline, will find these justifications acceptable; or perhaps these courts have other reasons for deferring to a PTR, which they cannot or do not wish to divulge. Unfortunately, there are only a few judgments in which such arguments of justification are stated *explicitly*. In some cases referring to PTRs, the judges say little or nothing about why they accord PTRs a certain relevance for the outcome of the dispute.[84] It is possible that these domestic courts rely on similar justifications as those judgments referring to 'reasonableness' or 'common sense'. Overall, what becomes apparent is the confusion among domestic courts in dealing with PTRs. Most courts do not see how they could logically ignore substantively relevant PTRs, but at the same time struggle with making a decision on exactly how much influence they should accord to them, and how they can defend this course of action in an acceptable manner.

[81] *Castlewood Products* (District Court and Court of Appeals).

[82] *Born Free USA v Norton*, 278 F.Supp.2d 5 (D.D.C.), 8 August 2003.

[83] *Stichting The Black Fish c.s. tegen de staatssecretaris van Economische zaken, Landbouw en Innovatie (Orka)*, LJN: BU5150 (Rb. Amsterdam), Voorlopige Voorziening [provisional order], 21 November 2011.

[84] See ch 4, section B.

i. Logic and Reasonableness

Upon closer inspection, some of the reasoning of domestic courts evolves in line with what is 'reasonable'. Sometimes, the judges even rely on pure 'logic' or 'common sense'.[85] For instance, in the *Lac Sorobon* case, the Dutch Crown Court (Council of State) concluded that because Article 3.1 Ramsar Convention offered little guidance on what that provision requires concretely, this was all the more reason for it to rely on the resolutions adopted to clarify it.[86] In other words, because this is all we have, it cannot but be decisive for determining what the obligations in Article 3.1 Ramsar Convention require. This can be countered by the argument that if the parties intended the PTRs to be decisive for the interpretation of Article 3.1, they could have phrased it in more mandatory language. As the parties were not able to agree on more mandatory language, why should it be decisive for what Article 3.1 requires?

In *Castlewood Products*, the Court of Appeals reasoned that '[t]here would be no point in the contracting states agreeing on resolutions only to then completely ignore them. Therefore, while not binding, *it was surely reasonable* for FWS and APHIS to look to the CITES resolutions for guidance in interpreting the regulations implementing CITES'.[87] The judgment of a US District Court in *Born Free v USA* simply states that '[u]nder the guidance of Res. Conf. 5.10 [CITES COP], it is *reasonable* for FWS to conclude that this is not a setting in which commercial aspects of the zoos' purposes predominate over non-commercial aspects'.[88] However, such reasoning overlooks that it is quite a leap to go from 'completely ignoring' a resolution towards concluding that government organs have conducted themselves lawfully because they did exactly what a resolution recommended.

The *FRC Intern* case concerned a US company claiming that it had 'recovered' halon so that it would qualify for a *tax* exemption for ozone-depleting substances 'diverted or recovered in the United States as part of a recycling process'.[89] In fact, the plaintiff company had 'recovered' halon by removing it from shipping containers in which it had been put by a Chinese company that had actually removed it

[85] Noting the same trend in domestic courts' application of IEL in general: Carl Bruch, 'Is International Environmental Law Really Law? An Analysis of Application in Domestic Courts' (2006) 23 *Pace Environmental Law Review* 423, 428, 452 ('In many cases, though, the precise role of international law is ambiguous, vague, or inconclusive. In these instances, the decisions consider, cite, and discuss international environmental law in support of the ultimate holding, but the weight that the court accords international environmental law is unclear. It could serve as a cause of action, a rule of decision, an interpretive aid, or a principle of national law notwithstanding the international status of the principle, or as "commonsense".').

[86] *Lac Sorobon*, para 2.2.3.5 ('"Deze aanbevelingen, resoluties en richtlijnen" zijn bij de interpretatie en invulling van de verplichtingen die uit artikel 3 voortvloeien, te meer van belang, omdat de bepaling zelf ten aanzien van de inhoud van die verplichtingen weinig houvast biedt.').

[87] *Castlewood Products Llc v A Norton*, 365 F3d 1076 (DC Cir), 30 April 2004, para 44.

[88] *Born Free USA*, p 16.

[89] 26 U.S.C. § 4682(d)(1).

from fire extinguishers in China. The US District Court relied on Montreal MOP Decision IV/24 on *Recovery, reclamation and recycling of controlled substances* to determine what constitutes 'recovery' of ozone-depleting substances. Although the District Court Judge acknowledged that the Decision was 'certainly not binding on this court', his judgment followed the Decision because it was 'helpful'.[90]

ii. Effectiveness in the Light of the Object and Purpose of the MEA

Other domestic courts have reasoned that the object and purpose of an MEA would be more effectively served if the rules suggested by a relevant PTR are followed. In this vein, a US District Court concluded in *Conservation Force v Salazar* that an interpretation of CITES by the standard contained in CITES COP Resolution 12.3 should prevail because, '[i]f plaintiffs were permitted to have their trophies returned or retroactive export permits issued, the underlying purpose of CITES would be undermined'.[91]

Dissenting Judge Laws in the UK *Greenpeace* case argued that following CITES COP Resolution 10.2(h) in reaching judgment would better serve the object and purpose of CITES:

> The Convention, though certainly it seeks to support viable international trade, is first and foremost intended as a legal antidote to some of the damage done by man's exploitation of nature's resources. That *purpose* must, in my judgment, serve as the most influential factor in the interpretation of the [EU] Regulation, … which I have set out. For these reasons I prefer the construction advanced in Greenpeace's modified argument.[92]

Greenpeace UK had argued that, based on Resolution 10.2, the UK importing authorities were under an obligation to refuse the importation of the mahogany shipment because they knew that the Brazilian exporting authorities were not satisfied at the time that the exports were no violation of Brazilian conservation laws, even though they formally issued an export permit.[93] Judge Laws argued that this Greenpeace argument should be followed, because of his understanding of the object and purpose of CITES.

Arriving at an interpretation in view of the object and purpose of a convention is in accordance with most international and domestic rules of treaty interpretation, including Article 31.1 VCLT. But these justifications fail to appreciate that

[90] *FRC Int'l, Inc. v United States*, 82 American Federal Tax Report 2d. 98-7074 (N.D. Ohio), 29 October 1998.

[91] *Conservation Force v Salazar*, 677 F.Supp.2d 1203 (N.D.Cal.), 30 December 2009, p 1210.

[92] *R (on the application of Greenpeace Ltd) v Secretary of State for the Environment, Food and Rural Affairs*, EWCA Civ 1036 (Civil Division), 25 July 2002, Dissent of Laws, LJ, para 34.

[93] CITES COP Res Conf 10.2(h), *Permits and Certificates* states that 'Parties not authorise the import of any specimen if they have reason to believe that it was not legally acquired in the country of origin'. See *Greenpeace*, para 32.

the object and purpose rarely clearly point at an interpretation provided by a PTR, rather than at a rival interpretation of the MEA provision in question. It could be equally argued that the exporting authorities are in a better position than the importing authorities to determine whether a specimen was traded in violation of the laws of the exporting state. Likewise, in response to the consideration in *Conservation Force v Salazar*, there are heated debates inside and outside CITES whether allowing for limited export of hunting trophies is supportive or detrimental to the survival of a species.[94] At the very least, judges should be very careful with these kinds of justification.

iii. Input (Il)Legitimacy of PTR Adoption

Domestic courts have also tapped into input-legitimacy arguments to either deny or allow for a PTR's application to government conduct. Judges sometimes make their own (very brief) analysis of the type of decision making on the PTR at hand in the international plenary body concerned. The number of domestic court cases in which input legitimacy (in a broad sense) is explicitly discussed are limited, but it can be assumed that it plays a role in more cases even if it does not find its way into the judgment. Unfortunately, these analyses (can) go only so far, looking at the formal decision-making mode rather than how it functions in practice.

In the already discussed *Lac Sorobon* case, the Council of State stated that the 'resolutions and recommendations under the Ramsar Convention *were unanimously adopted* by an organ – the Conference of the Parties – *in which all treaty parties* – including the Kingdom of the Netherlands – *are represented*' (emphasis added).[95] This line of argument shows a clear parallel with the reasoning of the majority of the ICJ in the *Whaling in the Antarctic* case, where adoption by consensus was explicitly introduced as a condition for IWC resolutions and guidelines to qualify as subsequent agreements.

In *NRDC v EPA*, a US Court of Appeals, in contrast to the Dutch Council of State, cited legitimacy *concerns* as a reason to *deny* application of the *Critical Use Criteria* and *Exemptions* to the lawfulness of executive acts. The judges voiced the constitutional concern that '[i]f the "decisions" are "law" – enforceable in federal court like statutes or legislative rules – then Congress either has delegated lawmaking authority to an international body or authorised amendments to a treaty without presidential signature or Senate ratification, in violation of Article II of the Constitution'.[96] The judges thus expressed a worry that the US Congress had

[94] *The Role of Hunters in CITES Implementation*, Keynote address by John E Scanlon, Secretary-General, CITES, for the opening session of the 58th General Assembly of the International Council for Game and Wildlife Conservation (CIC), Saint Petersburg, 12–15 May 2011, at: https://cites.org/eng/news/sg/2011/20110512_SG_CIC.php.

[95] *Lac Sorobon*, para 2.2.3.5.

[96] *Natural Resources Defense Council v Environmental Protection Agency (Judgment after rehearing)*, 464 F.3d 1 (DC Cir), 29 August 2006, p 13.

lost decision-making power to the Montreal MOP, without using the constitutionally prescribed procedures for such a delegation.

In the aforementioned case of *FRC Intern*, a Court of Appeals affirmed the District Court's decision, stating merely that Montreal MOP Decision IV/24 contained '[t]he *accepted* definition of "recovery" among the parties to the Protocol' (emphasis added),[97] thus implying that because the treaty parties had agreed upon the adoption of the Decision, it was legitimate to consider that definition leading for the interpretation of a US law granting tax advantages to businesses for 'recovering' halon.

It is impossible to verify if the judges of the Dutch Council of State in the *Lac Sorobon* case really *believed* that the legitimacy provided by the consensual process of adopting PTRs made reliance on the Ramsar Guidelines difficult to escape, or that it was in fact persuaded by the sensibility of the Environmental Impact Assessment prescribed by the Ramsar PTRs in question, and needed a justification. It is likewise impossible to verify if the US Court of Appeals in *NRDC v EPA* really *believed* that the lack of legitimacy of a – very similar – consensual process forced it to refuse to rely on the Montreal Protocol MOP Decisions to reach its decision, or that it had its own reasons for not tying the hands of the US Government in regulating production and consumption of methyl bromide, an ozone-depleting substance.

iv. Inconsistent Practice

Consistent practice may strengthen or diminish the authority of PTRs in the domestic legal orders over time.[98] However, there is as of yet little evidence of such consistent practice, neither within single jurisdictions, nor in all the reviewed domestic legal orders together.

There are roughly two ways in which practice could have an effect on the domestic authority of PTRs beyond their case-by-case application. First, by consistently applying or refusing to apply PTRs *without providing justification*, justifications would appear not to be needed. Second, by consistently applying or refusing to apply PTRs on the basis of fulfilling additional justifications, these repeatedly referred-to justifications could turn into formal *criteria* that PTRs need to meet in order to have authority.

Both scenarios require a certain consistency or perhaps a decision by a supreme court. But cases are relatively few, judgments rarely refer to the treatment of PTRs in previous judgments,[99] and in the jurisdictions with more than just a few cases (the United States primarily) the justifications advanced are widely divergent.

[97] *FRC Intern, Inc. v US*, 278 F.3d 641, (C.A.6 Ohio), 30 January 2002, p 643.

[98] For discussing this phenomenon in the context of the domestic application of IEL generally, see again Bruch, 'Is International Environmental Law Really Law?', 455 ('The first decisions interpreting or applying international law might be ambiguous for the reasons cited above, with subsequent decisions taking increasingly clear interpretations that build upon the earlier decisions.') (footnote omitted).

[99] Just once, a US District Court referred to the Court of Appeals judgment in the *Castlewood* case. See *Franks v Salazar*, 816 F.Supp.2d 49 (D.D.C.), 6 October 2011, p 64.

Moreover, very similar PTRs have been found legitimate and illegitimate. Often, judges are silent on why they treat PTRs a certain way, so it is difficult to know whether they rely on precedents or not. The issue of PTRs' authority is hardly ever treated rigorously in domestic court judgments, and that means that every new court tends to consider the issue anew.[100] For instance, in the United States, where precedent plays an important role, the existence of such widely diverging judgments makes it difficult to regard any as 'persuasive authorities'.[101] Accordingly, it is highly questionable that the authority of PTRs has already stabilised. National courts still have much freedom of action in justifying whether to merely take PTRs into account, or to actually make them determinative of the environmental standard applied in a case.

C. Conclusion

Social legitimacy and the social pressures in which it translates are the crucial missing link between PTRs the COP is merely 'competent' to adopt and PTRs with authority in the functioning of regime bodies; between PTRs that merely need to be taken into account and PTRs that states actually must act in accordance with; and between PTRs that are 'recommendations' on paper but mysteriously take centre stage in the judgments of international and national courts. Likewise, social legitimacy and social pressures explain why the authority of one and the same PTR can be so very different in different normative orders. Chapter three concluded that none of the relevant normative orders considers PTRs to be (legally) binding. Chapter four concluded that there is much similarity between the doctrines of interpretation developed in the international and national legal orders with regard to the treatment of PTRs. So these factors – which are comparable across the board – do not explain their compartmentalised authority, which rather is a direct result of the role of social legitimacy.

The next and final part takes this fact – the central role of social legitimacy for the authority of PTRs – and looks at it through a critical lens. Is the authority of PTR based on social legitimacy somehow different than authority based on the binding character of law? Or is it in any way more vulnerable and volatile? If the latter, what does that mean for the procedural rights of those affected by such PTRs? And if social legitimacy becomes such a decisive factor, is there sufficient reason to agree with the beliefs of state representatives and judges from a normative viewpoint? Are PTRs really that legitimate, considering the procedures of their adoption and the effectiveness of their content? Or do those judges that have been critical of the legitimacy of PTRs have a point?

[100] Harlan G Cohen, 'Theorizing Precedent in International Law' in Andrea Bianchi, Daniel Peat and Matthew Windsor (eds), *Interpretation in International Law* (OUP, 2014), 17 ('the less clear the precedent and the more ad hoc the interpretation appears to be, the easier it will be to distinguish').

[101] Using this term here because it is particular to the US legal system.

PART III

Critical Perspectives on the Authority of Environmental Post-Treaty Rules

6

Vulnerable Authority: Discretion in Domestic Implementation and Violation of Procedural Principles

Having explained the various sources that determine the degree of authority of environmental post-treaty rules, the final part of this study begins with an inquiry into the consequences of social legitimacy being such an important source. In what respects might such authority be different, and how does that difference affect the effectiveness of national implementation and the procedural rights of the addressees of such rules? What are the consequences of such important environmental rules having compartmentalised and ambiguous authority, resting to such an extent on legitimacy beliefs?

There appear to be two main consequences. First, it allows broad discretion to governments in the domestic implementation of such a crucial part of international environmental law. The manner in which the authority of PTRs is built up threatens to 'commodify' international environmental law into a thing that governments maintain overwhelming control over, without NGOs, individuals or companies being able to invoke it against the government, or defend themselves against its application against them. The ambiguous authority of PTRs thus negatively affects the role that civil society and private parties might play in the effective implementation of IEL. Second, it leads to the infringement of crucial procedural principles such as legal certainty, legality and the duty to state reasons. Perhaps worst of all, these vulnerabilities and downsides of international rules' authority resting on social legitimacy are not coincidental. They are the result of purposeful choices of states.

A. Is Authority Based on Social Legitimacy Different?

What are the consequences of authority resting directly on social legitimacy? To be clear, authority based partly or even entirely on social legitimacy rather than on legal obligation need not affect the degree of authority.[1] This was observed extensively in chapter two. What is more, these observations support the position that authority based on social legitimacy, unmediated by legal obligation, can even be stronger than based on legal obligation in the absence of social legitimacy. Ulfstein has remarked that states consider the difference between legally binding and non-binding international law 'to be fundamental,' illustrating his point with the supposedly more difficult negotiations when 'binding consequences' are at stake.[2] For the international legal order, that difference is indeed a real one, but that is not the case in the internal normative orders.

For the internal normative orders, the difference is to be found not so much in the degree of authority of the norms. Rather, it is to be found in the language of compliance rather than of breach and violation, and in the nature of the consequences of non-compliance. The Kyoto COP/MOP *Compliance Procedures*, for instance, profess to 'aim at the restoration of compliance to ensure environmental integrity' and to 'provide for an incentive to comply'.[3] There is much debate about the binding consequences of non-compliance and the role of the plenary treaty meetings in making the final decision about such consequences.[4] In this respect, regimes differ greatly.[5] Considering these aspects of compliance procedures, it is possible that the authority of the *outcomes* of compliance procedures is weaker. A further examination of that possibility falls outside the scope of this thesis.

The consequences of the role that social legitimacy plays for the authority of PTRs in the international and national legal orders are different. This practice fits Zürn's 'reflexive' theory of authority and Krisch's theory of 'liquid' authority. Outside the internal normative orders, the (social) legitimacy of PTRs is subject to more contestation. As a result, authority is more contested as well. The classic standards for what constitutes authority, such as wording and legal obligation, no longer provide an answer, while the new standards are still contested. Authority is thus no longer 'internalised':[6] At least in the early stages of a new type of

[1] Nico Krisch, 'The Structure of Postnational Authority' (2015), at http://papers.ssrn.com/sol3/papers.cfm?abstract_id=2564579, 11 ('they are able to flow and are thus more difficult to grasp, though not for that matter necessarily less weighty or impacting').

[2] Geir Ulfstein, 'Reweaving the Fabric of International Law? Patterns of Consent in Environmental Framework Agreements, Comment by Geir Ulfstein' in Rüdiger Wolfrum and Volker Röben (eds), *Developments of International Law in Treaty Making* (Springer, 2005), 151. He gives the example of 'the difficult negotiations regarding "binding consequences" under article 18 of the Kyoto Protocol'; Daniel Bodansky, *The Art and Craft of International Environmental Law* (Harvard University Press, 2010), 101.

[3] Kyoto COP/MOP Decision 27/CMP.1, *Compliance Procedures*, s VI.

[4] Jan Klabbers, 'Compliance Procedures' in Daniel Bodansky, Jutta Brunnée and Ellen Hey (eds), *The Oxford Handbook of International Environmental Law* (OUP, 2007), 998–99.

[5] The Enforcement Branch of the Kyoto Protocol Compliance Committee can, for instance, attach consequences to its decisions that are executed independent of the non-complying party's influence ('shall apply the following consequences'). See Kyoto COP/MOP Decision 27/CMP.1, *Compliance Procedures*, s XV. The Kyoto COP/MOP's approval of such consequences is not required. See Kyoto COP MOP Decision 27/CMP.1, *Compliance Procedures*, s XII.

[6] Michael Zürn, 'From Rule to Authority – Why We Enter a Phase of Reflexive Legitimacy', Paper distributed for a presentation at the University of Amsterdam, 17 March 2014 (on file with author), 5.

instrument, each time a court is confronted with one, it has to face 'conflicts over which justification is appropriate for which form of … authority'.[7] As the above examination of the practice shows, those 'early stages' can take a long time. In order to establish itself and gain recognition, such authority has recourse to sources like expertise, moral principles and values, or problem-solving capacity. Krisch observes that formal institutions, too, will increasingly make such claims 'to complement their rational-legal authority'.[8] But authority grounded in such sources 'is typically more vulnerable to societal challenge and will reflect a lower degree of consolidation, allowing for more rapid change'.[9]

This vulnerable authority, as the next section lays out in more detail, leaves wide discretion to governments whether or not to act in accordance with PTRs. This freedom of action turns international environmental law into norms that governments can switch on and off at will – particularly when shaping and implementing domestic environmental policies – threatening both the effectiveness of the domestic implementation of international law and important procedural protections of weaker states, citizens, NGOs and companies.

B. Wide Governmental Discretion

1. The Commodification of International Rules

In 'The Commodification of International Law', Klabbers complains that, nowadays, 'the argument is increasingly heard' that international cooperation and regulation 'can also be done outside international law altogether. … [I]t would remain outside the realm of law and, instead, bind on a different level or, more accurately, *under a different normative system*' (emphasis added).[10] As a result, Klabbers agitates, law has turned into a commodity 'to be used when desired, and to be disused when deemed unproductive'.[11]

It is not difficult to see certain aspects of the PTR practice as falling squarely within the scope of these observations. PTRs are highly authoritative within the internal order of the treaty bodies – 'a different normative system' – yet their authority outside of that order is contested and ambiguous. And the choice for the 'form' of PTRs is indeed a purposive choice. As treaty law expert Fitzmaurice observes, '[p]arties' ambiguity in this respect [of form, TS] is, indeed, often more

[7] ibid, 17.
[8] Krisch, 'The Structure of Postnational Authority', 13.
[9] ibid, 14.
[10] Jan Klabbers, 'The Commodification of International Law' in Hélène Ruiz Fabri, Emmanuelle Jouannet and Vincent Tomkiewicz (eds), *Select Proceedings of the European Society of International Law* (Hart Publishing, 2008) 341, 342–43.
[11] ibid, 343; Nico Krisch, 'The Decay of Consent: International Law in an Age of Global Public Goods' (2014) 108 *American Journal of International Law* 1.

or less intentional'.[12] Similarly, in a general study on non-binding environmental instruments, Friedrich states that COP decisions 'are deliberately used as another option, … even when comparatively flexible *binding* instruments are also available'.[13] The Montreal Protocol adjustment mechanism, for instance, underlines that it is possible for the parties to select a binding legal form. Not opting for a legal form is therefore rarely purely accidental or imposed by legal impossibilities.

To be sure, the choice for the non-legal form may result in part from lack of agreement on the substance of the rules.[14] There are many explicit enabling clauses in the Kyoto and Cartagena Protocols where the reason for postponing rule making to the post-treaty phase was a lack of agreement during the Protocols' negotiations.[15] But this makes the choice no less 'intentional': owing to the lack of agreement, the parties choose a type of instrument that is only binding among themselves, so that the consequences of its violation remain within the (collective) control of state representatives.

All of this only matters insofar it has undesirable consequences. In the case of PTRs, the term 'commodification' is overly dramatic – considering that within the internal normative orders, the authority of PTRs is high and real, and can certainly not be easily switched on and off as if it were a commodity that can be bought and sold. The more pressing question is whether the choice for PTRs rather than legally binding norms leaves the freedom of action of governments in their *domestic* legal orders intact to the point of such a full discretion that effective implementation of international law suffers, and procedural principles are violated.

Klabbers' concerns with the increasing use of instruments that bind only under a different normative system[16] (and not in the international or national legal orders), concentrate on what he calls the 'duck paradox' of setting up parallel normative orders: 'The more people started to think about what it could mean to conclude a morally binding agreement, or a politically binding agreement[, or soft law], the more the picture that emerged started to look like the very same international legal order they tried to escape from.' 'It looks like a duck, walks like a duck, and quacks like a duck; it is just that its name has changed.'[17] The authority of PTRs in the internal normative orders fits this duck metaphor perfectly. In the place of legal constraints have come social practices of

[12] Malgosia Fitzmaurice, 'Compliance with Multilateral Environmental Agreements' (2007) 20 *Hague Yearbook of International Law* 19, 24.

[13] Jürgen Friedrich, *International Environmental 'soft Law': The Functions and Limits of Nonbinding Instruments in International Environmental Governance and Law* (Springer, 2013), 45–46 ('The nonbinding instruments … are deliberately used as another option.').

[14] Fitzmaurice, 'Compliance with Multilateral Environmental Agreements', 24, fn 12.

[15] For the Cartagena Protocol, see René Lefeber, 'Creative Legal Engineering' (2000) 13 *Leiden Journal of International Law* 1.

[16] To begin with, he fears that choosing non-legally binding instruments 'runs the risk of undermining whatever respect for the law may be left'. Klabbers, 'The Commodification of International Law', 343 (echoing Prosper Weil's critique of some 20 years earlier).

[17] ibid, 345, 347. Klabbers discusses soft law in a separate section, but to make the same point.

international implementation that cannot be escaped, thus affecting the freedom of states, the fear of loss of privileges, and deference to PTRs in the context of compliance control. As Klabbers remarks specifically about the compliance procedures of the Montreal Protocol, 'once again, the paradox of the duck sets in: the more developed the compliance procedures become, the more they look like traditional enforcement mechanisms'.[18]

For Klabbers, this paradox of the duck entails several critiques, only two of which should concern us here. Despite the duck paradox – i.e. that *within* the normative system where they originate they basically function like law – non-legally binding instruments have two important undesirable consequences. One is that, although relocating rule making to these other normative orders is often said to be in the general interest (because it is a more flexible and therefore more effective road to a solution), it seems to him that the interest lies primarily in gaining control over the process for powerful states,[19] and inducing deference to the outcomes by weaker states.[20] He also notes that parliaments are much more easily circumvented through using non-legally binding instruments, for which parliamentary consultation is usually not constitutionally required.[21] Sections B and C of this chapter further examine these (normative) legitimacy concerns.

The other, Klabbers argues, is that choosing a 'policy option' other than law turns rules into commodities. By choosing instruments that have authority within their separate normative orders, but much less so in the international and national *legal* orders, states free themselves from interventions by companies, citizens and NGOs. They *replace international law by a normative system binding between states, but emphatically not between states and others.* As Benvenisti expresses it, 'the lack of formal treaties may make it more difficult for individuals who are affected either by the adopted policy or by the deviation from that policy, to challenge it (in the former case), or invoke it (in the latter case), in domestic courts'.[22] States can pressure each other to comply with them, and can affect individuals by implementing these rules, but individuals cannot complain because, officially, there is no law that affects them.[23] Thus, by localising authority within the internal normative orders, states might achieve – with or without intent – an escape from it outside of that normative order. There, they can use or not use these instruments more or less at will, and can deny being bound by them vis-à-vis private actors, other states, NGOs, and their parliaments.

This final critique squarely applies to the practice of PTRs. By not opting for a legally binding form to agree on the all-important details of their obligations,

[18] ibid, 350.
[19] ibid, 345.
[20] ibid, 350.
[21] ibid, 346–47.
[22] Eyal Benvenisti, '"Coalitions of the Willing" and the Evolution of Informal International Law' (2006) *Tel Aviv University Legal Working Paper Series* 31, 20.
[23] Klabbers, 'The Commodification of International Law', 346.

governments in effect preclude an effective judicial review by independent third parties such as international and national courts, particularly one that may come with legal consequences attached. At the same time, by not making PTRs explicitly *non*-binding either, states can still rely on them when taking action against private actors. In the internal normative order, states want to be able to include at least some PTRs in compliance assessments, unchallengeable by individual governments. It does not suit governments if PTRs have limited or no authority there. By not giving PTRs an explicitly non-legally binding status, leaving PTRs to exist in 'legal purgatory', it is precluded that assessment by compliance committees in the internal legal orders becomes impossible. The point is not that treaty parties want *no* compliance assessment to take place; the point is that they want to maintain control over the conditions under which the assessment takes place, not leave it to unpredictable courts. Governments want to have their cake and eat it too. As Klabbers says, they want to have all of law's virtues, but none of its vices.[24]

2. Governmental Discretion in Domestic Legal Orders

The 'vices' that states are able to escape are the NGOs, companies and citizens trying to invoke PTRs against governmental agencies, or trying to challenge the invocation of PTRs by governmental agencies against them. The extensive exploration of national court practice in this thesis has made that abundantly clear.

The low authority of PTRs in the national legal orders entails that governments have wide discretion how to deal with their national implementation, short of risking a finding of non-compliance by treaty bodies. In theory, the discretion partly lies with domestic courts, since the courts have the power to decide on the place of new instruments in the legal system. But domestic courts have failed to take a systematic approach towards PTRs that would have made their authority more stabilised. In essence, courts pass their discretion onwards to the domestic administrative authorities. Instead of using their interpretive discretion to take up a role in the reparation of constitutional imbalances, as witnessed in other areas by Benvenisti, by confronting administrative authorities with their international commitments or by refusing to let those authorities get away with basing their domestic executive action on non-binding international decisions, these courts continue the old practice of deference.[25]

In most instances, national courts are choosing the 'safest' way out and *find in favour of the government's position*, whether the government points to a PTR

[24] ibid, 348.

[25] Eyal Benvenisti, 'Reclaiming Democracy: The Strategic Uses of Foreign and International Law by National Courts' (2008) 102 *American Journal of International Law* 241.

in defence of its conduct, or denies its authority instead. If the dispute involves a government agency having acted in accordance with a PTR to the detriment of a private actor, domestic courts almost always agree with the government that it was *allowed* to do so. If the dispute involves a private actor claiming a government agency should have acted in accordance with a PTR, domestic courts almost always agree with the government that it did not *have* to.

In the following cases, governments were found to be *allowed* to adopt an executive act or policy by domestic courts because the act or policy was in accordance with a relevant PTR (for the sake of brevity, the precise names of the various governmental actors and agencies are replaced by the term 'government'):

1. *Castlewood Products District Court*: The US Government was permitted to confiscate shipments of mahogany because it was 'instructed' to do so by a CITES COP Resolution.
2. *Castlewood Products Court of Appeals*: The US Government's confiscation of shipments of mahogany was found to be 'reasonable' on the basis of a CITES COP Resolution.
3. *Orka*: The State of the Netherlands acted lawfully in disposing of a confiscated Orca in light of the recommendations in the CITES COP *Disposal of Confiscated Specimens* Resolution.
4. *Born Free*: The same argumentation applies as in *Castlewood Products Court of Appeals*: '[U]nder the guidance of Res. Conf. 5.10, it is reasonable for [the US Fish and Wildlife Service] to conclude that this is not a setting in which commercial aspects of the zoos' purposes predominate over non-commercial aspects.'[26]
5. *FRC Intern*: The US Government was allowed to consider the definition of 'recovery' adopted by the Montreal MOP leading for the interpretation of a US law providing tax advantages for the 'recovery' of the ozone-depleting substance halon.
6. *Conservation Force v Salazar*: The US Government was allowed to confiscate hunting trophies in accordance with CITES Resolution 12.3, because to decide otherwise would go against the object and purpose of CITES.
7. *Franks v Salazar*: The US Government's confiscation of elephant trophies is supported by CITES Resolution 2.11, but when plaintiffs try to rely on it, 'CITES Resolutions do not create enforceable legal standards'.[27]
8. *Cayman Turtle Farm*: Decided in favour of the US Government, in part because the government's 'more strict definition of "closed-cycle" comports with the terms and underlying policy of the resolution adopted by the parties to the Convention'.[28]

[26] *Born Free v USA*, p 16.
[27] *Franks v Salazar*, p 64.
[28] *Cayman Turtle Farm, Ltd v Andrus*, 478 F. Supp. 125 (D.D.C.), 29 May 1979, p 133–34.

In the following cases, governments were found *not to be prohibited* from adopting an executive act or policy by domestic courts, regardless of that executive act or policy not being in accordance with a relevant PTR:

9. *One Etched Tusk*: The US Government was not obliged to act in accordance with CITES Resolution 12.3 to determine whether an elephant tusk no longer constituted a hunting trophy, because it had been 'scrimshawed'.
10. *Face the Future*: The Dutch Government was found not to be under an obligation to subtract units from its assigned amount in accordance with the Kyoto COP/MOP *Accounting Modalities*.
11. *Greentree (FCA and Full Court)*: The Australian Government was found to have successfully listed the Gwydir site on the Ramsar List of Wetlands of International Importance, despite not having acted in accordance with the recommendations in the Ramsar COP *Designation Conditions*.
12. *NRDC v EPA*: The US Government was found not to be under an obligation to act in accordance with the Montreal MOP *Exemption Criteria* and *Decisions*.

In the *Face the Future* and *Greentree* cases, the recommendatory nature of the PTRs in question served as the main reason for declaring the governmental policy or act not to be prohibited. In the *One Etched Tusk* and *NRDC v EPA* cases, it was the PTR form that enabled the governmental agencies to ignore the relevant PTRs in their decision making.

The one case where an argument can be made that a governmental actor was reproached by a court for not acting in accordance with a PTR is the *Lac Sorobon* case. In fact, another outcome would have been impossible, because in *Lac Sorobon*, two governmental actors – the Bonaire Governor *and* the Bonaire Governing Council – held opposing views as to whether or not they should have acted in accordance with Ramsar COP resolutions and recommendations. The Dutch Council of State concluded that it was not unreasonable for the Governor to have relied on these Ramsar PTRs in quashing the Governing Council's decision to grant a licence without conducting an Environmental Impact Assessment in the manner recommended by these Ramsar PTRs. The other partial exception is the *minority* judge in *Greenpeace*, who argued that the course of action recommended in the CITES COP *Reason to Believe Paragraph* should have been followed by the UK Commissioners of Customs and Excise.

The difference in wording between PTRs is not an explanatory factor here. In *NRDC v EPA*, the relevant Montreal MOP Decisions were all phrased in highly mandatory and relatively precise language. By contrast, in all but one of the cases where the government was allowed to act in accordance with a PTR in constraining private actors, it concerned PTRs of a recommendatory nature, with the exception of the *FRC Intern* case.

Governments 'benefit' optimally from the so-called 'permissive' or 'entitling' effect that has often been ascribed to resolutions of international organisations and other non-legally binding instruments.[29] Because of the ambiguity in what kind of legal obligation a PTR creates exactly, courts can always find a plausible justification in favour of or against the prevalence of the PTR in question. Effectively, this precludes a real judicial review of government activities for which there exist relevant PTRs, while not hindering governments in acting against private actors on the basis of PTRs when they are inclined to do so. This situation is not incomprehensible from the perspective of the courts: for national courts, confronted with a type of instrument they have never before based their decisions on, it is safest to go with the government's view. Considering the discretion in applying PTRs or not, they otherwise risk being reproached for entering the realm of the executive.

PTRs are particularly vulnerable in states that traditionally give precedence to the text of the treaty in its interpretation. For instance, UK courts tend to lean more towards the 'ordinary language' of treaty provisions than towards subsequent agreements. The effect of this clearly shows in the two concurring opinions of the majority in *Greenpeace*. One of the two concurring judges, Justice Dyson, relies on what he considers to be 'the most natural interpretation of the language' of Article 4(3)(a) of the EU CITES Implementing Regulation, which 'interpretation also accords better with the opening words of Article 4.3 of the Regulation', so that: 'based simply on an analysis of the words of the Regulation and the Convention, I would hold that "in accordance with the Convention" in Article 4.3(a) of the Regulation means "in accordance with the requirements of Article VI of the Convention".'[30] Likewise, Lord Justice Mummery concluded 'that the respondents' arguments are more persuasive as a matter of the ordinary meaning of the text when read in context and that the legal and practical consequences of the respondents' arguments are more consistent with the evident policy of the documentary evidence provisions of the Regulation and of the Convention'.[31]

The compartmentalised authority of PTRs further presents fruitful territory for nationalist judicial tendencies towards the application of international law in some domestic jurisdictions.[32] Sloss generally distinguishes 'internationalist' (or 'transnationalist') and 'nationalist' attitudes,[33] and argues that these attitudes matter most in relation to what he calls 'vertical provisions', treaty provisions that regulate relations between states and private parties.[34] These different attitudes

[29] Prosper Weil, 'Towards Relative Normativity in International Law?' (1983) 77 *American Journal of International Law* 413, 416 ('without creating any obligation, a resolution is supposed at least to have *entitling* effects, so that any state acting in conformity with it could not thereby be committing an internationally unlawful act' (emphasis added)).

[30] *Greenpeace*, paras 43–45.

[31] *Greenpeace*, para 53.

[32] *cf* Daniel Bodansky and Jutta Brunnée, 'Introduction: The Role of National Courts in the Field of International Environmental Law' in Michael Anderson and Paolo Galizzi (eds), *International Environmental Law in National Courts* (BIICL, 2002), 13.

[33] David Sloss, 'Domestic Application of Treaties' in Duncan B Hollis (ed), *The Oxford Guide to Treaties* (OUP, 2012), 386.

[34] ibid, 380.

can have such an effect that they override the difference between monist and dualist states. Sloss suggests that judicial attitudes towards international instruments are most likely to lead to different outcomes where 'a private party invokes a vertical treaty provision as a constraint on government action'.[35] In such cases, internationalist judges tend to accept their 'independent responsibility to ensure that domestic government officials act in accordance with international treaty obligations',[36] 'whereas nationalist judges employ various rationales to refrain from applying treaties as a constraint on government action'.[37] PTRs make it easier still for nationalist judges to refrain from constraining government action.

Looked at through this lens, it is not difficult to discover a 'nationalist' attitude in some recent US judgments involving PTRs. Most of these judgments were rendered in the slipstream of the 'nationalist' *Medellin* judgment of the US Supreme Court and critical writings from conservative corners about international delegation. In both *NRDC v EPA* (Concurring Opinion Edwards, SCJ) and *One Etched Tusk*, US District Courts referred to the US Supreme Court decision in *Medellin*[38] to support their strict test for domestic application of international instruments.[39] The *NRDC v EPA* judgment refers to various conservative scholarly articles on international delegation to support its decision. These judgments resonate with a strong deference to the executive branch in the implementation of international instruments.

The choice for PTRs marginalises the role of civil society in the implementation of international environmental law. Since international courts and compliance procedures are not accessible for NGOs, businesses and individuals, national court procedures present the only opportunities for non-state actors to hold environmental treaty parties' governments to their detailed obligations. It is particularly important that NGOs and individuals can hold governments to their environmental commitments, because political pressure among states to comply with international environmental law is much lower than in many other areas of international cooperation. As opposed to areas such as trade, investment or intellectual property, when it comes to most areas of international environmental cooperation, powerful states are much less ready to consistently put their foot down politically and economically,[40] let alone that there is any group of states or international institutions to pressure *powerful* states into action.[41]

[35] ibid.

[36] ibid, 378.

[37] ibid, 380.

[38] The decision in *Medellin v Texas*, 552 U.S. 491, 128 S.Ct. 1346 (2008), 24 March 2008, has been widely interpreted as a serious restriction of treaty provisions that qualify as 'self-executive' according to US law on the domestic application of treaties. See Carlos Manuel Vázquez, 'Less Than Zero' (2008) 102 *American Journal of International Law* 529.

[39] *US v One Etched Ivory Tusk of African Elephant (Loxodonta Africana)*, 871 F.Supp.2d 128 (E.D.N.Y.), 17 May 2012, p 136; *NRDC v EPA* (Edwards, Senior Circuit Judge, concurring), p 11.

[40] Francesco Francioni, 'Realism, Utopia and the Future of International Environmental Law' in Antonio Cassese (ed), *Realizing Utopia: the Future of International Law* (OUP, 2012) 442, 447–48.

[41] The appliance of pressure by political or economic means has so far depended mostly on the incidental active backing by a number of powerful states of certain environmental interests out of

C. Infringement of Fundamental Procedural Principles

Apart from weakening domestic implementation compartmentalisation of authority, and the wide governmental discretion that it fosters, also creates a danger of infringements of fundamental procedural principles. Such principles include the duty to promulgate rules, the possibility to contest such infringements, legal certainty, the duty to state reasons, but also the right to be heard – for instance through participation in and consultation on decision making on rules one is specifically concerned with.

The PTR practice falls within the Global Administrative Law project's definition of 'administrative action' at the global level.[42] The notion that administrative principles have started to emerge, and should emerge, in response to the increase in administrative type instruments originating at the international level, finds increased support. 'Global administrative law'[43] originates in the application of domestic administrative and comparative administrative principles to intergovernmental regulatory decisions that affect domestic regulations and situations.[44] As a result, international organisations may have to adapt their rule-making processes to those principles in order to ensure future domestic compliance with their rules, thus stimulating the development of new international procedural mechanisms.[45] Underdeveloped seeds of core procedural principles are indeed found in *some* international organisations and other international bodies, including environmental bodies,[46] and in *some* domestic court cases concerning the domestic implementation of decisions of international institutions.[47] These principles do not yet form a single body of laws and principles applicable to all international administrative action.[48] Still, there is much agreement that certain *core*

temporary preference or self-interest. Kal Raustiala, 'Compliance & Effectiveness in International Regulatory Cooperaton' (2000) 32 *Case Western Reserve Journal of International Law* 387, 404–05; Kyle W Danish, 'International Relations Theory' in Daniel Bodansky, Jutta Brunnée and Ellen Hey (eds), *Oxford Handbook of International Environmental Law* (2007) 205, 208 ('the few regimes that have been associated with changed state behaviour have also had the active backing of a powerful ('hegemonic') state'); Scott Barrett, *Why Cooperate? Incentives to Supply Global Public Goods* (OUP, 2007), 76–77.

[42] Admittedly, the GAL project defines 'administrative action' very broadly. Benedict Kingsbury, Nico Krisch and Richard B Stewart, 'The Emergence of Global Administrative Law' (2005) 68 *Law and Contemporary Problems* 15, 17.

[43] ibid, 17, 28 ('the mechanisms, principles, practices, and supporting social understandings that promote or otherwise affect the accountability of global administrative bodies, in particular by ensuring they meet adequate standards of transparency, participation, reasoned decision, and legality, and by providing effective review of the rules and decisions they make').

[44] ibid, 16.

[45] ibid.

[46] Francesca Spagnuolo, 'Diversity and Pluralism in Earth System Governance: Contemplating the Role for Global Administrative Law' (2011) 70 *Ecological Economics* 1875, 1875–76.

[47] Examples in *European Journal of International Law* (2006) Vol 17, Issue 1.

[48] Nico Krisch, 'The Pluralism of Global Administrative Law' (2006) 17 *European Journal of International Law* 247.

administrative principles *should* apply to the rule making and decision making of international institutions, from the viewpoint of western conceptions of good administration, and considering the shifting of the centre of gravity of international as well as EU rule making from treaties and legislation towards post-treaty and post-legislative instruments.[49]

The 'existing or possible principles and rules' of GAL focus on 'transparency, participation, reasoned decision-making, and assurance of legality in global governance'.[50] More specifically, they identify as emerging as well as normatively desirable, principles of procedural participation, transparency, reasoned decision making, (judicial) review, proportionality and legitimate expectations.[51] Brunnée and Toope have suggested that international rule making should adhere to Fuller's eight criteria of legality.[52] These criteria include the requirements that laws should be general, promulgated (accessible to the public), not retroactive, clear, not contradictory, not demand the impossible, remain relatively constant, and actions of officials operating under the law should be congruent with it.[53]

From this literature, three administrative or procedural principles emerge that most obviously raise questions about various stages in the PTR practice. The ambiguity that surrounds the type of legal obligation that PTRs create is the source of much of the procedural trouble, as will be discussed in more detail below. It conflicts directly with the duty to state the law, the duty to state reasons and the principles of legal certainty and legitimate expectations. The principles of promulgation and legality are likewise compromised by the ambiguity in that this makes it even harder to know whether, and which, PTRs are part of the relevant legal sources.[54] From a strict viewpoint of legality, the procedural standards to be applied to compliance bodies and domestic courts with regard to these four procedural issues are different, and differ moreover between the various domestic jurisdictions. The section looks at the practice of applying PTRs to individual cases through the lens of those widely accepted procedural principles identified by the GAL project, where possible supported by applicable legal principles – such as the rules and principles of the Aarhus Convention on Access to Information, Public Participation in Decision-Making and Access to Justice in Environmental Matters.[55]

[49] For the argument that EU 'post-legislative guidance' requires a re-thinking of European Administrative Law see Joanne Scott, 'In Legal Limbo: Post-Legislative Guidance as a Challenge for European Administrative Law' (2011) 48 *Common Market Law Review* 329. Particularly as regards re-thinking accountability mechanisms, see Emilia Korkea-aho, 'Laws in Progress? Reconceptualizing Accountability Strategies in the Era of Framework Norms' (2013) 2 *Transnational Environmental Law* 363.

[50] Kingsbury, Krisch and Stewart, 'The Emergence of Global Administrative Law', 29.

[51] ibid, 37–42.

[52] Jutta Brunnée and Stephen J Toope, *Legitimacy and Legality in International Law* (CUP, 2010), '*Legitimacy and Legality*', ch 1.

[53] Lon L Fuller, *The Morality of Law* rev edn (Yale University Press, 1969), 33–94; Lon L Fuller, 'Positivism and Fidelity to Law – A Reply to Professor Hart' (1958) 71 *Harvard Law Review* 630.

[54] Fuller, *The Morality of Law*, 50.

[55] Convention on Access to Information, Public Participation in Decision-Making and Access to Justice in Environmental Matters (adopted 25 June 1998, entered into force 30 October 2001) 2161 UNTS 447 (Aarhus Convention).

1. The Principle of Promulgation

Law must be publicly promulgated. It must be accessible to the public, enabling citizens to know what the law requires. Most PTRs in force are accessible on the internet on the websites of the various MEAs, and can technically be reached with a few mouse-clicks. However, it is not always easy to understand the normative relationship between consecutive resolutions relating to the same or related topics. In the *Lac Sorobon* case, the Dutch Crown Court (Council of State) referred to five different Ramsar PTRs adopted at five different meetings of the Ramsar COP, all related to the topic of Environmental Impact Assessments and 'wise use'.[56] In the *Greentree* case, the Australian Federal Courts also consulted a whole series of Ramsar documents, together constituting the Designation Conditions, needing an entire seven pages to set out all relevant sections.[57] Guidelines on CITES import requirements are found in resolutions on such varying topics as *Permits and Certificates* and *Compliance and Enforcement*. The CITES Handbook[58] contains more than a thousand pages describing how various resolutions have created layer upon layer of guidelines. Admittedly, the Handbook prints resolutions that are no longer in force in a different colour, but that still leaves a hugely complex document. PTRs under the Montreal and Kyoto Protocol also run into hundreds and hundreds of pages of regularly updated PTRs and Handbooks. Moreover, the requirement of promulgation goes beyond mere availability. It also includes the requirement that there is a way for private actors to identify which of the many PTRs are in fact relevant to their rights and obligations.[59]

In at least one domestic court case, plaintiffs made the claim that they had no way to be aware that the governmental authorities would interpret implementing legislation in line with PTRs. In *Castlewood Products* (Court of Appeals), the plaintiffs claimed 'that they did not have notice of the Government's interpretation'. The Court of Appeals declared the claim to be meritless with the argument that '[i]t is clear that signatories may only issue export permits for Appendix III goods upon determining that they were legally obtained'. However, the whole point of the *Castlewood Products* case (and the UK *Greenpeace* case) was whether CITES COP resolutions can provide reasons not to grant an import permit *additional* to the ones listed in the Convention. As far as the Convention is concerned, once an export authority has granted a permit for export, a trader may assume that the Management Authority of the country of export concluded that the specimens were 'not obtained in contravention of the laws of that State for the protection of

[56] *Lac Sorobon*, para 2.2.3.3.
[57] *Greentree* (FCA), pp 24–30.
[58] Willem Wijnstekers, *The Evolution of CITES* (2011).
[59] With regard to the UNFCCC Copenhagen Accord, for instance, Brunnée and Toope remark that it is problematic in light of the promulgation criterion, because by merely 'taking note' of the Accord, the UNFCCC parties were 'leaving its future and precise relationship to the convention uncertain'. Brunnée and Toope, *Legitimacy and Legality*, 211.

fauna and flora' (Article V.2(a) CITES). So, on the basis of the Convention *alone*, it was not at all clear to traders that the issuing of an export permit upon a (Brazilian) judicial determination that export was not in contravention with Brazilian law could later be challenged by the authorities in the country of import.

2. The Duty to State the Law and to State Reasons

Another important procedural or administrative principle is that decisions of law-applying bodies should be *reasoned*:[60] they should state the law and should state reasons.[61] The importance of this principle for environmental decision making by national courts is recognised in Article 6.9 of the Aarhus Convention.[62] Article 3.7 of the Aarhus Convention also requires that the (primarily European) parties to this Convention promote the application of the Aarhus principles in *international* decision making.[63] The 'reasons and considerations on which the decision is based', at the very least, include the reasoning as regards the applicable law. Yet, such reasons and considerations are exactly what is missing in many compliance procedures and domestic court judgments.

First, as was observed, compliance bodies provide no reasons for why PTRs should be included in controlling compliance with the treaty. Compliance bodies simply refer to PTRs in their determination of the proper standard for compliance control, and then measure the record of the individual party in question against this standard. In other words, the precise standard for compliance control is *almost entirely* derived from PTRs. But compliance bodies do not explain the legal connection between a PTR and its underlying MEA, thereby implicitly denying a concurrent role for other means of interpretation. The argumentation of the Enforcement Branch of the Kyoto Protocol in the case of Croatia is quite extraordinary in this respect, because the Branch *does* explain extensively why *UNFCCC COP* decisions have no legal relevance for compliance with the Kyoto Protocol, but says nothing about the legal relevance of *Kyoto* PTRs.[64]

Many national courts similarly provide no or very incomplete reasons as to why PTRs deserve a certain legal weight in a decision. Some courts are completely silent, like the compliance bodies, and just ignore PTRs without providing a reason, or apply them without any justification. Other courts mention the general

[60] Kingsbury, Krisch and Stewart, 'The Emergence of Global Administrative Law', 39.

[61] ibid, 39; Benedict Kingsbury, 'The Concept of 'Law' in Global Administrative Law' (2009) 20 *European Journal of International Law* 23, 47–48.

[62] Art 6.9 Aarhus Convention: 'Each Party shall make accessible to the public the text of the decision along with the reasons and considerations on which the decision is based.'

[63] Art 3.7 Aarhus Convention: 'Each Party shall promote the application of the principles of this Convention in international environmental decision-making processes and within the framework of international organizations in matters relating to the environment.'

[64] Kyoto Protocol Compliance Committee, Enforcement Branch, CC-2009-1-8/Croatia/EB, 26 November 2009.

rule of interpretation that subsequent agreements should be taken into account in the interpretation of treaties, but then fail to explain why, in the given case, they give more or less weight to PTRs compared to other means of interpretation of the underlying treaty. This analysis applies, for instance, to the decision in *Castlewood Products I*, where the US District Court leaps from the assertion that CITES Resolutions 10.2 and 11.3 are 'post-ratification understandings' to the conclusion 'that mutual assistance in the enforcement of their respective environmental laws is expected' of the parties.[65] That this leap cannot just be made without justification can be deduced from those courts that *do* make an attempt at finding additional justifications.

Those national courts that *do* provide reasons why a PTR should or should not have (decisive) legal relevance often provide reasons that are weakly substantiated. Examples are the flat-out rejection of any domestic legal relevance of CITES resolutions in the US District Court judgment in *One Tusk*, because they 'are not binding as a matter of domestic law unless those instruments are self-executing or Congress takes an action to incorporate them into domestic law'.[66] This flatly contradicts the US Supreme Court's case law, holding that this type of resolution – while not binding – is, in some manner, relevant for the interpretation of the underlying treaty.[67] Likewise, one could refer to the incredibly short references to respectively the supposed legitimacy or illegitimacy of PTRs in the *Lac Sorobon* and *NRDC* cases. The small number of cases involving various types of *international* governance below the level of formal sources of international law perhaps makes it difficult to develop solid reasoning regarding the legal relevance of each. Therefore, dealing with PTRs remains very much an *ad hoc* issue, requiring judicial improvisation in each case, which inevitably leads to poor reasoning.

3. The Principle of Legal Certainty

A final administrative law principle infringed by the PTR practice is that of legal certainty or predictability. Infringements of this overarching and fundamental principle are closely related to shortcomings in complying with the duty to state the law and to state reasons, and with the duty of promulgation. A consequence of the large discretion that national courts leave to governments, and the inconsistency in the treatment of the same or very similar PTRs even within single countries, is that individuals, environmental NGOs and businesses can never reasonably know in advance what role PTRs will play in the decisions of administrative authorities and courts. In the United States, the *One Etched Tusk* and *Castlewood* cases came

[65] *Castlewood Products v Norton*, 264 F.Supp.2d 9 (D.D.C.), 16 April 2003, p 12.
[66] *One Etched Tusk*, p 136.
[67] *Zicherman v Korean Air Lines Co*, 516 U.S. 217, 116 S.Ct. 629 (1996), 16 January 1996.

to completely opposite conclusions regarding the legal weight to be accorded to PTRs, yet there was no discernible difference between the respective CITES resolutions at issue.

D. Conclusion

To conclude, the ambiguities in the authority of PTRs cause a number of related frictions with fundamental procedural principles, while the sprawling number of complexly related PTRs challenges the principle of promulgation. To address these issues, two types of solution are imaginable. On the one hand, compliance bodies and courts could provide (better supported) justifications for how they treat PTRs than they currently do. For national courts, this will mean a rather high research burden to make informed choices about the complex issue of legitimacy. On the other hand, one could think in the direction of MEAs or specific enabling clauses providing more clarification about the obligatory character of the PTRs adopted on their basis, following the so-far unique example of Article 2(9) of the Montreal Protocol. Or, as Bruch suggests, 'a country can clarify the legal status of international environmental law within its legal system (eg, through constitutional provisions)'.[68] But that would involve a choice for states to have the virtues *and* the vices of law, a choice they might not be willing to make.

[68] Carl Bruch, 'Is International Environmental Law Really Law? An Analysis of Application in Domestic Courts' (2006) 23 *Pace Environmental Law Review* 423, 459.

7

Challenges to the Normative Legitimacy of Environmental Post-Treaty Rules

This chapter addresses the main normative legitimacy concerns that arise in the practice of developing international environmental law through post-treaty rules. Since social legitimacy is so important for PTRs' authority, there is a need to examine legitimacy from a normative viewpoint: are exercises of authority not just believed by an elite set of state representatives to be legitimate, but also *justified* from more objective input and output legitimacy perspectives?

To set the conceptual stage, this chapter takes a normative legitimacy perspective, defined as the *justification of authority from the viewpoint of one or more widely accepted political theories and philosophies.*[1] The existence of sufficient justification can be assessed through applying normative yardsticks (called 'grounds of legitimacy') of an input or output legitimacy nature. In applying these yardsticks, the actual beliefs of various groups of subjects about the extent to which PTRs comply with those yardsticks (social legitimacy) are not taken into account. Normative legitimacy is concerned with 'when an organization *should* be regarded as legitimate, rather than on whether it *is* regarded as legitimate'.[2]

Within the two main grounds of legitimacy, Steffek notes, '[t]here is a wide variety of possible criteria for assessing what constitutes legitimate governance. These criteria change over time and they remain contested.'[3] In this study, the yardsticks used to assess input legitimacy include the respect for sovereign

[1] Rüdiger Wolfrum and Volker Röben, *Legitimacy in International Law* (Springer, 2010), 6; Robert O Keohane and Allen Buchanan, 'The Legitimacy of Global Governance Institutions' in Rüdiger Wolfrum and Volker Röben (eds), *Legitimacy in International Law* (Springer, 2008), 62; Daniel Bodansky, 'The Concept of Legitimacy in International Law' in Rüdiger Wolfrum and Volker Röben (eds), *Legitimacy in International Law* (Springer 2010), 310; Daniel Bodansky, 'The Legitimacy of International Governance: A Coming Challenge for International Environmental Law?' 1999 *American Journal of International Law* 596. Others speak of the (moral) *right to rule*. See Keohane and Buchanan, 'The Legitimacy of Global Governance Institutions', 25.

[2] Julia Black, 'Constructing and Contesting Legitimacy and Accountability in Polycentric Regulatory Regimes' (2008) 2 *Regulation & Governance* 137, 145.

[3] Jens Steffek, 'Discursive Legitimation in Environmental Governance' (2009) 11 *Forest Policy and Economics* 313, 314.

equality and individual state consent in the practice of PTR adoption, the room for interests not identical to the interests of (individual) states – such as global interests or the interests of sub-state groups – and the impact of the PTR practice on the national *trias politica*. For output legitimacy, the primary yardstick is the effectiveness of PTRs in light of the MEA's object and purpose. It is operationalised by looking at the extent to which PTRs are supporting the realisation of the environmental objectives laid down in the underlying MEA (rather than softening the obligations of treaty parties or more generally serving their parochial, non-environmental interests).

The subjects of legitimacy[4] are not identical for each yardstick of normative legitimacy. Input theories of *democratic* legitimacy generally 'elaborate on how the interests, values and ideas of citizens are channelled into the political process',[5] but input legitimacy can also concern the interests of states. In examining sovereign equality and inclusiveness of the consensual decision-making process, the subjects towards whom the exercise of authority must be justified, are, in the first place, the individual treaty parties. For the room for interests not identical to the interests of (individual) states, such as global interests beyond the state or the interests of sub-state groups, the subjects include the treaty parties' respective national populations, parts of national populations that are specially affected by the environmental issue in question, or even the interests of the global citizenry. For output legitimacy too, the interests of states are less relevant than the interests of those ultimately affected by global environmental policies.

Three observations made in the previous chapters call for the analysis of the legitimacy of PTRs, on the basis of various legitimacy grounds. The first authority finding that raises legitimacy questions is the category of PTRs with a high degree of authority over the treaty parties in the orders of the treaty bodies.[6] It is well established that (serious) exercises of authority require legitimation,[7] and that the question of legitimacy has become pressing with the rise of exercises of authority beyond the state.[8] Drawing PTRs with high degrees of authority into the spotlight

[4] The subjects of legitimacy are the various addressees of the object that normatively should submit to them (from the perspective of normative legitimacy), or that socially believe they should (from the perspective of social legitimacy). Christopher A Thomas, 'The Uses and Abuses of Legitimacy in International Law' (2014) 34 *Oxford Journal of Legal Studies* 729, 747.

[5] Jens Steffek, 'The Output Legitimacy of International Organizations and the Global Public Interest' (2015) 7 *International Theory* 263, 264.

[6] Nico Krisch, 'The Structure of Postnational Authority' (2015), at http://papers.ssrn.com/sol3/papers.cfm?abstract_id=2564579, 14 ('Understanding a practice as authority … provides a trigger for a number of follow-on questions, especially as regards accountability and legitimacy, which in contexts without "authority" appear less pressing.').

[7] Keohane and Buchanan, 'The Legitimacy of Global Governance Institutions', 33.

[8] See, eg, Michael Zürn, Martin Binder and Matthias Ecker-Ehrhardt, 'International Authority and Its Politicization' (2012) 4 *International Theory* 69, 70; Joost Pauwelyn, Ramses Wessel and Jan Wouters, 'When Structures Become Shackles: Stagnation and Dynamics in International Lawmaking' (2014) 25 *European Journal of International Law* 733, 743 ('the most pressing problems of informal lawmaking, accountability and legitimacy, arise as a consequence of its effectiveness').

is especially urgent, since, like many instruments of global governance, they 'operate in the background, drawing little attention but from a small set of insiders and close observers'.[9] The primary yardsticks of legitimacy to look at in relation to this finding are those related to the input legitimacy of the adoption of PTRs. But authoritative PTRs also put high demands on output legitimacy.

PTRs' ambiguous or even low degrees of authority in the international and national legal orders, particularly of recommendatory PTRs, perhaps counter-intuitively also raises legitimacy problems, especially of output legitimacy (effectiveness). If the effective implementation of PTRs due to their recommendatory wording rests on volatile factors such as persuasiveness, political expediency, and willingness to contribute economic means, the output legitimacy of these PTRs may receive a severe blow when such factors diminish. The ambiguous legal status of PTRs with a more mandatory wording can raise similar legitimacy problems of ineffective implementation. Moreover, the application of PTRs by administrative agencies *despite* their ambiguous authority raises the question of the legitimate basis of those actors' discretionary powers in this respect.

Finally, it was found that the authority of PTRs in the internal normative orders, to a large extent, rests on their social legitimacy among a sufficiently dominant part of the treaty parties, translated into social pressures. It was also found that international and national courts tend to justify the application or non-application of PTRs by pointing at various legitimacy considerations. These findings, in a more direct and urgent sense, raise the question of whether this social legitimacy and these legitimacy considerations survive normative scrutiny.

It must be noted immediately that, while this chapter finds some serious challenges to the input and output legitimacy of particular post-treaty rules, the examples discussed are too few to allow for general conclusions regarding the legitimacy of the PTR practice. This chapter thus foremost sets a research agenda, and the outlines of an approach for executing it, and discusses those characteristics of the PTR practice that can lead to legitimacy problems without appropriate safeguards. What can be concluded at this point is that problems are most serious and widespread for UNFCCC and Kyoto Protocol PTRs, both in terms of input and output legitimacy. It is likely that this will extend to future PTRs under the Paris Agreement. The practices of the other three regimes have less serious input legitimacy problems, but each has produced PTRs on important topics that are of questionable output legitimacy. These instances do deserve close attention, however, considering that the primary rationale for PTRs is that, in exchange for a weaker link to state consent – lower input legitimacy – they were supposed to make international environmental law more effective (output legitimacy). Equally worrisome is the superficial character of courts' legitimacy considerations, and their failure to act as a counterweight to the dominance of executive branches in the PTR practice.

[9] Krisch, 'The Structure of Postnational Authority', 14.

Like authority, legitimacy is a matter of degree.[10] And clearly, when comparing the PTR process with the making of international environmental law as a whole, 'one is not comparing a defective process against an ideal, but rather two imperfect institutional alternatives'.[11] However, the less legitimate side to the PTR practice has thus far received insufficient structured attention in the literature, which initially strove to point out positive legitimacy aspects, in order to show the relevance of the (previously little known) role of PTRs for effective global environmental governance.[12] For these reasons, in this chapter, the choice is made to address a number of legitimacy concerns in theory and in practice, so as to illustrate the challenges that practitioners and the public should be aware of. The aspiration is that those involved in the PTR practice can take note of these concerns, and improve the practice's inclusiveness, procedures and effectiveness.

A. Input Legitimacy

Input legitimacy focuses on the strength of the link between the addressees of an exercise of authority on the one hand and those involved in the exercise of authority on the other. This link usually consists of some form of consent.[13] But *whose* consent matters? Who are identified as the subjects of input legitimacy?

First, in the traditional *state-centric* view on the input legitimacy of international law making, the subjects of legitimacy are sovereign states. This is expressed in the long-established international law principle of sovereign equality.[14] If sovereign equality is restrictively interpreted, it merely concerns the juridical equality of states, a relatively low threshold that can uphold very unequal law-making processes in practice. Therefore, an account that takes sovereign equality seriously as a yardstick for input legitimacy from a state-centric view should go beyond the formal juridical equality and look at the actual inclusiveness of law-making practices among states. From this angle, the most problematic part of the PTR practice is the *consensual process* through which PTRs are adopted.

[10] Peter G Stillman, 'The Concept of Legitimacy' (1974) 7 *Polity* 32, 43.

[11] Gregory Shaffer and Daniel Bodansky, 'Transnationalism, Unilateralism and International Law' (2012) 1 *Transnational Environmental Law* 31, 38.

[12] See, eg, Jutta Brunnée, 'Reweaving the Fabric of International Law? Patterns of Consent in Environmental Framework Agreements' in Rüdiger Wolfrum and Volker Röben (eds), *Developments of International Law in Treaty Making* (Springer, 2005), 122 (stressing that 'COPs and the continuous interaction that they facilitate may be particularly suited to fostering shared understandings and legitimate norms'). But see *contra* Annecoos Wiersema, 'The New International Law-Makers? Conferences of the Parties to Multilateral Environmental Agreements' (2009) 31 *Michigan Journal of International Law* 231, 283–86; and Günther Handl, 'International "Lawmaking" by Conferences of the Parties and Other Politically Mandated Bodies' in Rüdiger Wolfrum and Volker Röben (eds), *Developments of International Law in Treaty Making* (Springer, 2005), 140–43 ('the need intensifies for certain safeguards or techniques to compensate for the loss of legitimacy associated with the abandonment of states' (specific) consent as a condition of 'bindingness').

[13] Bodansky, 'The Legitimacy of International Governance', 612.

[14] Art 2(1) Charter of the United Nations (adopted 26 June 1945, entered into force 24 October 1945) (UN Charter).

A second, *cosmopolitan* view on input legitimacy emphasises the importance of global interests being represented in the rule-making process next to state-specific interests, with the former even having greater importance. According to the cosmopolitan view of IEL, there should be more influence for global public interests on the rule-making process.[15] Particularly for issues of global relevance such as climate change, biodiversity, ocean pollution and the ozone-layer, cosmopolitans argue that the global public interest should prevail over state-specific interests. To achieve that in input legitimacy terms, 'the emphasis clearly is on mechanisms … that allow for political representation of and accountability to the citizens of the world'.[16] The problematic aspect in the process of adopting PTRs from this cosmopolitan perspective is that state-specific interests tend to thrive in the consensual process, whereas global interests tend to fade into the background. Yet, how global interests could be represented, and by whom, is still an important bone of contention. While some '[c]osmopolitans … argue for new transnational avenues of citizen participation and representation',[17] it is not yet clear how such representation should be shaped so that it would truly represent global interests or global citizenry.

Third, the input legitimacy of international rule-making should be approached from the angle of the *national populations* of the respective treaty parties. According to, amongst others, liberal internationalists, democratic systems will, at least for some time, remain necessarily confined to the borders of the nation state. Democratising international rule making is likely to run into limits far short of what even basic notions of democracy require.[18] It should therefore be accepted that states will continue to be the primary vehicles for democracy for a while.[19] International rule making need not necessarily conflict with national democracy as it can complement the externalities of domestic legislation. But safeguards must prevent that international rule making upsets valuable domestic democratic systems. From this angle, a problematic aspect of the PTR practice is the almost exclusive role of national *executive branches* compared to the other domestic branches of government in almost all stages of the PTR cycle after the initial parliamentary approval to give state consent to the MEA.

[15] Jonas Ebbeson, 'Public Participation' in Daniel Bodansky, Jutta Brunnée and Ellen Hey (eds), *Oxford Handbook of International Environmental Law* (OUP, 2007) 681, 687.

[16] Steffek, 'The Output Legitimacy of International Organizations', 280. Important representatives of the cosmopolitan view are John Dryzek, *Deliberative Global Politics* (Polity Press, 2006); Mathias Koenig-Archibugi, 'Is Global Democracy Possible?' (2011) 17 *European Journal of International Relations* 519; Terry Macdonald, *Global Stakeholder Democracy: Power and Representation beyond Liberal States* (OUP, 2008).

[17] Steffek, 'The Output Legitimacy of International Organizations', 287.

[18] Robert O Keohane, Stephen Macedo and Andrew Moravcsik, 'Democracy Enhancing Multilateralism' (2009) 63 *International Organization* 1, 2; Steffek, 'The Output Legitimacy of International Organizations', 280.

[19] Christian Tomuschat, 'International Law: Ensuring the Survival of Mankind on the Eve of a New Century: General Course on Public International Law' (2001) 281 *Receuil des Cours* 13, 162.

1. The Insufficiency of State Consent to the Underlying Treaty

In a widely read 1999 article, Bodansky firmly established that individual state consent can no longer suffice for the legitimation of most international environmental governance. He noted that, in most of international environmental governance, states give formal consent only to 'an ongoing *system* of governance' rather than to particular obligations or decisions.[20] While most of international environmental *law* (i.e. treaties) is specifically consented to,[21] the sharp edges of the content of the obligations are found in PTRs, the products of the 'ongoing system of governance'. At first glance, it seems to be a sensible argument that the individual consent given to a general system of governance by ratifying an environmental treaty and establishing a Conference of Parties with decision-making powers would extend to any subsequent PTRs, by means of consent to the enabling clauses. But this argument loses its strength because, as explained in chapters one and three, enabling clauses hardly ever come close to predisposing the range of substantive outcomes eventually laid down in PTRs.[22] PTRs interpret, modify or fill gaps in the underlying MEA; they are never just 'clarifications' of what the parties already meant. Moreover, PTRs are not only adopted in the direct aftermath of an MEA's adoption, but for decades afterwards, without renewal of the initial consent.

Bodansky's second argument was that modern IEL, MEAs and PTRs alike have significant implications for sub-state actors, for whom state consent among sovereign nations may have insufficient legitimising effect. Historically, international law primarily concerned the relations between states. Yet, 'international environmental law continues to grow more like domestic environmental law', and 'addresses subjects that, in the past, were addressed by national law'.[23] Environmental subjects previously governed by domestic legislation have now become subject to international law and other international rules. These developments raise the question if a legitimacy device such as state consent, which was developed for foreign policy type issues, is at all sufficient.[24]

Considering these observations – still very much valid – examination of input legitimacy must focus directly on the adoption and application of PTRs *by* the ongoing systems of governance, and cannot be satisfied with consent *to* the

[20] Bodansky, 'The Legitimacy of International Governance', 605.

[21] ibid.

[22] ibid, 604, 608–09. As Marmor says about changes in institutions and practices, 'some changes are such that one can be expected to have consented to; after all, one cannot expect that an institution one joins will remain unchanged forever. But some institutional changes that occur can be such that they undercut one's commitment; it is sometimes appropriate to react to a change by saying that 'this is not what I signed up for'. Marmor, 'An Institutional Conception of Authority', 251.

[23] Bodansky, 'The Legitimacy of International Governance', 606, 610–11.

[24] ibid, 611.

ongoing systems of governance alone. More attention must be paid to how exactly individual states are represented in this system, and whether specially affected states have opportunities for involvement. Considering Bodansky's second point, attention should also be paid to which parts of the state represent the state in this system. All this is not to say that the role of state consent is negligible for input legitimacy: It ensures the legitimate *existence* of rule-making powers of the COP, but not the *exercise* thereof.

2. The Reality of Consensual Decision Making

a. Adopting PTRs by Consensus

The various enabling clauses in MEAs leave serious doubts about the required mode of decision making. The general clauses on the functioning of plenary treaty meetings do not provide much clarity either. Such phrases as 'the parties decide',[25] 'the Conference of the Parties shall be competent',[26] and 'the COP/MOP shall take a decision'[27] do not explicitly state whether a unanimous vote, consensus, or majority voting is required when the COP, COP/MOP or MOP adopts rules. Only the Ramsar Convention explicitly stipulates that 'recommendations, resolutions and decisions' are to be adopted 'by simple majority of the Contracting Parties present and voting'.[28] In the absence of specified decision-making arrangements in the treaty, plenary treaty meetings decide by consensus.[29]

For every MEA studied here, except for the UNFCCC/Kyoto Protocol, the COP, COP/MOP or MOP has indeed by consensus adopted a set of Rules of Procedure that governs among others the adoption of PTRs. Adoption of each PTR thus at least formally has to comply with the Rules of Procedure that plenary treaty meetings have agreed to, particularly the procedures for decision making.

[25] Art 2H.5 Montreal Protocol on Substances that Deplete the Ozone Layer (adopted 16 September 1987, entered into force 1 January 1989) 1522 UNTS 3 (Montreal Protocol).

[26] Art 6.2 Convention on Wetlands of International Importance especially as Waterfowl Habitat (adopted 2 February 1971, entered into force 21 December 1975) 996 UNTS 245 (Ramsar Convention).

[27] Various provisions in the Kyoto Protocol to the United Nations Framework Convention on Climate Change (adopted 11 December 1997, entered into force 16 February 2005) 2303 UNTS 162 (Kyoto Protocol) and the Cartagena Protocol on Biosafety to the Convention on Biological Diversity (adopted 29 January 2000, entered into force 11 September 2003) 2226 UNTS 208 (Cartagena Protocol).

[28] Art 7.2 Ramsar Convention.

[29] One might read a sanctioning of that practice into the phrasing of most explicit enabling clauses that '[t]he Conference of the Parties shall decide', which neither gives a hint of the positive consent of every individual treaty party being required, nor indicates that anything less than consensus is sufficient. Another sanctioning of the practice of consensus follows from the fact that, for instance, the UNFCCC and the Convention on Biological Diversity require the *Rules of Procedure* to be adopted by consensus. Art 7.2(k) United Nations Framework Convention on Climate Change (adopted 9 May 1992, entered into force 21 March 1994) 1771 UNTS 107 (UNFCCC); Art 22.2(e) Convention on Biological Diversity (adopted 5 June 1992, entered into force 29 December 1993) 1760 UNTS 79 (CBD).

The various framework agreements and protocols[30] prescribe that the adoption of Rules of Procedure shall be done by consensus. An example is Article 11.3(a) Montreal Protocol, prescribing that '[t]he Parties … shall … adopt by consensus rules of procedure for their meetings'. The Vienna Convention on the Ozone Layer, the UNFCCC, the Kyoto Protocol, the CBD and the Cartagena Protocol all contain similar rules. The Ramsar Convention and CITES are silent on a particular procedure required for adopting Rules of Procedure, but foresee that such Rules shall or may be adopted.[31]

The UNFCCC COP and the Kyoto COP/MOP have never been able to reach consensus on the adoption of a Rule of Procedure foreseeing in 'specified majorities required for the adoption of particular decisions', as Article 7.3 UNFCCC allows for. The UNFCCC/Kyoto Protocol Rules of Procedure are therefore, in practice, applied with the exception of Rule 42 on voting.[32] As a result, the Kyoto COP/MOP has had to fall back on consensual decision making by default.[33]

The Ramsar, CITES, and Montreal Rules of Procedure formally allow recourse to voting with qualified,[34] or in exceptional cases even simple, majorities.[35] However, the Ramsar Convention and CITES Rules of Procedure make it quite clear that voting is a last resort after seeking consensus. For instance, the Ramsar Rules of Procedure state that '[t]he Parties shall make every effort to reach agreement on all matters of substance by consensus'.[36] Perhaps a bit more cautiously, Rule 21.1 of the CITES Rules of Procedure provides that '[t]he Conference shall as far as possible decide on draft resolutions and other documents by consensus'.[37]

[30] Or, sometimes, their underlying framework agreements do so as well. See, eg, Art 13.5 Kyoto Protocol: 'The rules of procedure of the Conference of the Parties and financial procedures applied under the [UNFCCC] shall be applied *mutatis mutandis* under this Protocol, except as may be otherwise decided by consensus by the Conference of the Parties serving as the meeting of the Parties to this Protocol.'

[31] Art 6.4 Ramsar Convention: 'The Conference of the Contracting Parties shall adopt rules of procedure for each of its meetings.' Art XI.5 Convention on International Trade in Endangered Species of Wild Fauna and Flora (adopted 3 March 1973, entered into force 1 July 1975) 993 UNTS 243 (CITES): 'At any meeting, the Parties may determine and adopt rules of procedure for the meeting.'

[32] UNFCCC COP 2, Geneva, 8–19 July 1996, para 2: 'As decided by the Conference of the Parties (COP) at the start of its first session, the draft rules of procedure are at present being applied by the COP and its subsidiary bodies, with the exception of draft rule 42: "Voting" (see FCCC/CP/1995/7, para 10), which appears in bold type in the present document'.

[33] To this date the lack of a Voting Rule in the case of the UNFCCC and the Kyoto Protocol is being interpreted in the UNFCCC COP and Kyoto COP/MOP as a continuation of the consensus requirement. See, eg, *UNFCCC Guide for Presiding Officers*, Revised November 2011, at http://unfccc.int/resource/docs/publications/guide_presiding_officers.pdf, 8.

[34] Rule 40 of the Montreal Protocol Rules of Procedure requires a two-thirds majority; Rule 26 of the CITES Rules of Procedure requires a two-thirds majority; Rule 40 of the CBD and Cartagena Protocol Rules of Procedure requires a two-thirds majority (however, this last Rule is still bracketed).

[35] Art 7.2 Ramsar Convention.

[36] Ramsar COP, *Rules of Procedure of the Ramsar Conference of the Contracting Parties* (Rev. COP 11), Rule 40.1.

[37] CITES COP, *Rules of Procedure of the Conference of the Parties* (Rev. COP 14).

By contrast, the Montreal Protocol Rules of Procedure do not contain such a 'last resort' clause. Decisions on matters of substance 'shall be taken by a two-thirds majority vote of the Parties present and voting'.[38] However, when analysing actual Montreal MOP decisions, there are often references to consensus. For instance, in relation to *Critical-Use Exemptions*, MOP decisions frequently emphasise the need for the Technical and Economic Assessment Panel to 'develop its recommendations in a consensus process'.[39] The same is true for MOP decisions relating to the financial mechanism.[40] While there is no *formal* need first to make every effort to achieve consensus before resorting to a vote, in the reports of meetings, frequent referrals can be found to the need to find consensus on various topics, and even indications that decision making by consensus is part of the 'customary' practice of the Montreal MOP.[41] Indeed, every Report of the Montreal MOP contains a paragraph that emphasises that '[t]he parties agreed to follow their customary procedures'.[42] In other words, even in the Meetings of the Parties of the Montreal Protocol, there is an unwritten rule that the Parties should exhaust all options to reach consensus before resorting to a vote.

Of such arrangements as found in the Ramsar and CITES Rules of Procedure, it is often said that the 'shadow of a vote' hangs over the treaty parties. The idea is that 'the technically possible vote serves thus as an incentive to reach consensus', because 'the rules of procedure … might be invoked for requesting a vote should the result by consensus not be forthcoming'.[43] In practice, even in the regimes where voting is formally possible, or even formally mandated as in the case of the Montreal Protocol, plenary treaty meetings hardly ever decide otherwise than by consensus. For instance, at Ramsar COP VIII in 2002, 45 resolutions and recommendations on substantive issues were adopted by consensus and none by voting.[44]

[38] Vienna Convention COP, *Rules of procedure for meetings of the Conference of the Parties to the Vienna Convention and Meetings of the Parties to the Montreal Protocol*, Rule 40.2. In the Montreal Protocol text, there are a number of more isolated references to consensual decision making, notably for the adoption of financial rules and for adjustments of the annexes banning ozone-depleting substances. In both cases, the parties 'shall make every effort to reach agreement by consensus' before resorting to qualified majority voting. See Arts 2.9(c) and 10.9 Montreal Protocol.

[39] Montreal MOP Decisions XIX/9, XX/5, XXI/11, XXII/6, XXIII/4, XXIV/5.

[40] See, eg, Montreal MOP Decision II/8, *Financial mechanism*.

[41] *Report of the Twenty-Fifth Meeting of the Parties to the Montreal Protocol on Substances that Deplete the Ozone Layer*, Bangkok, 21–25 October 2013, para 106: 'Several representatives expressed disappointment at that stance, emphasizing that all customary procedures of Montreal Protocol meetings had been followed, namely that the time and venue of the contact group had been well publicised and that interested parties had come together to discuss their differing views. Through compromise, they had succeeded in reaching consensus.'

[42] *Report of the Twenty-Fifth Meeting of the Parties to the Montreal Protocol on Substances that Deplete the Ozone Layer*, Bangkok, 21–25 October 2013, paras 20, 179.

[43] Karl Zemanek, 'Majority Rule and Consensus Technique in Law-Making Diplomacy' in Ronald St J MacDonald and Douglas M Johnston (eds), *The Structure and Process of International Law* (Martinus Nijhoff Publishers, 1986), 863.

[44] Not counting Ramsar COP Res VIII.46, *Thanks to the people and governments of Spain*. See *Report of the 8th Meeting of the Conference of the Contracting Parties*, Valencia, Spain, 18–26 November 2002.

When a widespread and consistent practice of consensual decision making develops in a regime, particularly with regard to weighty issues, pulling the emergency brake of voting may be regarded as a particularly hostile move, and could mean a death sentence for the post-treaty rules in question, even if formally adopted. If qualified majority voting is not a regular practice in a regime, its invocation is too politically charged and can trigger a backlash in the form of a refusal by the minority to implement and comply with the rule, even considering it as a breach of 'customary' practices.

b. What is Consensual Decision Making and How Should its Legitimacy be Assessed?

As this short overview shows, the demand that decisions should be taken 'by consensus' is well established in the practice of PTR adoption. But how should consensus be defined? Is there any convergence on the formal requirements of consensual decision making, and what does it look like in practice? These are important questions, because different appearances of consensual decision making would satisfy yardsticks of input legitimacy to quite different extents.

At least for the Kyoto Protocol regime, the Enforcement Branch of the Compliance Committee has confirmed that consensus should be understood in the same way as it is generally understood in international law making: '[T]he term is generally understood to refer to *the absence of a formal objection*' (emphasis added).[45] This sets consensual decision making apart from decision making by individual state consent, or decision making by unanimity.[46] Unanimity would require the individual expression of agreement by each treaty party representative. Unanimity is neither mentioned as a mode of decision making in any of the studied MEAs and their Rules of Procedure, nor is it found in practice.[47]

The idea behind consensus, and why – at least initially – there was so much enthusiasm about its usefulness for the negotiation of new treaties in legal scholarship,[48] is that it helps to get as many treaty parties as possible on board, which was then viewed as an important condition for successful treaties. On the arrival of the 'active' consensual method[49] of treaty-text adoption in the

[45] Kyoto Protocol Compliance Committee, Enforcement Branch, CC/EB/21/2012/1, 27 September 2012, Twenty-first meeting, 22–24 October 2012, Bonn, Germany, Annex, *Annotated list of stocktaking issues for the enforcement branch*, para 16.

[46] Zemanek, 'Majority Rule and Consensus Technique', 874.

[47] Occasionally, the Ramsar COP adopts PTRs 'by acclaim', which is a hybrid between consensus and unanimity.

[48] eg Barry Buzan, 'Negotiating by Consensus: Developments in Technique at the United Nations Conference on the Law of the Sea' (1981) 75 *American Journal of International Law* 324.

[49] 'Active consensus', as opposed to 'passive consensus', means that the Chairperson assumes an active role in producing negotiat*ing* texts, which would then gradually evolve into negotiat*ed* texts. ibid 334–35.

UNCLOS-negotiations, with a large role for the chairperson, international legal scholars wrote positive reviews about it, figuring that it had a chance at more effective decision making and more widespread support of states.[50]

There was and is much disagreement about the formal requirements of consensus.[51] Despite it being possible to describe what consensus requires more or less, it exists in a 'legal vacuum'.[52] Consensus generally means *the taking of decisions without a formal vote, in the absence of formal objection(s)*, after which a non-objecting state may 'be subjected to an argument that it is estopped by acquiescence from any subsequent objection to the draft'.[53] Discussions continue both inside and outside the plenary until consensus is reached, which is when no objections are made known to the chairperson any longer. Whether that is the case is in principle decided by the chairperson. And this is where the problems – of legal definition and otherwise – begin: there is a lack of formal and clear instructions to chairpersons on how and when they should determine whether there is an 'absence of formal objections'.

There is a lot of uncertainty about how much objection, and by whom, the consensus requirement can withstand. Chairpersons have often applied different understandings, including the following: one objection precludes consensus; more than one objection is needed; even a handful of objections is not enough; an 'overwhelming majority' suffices to declare consensus; parties may no longer object when they have not participated in consensus building; or, most remarkably, parties may be precluded from speaking in order to prevent consensus from failing. This final interpretation is squarely in violation of among others the UN General Assembly Rules of Procedure 'that the right of every member state to set forth its views in full must not be prejudiced by this procedure'.[54] The discussion flared up heavily during the negotiations of the Arms Trade Treaty (ATT) in 2013, sending diplomats all over the world scrambling for information about whether they would be the next to be 'outvoted' by consensus.[55] In the course of

[50] Bruno Simma, 'Consent: Strains in the Treaty System' in Ronald St J MacDonald and Douglas M Johnstone (eds), *The Structure and Process of International Law* (Martinus Nijhoff Publishers, 1986), 485; Oscar Schachter, 'The Nature and Process of Legal Development in International Society' in Ronald St J MacDonald and Douglas M Johnston (eds), *The Structure and Process of International Law* (Martinus Nijhoff Publishers, 1983), 745; Buzan, 'Negotiating by Consensus'; Zemanek, 'Majority Rule and Consensus Technique', 875.

[51] Zemanek already found it difficult to define consensus: 'the object is too amorphous'; ibid 875. For the present, Dapo Akande, 'What Is the Meaning of "Consensus" in International Decision Making?' *EJIL Talk!* (2013); Antto Vihma, 'A Climate of Consensus: The UNFCCC Faces Challenges of Legitimacy and Effectiveness' (2011) 75 *The Finnish Institute of International Affairs*, March Issue.

[52] ibid 4.

[53] Richard H Steinberg, 'In the Shadow of Law or Power? Consensus-Based Bargaining and Outcomes in the GATT/WTO' (2002) 56 *International Organization* 339, 344.

[54] Annex V, *Rules of Procedure of the General Assembly*, para 104.

[55] In that negotiation, the objection of one state, Russia, ultimately prevented the formation of consensus. However, Russia's objections were preceded by objections of Syria, Iran, and North Korea;

the Arms Trade Treaty negotiations, Mexico stated dryly that 'there is no established definition of the term "consensus" in the United Nations'.[56]

In addition to the confusion as regards the legal requirements of consensus, that brief moment of a Chair's hammer coming down is also just the final part of the consensual *process* considered as a whole. Consensus is 'a process of negotiations and mediations'.[57] In this process, compromises are sought, coalitions are built, and often the weaker states or states that fail to find themselves in (stronger) coalitions are sidestepped. Frequently, it is even considered unfair for a treaty party not to participate in consensus building, only to raise its objection at the very last moment. In the context of the PTR practice, statements of such a nature were, for instance, made when India raised objections to a decision regarding the implementation of the Montreal Protocol vis-à-vis small island developing states, even though it had not attended the meetings of the 'contact group'![58]

Since consensus as a mode of adoption has flexible boundaries to say the least, consensus as such cannot serve as a yardstick of normative legitimacy, in the sense of: 'if the decision was taken by consensus it is (not) legitimate'. The legitimating potential of consensus depends too much on how consensus is interpreted in each case, and how the process leading up to the consensual decision is conducted. Instead, it is necessary to take individual instances of consensual decision making, and assess them against other yardsticks. It is also necessary to assess the process of consensus building as a whole, and not just the final decision-taking moment.

Particularly, it is suggested that the consensual process and decisions should be viewed along two yardsticks: (1) sovereign equality and inclusiveness among the treaty parties (requirements that follow from the traditional state-centric view); and (2) the yardstick of the representation of global interests, i.e. interests rising above the level of state-specific interests as chiefly represented by NGOs (requirements following from the cosmopolitan view) and groups not represented sufficiently by state representatives. In turn, these yardsticks can only be properly measured when the evaluated process is at least to some extent transparent.[59]

their objections had still been dismissed as *not* preventing consensus. It was Russia's protests against consensual adoption in the face of objections by the *other* three, upon which the Chairperson concluded that consensus was lacking. For details and discussion, see the Arms Trade Treaty Legal Blog, 'Iran, North Korea, and Syria shoot down the ATT … but only for now', Thursday 28 March 2013, at http://armstradetreaty.blogspot.co.uk/2013/03/iran-north-korea-and-syria-shoot-down.html; and Akande, 'What Is the Meaning of "Consensus"?'.

[56] Arms Trade Treaty Legal Blog, 'Iran, North Korea, and Syria shoot down the ATT'.

[57] Jens Evensen, 'Three Procedural Cornerstones of the Law of the Sea Conference: The Consensus Principle, The Package Deal and The Gentleman's Agreement' in: John Kaufmann (ed), *Effective Negotiation* (Martinus Nijholf Publishers, 1989), 78.

[58] *Report of the Twenty-Fifth Meeting of the Parties to the Montreal Protocol on Substances that Deplete the Ozone Layer*, Bangkok, 21–25 October 2013, para 106: 'Through compromise, they had succeeded in reaching consensus. They said that no representative of India had attended the meetings of the contact group and that it set a dangerous precedent to permit a party that had not attended a meeting of a contact group to reopen discussions on, or block, a decision in plenary session.'

[59] Frank Biermann and Aarti Gupta, 'Accountability and Legitimacy in Earth System Governance: A Research Framework' (2011) 70 *Ecological Economics* 1856, 1858; Aarti Gupta, 'Transparency as

The most important requirement from a state-centred view of input legitimacy remains that the consensual process should respect sovereign equality.[60] In the context of international law making, sovereign equality is often restrictively understood to mean that each state has one vote and that these votes should be of equal weight.[61] Although no vote is taken in the consensual process, formally, each state can prevent consensus by objection, without differentiation between powerful states and weak states. Once consensual processes deviate from that formal interpretation, as was the case in the Arms Trade Treaty negotiations, they openly fall short of sovereign equality. However, most deviations are not as flagrant, and inequality often arises in the *process* of consensus seeking. If the requirement of sovereign equality is to be meaningful for input legitimacy, it therefore needs to be expanded into a stronger version: it must extend to the process of consensus seeking.

In inclusive law making, all affected (state) parties are not only formally represented equally, but 'the views of all parties concerned must be taken into account and an attempt must be made to reconcile conflicting arguments'.[62] (Inclusiveness does not require that *outcomes* reflect all those views.) As all states in the world are affected – both ecologically and economically – by most of the rule-making decisions of environmental plenary bodies, it is evident that, at the very least, all treaty parties should be fully included in the consensual process. Their participation in the process should be effective and real. Although most of the research about disenfranchisement of developing countries and other smaller states has focused on the negotiation of treaties,[63] inclusiveness is at least as important at the stage of PTR adoption, because that is where the all-important detailed rules are agreed.

Of course, on the one hand, inclusiveness should not require that all parties have an exactly equal weight in the consensual process. Decision making in international law should to some extent reflect geopolitical and economic realities in order to be acceptable processes for the powerful states to participate in. Otherwise, there is a real risk that such states will flee the multilateral process,[64] exacerbating the 'decay of consent' that is already underway.[65] Indeed, increasingly, powerful states retreat into informal structures and 'minilateral' settings,[66]

Contested Political Terrain: Who Knows What about the Global GMO Trade and Why Does It Matter?' (2010) 10 *Global Environmental Politics* 32.

[60] Benedict Kingsbury, 'Sovereignty and Inequality' (1998) 9 *European Journal of International Law* 599.

[61] Kingsbury, 'Sovereignty and Inequality', 605.

[62] Pauwelyn, Wessel and Wouters, 'When Structures Become Shackles', 755.

[63] Ian M McGregor, 'Disenfranchisement of Countries and Civil Society at COP-15 in Copenhagen' (2011) 11 *Global Environmental Politics* 1.

[64] Jochen Von Bernstorff, 'Procedures of Decision Making and the Role of Law in International Organizations' (2008) 9 *German Law Journal* 1939.

[65] Nico Krisch, 'The Decay of Consent: International Law in an Age of Global Public Goods' (2014) 108 *American Journal of International Law* 1.

[66] Robyn Eckersley, 'Moving Forward in the Climate Negotiations: Multilateralism or Minilateralism?' (2012) 12 *Global Environmental Politics* 24.

such as in the negotiation of the *Copenhagen Accord* between the US and the BASIC countries.[67] On the other hand, when the accommodation of the geopolitically and economically leading countries leads to the near-complete disenfranchisement of less powerful states,[68] then that is another line that should not be crossed. That is especially the case when this concerns those states most affected by ecological deterioration, such as climate change (the Small Island Developing States), or loss of biodiversity. In other words, an inclusive but politically realistic decision-making process should achieve a certain balance between these extremes.

The merits as well as the problems of consensual decision making for sovereign equality and inclusiveness have received their share of attention in international relations, with a notable focus on UNCLOS, the GATT/WTO,[69] and the EU.[70] Contrary to (qualified) majority voting, the shift from 'one state, one vote' to a non-transparent process of negotiations is almost sure to guarantee that 'outcomes reflect underlying power'.[71] That became clear already during the negotiations of UNCLOS in the 1980s.[72] As Charney explains, 'the consensus approach permits the maintenance of an egalitarian procedure which in practice may assure that multilateral negotiations reflect the real geopolitical power of the participating nations'.[73] In other words, consensual decision making is a form of invisibly weighted voting that can be sold to home constituencies and the public as if it fully respects sovereign equality. Even an overwhelming majority can no longer threaten those powerful minority states to bring the matter to a vote.

There are at least four further reasons why consensual decision making gives such disproportionate power to powerful minorities. First, consensual decisions tend to concern *package deals*, which can only be accepted or objected to as a whole.[74] Package deals focus on reaching agreement between the big players first.

[67] Or, more generally, the G20 and the Major Economies Forum (MEF). Krisch, 'The Decay of Consent', 16.

[68] Dana R Fisher and Jessica F Green, 'Understanding Disenfranchisement: Civil Society and Developing Countries' Influence and Participation in Global Governance for Sustainable Development' (2004) 4 *Global Environmental Politics* 65.

[69] Steinberg, 'In the Shadow of Law or Power?'; Robert Kissack, 'Crisis Situations and Consensus Seeking: Adaptive Decision-Making in the FAO and Applying Its Lessons to the Reform of the WTO' in Thomas Cottier and Manfred Elsig (eds), *Governing the World Trade Organization: Past, Present and Beyond Doha* (CUP, 2011), 241.

[70] Dorothee Heisenberg, 'The Institution of "Consensus" in the European Union: Formal versus Informal Decision-Making in the Council' (2005) 44 *European Journal of Political Research* 65.

[71] Steinberg, 'In the Shadow of Law or Power?', 342.

[72] Akande, 'What Is the Meaning of "Consensus"?'.

[73] Jonathan I Charney, 'United States Interest in a Convention on the Law of the Sea: The Case for Continued Efforts' (1978) 11 *Vanderbilt Journal of Transnational Law* 39, 43. For a similar argument in relation to the WTO, see Steinberg, 'In the Shadow of Law or Power?', 344.

[74] In a package deal, 'critical issues, supported and contested by different negotiating parties, are matched in a complex compromise that has to be accepted as a whole, its components not being negotiable'. Zemanek, 'Majority Rule and Consensus Technique', 876.

To object to such a negotiated package requires a (smaller) state to explain that the package is fundamentally against its interests, in the full limelight of the plenary meeting.

Second, and closely connected, consensual processes operate in accordance with the logic of the '*information game*':[75] when powerful states table a proposal, weaker states must respond with a reasoned objection, or later on face the argument that they have acquiesced.[76] These reasoned objections in turn deliver information to powerful states, allowing them to come up with trade-offs that are just enough for weaker states to have the feeling that they have reached some result they can present at home. Often, these trade-offs are in the shape of (short-term) economic advantages, such as in the attempts of passing the *Copenhagen Accord* through the UNFCCC COP.[77]

Third, consensual decision making carries with it a considerable risk of *non-transparency*, which makes it very difficult to *assess* its inclusiveness. The consensual process drives parties to informal settings, because the logic and workings of the consensual process are 'based in no minor part on the secrecy and confidentiality of these negotiations'.[78] This 'creates an informal market of IOUs about which only the insiders are knowledgeable'.[79] In the climate change negotiations, a low point – in terms of transparency in combination with a lack of inclusiveness – was reached in the negotiation of the *Copenhagen Accord*. Brazil, China, India, South Africa and the United States negotiated an agreement behind closed doors,[80] and tried to get it adopted as a 'consensus' decision in the UNFCCC COP.

Fourth, the negotiating nature of the consensus process gives an important role to the chairperson, usually coming from the state organising the conference, such as Patricia Espinosa from Mexico in the case of the UNFCCC/Kyoto *Cancun Agreements*. There are many examples of chairs performing 'efficiency-enhancing interventions'.[81] As chairperson and organiser, this person and the country he or she represents have a high stake in reaching an outcome that is perceived

[75] As defined by Steinberg, consensus provides 'incentives and opportunities for collecting the information necessary for a successful agenda-setting process'. Steinberg, 'In the Shadow of Law or Power?', 361.

[76] ibid 363.

[77] Consider particularly the statement of the representative of Tuvalu, who stated that they were 'being offered money to betray our people and our future; however, our future is not for sale'. Kyoto COP/MOP, resumed 12th meeting, 3.10 am, http://cop15.meta-fusion.com/kongresse/cop15/templ/play.php?id_kongresssession?2755&theme?unfccc.

[78] Philipp Dann, 'The Political Institutions' in Armin Von Bogdandy and Jürgen Bast (eds), *Principles of European Constitutional Law* (Hart Publishing, 2009) 237, 248.

[79] Heisenberg, 'The Institution of "consensus" in the European Union', 70.

[80] Daniel Bodansky, 'The Copenhagen Climate Change Conference: A Postmortem' (2010) 104 *American Journal of International Law* 230, 234.

[81] Jonas Tallberg, 'The Power of the Chair: Formal Leadership in International Cooperation' (2010) 54 *International Studies Quarterly* 241, 259.

as successful, and are therefore inclined to provide as little room as possible to objectors. Moreover, it is unlikely that chairs are appointed who are not favoured by the key players.[82]

c. Input Legitimacy of Kyoto Protocol COP/MOP Decisions

Having established these *tendencies* of consensual decision making in politically high-profile negotiations, such as WTO Rounds, Climate Change Summits and the Arms Trade Treaty, the question is whether the same tendencies materialise in the PTR adoption process. After all, consensus is not inherently non-inclusive; it is susceptible to abuse. The obvious hypothesis is that the more politically charged or economically weighty a prospective PTR is, the greater the tendency towards disenfranchisement of smaller states, civil society and interests beyond states. Disenfranchisement can be most clearly noted in the negotiations of both the Marrakech/Bonn Agreements and the Cancun Agreements under the UNFCCC/Kyoto Protocol. Political disagreement is much more modest in the Montreal MOP. The recommendatory nature of many CITES and Ramsar COP PTRs may diminish the importance that treaty parties attach to objecting to PTRs that are not entirely in conformity with their interests. After all, they are easier to escape. But further research of the other three regimes is required before any conclusions can be reached. Here, two examples from the UNFCCC COP and the Kyoto COP/MOP show what can happen to the inclusivity of the consensual process if there is too much at stake.

The series of COP and COP/MOP decisions adopted in the wake of the Kyoto Protocol in order to achieve its ratification,[83] known as the *Bonn Agreements* or the *Marrakech Agreements*, constitute a first example. These *Agreements* include the *LULUCF* Decisions and the *Accounting Modalities* of chapter two, and many other PTRs crucial to the Kyoto system. Their import was such that Rajamani, a long-time commentator of the climate change negotiations, speaks of 'a re-negotiation of the Kyoto Protocol'.[84] The good news for input legitimacy was that because the negotiations of the Marrakech Agreements *preceded* ratification of the Kyoto Protocol, ratification could still be used as a legitimating device. This 're-negotiation' was too politically salient to be negotiated by consensus *after* individual state consent had been given. The bad news was that the so-called Umbrella Group (roughly consisting of Australia, Canada, Japan,

[82] ibid.

[83] See generally Gerhard Loibl, 'Conferences of Parties and the Modification of Obligations' in Matthew CR Craven and Malgosia Fitzmaurice, *Interrogating the Treaty: Essays in the contemporary law of treaties* (2005), 103; Hermann E Ott, 'The Bonn Agreement to the Kyoto Protocol – Paving the Way for Ratification' (2001) 1 *International Environmental Agreements: Politics, Law and Economics* 469.

[84] Lavanya Rajamani, 'Re-Negotiating Kyoto: A Review of the Sixth Conference of Parties to the Framework Convention on Climate Change' (2000) 21 *Colorado Journal of International Environmental Law and Policy* 201, 237.

Iceland, New Zealand, Norway, the Russian Federation, the US, and Ukraine) could threaten non-ratification to get their way.[85] This was particularly so from the moment it became clear that the US would not ratify,[86] necessitating ratification by all the others in the Umbrella Group in order to achieve the entry into force of the Protocol.

James Fry, adviser of Tuvalu and the Alliance of Small Island States, documented how various parties – such as Russia,[87] Japan[88] and Australia[89] – were able to apply pressure to insert paragraphs into decisions that were wholly designed for their individual situations. Individual states that were indispensable for the Protocol's entry into force endlessly pushed the various COP and COP/MOP decisions towards a point where meeting their emissions reductions hardly required any domestic policy changes.[90] Rajamani commented: 'After the developing countries had left, the main actors got down to business'.[91] When the dust settled, Fry concluded that 'it is evident that some parties are less dissatisfied than others. For the "less dissatisfied", the journey through the jungle provided an opportunity to minimise their obligations to reduce emissions of greenhouse gases'.[92]

A second example of flawed consensual decision making involving PTRs under the UNFCCC/Kyoto Protocol is the *Cancun Agreements* of 2010, an attempt to repair the multilateral process after the fiasco at Copenhagen. The *Cancun Agreements* consist of a range of post-treaty rules, addressing among others additional LULUCF activities, deforestation in developing countries (REDD), and a Green Climate Fund. The familiar pattern for multilateral consensual negotiations of high political salience unfolded: 'The final deal was drafted to ensure that compromises, where struck, did not breach red lines for the key players,' writes Rajamani.[93] 'Notwithstanding the avowals to transparency and inclusiveness, the final days were marked, as ever, by closed-door Ministerial consultations on discrete pieces of text sown together by the Mexican Presidency'.[94]

[85] Ian Fry, 'Twists and Turns in the Jungle: Exploring the Evolution of Land Use, Land-Use Change and Forestry Decisions within the Kyoto Protocol' (2002) 11 *RECIEL* 159, 159.

[86] Office of the Press Secretary of the White House, 'Text Of A Letter From The President To Senators Hagel, Helms, Craig, And Roberts' (13 March 2001).

[87] The so-called 'Russian Fix' allowed Russia a high tonnage for joint implementation of its emissions obligations.

[88] Fry, 'Twists and Turns in the Jungle', 165 ('In an act of political desperation, [chairman] Pronk introduced a special concession for Japan in the run up to COP-6bis. This concession added a new accounting sub-rule that would allow only Japan to be exempt from the 85% cap on forest management activities.').

[89] Another part of the LULUCF decision 'gives Australia the opportunity to maximize its base year emissions (1990) from land-use change activities (land clearing for agriculture)'; ibid 168.

[90] Rajamani, 'Re-Negotiating Kyoto', 235.

[91] ibid 235.

[92] Fry, 'Twists and Turns in the Jungle', 159.

[93] Lavanya Rajamani, 'The Cancun Climate Agreements: Reading the Text, Subtext and Tea Leaves' (2011) 60 *International and Comparative Law Quarterly* 499, 514.

[94] ibid 514.

Yet, this time, a small number of 'unimportant' treaty parties led by Bolivia (the ALBA countries),[95] disappointed with the lack of real progress, dared to preclude the adoption of a set of PTRs that had to convey the image to the outside world that the multilateral process was afloat again. Rather than turning away from the process, as they have been accused of, Bolivia asked for the floor of the plenary at least three times. The first time, it was rejected. The second and third times, it made serious and unequivocal objections to the adoption of the Agreements, providing well-argued and substantive reasons that were not even based on its own particular interests.[96] Chair Espinosa and the chairs of the *Ad Hoc* Working Groups, however, declared the objections of Bolivia not to prevent the successful formation of consensus, and adopted the *Agreements*.[97] Espinosa ruled that the support of all other treaty parties meant that consensus had been achieved, because 'consensus does not mean unanimity'. (While that observation is true, it is beside the point: unanimity would have required all treaty parties to *express* their agreement.) The point made by Bolivia was not that it should be able to veto the consensus on its own. It was 'not opposed to consensus emerging from a democratic discussion'.[98] Rather, Bolivia wanted to make the statement that the consensual process as a whole had been violated at Cancun.[99] Parts of the *Cancun Agreements* were never discussed, let alone negotiated, by the COP as a whole. The formal sessions met to adopt but not to negotiate the texts emerging from Ministerial consultations.[100] As observed in the context of other consensual international law-making processes, the UNFCCC COP and Kyoto COP/MOP consensus-seeking process quickly slides from an inclusive to a non-inclusive mode as soon as the political salience of the issues increases.[101] Yet Espinosa hailed the *Cancun Agreements* as launching 'a new era of international cooperation on climate change'.[102]

[95] The nine ALBA countries were Antigua and Barbuda, Bolivia, Cuba, Dominica, Ecuador, Nicaragua, Saint Vincent and the Grenadines, Venezuela and Saint Lucia.

[96] Amongst others, 'Submissions from Bolivia', 21 February 2011, documented in Ad Hoc Working Group on Long-term Cooperative Action under the Convention, Fourteenth session, Bangkok, 5–8 April 2011, and Bonn, 6–17 June 2011, *Views on the elaboration of non-market-based mechanisms*, pp 3–5.

[97] Rajamani, 'The Cancun Climate Agreements', 515. Something similar had already happened when in 1997 Saudi Arabia's protests over the Kyoto Protocol itself were ignored. Kati Kulovesi, 'Different Views on Consensus: Legality of the Cancun Agreements?' *Point Carbon*, 23 December 2010; Rajamani, 'The Cancun Climate Agreements'.

[98] On Demand Webcast, COP-16, resumed 9th meeting (10 December 2010), once available at http://webcast.cc2010.mx/grid_en.html, no longer accessible.

[99] See, for an analysis of the extent to which Bolivia and the other ALBA countries could claim to represent the global citizenry in making these protests, Hayley Stevenson, 'Representing Green Radicalism: The Limits of State-Based Representation in Global Climate Governance' (2013) 40 *Review of International Studies* 177.

[100] Rajamani, 'The Cancun Climate Agreements', 517.

[101] ibid 518.

[102] See On Demand Webcast, COP-16, resumed 9th meeting (10 December 2010), once available at http://webcast.cc2010.mx/grid_en.html, no longer accessible.

d. Consensus and Global Interests

From a cosmopolitan perspective, input legitimacy could be improved through greater inclusiveness of global interests, represented as faithfully as possible by globally organised civil society. Acknowledging the legitimacy problems that would come with a *too* prominent role for, in one way or another, biased 'global' NGOs,[103] at least a number of these NGOs – when viewed collectively – represent views that rise above the interests of a particular state, and are thus not otherwise represented.[104] NGOs also in part represent the interests of smaller states, and are more single-mindedly focused on the issues being negotiated. In other words, while it is far from advocated here that NGOs should be the dominant actors in the making of PTRs, NGO influence has a potential for balancing the 'national interest'-based negotiations between the powerful states. But the consensual process hurts the role of global interests as represented by NGOs in at least three ways, and thus threatens to diminish the input legitimacy that such representation can bring to the table.

First, the legal arrangement of NGO participation in the work of Conferences of the Parties[105] falls far short of guaranteeing any kind of inclusivity. Most MEAs contain a provision similar to the following (Article XI.7 CITES):

> Any body or agency technically qualified in protection, conservation or management of wild fauna and flora, in the following categories, which has informed the Secretariat of its desire to be represented at meetings of the Conference by observers, shall be admitted unless at least one-third of the Parties present object:
>
> (a) international agencies or bodies, either governmental or non-governmental, and national governmental agencies and bodies; and
>
> (b) national non-governmental agencies or bodies which have been approved for this purpose by the State in which they are located.
>
> Once admitted, these observers shall have the right to participate but not to vote.[106]

MEAs thus provide a basic participatory possibility, although 'narrowly defined, qualified, and conditioned'.[107] (And note the mere one-third of the parties needed to exclude an NGO.) In any case, these arrangements do not 'include the means and procedures by which the acts and decisions of the institution may be challenged'.[108] NGOs are still at most information providers and agenda-setters, not decision makers.[109]

[103] *cf* the nuanced but ultimately not defeating criticism of Steffek, 'The Output Legitimacy of International Organizations', 286.

[104] The argument is not that global interest representation should replace state-specific interest representation; the argument is that the two should complement each other. Ebbeson, 'Public Participation', 688–89.

[105] ibid, 690.

[106] Art XI.7 CITES.

[107] Ebbeson, 'Public Participation', 691.

[108] ibid, 683.

[109] Kal Raustiala, 'The 'Participatory Revolution' in International Environmental Law' (1997) 21 *Harvard Environmental Law Review* 537.

Second, the package deals that are typically the product of consensual decision making risk having the effect of shutting out the input of any interests that rise above the level of individual state interests. In the tit-for-tat process, there is little room for taking into account global interests, even apart from NGO access. That means that there is less interest among the negotiating state representatives for the views of NGOs that advocate solutions which do not necessarily connect to the interests of particular states, and are more single-mindedly aimed at the environmental issue in question.[110]

Third, in a more physical way, when negotiations towards consensus approach their apex, civil society tends to be shut out of the conference building, as happened during the Copenhagen Climate Summit.[111] Non-transparency not only blurs the view of observers and the public of the various positions advocated by state representatives, but also directly impacts the capacity of NGOs to influence the evolving negotiations by placing the intermediate outcomes into context for the media and the public. While free to visit the official plenary meetings, NGOs are much less welcome in the informal negotiating sessions where the deals are made, unless they manage to be part of a government delegation, as happened in the final days of the Copenhagen Climate Summit.[112] NGOs' massive presence and intense engagement in all sorts of side-shows[113] should not be confused with real inclusion in the process. Altogether, the consensual process tends to threaten meaningful participation of those representing the global public interest, although examination of particular regimes in addition to the climate change regime would be needed to reach more solid conclusions. Within the CITES regime, for instance, the IUCN (a hybrid non-governmental/governmental organisation) plays an important role as provider of advice to the CITES parties on amendments of the Appendices.

3. Courts' Misunderstanding of the Consensual Process

Bearing in mind the problems with consensual decision making and its case-by-case differences for input legitimacy, it is remarkable that there are many occasions on which national and international courts heavily rely on the mere fact that a PTR was adopted 'by consensus'. In the *Whaling* case, the International Court of Justice went as far as stating generally that recommendations of the International Whaling Committee (IWC), 'when they are adopted by consensus or unanimous vote,

[110] Anne Peters et al (eds), *Non-State Actors as Standard Setters* (CUP, 2009), 517.

[111] McGregor, 'Disenfranchisement at COP-15 in Copenhagen', 4; Dana R Fisher, 'COP-15 in Copenhagen: How the Merging of Movements Left Civil Society Out in the Cold' (2010) 10 *Global Environmental Politics* 11, 11.

[112] McGregor, 'Disenfranchisement at COP-15 in Copenhagen', 3–4.

[113] Ebbeson, 'Public Participation', 683.

they may be relevant for the interpretation of the Convention or its Schedule'.[114] The Court fails to acknowledge any difference between unanimity and consensus. This misunderstanding becomes even clearer when the Court strikes out a number of IWC resolutions because they were adopted 'without the concurrence of Japan'.[115] But consensus does not necessitate concurrence, only acquiescence.

The Court fails to signal that not all adoptions by consensus can bring the same degree of legitimation. Rather than as a material requirement, which can be fulfilled to a greater or lesser extent, the Court turns consensus into a formal, black and white requirement. In fact, the notion of 'between the parties' in Article 31.3(a) VCLT served better than 'consensus' in forcing a court to look what really happened during a subsequent agreement's adoption process. In *Whaling*, it has simply become a question of ticking off the box 'consensus'.

The problems with this formalistic approach are drawn into further focus by the Court's dismissal of IWC resolutions that were *not* adopted by consensus. On those resolutions, the Court states that they 'were adopted without the support of all States parties to the Convention'.[116] Although it is safe to say that majority resolutions did *not* receive the support of all treaty parties, the *reverse* is not necessarily true for consensus decisions. It is well known that a significant reason for Japan to withdraw its objection to the moratorium on commercial whaling in 1986 was the prospect of trade sanctions being imposed against it by the United States in the shape of a reduction of Japan's million tonnes fish quota in Alaskan waters.[117] If Japan withdrew its objection to the moratorium on commercial whaling under threat, then, in all likelihood, Japan failed to express objections to Resolution 1986-2 – the Resolution that made the difference in the *Whaling* case – for similar reasons. After all, Resolution 1986-2 was adopted in the same year that Japan withdrew its objection, and agreed to the scientific whaling solution.[118] One could maintain that Japan made its own choice in balancing the economic (and political) pros and cons of whales versus the size of its Alaskan fish quota, and that these kinds of dilemma are not unusual in international law making. However, the point remains standing that adoption by consensus in itself says little about the nature of the process preceding it.

The previously discussed judgment in the case of *Lac Sorobon* of the Netherlands' Council of State more or less repeats the mistakes of the *Whaling* judgment. The judges are apparently under the impression that all the relevant

[114] *Whaling in the Antarctic (Australia v Japan: New Zealand intervening)* (Judgment) [2014] ICJ Rep 226, para 46.

[115] *Whaling in the Antarctic*, para 83.

[116] *Whaling in the Antarctic*, para 83.

[117] Richard Black, 'Did Greens help kill the whale?' *BBC News website* (London, 16 May 2007) http://news.bbc.co.uk/2/hi/science/nature/6659401.stm, accessed 29 August 2018. See also various Japanese official government documents, the *National Diet Debates*.

[118] IWC Resolution 1986-2, *Resolution on Special Permits for Scientific Research*, 38th Annual Meeting, 1986 (Rep. int. Whal. Commn 37).

Ramsar PTRs were 'adopted unanimously' by the Ramsar COP, 'in which all treaty parties, including the Kingdom of the Netherlands, are represented'.[119] The Council thus overlooked the fact that all the referenced COP decisions were adopted by consensus, not unanimity. The judgment does not convey that the Council examined the Reports of the various meetings of the COP to look for any signs that the Netherlands perchance made expressions of support for the decisions, merely abstained from protest after having voiced serious concerns, or even participated in the discussions over these particular decisions at all.

In another already much-cited case, *NRDC v EPA*, the US Court of Appeals left the consensual process equally unscrutinised,[120] but to arrive at the opposite conclusion to the *Lac Sorobon* court. The Court initially gave a sound description of the Montreal Protocol PTRs on methyl bromide: 'postratification side agreements reached by consensus among 189 nations'.[121] Still, it apparently saw no reason to delve into the circumstances of the particular consensus decisions in considering whether or not to accord the *Exemption Decisions* any weight. Had the Court done so, it would have found that the US was particularly well represented at the meetings,[122] and received by far the largest exemption of methyl bromide production and consumption for the years at issue.[123] In fact, the United States was one of the treaty parties for which the possibility of methyl bromide exemptions was inserted into the treaty text in the first place.[124]

To summarise, despite their appeal to legitimacy considerations in determining the weight to be accorded to PTRs, the engagement of international and national courts with the realities of the consensual process is very limited. The point is not that courts necessarily *have to* make an input legitimacy assessment a part of the decision of how much weight to accord to PTRs. Quite the contrary, they should be very careful in doing so. Yet, once they engage in such an exercise, they should not take a formalistic approach, and examine the reality of the particular consensual PTRs at issue.

[119] *Lac Sorobon*, para 2.2.3.5.

[120] John H Knox, 'Natural Resources Defense Council v. Environmental Protection Agency 464 F.3d 1' (2007) 101 *American Journal of International Law* 471, 477 ('one could wish that the court would have carefully analyzed the issue itself before pronouncing upon it').

[121] *NRDC v EPA*, p 12.

[122] Brian J Gareau, 'Dangerous Holes in Global Environmental Governance: The Roles of Neoliberal Discourse, Science, and California Agriculture in the Montreal Protocol' (2008) 40 *Antipode* 102, 119 ('the 2004 1st Extraordinary Meeting of the Parties to the Montreal Protocol (1st ExMOP), a meeting designed solely to discuss the critical use nominations of the US and several other core countries').

[123] The exemption to the United States may eventually have risen above the 30 per cent maximum exemption indicated by the Protocol, Art 2H.5, towards 32 per cent. Gareau, 'Dangerous Holes in Global Environmental Governance', 112.

[124] The phase-out of methyl bromide was introduced by the Copenhagen Amendment of 1992, an amendment to the Montreal Protocol agreed by the Fourth Meeting of the Parties (Copenhagen, 23–25 November 1992).

4. Executive Branch Dominance

The decision in *NRDC v EPA* also touches on another important aspect of the input legitimacy debate, the second point in Bodansky's article. Taking national populations – affected persons in particular – rather than states as the ultimate subjects of legitimacy, attention shifts to the impact of PTR practices on domestic power configurations in the making and implementation of international environmental law. The *NRDC* judgment can be linked to a widely shared observation that delegations of what used to be domestic legislative competences to international plenary meetings risk upsetting the national constitutional balance of power in determining the laws applicable in the national legal order. Power shifts from the national *trias politica* to a collective of executive branch representatives. This dominant role of the executive is obviously not unique to international environmental law;[125] it is found in many other areas of intergovernmental cooperation.[126] However, for PTRs, this dominance is – again – particularly problematic since the underlying MEAs to which national parliaments have given their approval to ratify, at least in democratic states, allow for few predictions about the eventual direction in which executive branches will develop the regime through PTRs.

The view has long been defended that the external representation of the state by the executive does not upset the national balance of powers. That view held sway as long as external representation of the state also concerned matters largely unconnected to internal matters and internal regulation.[127] This changed when international environmental law and governance became no longer just concerned with issues such as transboundary harm, increasingly addressing both intra-state conduct and global environmental issues beyond interstate disputes.[128] The almost exclusive role of the executive branch in developing that law together with other executive branches around the world has, however, remained unchanged, if not increased.

The dominance of the executive branches in the various stages of PTR practice is truly overwhelming.[129] A picture takes shape of an international collective of executive branch representatives (i.e. the COPs, COP/MOPs and MOPs) making international environmental rules, assisted by expert bodies appointed by the same executive branches from their midst; subject to compliance control by bodies that are mostly peopled by government experts nominated by the same collective of

[125] Nico Krisch, *Beyond Constitutionalism: The Pluralist Structure of Postnational Law* (OUP, 2010), 18–19.

[126] Eyal Benvenisti and George W Downs, 'National Courts, Domestic Democracy, and the Evolution of International Law' (2009) 20 *European Journal of International Law* 59, 61–62, 65.

[127] Eyal Benvenisti, 'Reclaiming Democracy: The Strategic Uses of Foreign and International Law by National Courts' (2008) 102 *American Journal of International Law* 241, 245–47.

[128] Bodansky, 'The Legitimacy of International Governance', 610–11.

[129] *cf* Anna Huggins, 'The Desirability of Depoliticization: Compliance in the International Climate Regime' (2015) 4 *Transnational Environmental Law* 101.

executive branch representatives; and implemented domestically by governmental agencies without effective judicial review or parliamentary oversight.

That the COPs, COP/MOPs and MOPs are executive branch collectives is obvious. But these plenary treaty meetings consult subsidiary organs also manned by governmental experts from those same executive branches. A close examination of, for instance, the UNFCCC *Roster of Experts* reveals that almost all expert reviewers work in government departments for their national governments, and a large number are involved in the preparation of their own country's emissions inventory.[130] COPs, COP/MOPs and MOPs extensively consult a wide variety of subsidiary bodies before adopting PTRs. The 'technical' discussions in these bodies inevitably influence the normative processes taking place in the plenary meetings.[131] For instance, the Animals and Plants Committees under CITES 'provide technical support to decision-making', including the 'drafting [of] resolutions on animal and plant matters for consideration by the Conference of the Parties'.[132] The CITES COP appoints members in accordance with regional representation per continent. Ideally, they are associated with a national Scientific Authority, which is usually a government agency.[133]

Some subsidiary bodies also have implementing and even rule-making tasks they conduct fairly independently. One of the most pertinent examples is the Clean Development Mechanism Executive Body (CDM EB).[134] Article 12.9 Kyoto Protocol subjects participation under the CDM 'to whatever guidance may be provided' by the CDM EB. The members of the CDM EB are elected by the Kyoto COP/MOP. The members need not be government-employed. The one requirement is that they '[p]ossess appropriate technical and/or policy expertise'.[135] However, of the membership at the time of consulting the website, 13 were simultaneously employed by their national executive branch, three were self-employed or university employees, and three – while not government-employed – were also part of their national delegations to the UNFCCC.[136]

Expert review[137] and compliance control, including of compliance with PTRs, are also performed by executive branch representatives. The example of the Kyoto

[130] *UNFCCC Roster of Experts*, www4.unfccc.int/sites/roe/Pages/Home.aspx. For further discussion of the Expert Review Teams (ERTs) see Huggins, 'The Desirability of Depoliticization', 109.

[131] Thomas Gehring, 'International Environmental Regimes: Dynamic Sectoral Legal Regimes' (1990) 1 *Yearbook of International Environmental Law* 35, 37.

[132] At www.cites.org/eng/disc/ac_pc.php. Other examples are the Ramsar Convention's Scientific and Technical Review Panel (see Recommendation 4.7 and Resolution 5.5.) and the CBD's and Cartagena Protocol's version of the SBSTA.

[133] CITES Res. Conf. 11.1 (Rev. COP16), *Establishment of committees*.

[134] The CDM has become one of the greatest failures of the Kyoto Protocol. Its contribution to emissions reduction as well as to sustainable development is widely called into question. See, eg, the report of the World Bank Independent Evaluation Group, *Climate Change and the World Bank Group, Phase II: The Challenge of Low-Carbon Development*, p 72.

[135] In accordance with para 8(c) of the CDM *Modalities and Procedures*.

[136] See CVs at http://cdm.unfccc.int/public_inputs/EB/index.html.

[137] See a similar argument concerning the many roles played by a single government-appointed expert body in Huggins, 'The Desirability of Depoliticization', 104–05, 118.

Protocol Compliance Committee exemplifies this.[138] The Committee's members are elected by the Kyoto COP/MOP upon nominations of individuals by their own state.[139] Members 'shall have recognised competence relating to climate change and in relevant fields such as the scientific, technical, socio-economic or legal fields'.[140] Members of the Enforcement Branch must have experience in the legal field.[141] Both branches of the Compliance Committee (Facilitative and Enforcement) shall be representative of the UN regions, of the treaty parties with and without targets under the Kyoto Protocol, and of the special interest of the small island developing countries in the issue of climate change.[142] Lefeber and Oberthür, writing when respectively a current and a former member of the Enforcement Branch, point to some conditions and measures to prevent undue influences on Committee members once elected.[143] At least formally, Committee members 'shall serve in their individual capacities',[144] and shall 'act in an independent and impartial manner and avoid real or apparent conflicts of interest'.[145]

Added up, a picture emerges of a very dominant role of the executive in the development, negotiation, adoption, and compliance control of PTRs. (It is not possible to make reservations to MEAs.)[146] Only the legislators of the most powerful treaty parties might retain a *de facto* veto over their executive branches, because these executive branches can prevent consensus in the COP on their own.

Dann summarises the widely shared view that there are various factors that hamper national parliaments in effectively exercising control over external representation by the executive. In fact, many of these obstacles are precisely related to the consensual process.[147] These are delegations by *multiple* principals[148] to a *collective* of executive branch representatives, that are difficult to reverse unilaterally without withdrawing from the multilateral process *altogether*.[149] The long-term

[138] For the Kyoto Protocol Expert Review Teams, see again Huggins, 'The Desirability of Depoliticization', 111; Taryn Fransen, 'Enhancing Today's MRV Framework to Meet Tomorrow's Needs: The Role of National Communications and Inventories' (2009) *World Resources Institute Working Paper* 8.

[139] Kyoto COP/MOP Decision 27/CMP.1, *Procedures and Mechanisms Relating to Compliance under the Kyoto Protocol*, Annex, sections IV and V.

[140] Kyoto COP/MOP Decision 27/CMP.1, para 6.

[141] Kyoto COP/MOP Decision 27/CMP.1, s V, para 3.

[142] Kyoto COP/MOP Decision 27/CMP.1, ss IV and V. At the time of writing, the Kyoto Protocol website did not provide backgrounds of the Committee members.

[143] Sebastian Oberthür and René Lefeber, 'Holding Countries to Account: The Kyoto Protocol's Compliance System Revisited after Four Years of Experience' (2010) 1 *Climate Law* 133, 139.

[144] Kyoto COP/MOP Decision 27/CMP.1, section II.6.

[145] *Rules of Procedure of the Compliance Committee of the Kyoto Protocol*, rule 4.1. Annexes to Decisions 4/CMP.2 and 4/CMP.4 on the Compliance Committee, FCCC/KP/CMP/2006/Add.1 (2 March 2007), 17, and FCCC/KP/CMP/2008/11/Add.1 (19 March 2009), 14.

[146] See, eg, Art 18 Montreal Protocol.

[147] Philipp Dann, 'The Political Institutions', 268.

[148] Krisch, '*Beyond Constitutionalism*', 19.

[149] See, eg, Art 19 Montreal Protocol: 'Any Party may withdraw from this Protocol by giving written notification to the Depositary at any time after four years of assuming the obligations specified in paragraph 1 of Article 2A.'

consensual process in which the executives are represented makes parliaments into spectators on the sidelines. 'This deprives them of inside information, creates a timetable not geared towards the working rhythm of national parliaments and often prevents accumulation of in-depth expertise'.[150] Second, the confidentiality and non-transparency of the consensual process 'poses another major problem for control through the national parliaments'.[151] Third, the logic of the consensual process requires that 'every party has to be free to compromise and cannot be bound to a rigid mandate from their constituency'.[152] Detailed upfront mandates by parliaments do not work.[153]

Obviously, there are various PTRs dealing with topics best placed with expert bodies. The argument is not that rule making that affects many states and requires expert knowledge should not be delegated *away* from the national legislator. Also, to note executive dominance is not necessarily to argue for greater influence of other *domestic* forces over the international phases of the PTR process. This is a dead end in a globalised world in need of global rules,[154] and would mostly subject the process to (certain) national rather than global interests even more than it already is. Rather, checks and balances should be put in place at the *international* level, for instance by appointing more independent experts and compliance officials.

At the national level, courts could act as more of a counterweight than they currently do. Benvenisti observes a growing role of national courts in repairing constitutional imbalances resulting from global governance, noting how 'courts invoke international law … because they wish to protect or even reclaim the domestic political space that is increasingly restricted by the economic forces of globalization and the delegation of authority to international institutions'.[155] Such a role is 'fully justified under democratic theories that conceive of the court as a facilitator of democratic deliberation'.[156] In the case of PTRs, however, so far national courts tend to be deferential to governmental authorities as regards the application of PTRs. National courts will have to do better than that if they are to play a restorative role in the national balance of powers.

B. Output Legitimacy

Shortcomings in the input legitimacy of global governance are, to some extent, the price to be paid for more flexible, and thus potentially more effective governance.

[150] Dann, 'The Political Institutions', 268.
[151] ibid.
[152] ibid.
[153] ibid.
[154] Krisch, '*Beyond Constitutionalism*', 15, 17–22.
[155] Benvenisti, 'Reclaiming Democracy: National Courts', 244.
[156] ibid 273.

Effective governance may compensate small weaknesses in input legitimacy with 'output legitimacy'. Scharpf famously contrasted between input legitimacy as 'government *by* the people' and output legitimacy as 'government *for* the people', with the latter deriving legitimacy from 'a capacity to solve problems that require collective solutions' (emphasis added).[157] At the same time, there are important limits to the compensatory force of output legitimacy. Not only will there often be disagreement about how much effectiveness is needed to achieve a reasonable degree of output legitimacy; every policy also has winners and losers.

In relation to a set of rules adopted on the basis of a treaty – such as environmental PTRs – output legitimacy may range from the modest achievement of such rules being *prima facie* in line with the object and purpose of a treaty, all the way to more or less solid proof that such rules are contributing to the effective solution of the problem in question. Such 'problem-solving effectiveness',[158] sometimes called 'environmental effectiveness', is often difficult to prove in terms of outcome as well as causality. Absent such proof, the text of a PTR should at the very least show a real and genuine *effort* to solve the problem concerned, in order not to *de*legitimise the PTR practice. The following sections, after first defining in more detail how the effectiveness of PTRs can be assessed without empirical research, show that too many PTRs do not contribute to the effectiveness of international environmental law. This findings questions the extent to which the authority of PTRs should be based on beliefs of state representatives and courts in their output legitimacy.

1. Analysing Effectiveness *Ex Ante*

Not all kinds of effectiveness contribute to normative output legitimacy. Only effectiveness in relation to certain goals, which further the *public* interest, counts from a normative perspective on output legitimacy.[159] And only the effectiveness of (environmental) problem solving can make real contributions to output legitimacy, as opposed to legal or compliance-effectiveness and behavioural effectiveness.[160]

Legal or compliance effectiveness focuses on the question of 'whether outcomes conform to what a legal rule requires'.[161] This can, for instance, consist of the

[157] Fritz Scharpf, 'Problem-Solving Effectiveness and Democratic Accountability in the EU' (2003), *Max Planck Institut für Gesellschaftsforschung Working Paper* 2003/1.

[158] Daniel Bodansky, *The Art and Craft of International Environmental Law* (Harvard University Press, 2010), 256–58.

[159] Steffek, 'Discursive Legitimation in Environmental Governance', 316.

[160] Ronald B Mitchell, 'Compliance Theory: Compliance, Effectiveness, and Behaviour Change in International Environmental Law' in Daniel Bodansky, Jutta Brunnée and Ellen Hey (eds), *Oxford Handbook of International Environmental Law* (OUP, 2007), 893.

[161] Bodansky, *Art and Craft*, 253.

adoption of national legislation or the reaching of a prescribed target. A conclusion that an MEA or PTR is legally complied with, need not indicate any progress at the environmental level,[162] and may not even indicate a change of behaviour at all, as states tend to agree to obligations they already comply with.[163] For instance, even if all Kyoto parties had reached their 2008–2012 targets, that would still have been a far cry from the 2 degrees Celsius temperature increase 'agreed' to be safe. For the purpose of output legitimacy, compliance effectiveness is a modest factor in the long run. It can create a short-term appearance of output legitimacy before enough time passes that the environmental effectiveness can be evaluated.

Behavioural effectiveness focuses on the question whether the law or something else has caused states' behaviour to change.[164] A state may be in compliance with an MEA or PTR because of other reasons than that the law prescribes it, such as the economic crises contributing to some Kyoto Protocol developed country parties reaching their targets for the 2008–2012 period.[165] To discern the behavioural effectiveness of a treaty, an attempt must be made to separate the treaty's causal mechanisms from other causes of behavioural change.

Finally, *problem-solving* effectiveness focuses on the degree to which an instrument's objectives are achieved, or more generally solves the environmental problem it addresses.[166] Even a treaty provision that has a behavioural effect on the treaty parties might still require too little behavioural change, or require the wrong behaviour, to actually solve the environmental problem. For instance, if *illegal* trade in endangered species is the greater threat to biodiversity, then the proper implementation of the CITES import and export system may have a behavioural effect on the *legal* trade in these species, but problem-solving effectiveness is still rather low.[167]

A legal study does not dispose of the methodological tools to look into the behavioural and problem-solving effectiveness of PTRs in practice *ex post*, either singled out from the underlying MEA, or in conjunction with the MEA. This does not mean that such studies would not be necessary. Several political science studies on the (comparative) effectiveness of MEAs exist.[168] No studies exist, however, that *single out the particular contribution of PTRs*.

[162] ibid 254.

[163] George W Downs, David M Rocke and Peter N Barsoom, 'Is the Good News about Compliance Good News about Cooperation?' (1996) 50 *International Organization* 379, 380.

[164] Bodansky, *Art and Craft*, 253.

[165] Quirin Schiermeier, 'The Kyoto Protocol: Hot Air' (2012) 491 *Nature* 656.

[166] Bodansky, *Art and Craft*, 253.

[167] ibid, 257.

[168] Amongst others David G Victor, Kal Raustiala and Eugene B Skolnikoff (eds), *The Implementation and Effectiveness of International Environmental Commitments: Theory and Practice* (1998); Helmut Breitmeier, *The Legitimacy of International Regimes* (Ashgate, 2008); Helmut Breitmeier and others, 'The International Regimes Database as a Tool for the Study of International Cooperation Acknowledgments' (1996), *International Institute for Applied Systems Analysis Working Paper* 1996/160; Jürg Vollenweider, 'The Effectiveness of International Environmental Agreements' (2012) 13 *International Environmental Agreements: Politics, Law and Economics* 343.

Legal methodology *does*, however, possess tools to look at expected environmental effectiveness *ex ante*, in the form of textual analysis of MEA provisions and objectives, PTRs and their accompanying documents, and negotiating reports. Through a number of examples from the PTR practice, *likely* problem-solving effectiveness can be assessed, *insofar it can be gathered from comparing the content of PTRs to the obligations and objectives laid down in MEAs*. The purpose of this exercise is to discover the various ways in which PTRs are used to transform or affect the underlying treaty obligations and objectives. For instance, some PTRs are clearly primarily aimed at bringing the parties at least a little bit closer to solving the environmental problem for which their underlying MEA was concluded. Some, however, are – more or at least as much – aimed at parochial state interests, such as making compliance easier for all or some of the parties, postponing action, and taking off the sharp edges of the treaty.

By focusing on the clearest examples, even without extensive *ex post* empirical research, it is obvious that the functions that PTRs fulfil for the parties are far from homogenous. This approach is not just methodologically feasible; it also makes more sense for the analysis of the output legitimacy of *PTRs separately*, because it would be very difficult to distinguish the problem-solving effectiveness of PTRs from that of MEAs in *ex post* research.

The focus on environmental problem-solving effectiveness as the main determinant for output legitimacy is in line with Scharpf and Steffek's understanding that output legitimacy[169] should not just focus on the quality of the resulting decisions and their substantial rationality, but especially on their *public interest orientation* (emphasis added).[170] Normative output legitimacy cannot be what executive branch representatives make of it during COP negotiations.[171] The general provisions on Conferences and Meetings of the Parties found in most MEAs support this approach. According to these provisions, all COP, COP/MOP and MOP decisions have to improve the effectiveness of the MEA. Article 7 of the Kyoto Protocol, for instance, prescribes that COP/MOP recommendations 'are required for the achievement of the objective of the Convention',[172] or 'necessary for the implementation of the Convention'.[173] Similarly, Article XI.3(e) CITES states that the CITES COP 'may … where appropriate, make recommendations for improving the effectiveness of the present Convention'. If effectiveness is required from recommendations, it should certainly be required from the various 'rules, modalities and principles' the adoption of which is specifically enabled by various Kyoto Protocol Articles. Even more unequivocal is Article 11.4(j) Montreal Protocol, which states that one function of the MOP 'shall be to … consider and undertake any additional action that may be required for the

[169] Steffek, 'The Output Legitimacy of International Organizations', 267–69.
[170] ibid 264.
[171] ibid 263–64, 267.
[172] Art 7.2(m) Kyoto Protocol.
[173] Art 7.2(g) Kyoto Protocol.

achievement of the purposes of this Protocol'. The least that may be asked from PTRs is that they do not run counter to the underlying treaty's objectives or obligations.

Generally, two competing views of PTRs are possible when it comes to evaluating their contribution to the effectiveness of international environmental governance along these lines. In one sense, PTRs are flexibly adoptable instruments that the treaty parties use to make progress from the vague and general objectives they can arrive at in treaty form initially, towards more specific, precise, elaborate and – over time – innovative prescriptions on how to define and meet those objectives. The use of PTRs helps to protect MEAs from becoming obsolete, which was a great danger for earlier, more static environmental agreements.[174] For instance, the criteria adopted by the CITES COP[175] are widely believed to have made the process of listing species on the CITES Appendices more scientifically sound and based on information rather than on parochial interests.[176] Likewise, under the Montreal Protocol, the MOP adopted many consecutive decisions that accelerate the phase-out of controlled ozone-depleting substances, thus no doubt contributing to the objective of decreasing ozone depletion.[177] Under the Ramsar Convention, PTRs were used to make the transition to an ecosystems approach, rather than the outdated wetland-species based approach.[178] Such PTRs are truly what Shaffer and Pollack would call 'complements', bringing the parties closer to the objectives and obligations formulated in the underlying MEAs.

However, in opposition to the role of PTRs as the key to progress and dynamism in international environmental law, the content of PTRs is not necessarily always 'deepening and thickening'[179] the parties' environmental obligations. In reality, PTRs have also been used to address other, sometimes diametrically opposed interests. In the terminology of Shaffer and Pollack, many PTRs are not complementing treaty objectives and provisions, but antagonising them, or simply maintaining the status quo. Antagonistic PTRs run counter to or undermine existing law or expectations about existing law.[180] In that sense, environmental post-treaty rules are no different from international environmental

[174] Peter H Sand, 'Whither CITES? The Evolution of a Treaty Regime in the Borderland of Trade and Environment' (1997) 8 *European Journal of International Law* 29, 32.

[175] CITES Res. Conf. 9.24 (Rev. COP 16), *Criteria for amendment of Appendices I and II.*

[176] Thomas Gehring and Eva Ruffing, 'When Arguments Prevail Over Power: The CITES Procedure for the Listing of Endangered Species' (2008) 8 *Global Environmental Politics* 123. More sceptical is Shaun A Goho, 'The CITES Fort Lauderdale Criteria: The Uses and Limits of Science in International Conservation Decisionmaking' (2001) 114 *Harvard Law Review* 1769.

[177] See the procedure of Art 2.9 Montreal Protocol.

[178] Peter Bridgewater, 'A New Context for the Ramsar Convention: Wetlands in a Changing World' (2008) 17 *RECIEL* 100.

[179] Wiersema, 'The New International Law-Makers?', 234 ('[a]lthough not all consensus-based COP activity has this effect').

[180] Gregory C Shaffer and Mark A Pollack, 'Hard vs. Soft Law: Alternatives, Complements, and Antagonists in International Governance' (2010) 94 *Minnesota Law Review* 706, 728, 743.

law generally.[181] This darker side of PTRs must most likely be linked to the observation made earlier that executive representatives are in charge of each and every step and phase in the interpretation and implementation of MEAs. As Simma suggests, '[t]he effect of such absence of a [neutral] "third party" [from treaty interpretation] could be a tendency towards considerable "relaxation" in the interpretation of demanding provisions of such a treaty'.[182] In the long run, such 'relaxation' cannot but come at the cost of the output legitimacy of environmental regimes.

2. PTRs as Complements

To give an example of a PTR that has boosted the output legitimacy of an international environmental regime, this section discusses the CITES COP *Listing Criteria*. The CITES species *Listing Criteria* are an example of a PTR that presented a huge step forward in depoliticising the listing process, making it turn more to consideration of the available biological information. In the early years of CITES, before the current *Criteria* were in force, the CITES Appendices reflected a preference for 'charismatic' and other politically expedient species.[183] As a result of the 1994 Listing Criteria, a higher number of species that require protection are now actually listed, and a number of species that were listed unnecessarily, from a biological viewpoint, have been removed. The *Criteria* leave less space for discretion, reducing the chances of arbitrarily different treatment of comparable species.[184] It no longer needs to be proved that a species' threat of extinction is specifically caused by international trade alone, as long as the regulation of international trade can help to ensure its survival.[185] From the perspective of CITES' main objective 'not to endanger further the survival' of 'all species threatened with extinction which are or may be affected by trade',[186] that is certainly a great step forward.

Gehring and Ruffing did in-depth research showing that the criteria have indeed brought the practice of listing closer to the objectives of CITES, due to the clearer distinction between which type of arguments are valid in the discussions

[181] Among others Caroline E Foster, 'Diminished Ambitions? Public International Legal Authority in the Transnational Economic Era' (2014) 17 *Journal of International Economic Law* 355; Radoslav S Dimitrov, 'Hostage to Norms: States, Institutions and Global Forest Politics' (2005) 5 *Global Environmental Politics* 1.

[182] Bruno Simma, 'Miscellaneous Thoughts on Subsequent Agreements and Practice' in Georg Nolte (ed), *Treaties and Subsequent Practice* (OUP, 2013) 46, 48.

[183] Gehring and Ruffing, 'When Arguments Prevail over Power', 130; Charlotte Epstein, 'The Making of Global Environmental Norms. Endangered Species Protection' (2006) 6 *Global Environmental Politics* 32, 49–50.

[184] Gehring and Ruffing, 'When Arguments Prevail over Power', 129–31.

[185] CITES Res. Conf. 9.24. *cf* Gehring and Ruffing, 'When Arguments Prevail over Power', 130; Goho, 'The CITES Fort Lauderdale Criteria', 1779–82.

[186] Art II.1 CITES ('Fundamental Principles').

about new listings in the COP. The role of the Secretariat in first assessing the merits of a listing proposal, before presenting it to the COP, is also beneficial.[187] Of course, parochial objections are to some extent still possible, but the likelihood that species are listed that should not have been listed from a biological viewpoint has decreased.[188] Equally important, many species are now listed that in the past could be blocked without much argumentation relating to the biological survival of the species. It turns out that parties are sensitive to the official role of biological information in the process, at least as long as such information is available.[189]

Despite the CITES *Listing Criteria* positive effects in the 1990s, observers have found that proposals to list commercially important species continue to be rejected in the CITES COP, regardless of fulfilling the biological criteria on most occasions.[190] For instance, at CITES COP 15 in 2010, bluefin tuna and several shark and coral species were proposed for listing, but rejected through secret votes in the COP, despite little controversy over their satisfaction of the biological criteria.[191] The procedures still allow for non-environmental objectives to prevail over environmental ones.[192] Although the criteria were a huge step forward in the 1990s, the COP will have to deliver more rigorous procedures as well, with more power for an independent organ in the listing process, guaranteeing that the criteria are truly followed, even where it hurts.

3. PTRs as Antagonists

There are many ways in which the wording of environmental PTRs makes clear that the parties are attempting to supplement or interpret treaty obligations in a way that is not primarily aimed at bringing the parties closer to reaching the environmental objectives, but rather at softening the obligations of the parties or at serving parochial interests. Such global governance instruments are 'antagonists', because they reverse the direction or change the spirit of an earlier instrument.[193] There are several kinds of antagonist PTRs: a rough division can be made between *marginal* PTRs, which leave the *status quo* intact; *parochial* PTRs, which serve non-environmental (read: economical) interests of particular parties; and *softening* PTRs, which reduce the environmental efforts required from all the parties.

[187] Gehring and Ruffing, 'When Arguments Prevail over Power', 133.

[188] Michael Bowman, Peter Davies and Catherine Redgwell, *Lyster's International Wildlife Law* 2nd edn (CUP, 2010), 492. CITES COP Res Conf 8.20, *Development of New Criteria for Amendment of the Appendices*.

[189] Gehring and Ruffing, 'When Arguments Prevail over Power', 146.

[190] Melissa Blue Sky, 'Getting On The List: Politics And Procedural Maneuvering In Cites Appendix I and II Decisions For Commercially Exploited Marine And Timber Species' (2010) 10 *Sustainable Development Law & Policy* 35, 40.

[191] ibid 35, 36–39.

[192] ibid 40; Gehring and Ruffing, 'When Arguments Prevail over Power', 145–46.

[193] Shaffer and Pollack, 'Alternatives, Complements, and Antagonists', 728, 743.

Some PTRs take such marginal steps that they create an image of progress rather than actually achieving much. As extensively shown in chapter four, the wording of PTRs may be such that it is clear that they contain mere optional recommendations, hortatory advice to states on how to conduct environmental policy in a certain issue area most effectively, if they are willing to do so. In this scenario, the *status quo* is simply maintained, or just slightly affected, unless individual states decide for themselves to follow these rules, or other states decide to apply pressure to that effect. Many examples of this type are found under the Ramsar Convention[194] and CITES. Consider the somewhat half-hearted recommendation of the CITES COP *Reason to Believe Paragraph* that 'Parties not authorise the import of any specimen if they have reason to believe that it was not legally acquired in the country of origin'.[195] Opinions are divided on the effectiveness of hortatory instruments, but clearly the language signifies a very low level of control intention.[196] Especially if not coupled with international compliance control, or in areas with little peer pressure and little consequences for non-compliance, the extremely cautious formulation of some resolutions makes their effectiveness almost completely dependent on volatile circumstances. Particularly for the Ramsar Convention, the number of hortatory resolutions can make it look more like a talking forum than an effective institution. Marginal PTRs neither really increase nor decrease output legitimacy.

More serious, however, are PTRs that soften the obligations of all the parties or meet the parochial, non-environmental interests of some parties. Such PTRs are primarily looking for the least burdensome way to implement the treaty text rather than in an environmentally effective way, or aim to safeguard certain economic over environmental interests. Primary examples are the Kyoto COP/MOP *Marrakech Accords*, a number of Ramsar COP resolutions on the 'wise use' of wetlands, the Montreal MOP *Critical Use Criteria* and *Exemptions*, and a number of CITES COP resolutions on the interests of exporting parties and hunters.

Often, the seeds for such softening or parochial PTRs are already found in the underlying enabling clauses, by explicitly or implicitly enabling exceptions. Article 2H.5 of the Montreal Protocol explicitly stipulates that '[t]his paragraph will apply save to the extent that the Parties decide to permit the level of production or consumption that is necessary to satisfy uses agreed by them to be critical uses'. The Protocol thus already builds in the space for PTRs that will clearly protect interests diverging from its environmental objectives. Most of the enabling clauses in the Kyoto Protocol do not invite PTRs that make the Protocol more effective either; rather, the enabling clauses on emissions trading, land use and forestry (LULUCF) and the Clean Development Mechanism all enable the parties to adopt rules that make reaching their targets as *efficient* as possible, at the cost of their effectiveness. The lack of definitions of 'wise use' and 'conservation'

[194] See ch 4, section C.2.
[195] CITES Res. Conf. 12.3, *Permits and Certificates*, para II(j).
[196] Bodansky, *Art and Craft*, 104.

in Article 3.1, or elsewhere in the Ramsar Convention, also opened the way for the parties to adopt PTRs advocating minimal understandings of what 'wise use' and 'conservation' demands. Not that this would necessarily be the result, but the possibility is created.

The example of the methyl bromide *Critical Use Exemptions* is a clear case of PTRs that merely aim to meet the parochial interests of a number of treaty parties – particularly the US – to continue using methyl bromide for certain agricultural purposes. At the Ninth MOP, the treaty parties decided that use of methyl bromide should qualify as 'critical' if 'the lack of availability of methyl bromide for that use would result in a significant market disruption' (read: a disadvantage for a developed country party's traders in agricultural products) and '[t]here are no technically and economically feasible alternatives or substitutes'.[197] As Gareau reports, having attended the meetings, the efforts on the part of the US were primarily driven by Californian strawberry traders, afraid of losing the competition with strawberry traders in developing country parties like China.[198] In other words, these exemptions had nothing to do with a more effective phase-out of ozone-depleting substances, but only with easing certain parochial economic concerns. In fighting out a petty trade dispute, the yearly emission of tens of thousands of tonnes of highly ozone-depletive methyl bromide could continue for another decade.[199]

The CITES COP, in turn, has introduced all sorts of exceptions accommodating the special interests of wildlife-exporting states and hunters, despite the progress it had made with the species-listing procedure. As Sand notes, '[n]ew definitions of indeterminate terms such as 'captive breeding' and 'artificial propagation', and the introduction of new exceptions such as 'ranching', enabled countries meeting the criteria so established to make legitimate use (including transnational shipments) of Appendix I species at agreed sustainable rates'.[200] The export quotas that were first introduced as an exceptional measure for African leopard skins and elephant tusks, and subsequently acted as safeguards to limit the consequences of 'downlisting' Appendix I species to Appendix II, eventually became a standard practice that replaced the specimen-by-specimen no-detriment finding that export authorities needed to perform before granting export permits, 'even though there is no reference to a quota system anywhere in the Convention'.[201]

The most eye-catching examples of softening of treaty obligations through PTRs are probably the already much-discussed *Marrakesh Accords*, adopted prior to the ratification of the Kyoto Protocol. An obvious aim of the *Accords*

[197] Montreal MOP Decision IX/6, *Critical-use exemptions for methyl bromide*, paras 1.a.i and ii.
[198] Gareau, 'Dangerous Holes in Global Environmental Governance', 104, 115–23.
[199] For the exemptions of 2016 and 2017, see http://ozone.unep.org/en/handbook-montreal-protocol-substances-deplete-ozone-layer/40705 (archived page).
[200] Sand, 'Whither CITES?', 41.
[201] ibid 42.

became the facilitation of ratification.[202] The sections on input legitimacy already discussed the implications this had for the consensual process. After three week-long negotiations in The Hague, Bonn, and Marrakesh, reaching the previously agreed-to emissions reductions targets had become considerably easier for some of the parties,[203] leading many scientists to calculate that total mitigation estimates had fallen from 5 per cent to 2.5 per cent overall reduction of greenhouse gas emissions.[204] No quantitative cap was placed on the use of emissions trading, the Clean Development Mechanism, or Joint Implementation.[205] Moreover, a number of COP/MOP decisions considerably increased the extent to which parties could rely on land use, land use change and forestry activities in meeting their targets.[206]

To be sure, all of these PTRs stay within the broad, open-textured boundaries of the underlying treaty texts. They do not openly violate the treaty. The point here is that, rather than narrowing those boundaries, as instruments that 'are required for the achievement of the objective of the Convention'[207] or 'necessary for the implementation of the Convention'[208] could be expected to do, the relevant PTRs widened them further. They do so by providing treaty parties with a wide array of tools to implement, for instance, the Kyoto Protocol, in a manner that interrupted domestic policies as little as possible and ultimately diminished the greenhouse gas reductions achieved by the Kyoto Protocol.

Compared to the previous examples, the series of Ramsar PTRs on wise use are an example of PTRs that soften the obligations of all the parties, rather than just some of them. The Ramsar COP has adopted very minimalist interpretations, arguably even modifications, of the obligations under Article 3.1 of the Convention. Article 3.1 Ramsar Convention requires that '[t]he Contracting Parties shall formulate and implement their planning so as to promote the *conservation* of the wetlands included in the List, *and* as far as possible the *wise use* of wetlands in their territory' (emphasis added).[209] Through COP resolutions, the Ramsar

[202] Ott, 'The Bonn Agreement to the Kyoto Protocol'; Michael Bothe, 'The United Nations Framework Convention on Climate Change – an Unprecedented Multilevel Regulatory Challenge' (2003) 63 *Zeitschrift für ausländisches öffentliches Recht und Volkerrecht* 239.

[203] Fry, 'Twists and Turns in the Jungle', 159.

[204] Michel G den Elzen and André P de Moor, 'Analyzing the Kyoto Protocol under the Marrakesh Accords; Christoph Böhringer, 'Climate Politics From Kyoto to Bonn: From Little to Nothing?!?' (2001) *Zentrum für Europäische Wirtschaftsforschung Discussion Papers* 2001/49; Fry, 'Twists and Turns in the Jungle'; Ott, 'The Bonn Agreement to the Kyoto Protocol'; Bernd Brouns and Tilman Santarius, 'Die Kyoto-Reduktionsziele Nach Den Bonner Beschlüssen' (2001) 51 *Energiewirtschaftliche Tagesfragen* 590.

[205] UNFCCC COP Decision 15/CP.7.

[206] Kyoto COP/MOP Decision 13/CMP.1, *Modalities for the accounting of assigned amounts under Article 7, paragraph 4, of the Kyoto Protocol*; Kyoto COP/MOP Decision 16/CMP.1, *Definitions, modalities, rules and guidelines relating to land use, land-use change and forestry activities under the Kyoto Protocol.*

[207] Art 7.2(m) Kyoto Protocol.

[208] Art 7.2(g) Kyoto Protocol.

[209] Art 3.1 Ramsar Convention.

Parties have gradually conflated conservation with wise use,[210] and have settled on wise use as the more relevant notion.[211] More and more, this wise use standard applies to all wetlands, whether listed or not, while – according to the treaty text – listed wetlands should enjoy the higher standard of conservation.[212] Wise use is a much less intrusive notion than conservation, because it emphasises human use of wetlands as least as much as conservation. It is also a vaguer concept than conservation.

The gravitation towards wise use also opened the way to giving pride of place to environmental impact assessments (EIAs).[213] The use of EIAs aims at balancing competing considerations of sustainable use, rather than excluding certain specific activities and setting minimum standards.[214] Moreover, EIAs tend to 'deal badly with cumulative effect because they are generated by, and necessarily focus on, proposals involving specific projects. And they can accommodate continued destruction of wetlands'.[215] The Ramsar COP has not prohibited certain activities, such as drainage or filling, even though such activities irreversibly damage wetlands and should therefore fall outside the parameters of wise use at all times.[216] Under the current framework, a party that conducts EIAs of a certain quality and then decides to license a development project anyway, fulfils its obligations under Article 3.1, even if the project would severely damage the wetland in question. To be clear, conservation does not mean preservation in some imagined proto state of nature. Of course, most wetlands are not entirely 'natural'; human beings have had a major impact on wetlands, and without further human involvement many wetlands may not survive.[217] However, recognising that active conservation policies rather than utopian and passive hands-off approaches are needed is not the same as allowing further exploitation of wetlands of international importance.

To summarise, from this – admittedly non-exhaustive – overview, it transpires that PTRs are far from homogenously aimed at bringing the parties closer to the implementation of the underlying MEA's objectives. As Sand has remarked, they often serve to make the pill taste less bitter: 'Well-meaning peer interpretation

[210] Ramsar COP Res VIII.14, *New Guidelines for management planning for Ramsar sites and other wetlands*, and VII.11, *Strategic framework and guidelines for the future development of the List of Wetlands of International Importance. cf* Bowman, Davies and Redgwell, '*Lyster's International Wildlife Law*', 416.

[211] ibid 415–17.

[212] David Farrier and Linda Tucker, 'Wise Use of Wetlands Under the Ramsar Convention: A Challenge for Meaningful Implementation of International Law' (2000) 12 *Journal of International Environmental Law* 21, 27.

[213] See, eg, Ramsar COP Res X.17, *Environmental Impact Assessment and Strategic Environmental Assessment: updated scientific and technical guidance.*

[214] Farrier and Tucker, 'Wise Use of Wetlands Under the Ramsar Convention'.

[215] ibid 40.

[216] ibid 36, 40.

[217] Bowman, Davies and Redgwell, *Lyster's International Wildlife Law*, 415; Farrier and Tucker, 'Wise Use of Wetlands Under the Ramsar Convention', 31–33.

may also soften 'hard' treaty rules (thereby weakening their effectiveness, while ostensibly easing compliance) to accommodate offenders'.[218] Any agreement needs some room for exceptions, sometimes even to accommodate particular parties. But plenary treaty meetings should be careful in using PTRs for parochial interests and all-round softening of obligations.

Only *environmental* necessities should qualify as reasons to make exceptions, such as changed scientific knowledge about optimal protection methods or differences between geographical areas in terms of which protection methods work best. Economic necessities, such as the US strawberry sector, the hardwood trade, the Japanese sushi industry, or developing projects in wetlands of international importance to boost tourism, should be reasons for exceptions as little as possible. Such exceptions do not even benefit a state as a whole, but often only special interests within its boundaries, while an understanding of output legitimacy that keeps in mind the public interest, warrants the 'presumption that political decisions benefit every citizen [or state] and not just a specific group of them'.[219] PTRs that are used to maintain minimal interpretations of treaty obligations for *all* the parties, such as those encountered under the Ramsar Convention, threaten to turn PTRs into vehicles for the very standstill that environmental lawyers hoped they could be used to prevent.

4. National Courts and the Effectiveness of PTRs

Keeping this overview of examples of PTRs with different aims in mind, it should be clear that national courts have to be careful in reaching quick conclusions about the relationship between PTRs and the object and purpose of the underlying MEAs.[220] Courts should be aware of the various kinds of PTRs in terms of effectiveness, particularly when justifying a decisive role for PTRs in reaching judgment, because they would support the underlying MEA's object and purpose. Mindful of Simma's warning that '[i]t is conceivable that subsequent practice can result in somehow deteriorating the *telos* of a treaty, and thus minimise its effect',[221] international and national courts should not hesitate to look beyond PTRs to examine their connection to that *telos*, but if they do so, to do so thoroughly.

[218] Peter H Sand, 'Institution-Building Compliance with International Environmental Law: Perspectives' (1996) 56 *Zeitschrift für ausländisches öffentliches Recht und Volkerrecht (ZaöRV)* 774, 780.

[219] Steffek, 'The Output Legitimacy of International Organizations', 272. One way to ensure that PTRs can only serve environmental necessities is to include an MEA provision that the COP can only adopt resolutions and recommendations that have a basis in science. Bodansky, *Art and Craft*, 188.

[220] As Marcelo Kohen proposes, 'caution must be exercised when identifying subsequent practice'. Marcelo Kohen, 'Keeping Subsequent Agreements and Practice in Their Right Limits' in Georg Nolte (ed), *Treaties and Subsequent Practice* (OUP, 2013), 34. See also *Whaling in the Antarctic* (Separate Opinion of Judge Greenwood), para 7.

[221] Simma, 'Miscellaneous Thoughts on Subsequent Agreements', 48.

In the already much-discussed *Lac Sorobon* case, the Council of State also argued that Ramsar COP 'recommendations, resolutions and guidelines are all the more important for the interpretation and filling in of the obligations flowing from Article 3 [Ramsar Convention], because the Article itself provides little indication of the content of those obligations'.[222] Such argumentation presupposes that the open-endedness of Article 3 is *in itself* sufficient to let *any* interpretation by the parties prevail over any other means and methods of interpretation. This position excludes the possibility that those recommendations or resolutions could be at odds with the terms of Article 3, or with the object and purpose of the Convention generally. If a national court is inclined to apply a PTR in light of the treaty's object and purpose, it should actually look at how that particular PTR serves the objects and purposes.

In the case of *Castlewood Products* – the case of the mahogany traders – the US Court of Appeals made a promising reference to the requirement in Article XI.3(e) CITES that the CITES COP may 'make recommendations for improving the effectiveness of the present Convention'.[223] Nevertheless, the Court subsequently fell back to the same reasoning as the Crown Court in *Lac Sorobon*, stating that the interpretations of the COP are 'reasonable' *because* '[t]here would be no point in the contracting states agreeing on resolutions only to then completely ignore them'. In fact, as this section showed, if a court decides to look at the object and purpose of a PTR, there might be very good reasons to ignore them.

5. The Consensual Process and Output Legitimacy

The assumption is often that giving up some input legitimacy can help to provide more effective governance, resulting in better output legitimacy. However, the examples discussed in the previous section illustrate that giving up the rigidity of state consent does not necessarily have that result. Consensual decision making also has a tendency to lead to the *status quo* or the lowest common denominator. The thriving of powerful states in the consensual process has much to do with this: dominant powers have a greater tendency toward the status quo.[224] To be sure, consensual decision making is not the root cause of disappointing outcomes – there may simply be a great deal of substantive disagreement among the treaty parties. However, the consensual process does little to preclude that disagreements remain visible in the outcomes.

A certain strand of constructivist scholars ('transformationalists') believe that highly inclusive regimes, which minimise initial obligations and use consensual

[222] *Lac Sorobon*, para 2.2.3.5.
[223] *Castlewood Products* (Court of Appeals), para 42.
[224] Nico Krisch, 'International Law in Times of Hegemony: Unequal Power and the Shaping of the International Legal Order' (2005) 16 *European Journal of International Law* 369, 375.

decision making, maximise outcomes in the long term.[225] Such regimes are supposedly fertile ground for reaching shared understandings over time through 'socialisation'. The idea is that, while states may at first diverge widely in their preferences in relation to a given (environmental) issue, their preferences are more likely to change over time in an inclusive, open-ended, consensual surrounding.[226] Transformationalists emphasise in particular 'the power of iterated dialogues that occur in negotiating rounds, conferences of the parties, and other regime-sponsored fora'.[227] Consensual decision making would be central to that 'iterative dialogue'.[228] They rarely specify, however, why exactly these processes would have that effect, except for the unproven statement that the 'atmosphere' of consensus building would 'depoliticise' the process.[229]

On the subject of PTRs in particular, Wiersema has submitted that they are 'deepening the scope of obligations'[230] and '*enrich those original legal obligations by thickening them*' (emphasis added),[231] 'contributing to implementation and effectiveness. It can add to the fullness of the obligations by adding to the text of the original treaty through interpretation and guidance'.[232] However, the previous section showed that PTRs can also make obligations weaker or leave them exactly as they are. The higher specificity and determinacy of PTRs may just mean that parties have agreed on a compromise solution, but need not reflect a higher degree of agreement on the objectives of the regime.

It is not surprising that such views nonetheless gained followers with respect to IEL during the late 1980s and the 1990s when there was a positive spirit about the prospects of international environmental governance, with the Rio Declaration, the UNFCCC and the CBD all being concluded in 1994.

[225] Broadly representative of the transformationalist perspective are Abram Chayes and Antonia Handler Chayes, *The New Sovereignty: Compliance With International Regulatory Agreements* (Harvard University Press, 1995); Marc A Levy et al, 'The Study of International Regimes' (1995) 1 *European Journal of International Relations* 267; Jutta Brunnée and Stephen J Toope, 'Environmental Security and Freshwater Resources: Ecosystem Regime Building' (1997) 91 *American Journal of International Law* 26; Patrick Széll, 'The Development of Multilateral Mechanisms for Monitoring Compliance' in Winfried Lang (ed), *Sustainable Development and International Law* (Graham & Trotman, 1995).

[226] Gehring, 'International Environmental Regimes', 37; Chayes and Chayes, *The New Sovereignty*, 229.

[227] Downs, Danish and Barsoom, 'The Transformational Model of International Regime Design', 475–76 ('a kind of hothouse in which interests change and agendas are altered in the direction of a greater commitment to address environmental problems').

[228] ibid 480–82.

[229] Brunnée and Toope, 'Environmental Security and Freshwater Resources', 43; Ryan Goodman and Derek Jinks, 'How to Influence States: Socialization and International Human Rights Law' (2004) 54 *Duke Law Journal* 621, 626, 639.

[230] Wiersema, 'The New International Law-Makers', 258.

[231] ibid 233.

[232] ibid 234, 245. A similar belief that PTRs are 'furthering implementation' is found with Jürgen Friedrich, *International Environmental 'Soft Law': The Functions and Limits of Nonbinding Instruments in International Environmental Governance and Law* (Springer, 2013), 45 ff, 134 (suggesting that, for all non-binding instruments, '[t]heir underlying purpose is mostly to promote change rather than preserve the status quo').

After intensive review, however, Downs, Danish and Barsoom submit that there is little evidence that this interactional[233] or transformational model of international cooperation – embodied amongst others by the consensual process – is succeeding.[234] In 14 'transformational' regimes – i.e. regimes set up in accordance with transformationalist logic – Downs et al found that 13 achieved no or a very low level of cooperation. Strikingly, in line with Downs, Danish and Barsoom, most breakthrough moments in the UNFCCC and Kyoto Protocol happened exactly by *bypassing* the consensus rule. The UNFCCC/Kyoto emissions trading mechanisms were made possible by an out-of-COP agreement between the EU and the US that was then quickly gavelled through the plenary.[235] The same story was relayed above with regard to the adoption of the Kyoto Protocol text and the *Copenhagen Accord*: circumventing the consensual process in the COP.

Downs et al's findings on the generally disappointing progress in many MEAs that combine open-ended norms, inclusive membership and consensual decision making fit well with the mixed findings concerning the effectiveness of PTRs above. A prominent example is the stalling of the consensual process in relation to two crucial sets of PTRs under the Cartagena Protocol on Biosafety. Years of interaction in the COP/MOP and subsidiary bodies apparently were not enough to make political preferences converge: in the iron grasp of decision making by consensus the PTRs were never adopted.

C. Conclusion

What is considered a legitimate PTR practice depends on the actors identified as the main subjects towards whom environmental post-treaty rules should be legitimated: states, the various national populations of the treaty parties, or the global citizenry. Whichever of these subjects is prioritised, however, the initial state consent to the ongoing system of governance (the PTR practice) is not enough to provide legitimacy. This is mostly the case because of the overt indeterminacy of the enabling clauses to which that consent is given, but also because of the wide-ranging consequences that some PTRs have for domestic regulation and sub-state groups. For states as legitimacy subjects, it was found that the way in which the consensual process is conducted in the Kyoto COP/MOP has on occasion directly violated the sovereign equality of states (particularly the *Copenhagen Accord*, the *Marrakech Agreements*, and the *Cancun Agreements*). For a stronger version of inclusiveness, the mechanisms of the consensual process – package

[233] Jutta Brunnée and Stephen J Toope, 'Interactional International Law: An Introduction' (2011) 3 *International Theory* 307.
[234] Downs, Danish and Barsoom, 'The Transformational Model of International Regime Design', 468.
[235] ibid.

deals, compromise, non-transparent dealing – give too much space to powerful treaty parties. The same mechanisms tend to easily crowd out the effective participation of global interest representatives as well. Again, this is most starkly visible in the Kyoto Protocol/UNFCCC practice.

A remarkable paradox about consensus in relation to input legitimacy can be observed when comparing a normative to a social perspective. While it often diminishes inclusiveness and room for global interests in practice, consensus succeeds rather well in conveying an *image* of legitimacy. Even those who had to swallow unwanted rules can stand straight and present the outcome as something they were part of ('pacification').[236] '[A] decision based on consensus *appears to be* a product of consent and in accord with the principle of sovereign equality of states'.[237] Differently put, consensual decision making is better at providing social legitimacy than normative legitimacy. However, the extent to which these dangers of the consensual process are materialising in PTR practices outside the UNFCCC COP and the Kyoto COP/MOP remain beyond the limited research performed for this section. For the moment, it can at most serve as a warning to build safeguards into the consensual process that can mitigate its non-inclusive tendencies.

Moving on to the respective national populations of treaty parties as legitimacy subjects, the dominance of national executive branches at all stages of the PTR process, from PTR adoption in the COPs to domestic implementation by administrative agencies and everything in between, is overwhelming. Expert bodies, performing wide-ranging tasks from advice on new PTRs to review of and compliance control over PTRs, are full of 'experts' from the executive branches and appointed by executive branches. These national executive branch representatives are not only largely unmonitored by their national parliaments, the loss in national balance of powers is not compensated with international checks either. Considering the global reach of the environmental issues concerned, addressing these input legitimacy problems should focus on the international level. Safeguards should be built to protect the inclusiveness of the consensual process, and checks implemented on the power of executive branch representatives through expert and compliance bodies with more independent members.

Environmental legal scholars should also adjust their views on the role that PTRs play for the effectiveness of international environmental governance. This chapter identified several prominent PTRs as serving parochial interests rather than advancing the environmental objectives of the underlying MEAs.

[236] Krisch, 'International Law in Times of Hegemony', 373–75.

[237] Steinberg, 'In the Shadow of Law or Power?', 345, 360–61. As Heisenberg states for the EU, '[p]aradoxically, the main justification to have consensual decision-making rather than hard voting has always been to solidify the legitimacy of the EU in the eyes of its citizens by not making the losers apparent. … [T]he rights of small Member States are less protected under a system of consensus decision-making than in voting. However, the decision-making process obscures this reality to the public.' Heisenberg, 'The Institution of "consensus" in the European Union', 83.

Various other PTRs generally soften the obligations of the treaty parties, have a marginal effect on obligations, or turn out to simply have been a way of postponing action. To be sure, numerous other PTRs have helped MEAs transition from obsolete systems to more scientifically sound and objective ones, prominently including the CITES COP *Listing Criteria* and the various Ramsar COP resolutions moving wetland conservation towards an ecosystems approach. This chapter far from concludes that all PTRs have output legitimacy problems. However, many of those landmark PTRs date back one or two decades already. Treaty parties have to continue to keep in mind the global public interest as embodied in MEA objectives and core provisions, and make the next moves forward towards environmental effectiveness.

Conclusion

The fragility of the balance between the merits and pitfalls of the post-treaty practice has resonated throughout this study. The flexibility of the process of PTR adoption has enabled numerous improvements in the quality of international environmental law. Yet, the possibilities for flexible change were shown to enable the softening of treaty obligations just as well as their strengthening. The rigidity of the 'one state, one vote' principle of individual state consent was substituted with the flexibility of consensual decision making, but also with the latter's tendency to favour powerful states. More detailed and meaningful rules have come at the cost of wide governmental discretion regarding their domestic implementation, and of the violation of procedural principles towards individuals and businesses. This discretion also causes serious difficulties for citizens and NGOs to perform a role in the effective implementation of IEL. In part, these conflicts are purposively amplified by states, in order to maintain control over the making and implementation of IEL. These concluding reflections begin by imagining some suggestions on how the negative effects of these conflicts could be diminished if states are willing to cooperate.

To counter the discretion of governments and its consequences for procedural principles and the effectiveness of implementation alike, a solution could be sought in moving towards 'standard instruments'. Such a move could facilitate the identification of instruments by which international authority is exercised, settle the degree of authority accorded to each of them, and make clear which procedural rules each 'standard instrument' would have to meet. According to its main proponent, Goldmann:

> A standard instrument is a combination of a rule of identification for authoritative instruments of a specific type and a specific legal regime that is applicable to all instruments coming under the rule of identification. … The *rule of identification* identifies specific instruments that belong to a certain category of authoritative acts to which the same legal regime applies. … The *legal regime* is the second element of standard instruments. It determines conditions for the validity and legality of the instruments that fall under the rule of identification … that relate to issues such as competence, procedure, or review.[1]

[1] Matthias Goldmann, 'Inside Relative Normativity: From Sources to Standard Instruments for the Exercise of International Public Authority' in Armin Von Bogdandy et al (ed), *The Exercise of Public Authority by International Institutions* (Springer, 2010), 679.

The first step, developing a series of *rules of identification*, is executed by applying a set of formal parameters – author, wording, addressee, etc – to distinguish between instruments exercising different degrees and types of authority over different subjects (for example, regime bodies, states, individuals). For instance, a mandatory instrument should have more authority than a recommendatory one. This is crucial, because it allows for the fine tuning of the conditions for validity and legality of different standard instruments in the second step: the development of a *legal regime* for each standard instrument, which fits with the degree and type of authority. For instance, an instrument affecting the position of states should have to meet different conditions than one (directly) affecting the position of individuals. Such legal regimes – not to be confused with 'environmental regimes' – can emerge from 'multiple rounds of exchange between theory and practice',[2] through a process of induction and deduction.

Historically, in European legal orders, standard instruments played a similar role of rendering a then fast-growing body of domestic administrative instruments more legitimate and effective as well as subject to judicial review.[3] Then, as now, the aim was *not* to turn international administrative-type instruments into formal sources of law.[4] The aim was to mitigate uncertainty, discretion and arbitrariness, to safeguard procedural rights of those affected by international administrative instruments, and to make the implementation of such instruments more effective and legitimate. Existing international law doctrines such as 'subsequent agreements' that have to be 'taken into account' lack the sophistication needed to make sense of the many different types of instruments falling within its purview.

The conceptualisation in chapter one of 'post-treaty instruments', 'post-treaty decisions' and external as well as internal 'post-treaty rules' already represented the first move in the direction of rules of identification for post-treaty instruments and its sub-types. These rules are not necessarily limited to *environmental* post-treaty rules: the same types can be found in the instruments adopted under the Framework Convention on Tobacco Control, or the interpretations adopted by the European Committee of Social Rights. Distinguishing further between recommendatory and mandatory phrased PTRs, the following five standard instruments can be conceived of (with examples from this study):

1. Internal operational[5] post-treaty rules (CITES COP *Listing Criteria*, Montreal MOP *Critical-Use Criteria*, Ramsar COP *Designation Conditions* and *Identification Criteria*);
2. Internal operational post-treaty decisions (CITES COP species listings, Ramsar COP wetland listings);
3. External mandatory post-treaty rules (Kyoto COP/MOP *LULUCF* Decisions and *Accounting Modalities*);

[2] ibid, 703.
[3] ibid, 680.
[4] ibid, 681.
[5] *cf* ibid, 697–99.

4. External recommendatory post-treaty rules (Ramsar COP *Wise Use Guidelines*, CITES COP *Reason to Believe Paragraph* and *Disposal of Confiscated Specimens* Resolution);
5. External post-treaty decisions (Montreal MOP yearly *Exemption Decisions*, CITES COP *Trade Suspensions*).

These five sub-types have different degrees and types of authority (for example, mandatory versus recommendatory, general rules versus specific decisions), and while some are aimed at the operation of regime bodies, others are aimed at states individually (internal operational rules versus external rules). Further or different specifications are possible, such as distinguishing between external PTRs that affect states, and those that affect individuals.

At present, as this study hoped to demonstrate, post-treaty instruments falling under the same type of standard instrument – or even the very same instrument – are applied very differently and arbitrarily in practice (*Castlewood Products* versus *Greenpeace*, *Orka* versus *One Etched Tusk*). At the same time, *recommendatory* PTRs are sometimes applied as if they have more authority in practice than *mandatory* PTRs (*Lac Sorobon* versus *NRDC v EPA*). From so far isolated practices, attempts should be made to slowly distil how much and what kind of authority different types of standard instruments usually have. National and international courts can then come to recognise more clearly the type of instrument they are dealing with. Developing rules of identification would obviously be more effective if practice from different national jurisdictions is combined, as this study attempted to do.

The second step – developing *legal regimes* – is the attachment of what Goldmann calls 'validity' or 'legality' conditions to each of these five types of standard post-treaty instruments. Each PTI would then have to meet the conditions of the legal regime attached to its standard type in order to be valid, as a threshold for possessing the authority that usually comes with that type. Developing such conditions would come down to *internalising* the input and output legitimacy tests that courts are now sometimes observed to perform randomly, into standardised conditions of validity. As a result, legitimacy tests can move from very subjective to more objective exercises, becoming less discretionary and creating more predictable expectations.

In terms of conditions of input legitimacy, for instance, international and national courts should consider developing more detailed requirements for legitimate consensual decision making. In its *Whaling in the Antarctic* judgment, the International Court of Justice made a first step towards internalisation of consensus as a condition for the taking into account of IWC resolution as subsequent agreements. However, consensus as such is too crude to make a meaningful distinction between more and less inclusive decisions. More detailed requirements are needed to make consensus a meaningful and objective condition of validity/legality.

Output legitimacy requirements can also be internalised into validity conditions, replacing vague concepts such as 'reasonable' now randomly found in the case law. A starting point could be the provisions in most MEAs that require recommendations of the plenary meetings to 'improve the effectiveness', 'promote the functioning' or 'achieve the purposes' of the MEA.[6] These provisions can be fused into a condition that PTRs must support the effectiveness of the MEA in order to make a successful claim to authority. Of course, there is always room for discussion about what the objectives of PTRs require, and so there should be. Nevertheless, the most egregious antagonistic PTRs could be filtered out in this way, such as the Montreal MOP's *Critical Use Exemptions*, which merely serve economic interests of certain parties and make the Montreal Protocol less rather than more effective.

At the same time, PTRs that *do* bring the parties closer to the object and purpose of the treaty should, by contrast, no longer be discretionary, but should rather automatically be applied by international and domestic courts, to the same extent as binding international law. Developing standard instruments thus has the potential to improve procedural principles such as legal certainty and the stating of reasons, and to improve IEL's effectiveness and legitimacy.

In this process towards standard instruments, there is a primary role for national courts to develop more sophisticated doctrines for the domestic application of post-treaty instruments (be it environmental or otherwise). So far, national courts have approached environmental post-treaty rules in a much too isolated manner, hardly considering previous jurisprudence from their own or foreign jurisdictions. There is also a role for governments to be more consistent and less opportunistic in their implementation of PTRs, for instance by no longer challenging the authority of PTRs as such. Compliance bodies should improve their adherence to Aarhus Convention rules such as to publish 'the reasons and considerations on which the decision is based',[7] as the treaty parties of the Aarhus Convention are already obliged to promote in international environmental decision-making processes.[8] Such practices would support the move towards standard instruments.

The advantages of standard instruments do not include a solution for the shortcomings of consensual decision making – both in terms of inclusiveness and effectiveness – that were pointed out in chapter six. Alternatives are not readily available. A genuine shadow of qualified majority voting, if consensus fails, would

[6] Respectively Art XI Convention on International Trade in Endangered Species of Wild Fauna and Flora (adopted 3 March 1973, entered into force 1 July 1975) 993 UNTS 243 (CITES), Art 6 Convention on Wetlands of International Importance especially as Waterfowl Habitat (adopted 2 February 1971, entered into force 21 December 1975) 996 UNTS 245 (Ramsar Convention) and Art 11 Montreal Protocol on Substances that Deplete the Ozone Layer (adopted 16 September 1987, entered into force 1 January 1989) 1522 UNTS 3 (Montreal Protocol).

[7] Art 6.9 Convention on Access to Information, Public Participation in Decision-Making and Access to Justice in Environmental Matters (adopted 25 June 1998, entered into force 30 October 2001) 2161 UNTS 447 (Aarhus Convention).

[8] Art 3.7 Aarhus Convention: 'Each Party shall promote the application of the principles of this Convention in international environmental decision-making processes and within the framework of international organizations in matters relating to the environment'.

no doubt make the *decision-making process* more effective and respect sovereign equality to a greater extent.[9] Efforts in this direction are not very successful so far. Papua New Guinea made a (failed) plea for majority voting in the UNFCCC COP and Kyoto COP/MOP.[10] In the other three regimes, the option of qualified majority voting is not used in practice. But even if actual qualified majority voting would enable decisions that powerful parties disagree with, and that aim higher than the lowest common denominator, it would be likely to negatively impact effectiveness. There is a serious risk that powerful treaty parties would ignore majority decisions they voted against. Already, there is a tendency of powerful states to flee even from *consensual* decision making in the plenary,[11] and from multilateral processes altogether.[12] Suggestions so far to improve the effectiveness of the consensual process, such as 'exclusion clauses', are not convincing.[13]

The most promising option to mitigate outright violations of the consensual process like the *Copenhagen Accord* or the *Cancun Agreements*, without a threat of non-compliance by powerful minorities, could be to introduce review procedures. Aggrieved states such as Bolivia should be able to file a request for review whether the requirements of consensus have been met or not.[14] Likewise, such a review should be possible when PTRs conflict with the MEA's objectives. An independent third party can prevent treaty parties from writing non-environmental objectives into the treaty through the back door of PTRs. The problem with solutions of this kind is that they run counter to the objective of powerful treaty parties to maintain control over all stages of the process. Until this unbalanced executive branch control diminishes, efforts to reform the PTR practice are unlikely to take hold.

[9] A famous plea for qualified majority voting in the context of international environmental law is Geoffrey Palmer, 'New Ways to Make International Environmental Law' (1992) 86 *American Journal of International Law* 259, 281. Also Günther Handl, 'International "Lawmaking" by Conferences of the Parties and Other Politically Mandated Bodies' in Rüdiger Wolfrum and Volker Röben (eds), *Developments of International Law in Treaty Making* (Springer, 2005), 140–43 (predicting that, in order to tackle the progressively serious deterioration of global environmental problems, non-consensual forms of decision making will become unavoidable).

[10] UNFCCC COP, *Revised proposal from Papua New Guinea and Mexico to amend Articles 7 and 18 of the Convention*, FCCC/CP/2011/4/Rev.1.

[11] Jochen Von Bernstorff, 'Procedures of Decision-Making and the Role of Law in International Organizations' (2008) 9 *German Law Journal* 1939, 786–87.

[12] Nico Krisch, 'The Decay of Consent: International Law in an Age of Global Public Goods' (2014) 108 *American Journal of International Law* 1.

[13] Meyer has suggested the *exclusion clause* to make consensual decision making more effective. He proposes that 'international legislatures' should have the ability to suspend the participation of 'hold-out states' in the consensual process, or even expel a member state or treaty party entirely in narrowly defined circumstances (including powerful states such as the United States). Timothy Meyer, 'From Contract to Legislation: The Logic of Modern International Lawmaking' (2014) 14 *Chicago Journal of International Law* 559, 608–10. The most immediate danger to this proposal is that this clause is likely to be used only against non-powerful states such as Bolivia or Venezuela.

[14] *cf* Handl, 'International "Lawmaking" by Conferences of the Parties', 142 ('the process must provide an opportunity for at least the restatement and re-examination of the minority viewpoint before and by an authroitative third party decision-maker and, conceivably, also allow for the adjustment of the majority decision').

The project of 'standard instruments', on the other hand, works from the bottom up. It creates legal certainty and less arbitrary and more effective implementation by building a sophisticated transnational jurisprudence, not dependent on the willingness of treaty parties.

*****

As of the end of January 2003, the US District Court observed in its judgment in *Castlewood Products* that 10 complete and one partial shipment(s) remained 'on hold' in the detention of US federal agencies,[15] while five others had been released.[16] In the *Greenpeace* case, however, all of the 584 cubic feet of bigleaf mahogany (or 811 cubic feet according to Greenpeace) were cleared through customs. As Lord Justice Mummery of the England and Wales Court of Appeal reflected:

> It is no doubt unfortunate that mistakes may be made by the issuing authority which cannot be put right and that the enforcement of [CITES] is less than perfect, but in an imperfect world I would accept the construction which the language of [CITES] naturally bears and which is consistent with the legitimate needs of certainty in commerce, as embodied in the documentary evidence provisions [of CITES].[17]

In other words, had the authority of the *Reason to Believe Paragraph* been less ambiguous, commercial certainty would not have been harmed by letting the *Paragraph* prevail over the language of CITES. The Lord Justice could not have hidden behind commercial certainty in giving priority to what he called the 'surface validity' of the permits.

The authority of CITES resolutions in national legal orders is still ambiguous over a decade later. But other more promising developments have occurred in the protection of tropical hardwood from international trade. At the time of the shipments, bigleaf mahogany was still listed on CITES Appendix III: South American 'range states' had listed it unilaterally, and the lowest level of trade controls applied. Shortly after the *Castlewood Products* and *Greenpeace* shipments, on 15 November 2003, the CITES COP finally placed bigleaf mahogany logs, sawn timber, veneer and plywood officially in Appendix II,[18] mandating stricter controls by both exporting and importing Management Authorities. Sixty-eight parties voted in favour of this listing decision, while 30 parties, including Brazil and most other exporters of mahogany, voted against.[19] This upgrade does not mean that importing Management Authorities can now look beyond

[15] *Castlewood Products* (District Court), p 11, fn 2.
[16] *Castlewood Products* (Court of Appeals), para 24.
[17] *Greenpeace*, Lord Justice Mummery, para 65.
[18] https://cites.org/eng/news/pr/2003/031111_mahogany.shtml.
[19] Luiz C Barbosa, *Guardians of the Brazilian Amazon Rainforest: Environmental Organizations and Development* (Routledge, 2015), 61.

the exporting Management Authority's assessment of the legality of the acquisition of the specimen. That still depends on the domestic authority of the *Reason to Believe Paragraph.*

Since the listing in Appendix II, coinciding with stronger conservation efforts by Brazil, legal exports of bigleaf mahogany had declined by a factor of 10.[20] 'However,' the CITES Secretariat concedes, 'significant progress remains to be made in most range States'.[21] It is also unclear how much of the previously legal trade has shifted to illegal trade. For instance, illegally logged mahogany can be disguised by labelling it as 'other tropical timber species',[22] or loggers can harvest more than their allotted quota. In the UK, *The Observer* recently reported, illegally harvested hardwood from Brazil continues to make its way to the stores.[23] With the changes in the Brazilian Government, forest protection has ceased to be a top priority. PTRs evidently cannot solve such complex problems entirely. Nevertheless, treaty parties should strive to make them as effective, legitimate and authoritative as possible.

[20] ibid, 63.
[21] See https://cites.org/eng/prog/mwg.php.
[22] Barbosa, *Guardians of the Brazilian Amazon Rainforest*, 63–64.
[23] James Tapper, 'Hardwood from illegal logging makes its way into UK stores; Deforestation is rife in the Amazon, Colombia and the Philippines, say environmental groups', *The Observer*, 26 June 2016.

BIBLIOGRAPHY

Abbott, Kenneth W et al, 'The Concept of Legalization' (2000) 54 *International Organization* 401.

Abi-Saab, Georges, 'The Security Council as Legislator and as Executive in Its Fight Against Terrorism and Against Proliferation of Weapons of Mass Destruction: The Question of Legitimacy' in Rüdiger Wolfrum and Volker Röben (eds), *Legitimacy in International Law* (Springer, 2010) 109.

Acheson, Ray, 'Starting Somewhere: The Arms Trade Treaty, Human Rights and Gender Based Violence' (2013) 22 *Human Rights Defender* 17.

Ahlborn, Christiane, 'The Rules of International Organizations and the Law of International Responsibility' (2011) 8 *International Organizations Law Review* 397.

Akande, Dapo, 'What Is the Meaning of "Consensus" in International Decision Making?' *EJIL Talk!* (8 April 2013).

Alvarez, José E, 'Limits of Change by Way of Subsequent Agreements and Practice' in Georg Nolte (ed), *Treaties and Subsequent Practice* (OUP, 2013) 123.

Alvarez, José E, *International Organizations as Law-Makers* (OUP, 2005).

Amerasinghe, Chittharanjan F, *Principles of the Institutional Law of International Organizations* 2nd edn (CUP, 2005).

Arato, Julio, 'Subsequent Practice and Evolutive Interpretation: Techniques of Treaty Interpretation over Time and Their Diverse Consequences' (2010) 9 *The Law & Practice of International Courts and Tribunals* 443.

Arato, Julio, 'Treaty Interpretation and Constitutional Transformation: Informal Change in International Organizations' (2012) 38 *Yale Journal of International Law* 289.

Arato, Julio, 'Subsequent Practice in the Whaling Case, and What the ICJ Implies about Treaty Interpretation in International Organizations' *EJIL: Talk!* (31 March 2014).

Arendt, Hannah, *Between Past and Future: Eight Exercises in Political Thought* (Penguin, 1968).

Aust, Anthony, *Modern Treaty Law and Practice* 2nd edn (CUP, 2007).

Aust, Helmut P, Alejandro Rodiles and Peter Staubach, 'Unity or Uniformity? Domestic Courts and Treaty Interpretation' (2014) 27 *Leiden Journal of International Law* 75.

Barbosa, Luiz C, *Guardians of the Brazilian Amazon Rainforest: Environmental Organizations and Development* (Routledge, 2015).

Barr, Michael S and Geoffrey P Miller, 'Global Administrative Law: The View from Basel' (2006) 17 *European Journal of International Law* 15.

Barnett, Michael N and Finnemore, Martha, 'The Politics, Power, and Pathologies of International Organizations' (1999) 53 *International Organization* 699.

Barrett, Scott, *Why Cooperate? Incentives to Supply Global Public Goods* (OUP, 2007).

Bauer, Steffen and Frank Biermann, 'The Debate on a World Environment Organization: An Introduction' in Steffen Bauer and Frank Biermann (eds), *A World Organization: Solution or Threat for Effective International Environmental Governance?* (Ashgate Publishing, 2005) 1.

Benvenisti, Eyal, '"Coalitions of the Willing" and the Evolution of Informal International Law' in Christian Calliess, Georg Nolte und Peter-Tobias Stoll (eds), *Coalitions of the Willing: Avantgarde or Threat?* (Heymann, 2007) 1.

Benvenisti, Eyal, 'Reclaiming Democracy: The Strategic Uses of Foreign and International Law by National Courts' (2008) 102 *American Journal of International Law* 241.

Benvenisti, Eyal and George W Downs, 'National Courts, Domestic Democracy, and the Evolution of International Law' (2009) 20 *European Journal of International Law* 59.

Bernstein, Steven, 'Legitimacy in International Environmental Governance' (2005) 1 *Journal of International Law & International Relations* 139.

Biermann, Frank and Aarti Gupta, 'Accountability and Legitimacy in Earth System Governance: A Research Framework' (2011) 70 *Ecological Economics* 1856.

Biermann, Frank and Bernd Siebenhüner, *Managers of Global Change: The Influence of International Environmental Bureaucracies* (MIT Press, 2011).

Birnie, Patricia, Alan Boyle and Patricia Redgwell, *International Law and the Environment* 3rd edn (OUP, 2009).

Black, Julia, 'Constructing and Contesting Legitimacy and Accountability in Polycentric Regulatory Regimes' (2008) 2 *Regulation & Governance* 137.

Bled, Amandine J, 'Business to the Rescue: Private Sector Actors and Global Environmental Regimes' Legitimacy' (2009) 9 *International Environmental Agreements: Politics, Law and Economics* 153.

Blue Sky, Melissa, 'Getting On The List: Politics And Procedural Maneuvering In Cites Appendix I and II Decisions For Commercially Exploited Marine And Timber Species' (2010) 10 *Sustainable Development Law & Policy* 35.

Bodansky, Daniel, 'The United Nations Framework Convention on Climate Change: A Commentary' (1993) 1 *Yale Journal of International Law* 451.

Bodansky, Daniel, 'The Legitimacy of International Governance: A Coming Challenge for International Environmental Law?' (1999) 93 *American Journal of International Law* 596.

Bodansky, Daniel, 'Is There an International Environmental Constitution?' (2009) 16 *Indiana Journal of Global Legal Studies* 565.

Bodansky, Daniel, *The Art and Craft of International Environmental Law* (Harvard University Press, 2010).

Bodansky, Daniel, 'The Concept of Legitimacy in International Law' in Rüdiger Wolfrum and Volker Röben (eds), *Legitimacy in International Law* (Springer, 2010) 309.

Bodansky, Daniel, 'The Copenhagen Climate Change Conference: A Postmortem' (2010) 104 *American Journal of International Law* 230.

Bodansky, Daniel and Jutta Brunnée, 'Introduction: The Role of National Courts in the Field of International Environmental Law' in Michael Anderson and Paolo Galizzi (eds), *International Environmental Law in National Courts* (BIICL 2002) 1.

Bodansky, Daniel, Jutta Brunnée and Ellen Hey, 'International Environmental Law: Mapping the Field' in Daniel Bodansky, Jutta Brunné and Ellen Hey (eds), *Oxford Handbook of International Environmental Law* (OUP, 2007) 1.

Bodnar, Alice L, 'NRDC v EPA: Testing the Waters of the Constitutionality of Delegation to International Organizations' (2007) 34 *Ecology Law Quarterly* 895.

Von Bogdandy, Armin and Jürgen Bast (eds), *Principles of European Constitutional Law* (Hart Publishing, 2009).

Böhringer, Cristophe, 'Climate Politics From Kyoto to Bonn: From Little to Nothing?!?', *Zentrum für Europäische Wirtschaftsforschung Discussion Papers* 2001/49.

Bothe, Michael, 'The United Nations Framework Convention on Climate Change – an Unprecedented Multilevel Regulatory Challenge' (2003) 63 *Zeitschrift für ausländisches öffentliches Recht und Volkerrecht* 239.

Bowman, Michael, Peter Davies and Catherine Redgwell, *Lyster's International Wildlife Law* 2nd edn (CUP, 2010).

Bowman, Michael J, 'The Ramsar Convention Comes of Age' (1995) 17 *Netherlands International Law Review* 1.

Boyle, Alan E, 'Saving the World? Implementation and Enforcement of International Environmental Law Through International Institutions' (1991) 3 *Journal of Environmental Law* 229.

Boyle, Alan E, 'Some Reflections on the Relationship of Treaties and Soft Law' (1999) 48 *International and Comparative Law Quarterly* 901.

Bradley, Curtis A and Judith G Kelley, 'The Concept of International Delegation' (2008) 71 *Law and Contemporary Problems* 1.

Breitmeier, Helmut, *The Legitimacy of International Regimes* (Ashgate, 2008).

Breitmeier, Helmut, Marc A Levy, Oran R Young and Michael Zürn, 'The International Regimes Database as a Tool for the Study of International Cooperation', *International Institute for Applied Systems Analysis Working Paper* 1996/160.

Bridgewater, Peter, 'A New Context for the Ramsar Convention: Wetlands in a Changing World' (2008) 17 *RECIEL* 100.

Bröllmann, Catherine, 'A Flat Earth? International Organizations in the System of International Law' (2001) 70 *Nordic Journal of International Law* 319.

Bromley, Mark, Neil Cooper and Paul Holtom, 'The UN Arms Trade Treaty: Arms Export Controls, the Human Security Agenda and the Lessons of History' (2012) 88 *International Affairs* 1029.

Brouns, Bernd and Tilman Santarius, 'Die Kyoto-Reduktionsziele Nach den Bonner Beschlüssen' (2001) 51 *Energiewirtschaftliche Tagesfragen* 590.

Brownlie, Ian, *Principles of Public International Law* 7th edn (OUP, 2008).

Bruch, Carl, 'Is International Environmental Law Really Law? An Analysis of Application in Domestic Courts' (2006) 23 *Pace Environmental Law Review* 423.

Brunnée, Jutta, 'COPing with Consent: Law-Making Under Multilateral Environmental Agreements' (2002) 15 *Leiden Journal of International Law* 1.

Brunnée, Jutta, 'Enforcement Mechanisms in International Law and International Environmental Law' in: Ulrich Beyerlin, Thilo Mahraun and Rudiger Wolfrum (eds), *Ensuring Compliance with Multilateral Environmental Agreements: A Dialogue Between Practitioners and Academia*, vol 237 (Springer, 2005).

Brunnée, Jutta, 'Reweaving the Fabric of International Law? Patterns of Consent in Environmental Framework Agreements' in Rudiger Wolfrum and Volker Röben (eds), *Developments of International Law in Treaty Making* (Martinus Nijhoff Publishers, 2005) 101.

Brunnée, Jutta, and Stephen J Toope, 'Environmental Security and Freshwater Resources: Ecosystem Regime Building' (1997) 91 *American Journal of International Law* 26.

Brunnée, Jutta, 'International Law and Constructivism: Elements of an Interactional Theory of International Law" (2000) 39 *Columbia Journal of Transnational Law* 19.

Brunnée, Jutta, *Legitimacy and Legality in International Law* (CUP, 2010).

Brunnée, Jutta, 'Interactional International Law: An Introduction' (2011) 3 *International Theory* 307.

Buga, Irina, *The Modification of Treaties by Subsequent Practice: The Implications of Practice Going Beyond the Limits of Treaty Interpretation* (Dissertation, Utrecht University, 2015).

Burgiel, Stanley W, 'The Cartagena Protocol on Biosafety: Taking the Steps from Negotiation to Implementation' (2002) 11 *RECIEL* 53.

Buzan, Barry, 'Negotiating by Consensus: Developments in Technique at the United Nations Conference on the Law of the Sea' (1981) 75 *American Journal of International Law* 324.

Caron, David D, 'The International Whaling Commission & The North Atlantic Marine Mammal Commission: The Institutional Risks of Coercion in Consensual Structures' (1995) 89 *American Journal of International Law* 154.

Cardesa-Salzmann, Antonio, 'Constitutionalising Secondary Rules in Global Environmental Regimes: Non-Compliance Procedures and the Enforcement of Multilateral Environmental Agreements' (2011) 24 *Journal of Environmental Law* 103.

Casini, Lorenzo and Benedict Kingsbury, 'Global Administrative Law Dimensions of International Organizations Law' (2009) 6 *International Organizations Law Review* 319.

Cassese, Sabino, "Administrative Law Without the State? The Challenge of Global Regulation" (2005) 37 *New York University Journal of International Law and Politics* 663.

Charney, Jonathan I, 'United States Interest in a Convention on the Law of the Sea: The Case for Continued Efforts' (1978) 11 *Vanderbilt Journal of Transnational Law* 39.

Chayes, Abraham and Antonia H Chayes, *The New Sovereignty: Compliance With International Regulatory Agreements* (Harvard University Press, 1995).

Chinkin, Christine M, 'The Challenge of Soft Law: Development and Change in International Law' (1989) 38 *International & Comparative Law Quarterly* 850.

Churchill, Robin R and Geir Ulfstein, 'Autonomous Institutional Arrangements in Multilateral Environmental Agreements: A Little-Noticed Phenomenon in International Law' (2000) 94 *American Journal of International Law* 623.

Clapp, Jennifer, 'The Privatization of Global Environmental Governance: ISO 14000 and the Developing World' (1998) 4 *Global Governance* 295.

Cohen, Harlan G, 'Theorizing Precedent in International Law' in Andrea Bianchi, Daniel Peat and Matthew Windsor (eds), *Interpretation in International Law* (OUP, 2014).

Conforti, Benedetto, *International Law and the Role of Domestic Legal Systems* (Springer, 1993).

Corten, Olivier and Pierre Klein, *The Vienna Convention on the Law of Treaties, A Commentary (Volume I)* (OUP, 2011).

Craig, Paul, and Grainne De Búrca, *EU Law: Text, Cases, and Materials* 5th Rev (OUP, 2011).

Crawford, James, 'A Consensualist Interpretation of Article 31(3) of the Vienna Convention on the Law of Treaties' in Georg Nolte (ed), *Treaties and Subsequent Practice* (OUP, 2013) 29.

D'Aspremont, Jean, 'Softness in International Law: A Self-Serving Quest for New Legal Materials' (2008) 9 *European Journal of International Law* 1075.

D'Aspremont, Jean, 'The Law of International Organizations and the Art of Reconciliation: From Dichotomies to Dialectics' (2014) 11 *International Organizations Law Review* 428.

Danish, Kyle W, 'International Relations Theory' in Daniel Bodansky, Jutta Brunnée and Ellen Hey (eds), *Oxford Handbook of International Environmental Law* (OUP, 2007) 205.

Dann, Philip, 'The Political Institutions' in Armin Von Bogdandy and Jürgen Bast (eds), *Principles of European Constitutional Law* (Hart Publishing, 2009) 237.

den Elzen, Michael G and Adrienne P de Moor, 'Analyzing the Kyoto Protocol under the Marrakesh Accords: Economic Efficiency and Environmental Effectiveness' (2002) 43 *Ecological Economics* 141.

Dimitrov, Radoslav S, 'Hostage to Norms: States, Institutions and Global Forest Politics' (2005) 5 *Global Environmental Politics* 1.

Djeffal, Christian, 'Commentaries on the Law of Treaties: A Review Essay Reflecting on the Genre of Commentaries' (2013) 24 *European Journal of International Law* 1223.

Downs, George W, Kyle W Danish and Peter N Barsoom, 'The Transformational Model of International Regime Design: Triumph of Hope or Experience?' (2000) 38 *Columbia Journal of Transnational Law* 465.

Downs, George W, David M Rocke and Peter N Barsoom, 'Is the Good News about Compliance Good News about Cooperation?' (1996) 50 *International Organization* 379.

Dryzek, John S, *Deliberative Global Politics* (Polity Press, 2006).

Dupuy, Pierre-Marie, 'Soft Law and the International Law of the Environment' (1991) 12 *Michigan Journal of International Law* 420.

Ebbeson, Jonas, 'Public Participation' in Daniel Bodansky, Jutta Brunnée and Ellen Hey (eds), *Oxford Handbook of International Environmental Law* (OUP, 2007) 681.

Eckersley, Robyn, 'Moving Forward in the Climate Negotiations: Multilateralism or Minilateralism?' (2012) 12 *Global Environmental Politics* 24.

Ehlermann, Claus-Dieter and Lothar Ehring, 'Decision-Making in the World Trade Organization: Is the Consensus Practice of the World Trade Organization Adequate for Making, Revising and Implementing Rules on International Trade?' (2005) 8 *Journal of International Economic Law* 51.

Enroth, Henrik, 'The Concept of Authority Transnationalised' (2013) 4 *Transnational Legal Theory* 336.

Epstein, Charlotte, 'The Making of Global Environmental Norms. Endangered Species Protection' (2006) 6 *Global Environmental Politics* 32.

Evensen, Jens, 'Three Procedural Cornerstones of the Law of the Sea Conference: The Consensus Principle, The Package Deal and The Gentleman's Agreement' in John Kaufmann (ed), *Effective Negotiation: Case Studies in Conference Diplomacy* (Martinus Nijhoff Publishers, 1989).

Faiman Hans, Elspeth, 'The Montreal Protocol in U.S. Domestic Law: A "Bottom Up" Approach to the Development of Global Administrative Law' (2013) 45 *New York University Journal of International Law and Politics* 827.

Farrier, David and Linda Tucker, 'Wise Use of Wetlands Under the Ramsar Convention: A Challenge for Meaningful Implementation of International Law' (2000) 12 *Journal of International Environmental Law* 21.

Favre, David S, 'Tension Points Within the Language of the CITES Treaty' (1987) 5 *Boston University International Law Journal* 247.

Ferrajolo, Ornella, 'State Obligations and Non-Compliance in the Ramsar System State Obligations and Non-Compliance in the Ramsar System' (2011) 14 *Journal of International Wildlife Law & Policy* 243.

Finkelman, André D, 'Agreements of the Parties to the Montreal Protocol: Law or Politics? An Analysis of Natural Resources Defense Council v. EPA' (2007) 93 *Iowa Law Review* 665.

Fisher, Dana R, 'COP-15 in Copenhagen: How the Merging of Movements Left Civil Society Out in the Cold' (2010) 10 *Global Environmental Politics* 11.

Fisher, Dana R, and Jessica F Green, 'Understanding Disenfranchisement: Civil Society and Developing Countries' Influence and Participation in Global Governance for Sustainable Development' (2004) 4 *Global Environmental Politics* 65.

Fitzmaurice, Malgosia, 'Expression of Consent to Be Bound by a Treaty as Developed in Certain Environmental Treaties' in Jan Klabbers and René Lefeber (eds), *Essays on the Law of Treaties: A Collection of Essays in Honor of Bert Vierdag* (Martinus Nijhoff Publishers, 1998) 59.

Fitzmaurice, Malgosia, 'Compliance with Multilateral Environmental Agreements' (2007) 20 *Hague Yearbook of International Law* 19.

Fitzmaurice, Malgosia, 'Treaties' in Rüdiger Wolfrum et al (ed), *Max Planck Encyclopedia of Public International Law* (Max Planck Institute/OUP, 2010).

Footer, Mary E, 'The Role of Consensus in GATT/WTO Decision-Making' (1996) 17 *Northwestern Journal of International Law & Business* 653.

Foster, Caroline E, 'Diminished Ambitions? Public International Legal Authority in the Transnational Economic Era' (2014) 17 *Journal of International Economic Law* 355.

Francioni, Francesco, 'Realism, Utopia and the Future of International Environmental Law' in Antonio Cassese, *Realizing Utopia: the Future of International Law* (OUP, 2012) 442.

Fransen, Taryn, 'Enhancing Today's MRV Framework to Meet Tomorrow's Needs: The Role of National Communications and Inventories' *World Resources Institute Working Paper* (June 2009).

Freestone, David and Charlotte Streck (eds), *Legal Aspects of Implementing the Kyoto Protocol Mechanisms: Making Kyoto Work* (OUP, 2005).

French, Duncan, 'Finding Autonomy in International Environmental Law and Governance' (2009) 21 *Journal of Environmental Law* 255.

French, Duncan, 'Sustainable Development' in Malgosia Fitzmaurice, David M Ong and Panos Merkouris (eds), *Research Handbook on International Environmental Law* (Edward Elgar, 2010) 51.

Friedrich, Jürgen, *International Environmental 'soft Law': The Functions and Limits of Nonbinding Instruments in International Environmental Governance and Law* (Springer, 2013).

Friedrich, Jürgen and Eva Julia Lohse, '"Spaces of Normativity" – Revisiting the Junctures of International and Domestic Administration in Times of New Forms of Governance: Modes of Implementing Standards for Sustainable Development and Their Legitimacy Challenges' (2008) 2 *European Journal of Legal Studies* 49.

Fromm, Daniel and Dinah Shelton, 'Natural Resources Defence Council v Environmental Protection Agency – Case Note' (2006) 525 *ILDC*.

Fry, Ian, 'Twists and Turns in the Jungle: Exploring the Evolution of Land Use, Land-Use Change and Forestry Decisions within the Kyoto Protocol' (2002) 11 *RECIEL* 159.

Fuchs, Christina, 'Convention on International Trade in Endangered Species of Wild Fauna and Flora (CITES) – Conservation Efforts Undermine The Legality Principle' (2008) 31 *German Law Journal* 1565.

Fuller, Lon L, 'Positivism and Fidelity to Law – A Reply to Professor Hart' (1958) 71 *Harvard Law Review* 630.

Fuller, Lon L, *The Morality of Law* Rev edn (Yale University Press, 1969).

Gardiner, Richard K, *Treaty Interpretation* (OUP, 2007).
Gareau, Brian J, 'Dangerous Holes in Global Environmental Governance: The Roles of Neoliberal Discourse, Science, and California Agriculture in the Montreal Protocol' (2008) 40 *Antipode* 102.
Gareau, Brian J, 'The Limited Influence of Global Civil Society: International Environmental Non-Governmental Organisations and the Methyl Bromide Controversy in the Montreal Protocol' (2012) 21 *Environmental Politics* 88.
Gehring, Thomas, 'International Environmental Regimes: Dynamic Sectoral Legal Regimes' (1990) 1 *Yearbook of International Environmental Law* 35.
Gehring, Thomas, 'How to Circumvent Parochial Interests without Excluding Stake-Holders: The Rationalizing Power of Functionally Differentiated Decision-Making', *BACES Discussion Paper* 2004/3.
——, 'Treaty-Making and Treaty-Evolution' in D Bodansky, J Brunnée and E Hey (eds), *The Oxford Handbook of International Environmental Law* (2007) 467.
Gehring, Thomas and Eva Ruffing, 'When Arguments Prevail Over Power: The CITES Procedure for the Listing of Endangered Species' (2008) 8 *Global Environmental Politics* 123.
Goho, Saun A, 'The CITES Fort Lauderdale Criteria: The Uses and Limits of Science in International Conservation Decisionmaking' (2001) 114 *Harvard Law Review* 1769.
Goldmann, Matthias, 'Inside Relative Normativity: From Sources to Standard Instruments for the Exercise of International Public Authority' in Armin Von Bogdandy et al (ed), *The Exercise of Public Authority by International Institutions* (Springer, 2010) 661.
Goldmann, Matthias, 'We Need to Cut Off the Head of the King: Past, Present, and Future Approaches to International Soft Law' (2012) 25 *Leiden Journal of International Law* 335.
Goldmann, Matthias and Armin von Bogdandy, 'The Exercise of International Public Authority through National Policy Assessment: The OECD's PISA Policy as a Paradigm for a New International Standard Instrument' (2008) 5 *International Organizations Law Review* 241.
Goodman, Ryan and Derek Jinks, 'How to Influence States: Socialization and International Human Rights Law' (2004) 54 *Duke Law Journal* 621.
Goote, Maas M, 'Non-Compliance Procedures in International Environmental Law: The Middle Way between Diplomacy and Law' (1999) 1 *International Law FORUM du Droit International* 82.
Green, Jessica F and Jeff Colgan, 'Protecting Sovereignty, Protecting the Planet: State Delegation to International Organizations and Private Actors in Environmental Politics' (2013) 26 *Governance* 473.
Gupta, Aarti, 'Transparency as Contested Political Terrain: Who Knows What about the Global GMO Trade and Why Does It Matter?' (2010) 10 *Global Environmental Politics* 32.
Habermas, Jürgen, *Communication and the Evolution of Society*, Thomas McCarthy tr (Beacon, 1979).
Habermas, Jürgen, 'Chapter 8. Does the Constitutionalisation of International Law Still Have a Chance?' in Jürgen Habermas, *The Divided West* (Polity, 2006).
Hafner, Gerhard, 'Subsequent Agreements and Practice: Between Interpretation, Informal Modification, and Formal Amendment' in Georg Nolte (ed), *Treaties and Subsequent Practice* (OUP, 2013) 105.
Halabi, Sam F, 'The World Health Organization's Framework Convention on Tobacco Control: An Analysis of Guidelines Adopted by the Conference of the Parties' (2010) 39 *Georgia Journal of International & Comparative Law* 121.
Hall, Rodney B, and Thomas J Biersteker (eds), *The Emergence of Private Authority in Global Governance* (CUP, 2002).
Handl, Günther, 'Compliance Control Mechanisms and International Environmental Obligations' (1997) 5 *Tulane Journal of Internationl & Comparative Law* 29.
Handl, Günther, 'International "Lawmaking" by Conferences of the Parties and Other Politically Mandated Bodies' in Rudiger Wolfrum and Volker Roben (eds), *Developments of International Law in Treaty Making* (Springer, 2005) 127.
Hart, Herbert LA, *The Concept of Law* (OUP, 1961).
Hawkins, Daryl et al (eds), *Delegation and Agency in International Organizations* (CUP, 2006).

Heisenberg, Dorothée, 'The Institution of "consensus" in the European Union: Formal versus Informal Decision-Making in the Council' (2005) 44 *European Journal of Political Research* 65.

Herkenrath, Peter, 'Ramsar Convention on Wetlands: 10th Conference of the Parties' (2009) 43 *Oryx* 170.

Hey, Ellen, 'The European Community's Courts and International Environmental Agreements' in: Michael Anderson and Paolo Galizzi (eds), *International Environmental Law in National Courts* (BIICL 2002) 65.

Hey, Ellen, 'Sustainable Development, Normative Development, and the Legitimacy of Decision Making' (2003) 19 *Netherlands Yearbook of International Law* 3.

Hey, Ellen, *Teaching International Law: State-Consent as Consent to a Process of Normative Development and Ensuing Problems* (Kluwer Law International, 2003).

Hollis, Duncan, 'NRDC v. EPA: Are IO Decisions Really Only Political Commitments?' *Opinio Juris* (5 September 2006).

Huggins, Anna, 'The Desirability of Depoliticization: Compliance in the International Climate Regime' (2015) 4 *Transnational Environmental Law* 101.

Hurd, Ian, 'Legitimacy and Authority in International Politics' (1999) 53 *International Organization* 379.

Hurd, Ian, 'Legitimacy, Power, and the Symbolic Life of the UN Security Council' (2002) 8 *Global Governance* 35.

Joyner, Christopher, 'Recommended Measures under the Antarctic Treaty: Hardening Compliance With Soft International Law' (1998) 19 *Michigan Journal of International Law* 401.

Kahler, Miles, 'Conclusion: The Causes and Consequences of Legalization' (2000) 54 *International Organization* 661.

Kalimo, Harri and Staal, Tim, '"Softness" in International Instruments – the Case of Transnational Corporations' (2014) 41 *Syracuse Journal of International Law and Commerce* 257.

Karl, Wolfram, *Vertrag Und Spätere Praxis Im Völkerrecht. Zum Einfluß Der Praxis Auf Inhalt Und Bestand Völkerrechtlicher Verträge* (Springer, 1983).

Karno, Valerie, 'Protection of Endangered Gorillas and Chimpanzees in International Trade: Can CITES Help?' (1990) 14 *Hastings International & Comparative Law Review* 989.

Keohane, Robert O, and Allen Buchanan, 'The Legitimacy of Global Governance Institutions' in: Rudiger Wolfrum and Volker Roben (eds), *Legitimacy in International Law* (Springer 2008) 62.

Keohane, Robert O, Stephen Macedo and Andrew Moravcsik, 'Democracy Enhancing Multilateralism' (2009) 63 *International Organization* 1.

Kingsbury, Benedict, 'Sovereignty and Inequality' (1998) 9 *European Journal of International Law* 599.

Kingsbury, Benedict, 'Weighing Global Regulatory Rules and Decisions in National Courts' (2009) 9 *Acta Juridica* 90.

Kingsbury, Benedict, 'The Concept of "Law" in Global Administrative Law' (2009) 20 *European Journal of International Law* 23.

Kingsbury, Benedict, Nico Krisch and Richard B Stewart, 'The Emergence of Global Administrative Law' (2005) 68 *Law and Contemporary Problems* 15.

Kissack, Robert, 'Crisis Situations and Consensus Seeking: Adaptive Decision-Making in the FAO and Applying Its Lessons to the Reform of the WTO' in Thomas Cottier and Manfred Elsig (eds), *Governing the World Trade Organization: Past, Present and Beyond Doha* (CUP, 2011).

Klabbers, Jan, 'The Redundancy of Soft Law' (1996) 65 *Nordic Journal of International Law* 167.

Klabbers, Jan, 'Compliance Procedures' in Daniel Bodansky, Jutta Brunnée and Ellen Hey (eds), *The Oxford Handbook of International Environmental Law* (2007) 995.

Klabbers, Jan, 'The Commodification of International Law' in Hélène Ruiz Fabri, Emmanuelle Jouannet and Vincent Tomkiewicz (eds), *Select Proceedings of the European Society of International Law* (Hart Publishing, 2008) 341.

Klabbers, Jan, *An Introduction to International Institutional Law* 2nd edn (CUP, 2009).

Klabbers, Jan, 'Goldmann Variations, Comment by Jan Klabbers' in Armin Von Bogdandy et al (eds), *The Exercise of Public Authority by International Institutions* (Springer, 2010) 713.

Knox, John H, 'Horizontal Human Rights Law' (2006) 105 *American Journal of International Law* 1.

Knox, John H, 'Natural Resources Defense Council v. Environmental Protection Agency 464 F.3d 1' (2007) 101 *American Journal of International Law* 471.

Koenig-Archibugi, Matthias, 'Is Global Democracy Possible?' (2011) 17 *European Journal of International Relations* 519.

Kohen, Marcelo, 'Keeping Subsequent Agreements and Practice in Their Right Limits' in Georg Nolte (ed), *Treaties and Subsequent Practice* (OUP, 2013) 34.

Korkea-aho, Emilia, 'Laws in Progress? Reconceptualizing Accountability Strategies in the Era of Framework Norms' (2013) 2 *Transnational Environmental Law* 363.

Koskenniemi, Martti, 'Breach of Treaty or Non-Compliance? Reflections on the Enforcement of the Montreal Protocol' (1992) 3 *Yearbook of International Environmental Law* 123.

Koskenniemi, Martti, 'The Mystery of Legal Obligation' (2011) 3 *International Theory* 319.

Krasner, Stephen D, 'Structural Causes and Regime Consequences: Regimes as Intervening Variables' (2009) 36 *International Organization* 185.

Krisch, Nico, 'International Law in Times of Hegemony: Unequal Power and the Shaping of the International Legal Order' (2005) 16 *European Journal of International Law* 369.

Krisch, Nico, 'The Pluralism of Global Administrative Law' (2006) 17 *European Journal of International Law* 247.

Krisch, Nico, *Beyond Constitutionalism: The Pluralist Structure of Postnational Law* (OUP, 2010).

Krisch, Nico, 'The Decay of Consent: International Law in an Age of Global Public Goods' (2014) 108 *American Journal of International Law* 1.

Krisch, Nico, 'The Structure of Postnational Authority' (2015), at http://papers.ssrn.com/sol3/papers.cfm?abstract_id=2564579.

Ku, Julian G, 'The Delegation of Federal Power to International Organizations: New Problems with Old Solutions' (2000) 313 *Minnesota Law Review* 71.

Kulovesi, Kati, 'Different Views on Consensus: Legality of the Cancun Agreements?' *Point Carbon* (23 December 2010).

Kuokkanen, Tuomas, 'Putting Gentle Pressure on Parties: Recent Trends in the Practice of the Implementation Committee under the Convention on Long-Range Transboundary Air Pollution' in Martti Koskenniemi (ed), *Nordic cosmopolitanism: essays in international law for Martti Koskenniemi* (2003) 315.

Láncos, Petra L, 'Flexibility and Legitimacy – The Emissions Trading System under the Kyoto Protocol' (2008) 9 *German Law Journal* 1625.

Lane, Jan-Erik, 'The Concept of Implementation' (1983) 86 *Statsvetenskaplig tidskrift* 17.

Lang, Andre and Joanne Scott, 'The Hidden World of WTO Governance: A Rejoinder to Richard H. Steinberg' (2010) 20 *European Journal of International Law* 1073.

Lang, Winfried, 'International Environmental Cooperation' in Gunnar Sjostedt and Uno Svedin (eds), *International Environmental Negotiations: Process, Issues and Contexts* (The Swedish Institute of International Affairs, 1993) 19.

Lefeber, René, 'Creative Legal Engineering' (2000) 13 *Leiden Journal of International Law* 1.

Linderfalk, Ulf, *On the Interpretation of Treaties: The Modern International Law as Expressed in the 1969 Vienna Convention on the Law of Treaties* (Springer, 2007).

Loibl, Gerhard, 'Conferences of Parties and the Modification of Obligations' in Matthew CR Craven and Malgosia Fitzmaurice, *Interrogating the Treaty* (Wolf Legal Publishers, 2005) 103.

Luhmann, Niklas, *Legitimation Durch Verfahren* (Suhrkamp, 1983).

Macdonald, Terry, *Global Stakeholder Democracy: Power and Representation beyond Liberal States* (OUP, 2008).

Marauhn, Thilo, 'Towards a Procedural Law of Compliance' (1996) 56 *Zeitschrift fur auslandisches offentliches Recht und Volkerrecht* 696.

Levy, Marc A et al, 'The Study of International Regimes' (1995) 1 *European Journal of International Relations* 267.

Marmor, Andrei, 'An Institutional Conception of Authority' (2011) 39 *Philosophy & Public Affairs* 238.

McGregor, Ian M, 'Disenfranchisement of Countries and Civil Society at COP-15 in Copenhagen' (2011) 11 *Global Environmental Politics* 1.
McRae, Kenneth D, 'Contrasting Styles of Democratic Decision-Making: Adversarial versus Consensual Politics' (1997) 18 *International Political Science Review* 279.
Meidinger, Errol, 'The Administrative Law of Global Private-Public Regulation: The Case of Forestry' (2006) 17 *European Journal of International Law* 47.
Meyer, Timothy, 'From Contract to Legislation: The Logic of Modern International Lawmaking' (2014) 14 *Chicago Journal of International Law* 559.
Mitchell, Ronald B, 'Compliance Theory: Compliance, Effectiveness, and Behaviour Change in International Environmental Law' in Daniel Bodansky, Jutta Brunnée and Ellen Hey (eds), *Oxford Handbook of International Environmental Law* (OUP, 2007) 893.
Morris, Justin and Nicholas J Wheeler, 'The Security Council's Crisis of Legitimacy and the Use of Force' (2007) 44 *International Politics* 214.
Murphy, Sean D, 'The Relevance of Subsequent Agreement and Subsequent Practice for the Interpretation of Treaties' in Georg Nolte (ed), *Treaties and Subsequent Practice* (OUP, 2013) 82.
Nollkaemper, André, 'Compliance Control in International Environmental Law: Traversing the Limits of the National Legal Order' (2002) 13 *Yearbook of International Environmental Law*.
Nollkaemper, André, *National Courts and the International Rule of Law* (OUP, 2011).
Nollkaemper, André, 'International Adjudication of Global Public Goods: The Intersection of Substance and Procedure' (2012) 23 *European Journal of International Law* 769.
Nollkaemper, André and Gerrit Betlem, 'Giving Effect to Public International Law and European Community Law before Domestic Courts. A Comparative Analysis of the Practice of Consistent Interpretation' (2003) 14 *European Journal of International Law* 569.
Nolte, Georg, 'Subsequent Agreements and Subsequent Practice of States Outside of Judicial or Quasi-Judicial Proceedings. Third Report for the ILC Study Group on Treaties over Time' in Georg Nolte (ed), *Treaties and Subsequent Practice* (OUP, 2013) 307.
Nolte, Georg (ed), *Treaties and Subsequent Practice* (OUP, 2013).
Oberthür, Sebastian, Thomas Gehring, 'Reforming International Environmental Governance: An Institutionalist Critique of the Proposal for a World Environment Organisation' (2004) 4 *International Environmental Agreements: Politics, Law and Economics* 359.
Oberthür, Sebastian, and René Lefeber, 'Holding Countries to Account: The Kyoto Protocol's Compliance System Revisited after Four Years of Experience' (2010) 1 *Climate Law* 133.
Ott, Herman E, 'The Bonn Agreement to the Kyoto Protocol – Paving the Way for Ratification' (2001) 1 *International Environmental Agreements: Politics, Law and Economics* 469.
Palmer, Geoffrey, 'New Ways to Make International Environmental Law' (1992) 86 *American Journal of International Law* 259.
Pan, Eric J, 'Authoritative Interpretation of Agreements: Developing More Responsive International Administrative Regimes' (1997) 38 *Harvard International Law Journal* 503.
Pauwelyn, Joost, Ramses Wessel and Jan Wouters, 'When Structures Become Shackles: Stagnation and Dynamics in International Lawmaking' (2014) 25 *European Journal of International Law* 733.
Peters, Birgit and Johan K Schaffer, 'Introduction: The Turn to Authority Beyond States' (2014) 4 *Transnational Legal Theory* 315.
Pitkin, Hanna, 'Obligation and Consent-II' (1966) 60 *American Political Science Review* 39.
Putnam, Robert D, 'Diplomacy and Domestic Politics: The Logic of Two-Level Games' (1988) 42 *International Organization* 427.
Rae, Donald W, 'The Limits of Consensual Decision' (1975) 69 *The American Political Science Review* 1270.
Rajamani, Lavanya, 'Re-Negotiating Kyoto: A Review of the Sixth Conference of Parties to the Framework Convention on Climate Change' (2000) 21 *Colorado Journal of International Environmental Law and Policy* 201.
Rajamani, Lavanya, 'The Cancun Climate Agreements: Reading the Text, Subtext and Tea Leaves' (2011) 60 *International and Comparative Law Quarterly* 499.

Raustiala, Kal, 'The "Participatory Revolution" in International Environmental Law' (1997) 21 *Harvard Environmental Law Review* 537.

Raustiala, Kal, 'Compliance & Effectiveness in International Regulatory Cooperaton' (2000) 32 *Case Western Reserve Journal of International Law* 387.

Raustiala, Kal, *Reporting and Review Institutions in Ten Multilateral Environmental Agreements* (UNEP, 2001).

Redgwell, Catherine, 'National Implementation' in Daniel Bodansky, Jutta Brunnée and Ellen Hey (eds), *The Oxford Handbook of International Environmental Law* (OUP, 2007) 922.

Reeve, Rosalind, 'The Convention on International Trade in Endangered Species of Wild Fauna and Flora (CITES)' in Geir Ulfstein, Thilo Marauhn and Andreas Zimmerman (eds), *Making Treaties Work: Human Rights, Environment and Arms Control* (CUP, 2007) 134.

Reuter, Paul, 'Sécurité Des Engagements Internationaux' in *Le développement de l'ordre juridique international. Mélanges Ganshof van der Meersch* (Economica, 1995).

Röben, Volker, 'Institutional Developments under Modern International Environmental Law' (2000) 4 *Max Plank Yearbook of United Nations Law* 436.

Romano, Cesare P, 'International Dispute Settlement' in Daniel Bodansky, Jutta Brunnée and Ellen Hey (eds), *Oxford Handbook of International Environmental Law* (OUP, 2007) 1036.

Rosenau, James N, 'Governance, Order, and Change in World Politics' in James N Rosenau and Ernst-Otto Czempiel (eds), *Governance Without Government* (CUP, 1992) 1.

Sand, Peter H, 'Institution-Building Compliance with International Environmental Law: Perspectives' (1996) 56 *Zeitschrift fur auslandisches offentliches Recht und Volkerrecht* 774.

Sand, Peter H, 'Whither CITES? The Evolution of a Treaty Regime in the Borderland of Trade and Environment' (1997) 8 *European Journal of International Law* 29.

Sand, Peter H, 'The Evolution of International Environmental Law' in Daniel Bodansky, Jutta Brunnée and Ellen Hey (eds), *The Oxford Handbook of International Environmental Law* (OUP, 2007) 29.

Sand, Peter H, 'Das Washingtoner Artenschutzabkommen (WA)' (2016) 54 *Archiv des Völkerrechts* 561–589.

Sarooshi, Dan, *International Organizations and Their Exercise of Sovereign Powers* (OUP, 2007).

Schachter, Oscar, 'The Invisible College of International Lawyers' (1977) 72 *Northwestern University Law Review* 217.

Schachter, Oscar, 'The Nature and Process of Legal Development in International Society' in Ronald St J MacDonald and Douglas M Johnston (eds), *The Structure and Process of International Law* (Martinus Nijhoff Publishers, 1983) 745.

Scharpf, Fritz W, 'Problem-Solving Effectiveness and Democratic Accountability in the EU', *Max Planck Institut für Gesellschaftsforschung Working Paper* 2003/1.

Schauer, Frederick, *Playing by the Rules: A Philosophical Examination of Rule-Based Decision-Making* (Clarendon Press, 1991).

Schauer, Frederick, *Thinking Like a Lawyer: A New Introduction to Legal Reasoning* (Harvard University Press, 2009).

Schauer, Frederick, *The Force of Law* (Harvard University Press, 2014).

Schermers, Henry G, and Niels M Blokker, *International Institutional Law: Unity within Diversity* 3rd rev'd edn (Springer, 1995).

Schwarzenberger, Georg, 'Myths and Realities of Treaty Interpretation: Articles 27–29 of the Vienna Draft Convention on the Law of Treaties' (1968) 9 *Virginia Journal of International Law* 1.

Scott, Joanne, 'In Legal Limbo: Post-Legislative Guidance as a Challenge for European Administrative Law' (2011) 48 *Common Market Law Review* 329.

Shaffer, Gregory C, and Daniel Bodansky, 'Transnationalism, Unilateralism and International Law' (2012) 1 *Transnational Environmental Law* 31.

Shaffer, Gregory C and Mark A Pollack, 'Hard vs. Soft Law: Alternatives, Complements, and Antagonists in International Governance' (2010) 94 *Minnesota Law Review* 706.

Shany, Yuval, 'Assessing the Effectiveness of International Courts: A Goal-Based Approach' (2012) 106 *American Journal of International Law* 225.

Siebenhüner, Bernd, 'The Biodiversity Secretariat: Lean Shark in Troubled Water' in Frank Biermann and Bernd Siebenhüner (eds), *Managers of Global Change: the Influence of International Environmental Bureaucracies* (2009) 265.

Simma, Bruno, 'Consent: Strains in the Treaty System' in Ronald St J MacDonald and Douglas M Johnstone (eds), *The Structure and Process of International Law* (Martinus Nijhoff Publishers, 1986) 485.

Simma, Bruno, 'Miscellaneous Thoughts on Subsequent Agreements and Practice' in Georg Nolte (ed), *Treaties and Subsequent Practice* (OUP, 2013) 46.

Sloss, David, 'Domestic Application of Treaties' in Duncan B Hollis (ed), *The Oxford Guide to Treaties* (OUP, 2012) 367.

Somek, Alexander, 'The Concept of "Law" in Global Administrative Law: A Reply to Benedict Kingsbury' (2010) 20 *European Journal of International Law* 985.

Sommer, Julia, 'Environmental Law-Making by International Organisations' (1996) 56 *Zeitschrift für ausländisches öffentliches Recht und Volkerrecht* 628.

Spagnuolo, Francesca, 'Diversity and Pluralism in Earth System Governance: Contemplating the Role for Global Administrative Law' (2011) 70 *Ecological Economics* 1875.

Spencer, Martin E, 'Weber on Legitimate Norms and Authority' (1970) 21 *The British Journal of Sociology* 123.

Spiro, Peter J, 'Accounting for NGOs' (2002) 3 *Chicago Journal of International Law* 161.

Staal, Tim, 'Exercising or Evading International Public Authority? The Many Faces of Environmental Post-Treaty Rules' (2016) 7 *Goettingen Journal of International Law* 303.

Steffek, Jens, 'Discursive Legitimation in Environmental Governance' (2009) 11 *Forest Policy and Economics* 313.

Steffek, Jens, 'The Output Legitimacy of International Organizations and the Global Public Interest' (2015) 7 *International Theory* 263.

Steinberg, Richard H, 'In the Shadow of Law or Power? Consensus-Based Bargaining and Outcomes in the GATT/WTO' (2002) 56 *International Organization* 339.

Stevenson, Hayley, 'Representing Green Radicalism: The Limits of State-Based Representation in Global Climate Governance' (2013) 40 *Review of International Studies* 177.

Stillman, Peter G, 'The Concept of Legitimacy' (1974) 7 *Polity* 32.

Sutter, Cristoph and Juan Carlos Parreño, 'Does the Current Clean Development Mechanism (CDM) Deliver Its Sustainable Development Claim? An Analysis of Officially Registered CDM Projects' (2007) 84 *Climatic Change* 75.

Széll, Patrick, 'The Development of Multilateral Mechanisms for Monitoring Compliance' in Winfried Lang (ed), *Sustainable Development and International Law* (Graham & Trotman, 1995).

Széll, Patrick, 'Decision Making under Multilateral Environmental Agreements' (1996) 26 *Environmental Policy and Law* 210.

Tallberg, Jonas, 'The Power of the Chair: Formal Leadership in International Cooperation' (2010) 54 *International Studies Quarterly* 241.

Thomas, Christopher A, 'The Uses and Abuses of Legitimacy in International Law' (2014) 34 *Oxford Journal of Legal Studies* 729.

Timoshenko, Alexandre S, 'Protection of Wetlands in International Law', *Legal Aspects of the Conservation of Wetlands* (IUCN, 1991).

Tomuschat, Christian, 'International Law: Ensuring the Survival of Mankind on the Eve of a New Century: General Course on Public International Law' (2001) 281 *Receuil des Cours* 13.

Treves, Tulio, 'Aspects of Legitimacy of Decisions of International Courts and Tribunals' in Rüdiger Wolfrum and Volker Röben (eds), *Legitimacy in International Law* (Springer, 2010) 169.

Ulfstein, Geir, 'Reweaving the Fabric of International Law? Patterns of Consent in Environmental Framework Agreements, Comment by Geir Ulfstein' in Rudiger Wolfrum and Volker Roben (eds), *Developments of International Law in Treaty Making* (Springer, 2005) 145.

Ulfstein, Geir, 'Treaty Bodies' in Daniel Bodansky, Jutta Brunnée and Ellen Hey (eds), *The Oxford Handbook of International Environmental Law* (OUP, 2007) 877.

Ulfstein, Geir, 'Treaty Bodies and Regimes' in Duncan B Hollis (ed), *The Oxford Guide to Treaties* (2012) 428.
Van Alstine, Michael P, 'The Role of Domestic Courts in Treaty Enforcement: Summary and Conclusion' in David Sloss (ed), *The Role of Domestic Courts in Treaty Enforcement* (CUP, 2009) 555.
Vázquez, Carlos M, 'The Four Doctrines of Self-Executing Treaties' (1995) 89 *American Journal of International Law* 695.
Ulfstein, Geir, 'Less Than Zero' (2008) 102 *American Journal of International Law* 529.
Venzke, Ingo, *How Interpretation Makes International Law: On Semantic Change and Normative Twists* (OUP, 2012).
Venzke, Ingo, 'Between Power and Persuasion: On International Institutions' Authority in Making Law' (2013) 14 *Transnational Legal Theory* 382.
Verschuuren, Jonathan, 'Ramsar Soft Law Is Not Soft at All – Discussion of the 2007 Decision by the Netherlands Crown on the Lac Ramsar Site on the Island of Bonaire [Translation of a Case Law Annotation in Dutch]' (2008) 35 *Milieu en Recht* 28.
Victor, David G, 'The Use and Effectiveness of Nonbinding Instruments in the Management of Complex International Environmental Problems' (1997) 91 *Proceedings of the Annual Meeting of the American Society of International Law* 241.
Victor, David G, Kal Raustiala and Eugene B Skolnikoff (eds), *The Implementation and Effectiveness of International Environmental Commitments: Theory and Practice* (MIT Press, 1998).
Vihma, Anto, 'A Climate of Consensus: The UNFCCC Faces Challenges of Legitimacy and Effectiveness' *Finnish Institute of International Affairs Briefing Paper* 75 (March 2011).
Villiger, Mark E, 'The 1969 Vienna Convention on the Law of Treaties – 40 Years After' (2009) 344 *Recueil des Cours* 1.
Virally, Michel, 'Review Essay: Good Faith in Public International Law (Reviewing E Zoller, Good Faith in Public Internatonal Law)' (1983) 77 *American Journal of International Law* 130.
Vollenweider, Jürg, 'The Effectiveness of International Environmental Agreements' (2012) 13 *International Environmental Agreements: Politics, Law and Economics* 343.
Von Bernstorff, Jochen, 'Procedures of Decision-Making and the Role of Law in International Organizations' (2008) 9 *German Law Journal* 1939.
Von Bogdandy, Armin, 'General Principles of International Public Authority: Sketching a Research Field' (2008) 9 *German Law Journal* 1909.
Von Bogdandy, Armin, Philip Dann and Matthias Goldmann, 'Developing the Publicness of Public International Law: Towards a Legal Framework for Global Governance Activities' in Armin Von Bogdandy et al (eds), *The Exercise of Public Authority by International Institutions, Advancing International Institutional Law* (Springer, 2010) 3.
Von Bogdandy, Armin and Matthias Goldmann, 'The Exercise of International Public Authority through National Policy Assessment: The OECD's PISA Policy as a Paradigm for a New International Standard Instrument' (2008) 5 *International Organizations Law Review* 241.
Von Bogdandy, Armin and Ingo Venzke, 'In Whose Name? An Investigation of International Courts' Public Authority and Its Democratic Justification' (2012) 23 *European Journal of International Law* 7.
Weber, Max, *Economy and Society* (University of California Press, 1978).
Weber, Max, *The Theory of Economic and Social Organization* tr AM Henderson and Talcott Parsons (The Free Press of Glencoe, 1964).
Weil, Prosper, 'Towards Relative Normativity in International Law?' (1983) 77 *American Journal of International Law* 413.
Werksman, Jacob, 'Consolidating Governance of the Global Commons: Insights from the Global Environmental Facility' (1995) 6 *Yearbook of International Environmental Law* 27.
Werksman, Jacob, 'The Conference of the Parties to Environmental Treaties' in Jacob Werksman (ed), *Greening International Institutions* (Earthscan, 1996) 55.
Wiersema, Annecoos, 'The New International Law-Makers? Conferences of the Parties to Multilateral Environmental Agreements' (2009) 31 *Michigan Journal of International Law* 231.

Wijnstekers, Willem, *The Evolution of CITES* 9th edn (International Council for Game and Wildlife Conservation, 2011).

Wolfrum, Rüdiger, 'Means of Ensuring Compliance with and Enforcement of International Environmental Law' (1998) 272 *Recueil des Cours* 9.

Woods, Ngaire, 'Good Governance in International Organizations' (1999) 5 *Global Governance* 39.

Zemanek, Karl, 'Majority Rule and Consensus Technique in Law-Making Diplomacy' in Ronald St J MacDonald and Douglas M Johnston (eds), *The Structure and Process of International Law* (Martinus Nijhoff Publishers, 1986) 858.

Zürn, Michael, 'From Rule to Authority – Why We Enter a Phase of Reflexive Legitimacy' (Paper distributed for a presentation at the University of Amsterdam, 17 March 2014, on file with author).

Zürn, Michael and Matthew Stephen, 'The View of Old and New Powers on the Legitimacy of International Institutions' (2010) 30 *Politics* 91.

Zürn, Michael, Martin Binder and Matthias Ecker-Ehrhardt, 'International Authority and Its Politicization' (2012) 4 *International Theory* 69.

INDEX

accountability:
global administrative law, 221–22
legitimacy of PTRs, 231
accounting modalities, 105, 108, 218, 270
authority of PTRs, 109–10, 110–11, 112
compliance, 109–12, 129–30
EU law, 110–11
input legitimacy, 242
national law of Netherlands, 110–11
specificity of language, 175–76
administrative law, *see* **global administrative law**
adoption of PTRs:
adoption by acclamation, 73
adoption by consensus, 52–55, 73, 230
state consent to international treaties, 232–33
see also consensual decision-making
allowing adoption, 217
not prohibiting adoption, 218
social legitimacy, 191
amendments of treaties, PTRs as, 123
Animal and Plant Health Inspection Services (APHIS) (USA):
shipments of mahogany, 1–3, 91, 203
annexes, *see* **convention-annex approach to amendment of MEAs**
authority defined:
development of environmental treaty norms, 9
freedom, effect on, 9–10
reference point, as a, 8–9
see also delegated authority of PTRs; interpretive authority of PTRs; vulnerability of authority
autonomy:
decision-making processes, 31–32, 35–36
lack of COP/MOP autonomy, 31–32, 120–21

behaviour change, 104–5
binding decisions of international organisations, PTRs as, 6, 43, 124
Born Free USA v Norton:
permissive authority, 180, 182
primarily commercial purposes resolution, 87–88, 111–12, 160, 203, 217
reasonableness, 203

commodification of international law, 213
authority of PTRs, 214–15
meaning in PTR context, 213–14
compliance with PTRs, 17–18, 129, 113–14
authority and compliance compared, 8–9
CITES resolution on *Compliance and Enforcement*, 84 85
'reason to believe', 88
compliance bodies, 9, 38, 63, 183
CITES resolution on *Compliance and Enforcement*, 84–85, 88
compliance control, 60, 250–51
Kyoto Protocol Compliance Committee, Enforcement Branch, 58–59, 62, 106, 212, 250–51
Montreal Protocol Implementing Committee, 97, 99–100
mandatorily phrased PTRs, 178–79
national compliance of specific areas/industries, 63–64
national courts compared, 198, 215–16
procedural standards, 222
recommendatory PTRs, 179
Croatia, 58–59, 192
duty to state reasons, 224–25
flexibility mechanisms, 174
input legitimacy, 250–52
internal normative order, 189–90, 212, 214–15
international dispute settlement procedures, 63
Kyoto Protocol Compliance Committee, Enforcement Branch, 58–59, 62, 106, 212, 250–51
Accounting Modalities, 106, 108, 109–10
Croatia, 58–59, 192
Removal Units, 106, 108
Montreal Protocol Implementing Committee, 97
Exemption decisions, 99–100
Montreal Non-Compliance Procedure, 99

national courts, 216–20, 263–64
compliance bodies compared, 198, 215–16
procedural standards, 222
national legal orders, 133
output legitimacy, 255
behavioural effectiveness, 254
legal or compliance effectiveness, 253–54
post-treaty decisions, 44
procedural PTRs, 18–19, 129
CITES, 130–31
Kyoto Protocol, 129–30, 132
Montreal Protocol, 132–33
Ramsar Convention, 131–32
Rules of Procedure, 191
social pressures, 187–88
see also expert review
Conferences of the Parties (COPs):
attendees, 30
competences of attendees, 30–31
autonomy, 35–36
intentions and practice, 32–34
law of international organisations, 34–35
origins, 30
'plenary treaty meetings', meaning of, 35
see also individual Multilateral Environmental Agreements; post-treaty instruments
consensual decision-making, 4, 35–36
adoption of Rules of Procedure:
CITES, 233–34, 235–36
Kyoto Protocol, 233–34
Montreal Protocol, 235, 235–36
Ramsar Convention, 233, 235–36
assessing legitimacy, 236–38
sovereign equality and inclusiveness, 238, 239–40
defining consensus, 236
Kyoto Protocol, 236
formal requirements, 237–38
legal requirements for consensus, 236–38
disproportionate power of minorities, concerns regarding:
information trade-offs, 241
non-transparency, 241
package deals, 240–41
power of the chairperson, 241–42
enabling clauses of Multilateral Environmental Agreements, 233
Kyoto Protocol decisions, 242–44
output legitimacy, 264–66
social pressures, 194
violations and mitigation of violations:
review procedures, introduction of, 273
standard instruments, introduction of, 272–73, 274
see also enabling clauses; input legitimacy
consent, *see* **consensual decision-making**
context and relevance of study, 11–14
choice of examples, 16–18
Convention on International trade in Endangered Species 1973 (CITES):
authority, 80–82
Imports of Elephants cases, 87–88
Kyoto/Montreal and Ramsar/ CITES compared, 111–14
primarily commercial purposes resolution, 85–88
reason to believe paragraph, 88–94
resolutions, 82–85
shipments of mahogany cases, 90–94
Whaling case, 86–87
compliance:
CITES resolution on *Compliance and Enforcement*, 84–85
'reason to believe', 88
consensual decision-making:
adoption of Rules of Procedure, 233–34, 235–36
convention-annex approach to amendment of MEAs, 25–26
COP, 3, 82
development of Convention:
convention-annex approach, 25–26
external PTRs, 82–83
mandatory quality and specificity, 171–73
origins, 80–81
output legitimacy, 199–200, 252–53
CITES COP *Listing Criteria*, 257–58
CITES *Reason to Believe* paragraph, 259
Permits and Certificates resolution, 4, 83–85
primarily commercial purposes resolution, 83, 85
Born Free USA v Norton, 87–88
commercial activities defined, 85–86
non-commercial activities distinguished, 86
Whaling case, 86–87
Imports of Elephants case, 87
procedural PTRs, 130–31
purpose, 81–82
'reason to believe' paragraph, 3, 88
compliance and enforcement, 88
exporting authorities, 88

importing authorities, 89
interpretation, as, 88–90
modification, as, 89
shipments of mahogany, 90–94
shipments of mahogany, 2
reason to believe paragraph, 90–94
varied mandatory quality and specificity of PTRs, 171–72
external resolutions, 173
internal resolutions, 172–73
wording of PTRs, 171–73

Convention on Wetlands of International Importance especially as Waterfowl Habitat 1971 (Ramsar Convention)
adoption of resolutions by acclamation, 73
adoption of resolutions by consensus, 73
authority:
designation conditions, 75–76
Greentree case, 78–80
identification and designation of wetlands of international importance, 68–73
identification criteria, 73–75
Kyoto/Montreal and Ramsar/ CITES compared, 111–14
Secretariat's role, 76–78
consensual decision-making:
adoption of Rules of Procedure, 233, 235–36
COP, 4, 70
designation conditions:
boundary descriptions, 75–76
external PTRs, 70
Greentree case, 78–80
identification criteria, 73–74
authority of identification criteria, 74
implicit enabling clauses, 38, 69–70
internal PTRs, 70
mandatory quality and specificity, 169–71
origins, 68–69
output legitimacy:
Wise Use, 261–62
Listing Criteria and Designation Conditions, 70–71
designation of wetlands, 71
international significance of wetlands, 71–73
reform, 76–77
procedural PTRs, 131–32
Secretariat's role, 77–78
varied mandatory quality and specificity of PTRs, 169–71
wetlands:
designation conditions, 75–76
identification criteria, 73–75
wording of PTRs, 169–71

convention-annex approach to amendment of MEAs:
CITES, 25–26
other MEAs, 26–27

critical-use criteria, 270
adoption by consensus, 235
authority of the criteria, 98–99
Montreal Non-Compliance Procedure, 99–100
US political pressure, 99
critical use defined, 98
exemptions, 51
bindingness in national courts, 101
exemptions for methyl bromide, 45, 95–98
explicit enabling clause, 97
country-by-country exemptions, 97–98

customary law, as, 124, 140–41
'commercial purposes', 86–87

decision-making, *see* **consensual decision-making**

degree of authority, 6, 8–9, 46, 56, 64, 165, 270–71
CITES, 171–73
delegation of authority, 128, 139, 142
gap-filling agreements, 102
high degrees of authority, 112, 228–29
internal normative orders, 64–65
international legal order, 65–66
Kyoto Protocol, 173–76
Montreal Protocol, 176–77
Ramsar Convention, 169–71
measuring legitimacy, 227–29
high degrees of authority, 228–29
low degrees of authority, 229
national legal orders, 66, 159–64

delegated authority of PTRs, 119–22, 138–39, 182–83
customary law, 124–25
decisions of international organisations, 124
internal normative orders of MEAs:
compliance with PTRs, 129–32
delegation and delegated acts compared, 126–29
international delegation theory, 120
national legal orders, 136–37
soft law, 124–25

treaties/treaty amendments, 122–24
see also enabling clauses
delegation, 6, 119
delegated acts compared, 126–29
enabling clauses, 126–27
international delegation theory, 120
see also delegated authority of PTRs
democratic legitimacy and effectiveness, 7–8, 228
direct applicability of PTRs:
monist states, 137–38
refusal of direct applicability, 138
discretion:
administrative agencies, 229
governmental discretion, 269–70
commodification of international rules, 213–16
national implementation of PTRs, 211, 216–20
national legal orders, 216–20
standard instruments to counterbalance, 269–70
vulnerability of PTRs, 219–20
legal certainty, impact on, 225–26, 270
national courts, 115
national legal orders, 216–20
compliance with PTRs, 133
dispute settlement, *see* **international dispute settlement**
doctrine of interpretation:
international legal order, 142–59
limited value, 184
national legal orders, 159–64
doctrine of sources, 119
limited value, 184
sources of authority of PTRs, 122–23
social legitimacy of PTRs, 6–7
domestic courts, *see* **national courts**
domestic legal orders, *see* **national legal orders**
duty to state the law and to state reasons, 224–25

emissions trading, 37–38, 45, 47, 103–11
authority of PTRs, 110–11
compliance procedures, 129–30
enabling clauses, 123–24, 259
EU law, 135
flexibility mechanism, 28, 42–43
see also Kyoto Protocol
enabling clauses, *see* **explicit enabling clauses; implicit enabling clauses**
Enforcement Branch (Kyoto Protocol Compliance Committee), 58–59, 65, 106, 109–10, 129–30, 132, 189, 192, 195, 224, 236, 251
environmental soft law, 3–4
PTRs as, 124–25, 196–97, 214–15
EU law:
incorporating PTRs, 14, 110–11, 114
executive branch's role:
compliance control, 250–51
executive dominance, 249–50
expert review, 250–51
making rules, 249–50
national balance of powers, 249
national courts deferential nature, 252
national parliaments' subsidiarity, 251–52
expert review, 109, 250–51
explicit enabling clauses, 17, 19, 36–37, 44, 123–24
critical-use exemptions, 96, 97–98, 112
granting authority to PTRs, 120
obligations of conduct, 127–28
PTRs supplementing/gap-filling, 49, 51–52, 112–13
subsequent agreements, 150–51
see also delegation
external PTRs, 23–24, 45
internal PTRs distinguished, 45–46
supplemental or gap-filling purpose, 51–52

Fish and Wildlife Services (FWS) (USA), 1, 87–88, 91, 115, 135, 161–62, 182, 217
flexibility mechanisms, 14, 28, 42–43, 104, 109–10, 127–28, 195
Kyoto Protocol *Flexibility Mechanisms* Decisions, 128, 150, 168–69, 173–76
framework-protocol approach to amendment of MEAs:
UNFCCC, 27–28
fundamental rights and procedural principles:
duty to state the law and to state reasons, 224–25
global administrative law, 221–22
infringement of, 226
principle of legal certainty, 225–26
principle of promulgation, 223–24

global administrative law, 221
duty to state the law and to state reasons, 224–25
fundamental procedural principles, 221–22

principle of legal certainty, 225–26
principle of promulgation, 223–24
global interests, 231
consensual processes impact on, 245–46
***Greentree* case,** 218
designation of wetlands, 78–80
lack of authority of PTR, 78, 111
language, 167–68
principle of promulgation, 223
PTRs as subsequent agreements, 160, 164
wording and terminology, impact of, 167–68

Her Majesty's Commissioners of Customs and Excise (Commissioners) (UK), 1–2

implementation and procedural rights, 7, 184–87
implicit enabling clauses, 17, 19, 37–39, 41, 46, 259
CITES, 38, 82
interpretive PTRs, 49
modifying PTRs distinguished, 50–51
Kyoto Protocol, 38, 106
post-treaty rules, 44
Ramsar Convention, 38, 69–70, 72, 169–70
see also delegation
***Imports of Elephants* cases:**
primarily commercial purposes resolution, 87–88, 111–12, 182, 202
input legitimacy:
cosmopolitan perspective, 231
democratic legitimacy, 228
ICJ, 197–200
international legal order, 198–99
justification for application of PTRs, 205–6
Kyoto Protocol decisions, 242–43
national legal orders, 205–6
national populations' perspective, 231
role of the executive, 249–52
social legitimacy, 198–99
state centric perspective, 230
state consent to international treaties, 232–33
see also consensual decision-making
Institute of Environmental and Renewable Sources (IBAMA) (Brazil), 1–3, 90, 93–94
interests:
global interests, 227–28, 231
consensus and input legitimacy, 245–46
national interests, 231
urgent national interests, 45, 70, 71–72, 169
state-specific interests, 231, 238
global interests compared, 245
internal normative orders, 61–62
authority of PTRs, 64–65, 188–90
compliance with PTRs, 189–90, 212, 214–15
degree of authority, 64–65
delegated authority of PTRs
internal normative orders of MEAs, 126–32
international environment regimes as, 57–58
examples, 58–60
rules of recognition, 58
measuring legitimacy, 228–29
social legitimacy, 188–95
epistemic authority of PTRs, 192–93
internal and external PTRs compared, 192
legitimate nature of process of adoption, 191
shared intention of bindingness of PTRs, 190–91
threats to social legitimacy, 193–95
social pressures:
legitimacy of PTRs, 194–95
internal PTRs, 23–24, 45
external PTRs distinguished, 45–46
International Court of Justice (ICJ), 144–46
challenges to PTRs, 196–97, 200
consensual process:
Lac Sorogon case, 247–48
Natural Resources Defence Council case, 248
Whaling case, 205, 246–47, 271
Costa Rica v Nicaragua, 157
justifications for applying PTRs, 197–200
Pulp Mills case, 151–52, 195–96
Whaling case, 147–48, 179, 195–96, 246–47
international dispute settlement, 62, 63
challenges to PTRs, 196–97, 200
international environmental regimes, 11–12, 193
authority, 57–61
internal normative orders, as, 57–58
examples, 58–60
rules of recognition, 58
legal orders, as, 60–61
multilateral environmental agreements, 24–25
convention-annex technique, 25–27
framework-protocol technique, 27–28
Montreal Protocol adjustment technique, 28–30

relationship between MEAs and PTRs, 46
clarification, PTRs as, 46–47
implementing decision, PTRs as, 47–48
regulatory acts, PTRs as, 48–52
international legal order, 62–63
authority of PTRs, 65–66
interpretive agreements, PTRs as:
subsequent agreements, 142–53
'taking into account', 153–59
social legitimacy:
ICJ application of PTRs, 197–200
input legitimacy, 198–99
international dispute settlement, 196–97
legal obligations of states, 195–96
output legitimacy, 199–200
subsequent agreements, PTRs as, 142–53
'agreement' defined, 144
'between the parties', 144–49
interpretation of treaties and application of provisions, 149–53
qualifying conditions, 143–44
subsequent agreement defined, 143
see also subsequent agreements
'taking into account':
ambiguity, 153–54
duty to cooperate, 154–55
'give due regard' compared, 155–56
good faith, 158–59
hierarchical interpretation, 157–58
legally binding compared, 156
meaning of legal obligation to take into account, 156–57
international organisations:
defined, 31–32
legal personality, 31–32
interpretation doctrine, *see* **doctrine of interpretation**
interpretive authority of PTRs, 182–83
implicit enabling clauses, 49
modifying PTRs distinguished, 50–51
international legal orders:
subsequent agreements, 142–53
'taking into account', 153–59
limitations to authority from wording, 178
Born Free case, 182
Lac Sorobon case, 181
mandatorily phrased PTRs, 178–79
national courts, 180
Orka case, 182
recommendatory wording, 179–80
mandatory quality and specificity:
CITES, 171–73
comparisons, 177–78
Kyoto Protocol, 173–76
mandatory quality, 166, 168
Montreal Protocol, 176–77
Ramsar Convention, 169–71
specificity, 166–67, 168–69
variations, 168–69
national legal orders, 159–60
legal obligation to accept PTRs, 163–64
not accepting PTRs as interpretive agreements, 161–62
relevance of PTRs as interpretive agreements, 162–64
subsequent practice, 160
taking into account, 160
subsequent agreements, PTRs as, 142–53
'agreement' defined, 144
'between the parties', 144–49
interpretation of treaties and application of provisions, 149–53
qualifying conditions, 143–44
subsequent agreement defined, 143
see also subsequent agreements
'taking into account', 160
ambiguity, 153–54
duty to cooperate, 154–55
'give due regard' compared, 155–56
good faith, 158–59
hierarchical interpretation, 157–58
legally binding compared, 156
meaning of legal obligation to take into account, 156–57
wording and terminology, impact of, 164–66
mandatory quality, 166, 168
specificity, 166–67, 168–69
interpretive PTRs, 49
modifying PTRs distinguished, 50–51

justification for application of PTRs, 202
international legal order:
ICJ's justifications, 197–200
input legitimacy, 198–99
output legitimacy, 199–200
Whaling case, 198, 200
Pulp Mills case, 199–200
national legal orders:
Castlewood Products case, 203
consistency of practice arguments, 206–7
FRC Intern case, 203–4, 206
input legitimacy arguments, 205–6
Lac Sorobon case, 205

National Resources Defence Council case, 205–6
object and purpose of MEAs, 204–5
reasonableness, 203–4
social pressures, 194–95

Kyoto Protocol to the United Nations Framework Convention on Climate Change 1998 (Kyoto Protocol):
authority of PTRs, 103–5, 106–7
Accounting Modalities decision, 105, 108, 109–10
emissions trading COP/MOP, 110–11
Kyoto/Montreal and Ramsar/CITES compared, 111–14
Land Use, Land-Use Change and Forestry decisions, 105, 107–8, 109–10
consensual decision-making:
adoption of Rules of Procedure, 233–34
defining consensus, 236
Kyoto Protocol decisions, 242–44
COP/MOP, 4
degree of authority, 173–76
Enforcement Branch (Kyoto Protocol Compliance Committee), 58–59, 62, 65, 106, 109–10, 129–30, 212, 250–51
Flexibility Mechanisms Decisions, 128, 150, 168–69, 173–76
implicit enabling clauses, 38, 106
input legitimacy, 242–43
mandatory quality and specificity of PTRs, 173–76
procedural PTRs, 129–30, 132
wording of PTRs, 173–76

***Land Use, Land-Use Change and Forestry* decisions,** 18, 105–9, 109–10
external PTRs, 45, 270
gap-filling agreements, 150
input legitimacy, 242
consensual decision-making, 243
modifying character, 113
output legitimacy, 259
wording, 112, 127–28, 175–76
see also accounting modalities
language, 11
CITES, 171–73, 182
CITES *Listing Criteria*, 168
enabling clauses, 123, 126–27
importance of language, 165–66
Kyoto Protocol, 112, 175–76
mandatory language, 17, 32, 43, 77, 111, 172
Kyoto Protocol, 112, 175–76
Montreal Protocol, 112, 176–77, 218
Montreal Protocol, 112, 176–77, 218
Ramsar Convention, 169–71, 203
recommendatory language, 111
'take into account', 153–54
treaty language, 161
'ordinary language' of treaty provisions, 219
PTRs contradicting treaty language, 53, 60, 89
see also explicit enabling clauses; implicit enabling clauses; wording of PTRs
last resort clauses, 234–35
legal certainty principle, 7, 225–26, 272
legal obligations of parties:
international legal orders, 142–59
legally binding instruments distinguished, 141
national legal orders, 159–64
social legitimacy, 186–87
legal personality, 31–32, 34, 124
legally binding instruments:
instruments affecting legal obligations distinguished, 141
legitimacy beliefs, *see* **implementation and procedural rights**
legitimacy deficits, *see* **democratic legitimacy and effectiveness**
legitimate expectations, 222
legitimation, 232–33, 247

mahogany, *see* **shipments of mahogany**
majority rule, 145–46, 149, 195, 240
Montreal Protocol Adjustment technique, 28–30
Rules of Procedure, 34, 198, 235–36
when consensus fails, 34–36, 272–73
management authorities:
CITES, 2–3, 81–82, 82–83, 223, 274–75
'primarily commercial purposes' resolution, 85
decision-making, 173
One Etched Tusk case, 161–62
shipments of mahogany, 2–3, 90–94
measuring legitimacy, 227–29
high degrees of authority, 228–29
internal normative orders, 228–29
international legal order, 228–29
low degrees of authority, 229
national legal orders, 228–29
social legitimacy, 229

Meetings of the Parties (MOPs):
attendees, 30
competences of attendees, 30–31
autonomy, 35–36
intentions and practice, 32–34
law of international organisations, 34–35
nature of MOPs, 31
origins, 30
'plenary treaty meetings', meaning of, 35
see also individual Multilateral Environmental Agreements; post-treaty instruments
methyl bromide, 17, 37
consensus decision-making, 248
critical use criteria for methyl bromide, 48, 95–96, 98–100, 166–67
exemption decisions, 100–3, 113
methyl bromide resolutions, 97–98
Montreal Protocol:
Critical-use exemptions for methyl bromide, 45, 47, 51, 61, 95–97, 176–77, 260
specificity, 166–67
National Resources Defense Council case, 100–3
modifying PTRs, 49
interpretive PTRs distinguished, 50–51
substantive limits, 52–53
transboundary movement of hazardous material, 53
validity of PTRs, 54–55
whaling, 53–54
monist states:
direct applicability of PTRs, 137–38
domestic validity, 136–37
legally binding nature of PTRs, 133–34
Montreal Protocol adjustment technique, 28–30
Montreal Protocol Implementing Committee, 97, 113
Exemption decisions, 99–100
Montreal Non-Compliance Procedure, 99
Montreal Non-Compliance Procedure, 65, 99, 129
Montreal Protocol on Substances that Deplete the Ozone Layer 1987 (Montreal Protocol):
authority, 95
critical use criteria for methyl bromide, 95–96, 98–100
exemption decisions, 100–3
Kyoto/Montreal and Ramsar/ CITES compared, 111–14
methyl bromide resolutions, 97–98
consensual decision-making, 4, 35–36
adoption of Rules of Procedure, 235, 235–36
degree of authority, 176–77
mandatory language, 112, 176–77, 218
mandatory quality and specificity, 176–77
methyl bromide:
Critical-use exemptions for methyl bromide, 45, 47, 51, 61, 95–97, 176–77, 260
specificity, 166–67
Montreal Protocol adjustment technique, 28–30
MOP, 4
procedural PTRs, 132–33
varied mandatory quality and specificity of PTRs, 176–77
Multilateral Environmental Agreements (MEAs):
amendment of MEAs:
substantive limits of PTRs, 52–55
authority of MEAs, 56
concept, 24–25
COPs, COP/MOPs and MOPs, 30–36
developing MEAs, 25
convention-annex technique, 25–27
framework-protocol technique, 27–28
Montreal Protocol adjustment technique, 28–30
enabling clauses, 4
explicit enabling clauses, 36–37
implicit enabling clauses, 37–39
plenary treaty meetings, 30–36
explicit enabling clauses, 36–37
implicit enabling clauses, 37–39
relationship with PTRs:
clarifying role of PTRs, 46–47
implementing role of PTRs, 47–48
regulatory acts, PTRs as, 48–52
see also post-treaty rules explained

national courts, *see* **national legal orders**
national legal orders, 63–64
adoption of PTRs:
allowing adoption, 217
not prohibiting adoption, 218
application of PTRs by national courts, 67, 201–2
justification for application, 202–7
authority of PTRs, 66, 66, 111–12, 114–15
application of PTRs by national courts, 67, 201–7
interpretive authority of PTRs, 159–64

legal reasoning, 66
practice of courts, 66–67
courts' deference to executive branches of government, 252
effectiveness of PTRs, 263–64
interpretive authority of PTRs, 159–60, 180
legal obligation to accept PTRs, 163–64
not accepting PTRs as interpretive agreements, 161–62
relevance of PTRs as interpretive agreements, 162–64
subsequent practice, 160
taking into account, 160
justification for application of PTRs, 202
Castlewood Products case, 203
consistency of practice arguments, 206–7
FRC Intern case, 203–4, 206
input legitimacy arguments, 205–6
Lac Sorobon case, 205
National Resources Defence Council case, 205–6
object and purpose of MEAs, 204–5
reasonableness, 203–4
legally binding nature of PTRs, 133–34
reference to MEAs ad PTRs, 135–36
transposition of MEAs and PTRs, 134–35
limitations to authority from wording, 180
monist states:
direct applicability, 137–38
domestic validity, 136–37
see also monist states
national implementation of MEAs, 63, 134
legal obligations of parties, 159–64
PTRs as interpretive agreements, 159–64
social legitimacy, 201–7
***National Resources Defense Council* case,** 112, 114–15, 136–37, 150
balance of national powers, 249
exemption decisions, 100–2, 205–6, 218
legitimacy of decisions, 102–3
interpretive agreements, PTRs as, 150, 161
normative legitimacy, 185, 196, 227–30, 266–68, 266–68
defining what constitutes legitimate governance, 227–28
input legitimacy, 230–31
adoption of PTRs by consensus, 233–36
consensual decision-making and assessing legitimacy, 236–42
consensus and global interests, 245–46
courts' misunderstanding of consensual process, 246–48
executive branch dominance, 249–52
individual state consent, 232–33
Kyoto Protocol COP/MOP decisions, 242–44
meaning, 227
output legitimacy, 252–53
antagonistic PTRs, 258–63
behavioural effectiveness, 254
complementary PTRs, 257–58
consensus process, 264–66
legal/compliance effectiveness, 253–54
national courts and effectiveness of PTRs, 263–64
problem-solving effectiveness, 254–57
normative orders and their relevance for international environmental law
internal normative orders, *see* internal normative orders
international legal orders, *see* international legal orders
national legal orders, *see* national legal orders

open-ended enabling clauses, *see* **implicit enabling clauses**
output legitimacy, 199–200, 252–53
assessing effectiveness, 253
behavioural effectiveness, 254
legal/compliance effectiveness, 253–54
problem-solving effectiveness, 254–56
CITES COP *Listing Criteria*, 257–58
CITES *Reason to Believe* paragraph, 259
consensual decision-making, 264–66
content of PTRs, 256–57
LULUCF case, 259–60
'marginal' PTRs, 259
Marrakesh Accords, 260–61
Montreal MOP *Critical Use Criteria and Exemptions*, 259
'parochial' PTRs, 259
Ramsar *Wise Use*, 261–62
role of PTRs, 256
'softening' PTRs, 259–60

package deals, 195
consensual decisions, 240–41, 246
Paris Agreement on Climate Change, 4, 14, 41, 103, 229
***Permits and Certificates* resolution (CITES),** 3, 4, 18–19, 81–82, 83–85, 223

plenary treaty meetings, 4, 30–36
explicit enabling clauses, 36–37
implicit enabling clauses, 37–39
see also Conference of the Parties; Meetings of the Parties
post-treaty decisions, 44, 270–71
post-treaty instruments, 270–71
commonalities, 39–40
developing standard instruments, 272–73
function, 42–43
input legitimacy conditions, 271
output legitimacy conditions, 271–72
terminology, 40–44
validity/legality conditions, 271
see also Conferences of the Parties; Meetings of the Parties
***primarily commercial purposes* resolution,** 38, 82–83, 85, 163, 168–69, 173
Born Free USA v Norton, 87–88, 111–12
commercial activities defined, 85–86
Imports of Elephants cases, 87–88
non-commercial activities distinguished, 86
recommendatory nature, 182
Whaling case, 86–87
promulgation principle, 222, 223–24, 226

Ramsar Convention, *see* **Convention on Wetlands of International Importance especially as Waterfowl Habitat**
regulatory acts, PTRs as, 48–49
PTRs as modification, 49
relationship between PTRs and MEAs:
PTRs as clarification of MEAs, 46–47
PTRs as implementing aids to MEAs, 47–48
relative legal normativity, 140
review procedures:
expert reviews, 250–51
mitigation of violations of consensual process, 273
procedural PTRs, 129

shipments of mahogany:
Brazil, from, 2–3
Castlewood Products case, 1, 91, 92–94, 115, 217, 264, 274–75
CITES, 2–3
Permits and Certificates resolution, 3, 4, 18–19
Greenpeace case, 1, 91–93, 94, 115, 204, 274–75
reason to believe paragraph, 88, 90–94, 115, 274–75
United Kingdom, to, 1, 90–94
United States, to, 1, 90–94
social legitimacy, 186–86, 207
authority's relationship with, 184–88, 211–13, 227–30
consequences of authority associated with social legitimacy, 211–13
criteria, 6–7
internal normative orders, 188–93
social pressures, 194–95
international legal order, 195–96
ICJ application of PTRs, 197–200
international dispute settlement, 196–97
national legal orders:
domestic dispute settlement, 201–2
effectiveness criteria, 204–5
(in)consistency, 206–7
input legitimacy, 205–6
national courts' applications of PTRs, 202–7
reasonableness criteria, 203–4
soft law, 3–5, 124–25, 214–15
sources doctrine, *see* **doctrine of sources**
standard instruments, 39–40, 269–73
state-specific interests, 231, 238
subsequent agreements, PTRs as, 6, 142–53
'agreement' defined, 144
'between the parties', 144–45
ICJ jurisprudence, 144
non-consensual PTRs, 145–49
Whaling case, 146–49
explicit enabling clauses, PTRs based on, 150
gap-filling/supplementing PTRs, 149–50
interpretation of treaties and application of provisions, 149–53
modification of treaty provisions, 151–52
qualifying conditions, 143–44
subsequent agreement defined, 143
terminology and meaning, 41–42
subsequent practice, 39, 141–42, 157–58, 160
definitions, 143
ICJ jurisprudence, 145–46
modification of treaties by, 52–53, 263
see also subsequent agreements
supplemental PTRs, 38, 43, 47, 49, 51–52, 104, 112, 128

'taking into account':
ambiguity, 153–54
duty to cooperate, 154–55
'give due regard' compared, 155–56
good faith, 158–59
hierarchical interpretation, 157–58

legally binding compared, 156
meaning of legal obligation to take into account, 156–57
transparency, 246
consensual decision making, 241, 252
global administrative law, 221–22
treaties, PTRs as, 122

UN Framework Convention on Climate Change (UNFCCC):
amendment approach, 27–28
see also Kyoto Protocol
urgent national interests, 45, 70, 71–72, 169

Vienna Convention on the Law of Treaties (VCLT):
'between the parties', 247
customary treaty law (Art. 31.3(a)), 33–34
modification of treaties by subsequent practice (Art. 38), 52–53, 151
national courts' interpretation of VCLT articles, 160–61
principle of systemic integration (Art. 31.3(c)), 59–60, 62, 86
subsequent practice, 143, 145, 158
modification of treaties by subsequent practice (Art. 38), 52–53
'taken into account', 153, 156
'subsequent agreements' (Art. 31), 6, 33–34, 39, 41, 79, 102, 143, 144–45, 149, 158
interpretive PTRs, 150
modification of PTRs by way of, 151
'taken into account', 153, 156
vulnerability of authority, 7
consequences of authority associated with social legitimacy, 211–13
discretion of governments, 219–20

***Whaling* case:**
consensual process, 205, 246–47, 271
International Court of Justice (ICJ), 147–48, 179, 195–96, 246–47
modifying PTRs:
substantive limits, 53–54
primarily commercial purposes resolution:
Australia's argument, 86–87
Japan's argument, 87
subsequent agreements:
'between the parties', 146–49
wording of PTRs, 164–66
authority, impact on, 164–66
CITES, 171–73
comparison, 177–78
Kyoto Protocol, 173–76
mandatory quality, 166, 168
Montreal Protocol, 176–77
Ramsar Convention, 169–71
specificity, 166–67, 168–69
varied mandatory quality and specificity of PTRs, 171–72
CITES, 171–73
commercial activities defined, 85–86
comparison, 177–78
critical use defined, 98
Greentree case, 167–68
international organisations defined, 31–32
Kyoto Protocol, 173–76
legal obligation to take into account, 156–57
levels of agreement, impact on, 127–28
limitations to authority from wording, 178
Born Free case, 182
Lac Sorobon case, 181
mandatorily phrased PTRs, 178–79
national courts, 180
Orka case, 182
recommendatory wording, 179–80
mandatory quality, 166, 168
Montreal Protocol, 176–77
'plenary treaty meetings', 35
Ramsar Convention, 169–71
recommendatory wording, 179–80
mandatory PTRs distinguished, 270–71
specificity, 166–67, 168–69
subsequent agreements, PTRs as, 41–42, 142–43
'agreement' defined, 144
'between the parties', 144–49
interpretation of treaties and application of provisions, 149–53
qualifying conditions, 143–44
subsequent agreement defined, 143
see also subsequent agreements
'taking into account'
ambiguity, 153–54
duty to cooperate, 154–55
'give due regard' compared, 155–56
good faith, 158–59
hierarchical interpretation, 157–58
legally binding compared, 156
varied mandatory quality and specificity of PTRs, 171–72
see also interpretive authority of PTRs; language

www.ingramcontent.com/pod-product-compliance
Ingram Content Group UK Ltd.
Pitfield, Milton Keynes, MK11 3LW, UK
UKHW020240290926
15470UKWH00002B/637

9 781509 925568